NEW YORK HISTORY

SUMMER 2023

D1291886

The New York State Museum is a program of The University of the State of New York | The State Education Department | Office of Cultural Education.

New York History (ISSN 0146-437x) is a peer reviewed journal published two times a year by Cornell University Press in partnership with The New York State Museum. Postage is paid at Ithaca, NY 14850 and additional mailing offices. POSTMASTER: Send all address changes to Cornell University Press, 512 East State Street, Ithaca NY 14850.

New York History is available in print and electronically Project Muse (http://muse.jhu.edu). Cornell University Press does not assume responsibility for statements of fact or opinions made by contributors. Unlicensed distribution of all materials (including figures, tables, and other content) is prohibited. Communications about subscriptions, back issues, reproductions and permissions, and other business matters should be sent to Cornell University Press (nyhjournal@cornell.edu). Digital and print subscriptions, for individuals and institutions, may be ordered via Project Muse (https://www.press.jhu.edu/cart/for-sale?oc=3729). Single print copies and print back issues are available for $20.00 and check should be made out to Cornell University Press. For subscriptions and individual issues, inquiries and orders may be made by email, nyhjournal @cornell.edu, or by mail: *New York History* Journal, Cornell University Press, 512 East State Street, Ithaca NY 14850.

Submitted articles should address, in an original fashion, some aspect of New York State history. Articles that deal with the history of other areas or with general American history must have a direct bearing on New York State history. It is assumed that the article will have some new, previously unexploited material to offer or will present new insights or new interpretations. Editorial communications, including article submissions, should be sent to the Editorial Board via email (NYHJ @nysed.gov) Suggested length is 20-30 double spaced pages (or between 6,000 and 9,000 words), including footnotes. All submitted articles must include a 100-word abstract summarizing the article and providing keywords (no more than 10). Authors must submit articles electronically, with all text in Word and all tables, figures, and images in formats supported by Microsoft Windows. Provision of images in proper resolution (no less than 300 dpi at 5" x 7"), securing requisite permissions, and the payment of any fees associated with images for articles are all the responsibility of the author. *New York History* employs, with some modification, footnote forms suggested in the *Chicago Manual of Style*. More detailed submissions guidelines are to be found on the research and collections page of the New York State Museum: http://www.nysm.nysed.gov/research-collections/state-history/resources/new-york-history-journal

Cover art: *Front: The End of Fascism*, Henry DiSpirito, linocut block, ca. 1940's. Courtesy Collection of the New York State Museum, H-2022.4.1. *Back: The Refugees*, Henry DiSpirito, plaster, ca. 1953. *The Mole*, Henry DiSpirito, carved stone (gabbro), ca. 1960. Courtesy Collection of the New York State Museum, H-2019.20.4 & .6, gift of the DiSpirito Daughters. Henry DiSpirito (1898-1995) immigrated to Utica, NY from Italy in 1921 after witnessing the horrors of the First World War and the rise of fascism. Trained as a stonemason, direct carving in stone became his preferred medium, but he also worked in other two and three-dimensional media, exploring themes related to immigration, animals, and nature.

CONTENTS

Volume 104, Number 1

EXHIBIT REVIEWS

LETTER FROM THE EDITORS

Robert Chiles, Devin R. Lander, Jennifer Lemak, and Aaron Noble

Dear Readers,

A consistent factor throughout New York's dynamic history has been the complex interactions between groups with divergent worldviews and conflicting ambitions. Such scenarios have proven at different times to be creative, exploitative, empowering, or contradictory. This issue offers a rich array of such interactions, with articles offering unique insights from diverse perspectives.

Articles by Jaap Jacobs and Anne-Clair Faucquez provide important insights into slavery in New Netherland. In "The Arrival of Enslaved Africans in New Amsterdam," Jacobs explores global and regional historical evidence to provide a revisionist timeline for the introduction of slavery into the colony, while Faucquez explores the community-building work of enslaved people in New Amsterdam and follows that crucial history into contemporary memory in "Community-Building in the History and Memory of Slavery in Dutch New York."

Articles by Timothy J. Shannon and Evan Haefeli offer new understandings of Indigenous diplomacy in colonial New York using neglected sources to provide new perspectives. Haefeli uses diverse sources, including Mohawk oral traditions, to reconstruct and contextualize the Haudenosaunee-Lenape treaty of 1669 in "The Great Haudenosaunee-Lenape Peace of 1669: Oral Traditions, Colonial Records, and the Origin of the Delaware's Status as 'Women.'" Shannon's contribution, "In the Bushes: The Secret History of Anglo-Iroquois Treaty Making," explores private journals and diaries to transcend the official records of negotiations and to reveal a cultural milieu that fused Indigenous and European customs to produce a cultural context for diplomacy. James W. Bradley and James B. Richardson III likewise explore the complex interactions between colonists and natives in "The Eagle, the Bell, and other Fragments from the Intersecting Stories of Queen Anne's Chapel and Fort Hunter," using the discovery of two unusual material objects to investigate the changing cultural relationships between European colonists and their Protestant Mohawk neighbors in eighteenth-century New York. Also exploring how diverging perspectives drove historical events in colonial New York, Steven G. Wapen notes the salience of conflicts between Oswego's military garrison and Lake Ontario fur traders on the eve of the Seven Years' War in "Determined Justice on the New York Frontier: The 1752 Mutiny and Desertion at Oswego."

New York State's more recent history is also marked by complex interactions, as demonstrated by Lawrence J. King in "Memorial Day's Interracial Legacy in Brooklyn, New York, 1878–1897," and by Stuart M. Blumin and Glenn C. Altschuler in their article "When Sunday Baseball Came to Brooklyn." King reveals a palpable sense of interracial solidarity that embodied Memorial Day celebrations in post–Civil War Brooklyn, weathering racial divides and championing remembrance's inclusivity in the late nineteenth century. Blumin and Altschuler analyze the social and cultural conflicts that led first to the prohibition—and then to the legalization—of Sunday Baseball in Brooklyn.

Combining these articles with Ashley Hopkins-Benton's Artifact NY feature—which uses a sewing machine to explore industrial life in twentieth-century Chinatown—and Lauren Roberts's Community NY feature exploring work on the 250th anniversary of the Battles of Saratoga, issue 104.1 provides fresh insights on life throughout the Empire State's rich history.

Excelsior!
THE EDITORS

CONTRIBUTORS

GLENN C. ALTSCHULER

STUART BLUMIN

JAMES W. BRADLEY

Glenn C. Altschuler is the Thomas and Dorothy Litwin Professor of American Studies at Cornell University. He is the author or coauthor of twelve books, including *Cornell: A History, 1940-2015*; *All Shook Up: How Rock 'n Roll Changed America*; *Ten Great American Trials*; *Rude Republic: Americans and Their Politics in the Nineteenth Century*; *The G.I. Bill: A New Deal for Veterans*; and *The Rise and Fall of Protestant Brooklyn: An American Story*.

Stuart Blumin is Emeritus Professor of American History at Cornell University and a former Director of the Cornell in Washington Program. He is the author of a number of books, including *The Emergence of the Middle Class: Social Experience in the American City, 1760–1900*; *The Encompassing City: Streetscapes in Early Modern Art and Culture*; *The Urban Threshold: Growth and Change in a Nineteenth-Century American Community*; and with Glenn Altschuler, *Rude Republic: Americans and Their Politics in the Nineteenth Century*; *The GI Bill: A New Deal for Veterans*, and most recently, *The Rise and Fall of Protestant Brooklyn: An American Story*. He is a former Trustee of the New York State Historical Association.

James W. Bradley, founder, and president of ArchLink, is an archaeologist, historian, and educator with more than forty years of experience in the public and private sectors. His fieldwork ranges from archaeological surveys on Alaska's North Slope and Cape Cod to urban salvage in downtown Boston. Bradley received his PhD from the Maxwell School at Syracuse University in 1979. He served on the staff of the Massachusetts Historical Commission from 1979 to 1990. From 1990 to 2001, he was director of the Robert S. Peabody Museum of Archaeology, Philips Academy in Andover, Massachusetts. He and his wife, Peggy, live in Charlestown, Massachusetts.

JAMES B. RICHARDSON III   **ANNE-CLAIRE FAUCQUEZ**   **EVAN HAEFELI**

James B. Richardson Iii received his PhD from the University of Illinois and is an emeritus professor of anthropology at the University of Pittsburgh and emeritus Chief Curator of Anthropology at the Carnegie Museum of Natural History. He was a crew member in the 1960s on excavations directed by William A. Ritchie in New York State and on Martha's Vineyard. A major research focus is on maritime adaptations and climate change on the coast of Peru and on Martha's Vineyard. He has also conducted archaeological research on historic sites on Martha's Vineyard and in western Pennsylvania. Among his publications are *People of the Andes* (Washington, DC: Smithsonian Institution Press, 1994) and *Discovering a Lost Vineyard House: The Archaeology and History of the John and Experience Mayhew House Site on Martha's Vineyard* (Vineyard Haven, MA: Martha's Vineyard Museum, 2021).

Anne-Claire Faucquez is Associate Professor in American Civilization and History at the University Paris 8. She has published *De la Nouvelle-Néerlande à New York: La naissance d'une société esclavagiste 1624–1712* (Paris: Les Indes savantes, 2021), which is translated into English as *From New Netherland to New York: The Birth of a Slavery Society 1624–1712*. She works on New York's colonial past and more specifically on the issues of class and race. Her new project deals with the writing and teaching of the history of slavery in nineteenth-century history books and textbooks. She is also interested in the memory and representations of slavery in the public space, such as in museums, monuments, and contemporary art.

Evan Haefeli, Professor of History at Texas A&M University, specializes in the histories of Native American and early modern European colonization. He has taught at Princeton, Tufts, the London School of Economics, and Columbia universities and has held a variety of fellowships, including from the National Endowment for the Humanities and the Institute for Advanced Study. His books include *New Netherland and the Dutch Origins of American Religious Liberty* (2012) and, with Kevin Sweeney, *Captors and Captives: The 1704 French and Indian Raid on Deerfield* (2003).

ASHLEY HOPKINS-BENTON

JAAP JACOBS

LAWRENCE KING

Ashley Hopkins-Benton is Senior Historian and Curator of Social History at the New York State Museum. Her research focuses include women's history, LGBTQ+ history, immigration history, and American sculpture. She is the author of *Breathing Life into Stone: The Sculpture of Henry DiSpirito*, and coauthor of *Votes for Women: Celebrating New York's Suffrage Centennial* and *Enterprising Waters: The History and Art of New York's Erie Canal*. She holds a MA in History Museum Studies from the Cooperstown Graduate Program and a BA in Art Education and Studio Art from SUNY Potsdam.

Jaap Jacobs holds a PhD from Leiden University and is affiliated with the University of St Andrews. He is a scholar of early American history, specifically the Dutch in the Americas in the early modern period. He has taught at Leiden University, the University of Amsterdam, Cornell University, the University of Pennsylvania, Harvard University, and the University of St Andrews. His publications on Dutch New York include *The Colony of New Netherland: A Dutch Settlement in Seventeenth-Century America* (Ithaca: Cornell University Press, 2009), and several articles. He is currently working on a biography of Petrus Stuyvesant.

Currently a First Lieutenant in the US Air Force, Lawrence King leads sixty-five airmen as Flight Commander in the 790th Missile Security Forces Squadron, 90th Security Forces Group at Francis E. Warren Air Force Base, Wyoming. King graduated from the U.S. Air Force Academy with a BS in History and subsequently earned a MA in History from New York University through the Air Force Institute of Technology's Civilian Institution Program. He specializes in Civil War veterans' social and racial experiences during the postbellum periods of Reconstruction and the Gilded Age.

LAUREN ROBERTS

TIMOTHY J. SHANNON

STEVEN G. WAPEN

Lauren Roberts earned a dual BA in Anthropology and American Studies from Skidmore College and a MA in Public History from the University at Albany. She currently serves as the Saratoga County Historian, a position she has held since 2009. Lauren also serves as the 2nd Vice President for the Association of Public Historians of New York State (APHNYS). In 2017, she coproduced the documentary *Harnessing Nature: Building the Great Sacandaga*, which chronicles the history of New York's largest reservoir. In 2019, Roberts signed on as cohost for the award-winning podcast *A New York Minute in History*. She currently serves as Chair of the Saratoga County 250th Anniversary Commission.

Timothy J. Shannon teaches Early American, Native American, and British history at Gettysburg College. His most recent book is *Indian Captive, Indian King: Peter Williamson in America and Britain* (2018).

Steven G. Wapen is a native of upstate New York and an independent historian with a special interest in the early French and Indian War in North America. He is retired following an extensive career in labor relations and human resources in the Northeast and Midwest. Wapen is a graduate of SUNY at Oswego and holds graduate degrees from the University at Albany, Cornell University, and Trinity College in Hartford, Connecticut. His MA thesis from Trinity College focuses on Oswego and is titled "Understanding the British Collapse: Opponent Information, Martial Cultures, and the 1756 French Victory at Oswego/Chouaguen." He is married and currently lives in Chaplin, Connecticut.

Determined Justice on the New York Frontier
The 1752 Mutiny & Desertion at Oswego

Steven G. Wapen

On the night of January 11, 1752, in the British garrison at Oswego, commander Capt. John Mills went to bed early around 9 p.m. Earlier that evening, Mills had drunk two small bowls of punch with Nathaniel Downing, a private doctor and garrison surgeon, known as the Doctor. The convivial visit between Captain Mills and the Doctor was later described by Mills as one of "a great Harmony and Friendship, nor had an Ill-natured expression ever past betwixt them."[1] All was well at his garrison, or so the captain thought.

Between 12 midnight and 1 p.m., Private Mark Sampson of Captain Marshall's independent company walked into Mills's unlocked room of the main garrison building with a candle in his hand and looked at his watch. A greatly startled Captain Mills asked Sampson what was the matter, and Sampson replied, "[You] should soon see."[2] And so began the January 11, 1752, mutiny and desertion at Oswego on the southeastern shore of Lake Ontario (figure 1). The Doctor later joined Sampson and several other mutineers in Captain Mills's quarters. In the wee hours of the morning, Mills was severely beaten on the head with a club and one of his arms was cut by a hanger, or short sword. He was verbally berated by members of the rebellious party, most notably by the Doctor. The insurgents seized all of Mills's weapons and then freely drank his spirits and wine. Finally, the captain was physically knocked down, placed in irons (handcuffs), restricted to his room, and placed under guard. Of all the mutineers, Captain Mills was most incensed with the Doctor who, Judas like, betrayed his commander just a few hours after their friendly visit of small talk and punch nightcaps. It was also the Doctor who vociferously, profanely, and falsely accused Mills of mistreating his men at the small garrison.

---

1. Minutes of a General Court of Inquiry at the City of Albany, July 18, 1753, CO5 1064, 133, British National Archives. The Minutes are a confusing document and require several readings to fully understand the mutiny and desertion's convoluted chain of events and wide cast of characters.
2. Minutes of a General Court of Inquiry at the City of Albany, July 18, 1753.

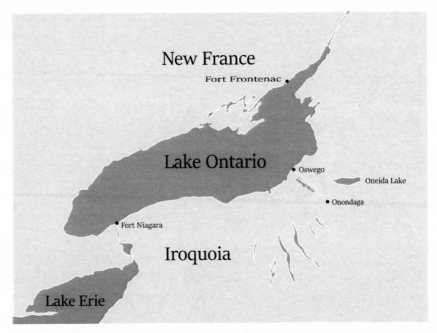

Figure 1. Map of Lake Ontario Watershed Showing Location of Oswego and other important settlements, ca. 1752. COURTESY GREG ROGERS, "PETITE POLITIQUE: THE BRITISH, FRENCH, IROQUOIS, AND EVERYDAY POWER IN THE LAKE ONTARIO BORDERLAND" (PHD DISS., UNIVERSITY OF MAINE, 2016), A.5, 287.

In early January 1752, Oswego was a small British fur trading post with an adjacent military garrison of some twenty soldiers, or sentries (figure 2). Ostensibly, Captain Mills and his troops were charged with protecting Oswego's fur trading community from French attack, while maintaining peaceful interactions between Albany fur traders and far west Native Americans. The British garrison upheld law and order at the frontier outpost. Thus, the 1752 mutiny and accompanying desertion were signal events that neutralized, albeit temporarily, British imperial authority. It transformed the garrison's role from martial protector and peacekeeper to impotent bystander.

The relationship between the British garrison and Oswego's fur traders was a complex one. The minutes of the court of inquiry held at Albany on July 18, 1752, is remarkable for the rich insights it offers on the rebellion and on relations between the military garrison and civilian fur traders. Perhaps most surprising is what the court of inquiry revealed concerning the root cause of the mutiny and desertion. It was quite unexpected. The principal cause of those events was not attributable to Captain Mills's soldiers. Rather, it came from a single unscrupulous personage within Oswego's fur trading community.

This article closely examines the testimonials of several mutineer deserters found in the minutes of the Albany court of inquiry. I argue that the path to British justice for the mutineers and deserters, while purposeful and determined, was ultimately incomplete.

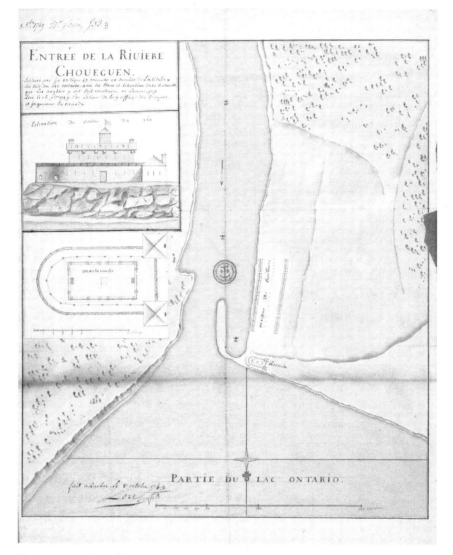

Figure 2. 1749 Map of Oswego, or Chouageun, by Gaspard-Joseph Chaussegros de Lery. View facing south with garrison structure and traders' houses depicted on lower right river bank. Enlargement of side and overhead views of fortification building appear in upper left corner. GASPARD-JOSEPH DE LERY AND CHOUAGUEN, YAHOO IMAGE SEARCH RESULTS, ACCESSED JULY 8, 2020.

The mutiny's top civilian conspirators successfully avoided the long arm of British colonial justice. In addition, the reputations of the British military and colonial New York, so vital in the mid-eighteenth century, suffered in the eyes of both their French rivals and their Native American allies. To lose a garrison to mutiny and desertion was a clear mark of command weakness and the absence of military discipline. Key provincial stakeholders wanted to distance themselves from the regrettable incident of January 11, 1752. These included New York governor George Clinton and William Johnson, frontier fur trader extraordinaire. Though both leaders had strong connections to Oswego, they desired to avoid public embarrassment by quickly putting those dark events behind them. To be sure, the records of New York's colonial history provide few references, and even fewer details, regarding the 1752 Oswego mutiny and desertion.

Fur Trade in Western New York

In the first half of the eighteenth century, Britain continued to expand its vast commercial empire westward in North America. This included the growing fur trade enterprise at Oswego. The primary motives for establishing Oswego's trade mart included securing the loyalty of New York's Six Nation Haudenosaunee as well as expanding the western fur trade with the far west, or the Great Lakes Indian nations.[3] The British recognized that cultivation of the western fur trade and related frontier security, or protection from French incursion, was contingent on successful diplomacy and good relations with the Iroquois Nations. Oswego's successful fur trade and frontier security were closely linked.[4] A military garrison was needed to protect the modest trading post, established in 1727, from external and internal threats.

From the onset, the question of financial support for the garrison created ongoing conflicts between New York's legislative Assembly in Albany and British authorities in London. The New York Assembly believed Britain should shoulder the cost of Oswego, while Britain felt it was the Assembly's responsibility. The net result of the dispute over the years was a failure to properly maintain the military outpost.[5] In fact, the Assembly's financial support for the garrison after 1740 was egregiously inadequate.[6] Up until the Seven Years' War (1756–63), British policy encouraged the provinces to pay for most of the costs of defending its citizenry and their commercial enterprises against all enemies.[7] Such was the expectation at Oswego with its fur business in the first half of the eighteenth century.

---

3. Johnson G. Cooper, "Oswego in the French-English Struggle in North America 1720–1760," (PhD diss., Syracuse University, 1961), 87.
4. Thomas E. Norton, *The Fur Trade in Colonial New York 1686–1776* (Madison: University of Wisconsin Press, 1974), 73, 78.
5. Cooper, "Oswego in the French-English Struggle," 70.
6. Norton, *The Fur Trade in Colonial New York*, 181.
7. Peter Way, "Locating the Lower Orders: Recovering the Lives of 18th Century Soldiers," in *Scholarship at UWindsor* 5 (2007): 19.

The Albany fur traders dominated at Oswego during this period. Many of them constituted a crude and wily bunch—very dishonest, dishonorable, and disloyal.[8] Apart from dealing with the vilest members of Oswego's fur trading community, there were plenty of other challenges for those managing the commercial fur business. The need for close oversight, paying the high costs of water transport, collecting traders' debts for trade goods secured on credit, and carefully timing when to obtain trade goods for transport to Oswego were a few of the gnarly hurdles encountered.[9]

The Crown's protection of Oswego's fur commerce consisted of New York Independent company soldiers under command of British officers. Though imperfect, this martial partnership was consistent with Britain's focus on protecting commerce over territory before the advent of the Seven Years War.[10] While minimizing violence between the Albany traders and Native Americans, the garrison was unable to check the traders' widespread fraudulent transactions with their far west Indian counterparts.[11] Similarly, Oswego's solitary seasonal commissary, or civil styled justice of the peace, could not reduce levels of shameless fraud at the popular trade mart. Large numbers of fur traders, combined with high volumes of transactions, effectively canceled efforts to control rampant cheating.[12] Other duties of the commissioners included the regulation of rum sales. They frequently tested rum supplies sold to Natives in order to discourage Oswego's traders from diluting their rum stocks with water.[13]

In a portent of things to come twenty years on, in the early 1730s Oswego trade commissioners feared garrison soldiers would mutiny, or easily surrender to the French, as conditions were so poor, characterized by inadequate supplies and overall lack of provincial support.[14] Moreover, in 1731, Joseph Clement, a new commissioner, complained of substandard conditions and mismanaged affairs. Clement pointed out that Lieutenant Smith, then garrison commander, and two noncommissioned officers died over winter 1731–32, and that several soldiers were sickly.[15]

Clearly, Oswego's garrison suffered from a pattern of inadequate support from the New York Assembly and concomitant poor troop morale among the New York Independent companies posted there. Nor could the garrison commander expect much help from those benefiting most from the fur business—the traders themselves. For example, when word of the outbreak of King George's War reached Oswego, the fur traders abandoned the

---

8. Norton, *The Fur Trade in Colonial New York*, 89.
9. Norton, 94.
10. Peter Way, "Militarizing the Atlantic World: Army Discipline, Coerced Labor, and Britain's Commercial Empire," *Atlantic Studies* 13, no. 3 (2016): 360.
11. Norton, *The Fur Trade in Colonial New York*, 170.
12. Norton, 170.
13. Norton, *The Fur Trade in Colonial New York*, 180.
14. Cooper, "Oswego in the French-English Struggle," 77.
15. Cooper, 77.

trading post in droves, opting instead for the for the relative safety of Albany. Collectively, they refused to defend Oswego against French attacks that, ironically, never materialized. Then New York governor George Clinton publicly chastised the fur traders for their disloyalty and rank cowardice.[16]

Following the trade-dormant years during King George's War (1744–48), Oswego enjoyed a brief resurgence of its fur business in 1749 and 1750. However, the trade dropped off again in 1752 when fur merchants turned their attention to exporting ginseng to Britain for higher profits.[17] The overall trajectory of Oswego's fur trade continued a downward slope, accompanied by diminishing economic and political power for Albany fur merchants and traders.[18] The 1755 opening of the larger-scale Seven Years War effectively brought an end to the earlier halcyon days of Oswego's fur enterprise. It never recovered after that conflict.[19]

Oswego Fur Traders

In order to understand the pivotal role certain fur traders played in causing the mutiny and desertion at Oswego, it is necessary to review conditions at the garrison and trading post in early 1752. Trade with far west Indian groups included the Miami, Potawatomi, Chippewa, Mississauga, Ottawa, and Huron Natives Americans (figure 3).[20] The fur trade at Oswego fell sharply during the War of Austrian Succession (1744–48). However, Lt. John Lindesay, Capt. John Mills's immediate predecessor at Oswego, reported on September 23, 1749, that 193 far west Indian canoes off-loaded 1,385 packs of furs that summer, valued at some 40,000 pounds sterling.[21] Clearly, the trade responded to years of pent-up demand. Nevertheless, the fur business was fickle, and traders Benjamin Stoddert and Thomas Butler both forecast a poor Oswego market to William Johnson in late May 1751.[22] Apart from the banner year of 1749, fewer far west Indians were willing to travel hundreds of miles by water with fur packs to trade for British manufactured goods in the early 1750s. The escalating cost of British goods was a deterrent exacerbated by threats of colonial duties on coveted items, such as rum and shrouds.[23] In addition, the French attempted to draw the Indian trade away from Oswego. In a September 7, 1750, letter from Lt. John Lindesay to William Johnson, Lindesay reported that the governor of New France encouraged his

---

16. Norton, *The Fur Trade in Colonial New York*, 183.

17. Norton, 98_99.

18. Norton, 120.

19. Norton, 99.

20. Norton, 152.

21. Frederick W. Barnes, "The Fur Traders of Early Oswego," *Proceedings of the New York State Historical Association* 13 (1914): 132.

22. Letter of Benjamin Stoddert to William Johnson, May 20, 1751, *The Papers of Sir William Johnson*, ed. Milton W. Hamilton and Albert B. Corey, 14 vols. (Albany: University of the State of New York, 1921–1965), 1: 336–37. Hereafter *Sir William Johnson Papers*.

23. Letter of William Johnson to Governor George Clinton, September 14, 1750, *Sir William Johnson Papers*, 9: 69.

Figure 3. *Winter Trade*, by Robert Griffing. Depicts mid-eighteent century frontier fur trading scene, emblematic of those common at Oswego. Note the stocks of woolen trade cloth on counter and rum tankards on table near fireplace. Both commodities were favored by far west Native traders in exchange for furs. COURTESY OF PARAMOUNT PRESS, INC. HTTPS://IMAGES.SEARCH.YAHOO.COM (OSWEGO FUR TRADE PAINTINGS, YAHOO IMAGE SEARCH RESULTS, ACCESSED JULY 8, 2020).

militia officers to convince far west Indians not to trade at Oswego. Lindesay related how a far west Native attempted to trade a pack of his furs for a silver armband but was prevented from doing so by a French militia officer who accompanied him on his visit to Oswego.[24]

Other factors also discouraged far west Indians from trading at Oswego. These could be ascribed specifically to the unethical business practices of the Oswego traders. The fur traders swindled the far western tribes unmercifully, perhaps to make up for profits lost during the lean war years (1744–48). Capt. John Bradstreet, interim commander at Oswego in 1755, during the British military mobilization there, stated that poor treatment of Native Americans by the traders over the past five years had ruined the fur trade. In fact, Bradstreet was surprised the aggrieved Indians had not exacted revenge by killing all the traders.[25] Similarly, William Johnson opined that severely cheated tribes would never return to Oswego but would trade with the French and were "among our most implacable enemies."[26]

---

24. Letter of Lt. John Lindesay to William Johnson, September 7, 1750, *Sir William Johnson Papers*, 1: 296–97.
25. Letter of Captain John Bradstreet to Sir Thomas Robinson, May 30, 1755, WO 5 46, 386. British National Archives.
26. Cooper, "Oswego in the French-English Struggle," 320.

Figure 4. *Delicate Balance of Honesty,* by Robert Griffing. Shows use of mid-eighteenth century frontier fur trading scales, emblematic of those found at Oswego trade mart. Provincial regulation of fur trade failed to control fraudulent practices of Albany traders at the remote outpost. COURTESY OF PARAMOUNT PRESS, INC. HTTPS://IMAGES.YAHOO.COM (OSWEGO FUR TRADE PAINTINGS—YAHOO IMAGE SEARCH RESULTS, ACCESSED JULY 8, 2020).

Johnson characterized Oswego's fur traders as being from Albany, Schenectady, or the Mohawk Valley who aimed for certain profits by trading a small volume of British trade goods for Indian supplied furs only three or four warm months of the year while remaining inactive for the balance.[27] In order to achieve "certain profits," the traders resorted to full-scale cheating. Standard methods used to maximize profits included the employment of altered weights (figure 4) to undervalue furs, the use of rum to get Natives intoxicated prior to trading, deceptive verbal flattery, outright theft of Indian furs, exchanges of watered-down rum for furs, and attempts to keep far west Indians in constant debt. Many unscrupulous traders believed a lower standard of ethics was required when dealing with Natives, which they expressed as "it's no Crime to cheat and gull an Indian."[28]

Not all Oswego fur traders shared the same opinion regarding Indian business interactions, however. Benjamin Stoddert, trader and agent for William Johnson in a postscript to his July 16, 1749, letter to Johnson, warned that Oswego's fur trading business should be taken over by a single company of ethical traders in order to return the Indians to the

---

27. Cooper, 319.
28. Wilbur R. Jacobs, "Unsavory Sidelights on the Colonial Fur Trade," *New York History* 34 (1953): 136.

market. Otherwise, the trade would by ruined by "Vile Steps taken [by the traders] to undermine each other . . . must give even the Savages a Damn'd mean opinion of us; especially over Honesty etc."[29] Thus, the Oswego fur trading community's predatory dealings targeted not only far west Natives but also the traders themselves and, eventually, extended even to Clinton's military complement at the garrison.

Of all the traders' shameless business practices, perhaps the most egregious was their kidnapping of innocent Native children who were then held as security to encourage the Indians' payment of debts owed the traders. Mercifully, New York governor George Clinton issued a proclamation on July 29, 1750, outlawing such activities and ordering the return of affected Indian children to their families.[30] The enforcement of Clinton's proclamation, however, remains unclear.

The prevailing demeanor of fur traders at Oswego in January 1752 was one of discontent. Indian relations were strained, profits were down, and unsold British trade goods were stored in sundry warehouses. Traders were concerned about rumors of the possible consolidation of their enterprises by a provincially sanctioned fur trading company. Such consolidation would likely put most of them out of business. Further, the traders had recently been prohibited by Governor Clinton's 1750 proclamation from using Indian children as security for debt payments. Last, the change in command at the Oswego garrison was not welcomed by all fur traders wintering over in 1751–52. The stage seemed perfectly set for trader-inspired mischief making.

Oswego Garrison

The garrison at Oswego that winter of 1751–52 totaled twenty-one men, including Capt. John Mills. It consisted of detachments from four New York Independent companies: Captain Marshall's company, Captain Rutherford's company, Captain Clarke's company, and Governor Clinton's company. The Independent Companies of New York were a unique military organization. They were not attached to the regular British Army, nor were they part of New York's colonial militia. Instead, the Independents were separate military formations loosely supported by the British Board of Trade and Plantations, Treasury, Pay Office, and the New York governor—as martial "stepchildren," of sorts.[31]

Operational support for the Independents was provided in joint fashion by the British

---

29. Letter from Benjamin Stoddert to William Johnson, July 16, 1749, *Sir William Johnson Papers*, 1:236–37.

30. Governor George Clinton, "A Proclamation Against Taking Indian Children as Security for Any Debt," June 29, 1750. Broadside, forbidding Indian traders from taking Indian children as sureties. Only known copy, held by the New York State Library, is mutilated. Ascribed to the press of James Parker by Evans, New York City, 1750. Reference: Evans 6567.

31. Stanley M. Pargellis, "The Four Independent Companies of New York," in *Essays in Colonial History Presented to Charles McLean Andrews* (New Haven: Yale University Press, 1931), 111.

home government and provincial New York. Britain paid the wages of the officers and soldiers, while the New York Assembly provided fortified barracks, firewood, and candles. Britain also supplied bedding, stores, and officers. And in the case of Oswego and its role as guardian of the fur trade there, New York victualed the small garrison. From its beginning in 1727 up to the 1752 mutiny, the British military presence at Oswego averaged around twenty soldiers and a commanding officer. Save for a brief spike to ninety-three soldiers in 1745 during the War of Austrian Succession, the garrison routinely billeted some twenty soldiers yearly. Food supplies were forwarded up to Oswego from the Albany area. Derick Petrie's October 12, 1754, receipt for his 1754–55 winter shipment of provisions to Oswego illustrates the limited variety of foodstuffs and dietary range supplied to the garrison. Since the garrison maintained about the same number of men in 1754–55 as it did in 1751–52, it is likely that the 1751–52 shipment resembled the one sent in 1754–55. Among the items shipped were fifteen skipple (skipple = 0.75 bushel) of Indian corn; thirty-three skipple of peas; 2,250 pounds of meal; seven barrels of pork; and one barrel of rum.[32]

Ostensibly, the main purpose of the garrison was to symbolically assert British imperial power on the New York frontier by protecting Oswego's commercial interests from French or French and Indian incursions. Secondarily, garrison soldiers upheld peace between the fur traders and far west Native Americans in an otherwise lawless environment. The responsibilities of garrison commander were considerable. That officer needed to ensure his soldiers were trained and prepared to defend the trading post against external threats. The officer also had to be strong enough to control the freewheeling and at times violent behavior of the fur traders and Indians. Moreover, the garrison's commander and soldiers were required to avoid conflicts of interest by not participating in the fur trade.

On January 29, 1752, Penelope Lindesay, recent widow of Lt. John Lindesay, late commander of the Oswego garrison, filed an affidavit with Robert Sanders, the mayor of Albany, certifying that she was about to receive a bounty from the King in recognition of Lindesay's service.[33] Apparently, Lindesay died sometime in 1751 and was replaced at the garrison by Capt. John Mills. The change in command was a significant event for the fur traders at Oswego as they, like the garrison soldiers, needed to adapt to the new commander. Previous understandings and working relationships between Lieutenant Lindesay and the traders were threatened by the arrival of Captain Mills.

Hints of future trouble on this score surfaced in early fall 1751. John Ackerman, a fur trader and, like Benjamin Stoddert, an agent to William Johnson, raised serious concerns in a September 21, 1751, letter to Johnson. For a time under Lieutenant Lindesay, Ackerman enjoyed the best of both worlds. He was a sergeant in Captain Clarke's Independent

32. Certification from Lt. Hitchen Holland that Provisions were delivered to Oswego by Derick Petrie for use by the Garrison, October 12, 1754 Document attached to April 25, 2020 email received by the author from Paul Lear, Director of Fort Ontario, Oswego, New York.
33. Affidavit of Penelope Lindesay, widow of Lt. John Lindesay, signed by John Sanders, Mayor of Albany, January 29, 1752, *Sir William Johnson Papers*, 1: 361–62.

company. But Clarke had approved Ackerman's assignment to Oswego as *both sergeant and fur trader*. Thus, at Oswego, Lindesay had allowed Ackerman to continue as a sergeant while enjoying the privileges of his fur trader status. Apparently, Captain Mills did not approve of Lieutenant Lindesay's previous arrangement and replaced Ackerman with another sergeant. Nevertheless, Mills kept him on the rolls as a garrison private, or sentinel. While content as a fur trader, Ackerman was extremely unhappy about the military demotion. In his letter, Ackerman appealed to Johnson to secure a release from Captain Clarke's Independent company and requested a signed discharge document from Captain Clarke. Clearly, Ackerman wanted to get out from under Captain Mills's command. In a closing line to Johnson, Ackerman wrote he "had been told by one that my life will be made Very uneasy to me [by Captain Mills] this Winter, which Gives me and My wife Great uneasiness."[34] Little did Ackerman realize at the time that his life would not be made uneasy by Mills but by fellow trader William Gough. John Ackerman was present at Oswego during the winter of 1751–52 and witnessed first-hand the garrison's January descent into mutiny and subsequent desertion.

Ackerman's dual status as garrison sergeant and active fur trader, sanctioned by both Capt. Thomas Clarke in Albany and Lt. John Lindesay at Oswego, stands as stark testament to Governor Clinton's slack administration and indifference to martial conflicts of interest. Given the unorthodox nature of Ackerman's arrangement, one could ponder the extent to which Lieutenant Lindesay and other Oswego soldiers might also have been involved in the fur trade. The New York Assembly issued a strict order to officers at all trading posts prohibiting them from engaging in the fur trade.[35] On the face of it, that might explain Captain Mills's demotion of Sergeant Ackerman, from noncommissioned officer to private. Mills may have simply enforced his interpretation of the Assembly's edict.

The reaction of other traders to Ackerman's demotion was likely not positive. Afterall, as a fellow trader, he was one of them and endured ongoing humiliation so long as he remained under Captain Mills's command. One trader in particular was the angriest of all with the transition to the new command, namely, William Gough (Gof or Goff). Gough was a physically imposing Albany trader, a crude bully, and a de facto leader of Oswego's fur trading community. As ruffian king, he dominated with a combination of physical intimidation, violence, and psychological terror. Doubtless, Gough saw Captain Mills as a major threat to Oswego's previously cozy garrison–fur trade arrangement. The "Ackerman demotion incident" of the fall of 1751 highlighted the captain's rejection of garrison involvement in the fur business. And as a result, Gough targeted Mills as a serious adversary to be marginalized.

Beset with a new commander and poorly trained and untested soldiers, William

---

34. Letter from John Ackerman to William Johnson, September 21, 1751, *Sir William Johnson Papers*, 1: 350–51.
35. Pargellis, "The Four Independent Companies of New York," 118.

Gough conspired with another civilian, Nathaniel Downing, known as "the Doctor," and several malcontented soldiers to foist a mutiny upon Captain Mills. Together, Gough, the Doctor, and their garrison conspirators would employ threats, intimidation, physical violence, and psychological terror to take control at Oswego. Through it all, Gough and his participating traders cleverly manipulated the garrison's most gullible soldiers do the insurrectionists' dirty work, so that they, not the fur traders, would be held accountable for.

January 11, 1752, Mutiny

On the evening of January 11, 1752, four soldiers from four New York Independent companies assaulted and confined Capt. John Mills and seized control of the British garrison at Oswego. The mutineers included Pvt. Mark Sampson of Captain Marshall's company; Cpl. William Barry, a.k.a. "the Corporal," of Captain Rutherford's company; Pvt. William Burchell, a.k.a. "the Drummer," of Captain Rutherford's company; Pvt. David Ray of Governor Clinton's company; and Nathaniel Downing, a.k.a. "the Doctor," a civilian contract surgeon to the garrison. The level of physical violence and verbal abuse directed at Captain Mills during the event is notable. Private Ray pushed Mills while the Corporal knocked him down with blows to the head using a large stick that opened bloody wounds. The Drummer then cut one of the captain's arms clear through his coat sleeve with a hanger. Throughout their violence, the mutineers cursed Mills that they would have no more soldiers flogged, as there was none of it in their respective Independent companies. When Mills called for the Doctor to dress his head wounds, Nathaniel Downing appeared and launched into a profanity-laced tirade accusing the captain of cheating his men of provisions and flogging them to force their desertions so he could take their allowances. The Doctor provided no evidence of Mills's alleged deeds, however. Downing told the captain that the mutineers swore they would desert to Cataraqui, a French fort due north of Oswego.[36]

A surprised Mills immediately recognized that the mutineers' allegations were meritless. Nevertheless, he was perplexed and quite angry at the abrupt turn of events that cold January evening. Most of the captain's anger focused on the treachery of Nathaniel Downing. Mills assumed the Doctor was a loyal colleague since they shared a visit earlier that evening over drams of rum punch. The garrison commander was lulled into a false sense of security by the Doctor and felt unforgivably betrayed by his false allegations. The surgeon's duplicitous behavior probably convinced Mills that this civilian doctor was a major force behind the uprising. But why would Oswego's civilian contract surgeon double-cross the garrison's commander with false accusations of abuse against his soldiers? Despite the Doctor's earlier veneered pleasantries on the night of the mutiny, it appears that Downing, like

---

36. Minutes of a General Court of Inquiry at the City of Albany, July 18, 1753, 133.

trader Gough, also disliked the garrison's new commander. Perhaps the Doctor got along better with Oswego's previous commander, the late Lt. John Lindesay.

Aspects of the 1752 Oswego mutiny draw parallels with the 1789 HMS *Bounty* mutiny. Both Captain Bligh of HMS *Bounty* and Captain Mills were taken prisoner in nighttime assaults, while they were sleeping. To halt the mutinies, Mills and Bligh made emotional appeals of loyalty and duty to their men, to no avail. In both insurrections, the planning was carefully kept secret. Neither captain suspected any threats from their subordinates. In fact, doors to their quarters were kept unlocked and no guards were posted. Not surprisingly, neither Mills nor Bligh attributed the origins of their respective mutinies to themselves. Despite treating his officers and crew poorly, Bligh believed the mutineers' desire to remain in Tahiti, rather than return to England, was the root cause of the Bounty mutiny.[37] For his part, Mills was befuddled by the actions of his garrison's ringleaders. Captain Mills had been assigned to Oswego only a few months prior to the mutiny and had no opportunity to get to know his men. By contrast, Captain Bligh was very familiar with veteran members of his crew, yet remained fooled by Fletcher Christian, the principal ringleader. In both instances, it appeared Mills and Bligh were not the best judges of people and were thus completely hoodwinked. Ostensibly, it was poor treatment of the men that instigated both revolts. While certainly true regarding Captain Bligh, this was not the case with Captain Mills at Oswego. Regardless, both captains suffered the outcomes of clandestine plotting and allegations of command mistreatment. While mutinies often arise as a result of scarcities in provisions, pay, clothing, and rum or related necessities, these were not factors in either the Oswego or the HMS *Bounty* rebellions.

The mutiny collaborators scheduled their uprising for early January 1752 during the fur trade's off-season. Such timing was intended to avoid any interference from the Oswego commissary, the singular provincial law enforcement officer assigned to the trade mart. Typically, the commissaries spent their off-seasons in the Albany area. When at Oswego, the commissary possessed legal authority and civil jurisdiction to apprehend the Doctor, Nathaniel Downing, William Gough, and other civilian fur traders implicated in inciting the garrison revolt. As a result, the timing of their January 11, 1752, mutiny was calculated to minimize that risk. By planning their insurrection for the off-season, the ringleaders ensured that the commissary was not in Oswego and thus unable to interfere with their insurrection design.

Oswego's mutineers took advantage of the event to seize Captain Mills's weapons, including his pistols, sword, and scimitar (Eastern curved sword). They also raided Mills's private stock of liquor taking whatever they wished.[38] The insurgents eventually cleaned

---

37. *William Bligh's Narrative of the Mutiny on the "Bounty"* (London: George Nicol, 1790), reproduced and accessed April 27, 2020, at http://law2.umkc.edu/faculty/projects/FTrials/Bounty/blighnarrative.html.
38. Minutes of a General Court of Inquiry at the City of Albany, July 18, 1753, 138.

out all the captain's valuables amounting to nearly 200 pounds sterling.[39] Pvt. John Colson, one of the mutiny leaders, forced Captain Mills to "give" him a new bob wig, four shirts, and three pairs of stockings as opportunistic rewards for guarding and protecting the captain from additional physical harm.[40]

Even Thomas Davis, a greedy fur trader supporting William Gough's subterfuge, got in on the plunder. Davis manipulated Pvt. Colson to act as his "go-between" in forcing Captain Mills to "sell" (give) two cows to Davis for "value received," meaning for gratis.[41] Pvt. Colson shortly thereafter traveled to Albany to report Captain Mills's alleged mistreatment of Oswego's soldiers and the subsequent mutiny to Capt. Hubert Marshall. Thomas Davis dutifully accompanied Colson as a guide on the Albany journey. As a fur trader from Albany, Davis knew the Mohawk Valley and way to Albany better than Colson did.

Though only a few members of Oswego's fur trading community actively promoted the military ringleaders in the 1752 mutiny, they carefully avoided any appearances of direct involvement. Direct conspiracy would subject them to provincial New York's judicial accountability and likely criminal prosecution. Thus, none of the traders was physically present at the scene of the mutiny when Captain Mills was assaulted, handcuffed, and detained. Nor did any of them depart Oswego with the mutiny's soldier-deserters or directly help them in that effort. The fur traders had no documented role in recruiting garrison men to join the mutiny against Captain Mills. Even the receipt that Mills signed under pressure on January 16, 1752, that "sold" two of his cows to Thomas Davis for gratis was backdated to January 10, 1752—one day before the date of the mutiny.[42] Moreover, members of Oswego's fur trading community were divided regarding the propriety of the garrison uprising. Two traders, John Ackerman and William Rickman, discussed thwarting the mutineers' initial scheme to steal British trade goods from Oswego and travel by batteau craft across Lake Ontario to sell them to French traders at Cataraqui.[43]

Only a day after the mutiny, on January 12, 1752, Captain Mills met with John Ackerman and William Barry, the Corporal. Mills told Ackerman he was duty-bound to alert in writing his commanding officer at Albany, Captain Marshall, of the mutiny. Likewise, William Gough and his complicit traders advised the garrison's mutineers to report their complaints and recent mutiny against Captain Mills as soon as possible.[44] Gough's advice was probably intended to insulate him and other involved traders from future culpability. In mid-January, the traders agreed to send Pvt. John Colson and fur trader Thomas Davis to Albany.[45] Colson, not the best of messengers, failed to deliver Mills's notice to Cap-

39. Minutes of a General Court of Inquiry at the City of Albany, July 18, 1753, 134.
40. Minutes of a General Court of Inquiry at the City of Albany, July 18, 1753, 134.
41. Minutes of a General Court of Inquiry at the City of Albany, July 18, 1753, 134.
42. Minutes of a General Court of Inquiry at the City of Albany, July 18, 1753, 134.
43. Minutes of a General Court of Inquiry at the City of Albany, July 18, 1753, 138.
44. Minutes of a General Court of Inquiry at the City of Albany, July 18, 1753, 136.
45. Minutes of a General Court of Inquiry at the City of Albany, July 18, 1753, 137.

tain Marshall. He also bungled the garrison's allegations of Captain Mills's mistreatment. At a small Schenectady outpost, Private Colson informed Sergeant Bayley and Captain Soumaien how Mills was handcuffed and held captive at the Oswego garrison. When asked who did this, Colson told Bayley and Soumaien *that all the soldiers* at the garrison did it.[46] Apparently lacking credibility, Colson and Davis made little impression in Schenectady. They garnered no sympathy during their presentation of the mutineers' complaints against Captain Mills.[47] Davis returned to Oswego on February 20, 1752.[48] Private Colson was arrested and returned under guard to the garrison around the same time. He was subsequently charged with mutiny by Captain Mills and detained. In the interim, the captain's command had been restored on February 1, 1752, following the arrival of respected fur trader Benjamin Stoddert.[49]

January 22, 1752, Desertion

Oswego's rebellious soldiers appeared to languish for two weeks following their January 11, 1752, mutiny. Perhaps they chose to wait until the ice on Lake Ontario broke up in March before they would attempt to desert to Cataraqui in absconded batteau boats laden with stolen British trade goods. Deserting overland in the dead of winter would not have been a wise course of action. Or perhaps they were waiting to learn how Private Colson and trader Davis's allegations of garrison abuse by Captain Mills was received by authorities in Albany. But the ringleaders and other soldier-mutineers probably sensed it was not safe to remain at the garrison. They likely knew the penalty for mutiny was capital punishment and grew restless. The soldier- mutineers may have thought their chances for survival were better attempting to desert to Cataraqui rather than staying at Oswego. Accordingly, the insurgents sprang into action and prepared to desert Oswego post haste.

On January 22, 1752, William Barry ("the Corporal"), William Burchell ("the Drummer"), and other mutineers marched Captain Mills and several nondeserting mutineers down to the west bank of the Oswego River. The corporal attempted to cajole Mills into swearing on a Bible not to prosecute the Doctor or any of the remaining nondeserting soldier-mutineers. The captain flatly refused. As he was in a hurry to flee the garrison, the corporal wisely declined to persist with his request.[50]

The insurgents' use of sworn oaths during the mutiny is reflective of a type of loyalty common to military organizations in the eighteenth century. Just as military recruits were sworn to loyalty in New York's Independent companies, Oswego's conspirators attempted

---

46. Minutes of a General Court of Inquiry at the City of Albany, July 18, 1753, 139.
47. Minutes of a General Court of Inquiry at the City of Albany, July 18, 1753, 139.
48. Minutes of a General Court of Inquiry at the City of Albany, July 18, 1753, 136.
49. Minutes of a General Court of Inquiry at the City of Albany, July 18, 1753, 132.
50. Minutes of a General Court of Inquiry at the City of Albany, July 18, 1753, 132.

to convert the soldiers from their traditional unit loyalty a to collective allegiance support-ing the insurrection. Because the garrison's soldiers were coerced with death threats by the ringleaders, they swore to join the mutiny. But for Captain Mills, a sworn conversion not to prosecute the Doctor and remaining ringleaders would have made him complicit in the very mutiny in which he was the victim.[51]

So, in feeling the long arm of British military justice nipping at their heels, a party of ten mutineers, led by the Corporal, deserted the Oswego garrison on January 22, 1752. Probably only the physically most fit and most "loyal" mutineers would have been allowed by the corporal to join the mutineer deserters. Their destination was Cataraqui, or Fort Frontenac, present day Kingston, Ontario. The group of deserters included Cpl. William Barry, Pvt. William Burchell, Pvt. John Dowgan, Pvt. Michael Finn, and Timothy Sullivan, all of Captain Rutherford's company; Pvt. Mark Sampson of Col. Marshall's Company; Pvt. David Ray, Pvt. James Reed, and Pvt. Peter Eybergen of the Governor Clinton's com-pany; and Pvt. Edward Burns of Captain Clarke's Company.[52] They traveled northeast to-ward Canada with inadequate provisions and several muskets but few other items of prac-tical value. Their journey was daunting and required trudging without snowshoes through nearly 100 miles of frozen wilderness. Oswego's green deserters were woefully unprepared for the challenge. Aside from the valuable wood cutting skills of Pvt. John Dowgan, the other mutineer deserters possessed no real wilderness survival training. Most critically, they lacked the hunting abilities to successfully acquire game in the wild.

The tremendous expenditure of energy from constant walking through deep snow, combined with constant shivering, burned thousands of calories and quickly melted off the deserters' fat reserves. Additionally, they suffered severe frostbite to their hands and feet. After approximately eight days, the Corporal's contingent of ten deserters separated into two parties. The first party needed to rest in a makeshift camp and included the Drummer (William Burchell), David Ray, Timothy Sullivan, and Edward Burns, all privates. The sec-ond party consisted of William Barry (the Corporal) and Pvts. James Reed, Peter Eybergen, Mark Sampson, John Dowgan, and Michael Finn. This group was pushed by the Corporal to continue their drive north. But only a day later with their provisions exhausted, the gnawing agony of human starvation caused the Corporal to order James Reed to shoot Mark Sampson with his musket. The five deserters consumed most of Sampson's body and carried away his hind quarters for later sustenance.[53] Only four days later, the Corporal co-erced Janes Reed to shoot Peter Eybergen. The party of four deserters proceeded to eat Ey-bergen's entire body and continued their desperate trek toward Cataraqui. After marching for seven more days, the Corporal ordered John Dowgan and Michael Finn to kill the pre-vious executioner, James Reed. When Dowgan and Finn refused, the Corporal took over

---

51. Minutes of a General Court of Inquiry at the City of Albany, July 18, 1753, 132.
52. Minutes of a General Court of Inquiry at the City of Albany, July 18, 1753, 143.
53. Minutes of a General Court of Inquiry at the City of Albany, July 18, 1753, 140.

and shot Private Reed. Reed's body was quickly cut into pieces and eaten by the group's remaining deserters. The next day, the Corporal attempted to murder Michael Finn, but Barry's musket misfired, and Finn escaped. When Finn rejoined the group a day later, the Corporal made several further attempts to kill him but was prevented by Dowgan.[54] Dowgan and Finn then separated from the Corporal. They decided to turn south and return to Oswego as their only chance for survival. Dowgan and Finn never saw the Corporal again. On their return trek they came across an old campsite of the group of four deserters they had left several days earlier that included William Burchell, David Ray, Timothy Sullivan, and Edward Burns. Dowgan and Finn found the Drummer's corpse with a gun shot and with all flesh stripped, except for his legs.

It was apparent that both deserting parties had resorted to grisly cannibalism in order to survive the overwhelming frozen wilderness. Only John Dowgan and Michael Finn managed to escape the brutal ordeal. It was a nightmare in which the deserters faced not only the challenges of harsh terrain and punishing weather but also the treachery of fellow deserters attempting to murder one another for their flesh. Dowgan and Finn finally arrived back at Oswego on February 22, 1752, a month after beginning their ill-fated journey to Cataraqui.[55] One of the first things Captain Mills did after he took them into custody was to get an account of their desertions as best they could recollect. As detainees of the captain, Privates Dowgan and Finn awaited military justice at future courts-martial trials.

When fur trader and agent to William Johnson, Benjamin Stoddert, visited Oswego on February 1, 1752, he helped restore Captain Mills's garrison command by promising to grant forgiveness to the remaining nondeserting mutineers. As a veteran and trusted trader, Stoddert's word strengthened Captain Mills's similar assurances of forgiveness. With joint promises extended by Mills and Stoddert, the soldiers returned to their regular garrison duty.

While at Oswego, Stoddert took time in March to track the northbound path of the deserters. Stoddert often sold British trade goods he received from Johnson directly to French traders at Cataraqui rather than to far west Indians.[56] Thus, Stoddert knew the way to Cataraqui quite well and may have wanted to learn if Oswego's deserters had lifted any of his merchandise to sell to the French. As he tracked the deserters' trail toward Canada, Stoddert made several grisly discoveries. In a March 24, 1752, letter to William Johnson, Stoddert noted he was with a party of Indians near Cataraqui and found the mangled body of Private William Burchell (the Drummer), the bones of others, and the skull of Mark Sampson that had apparently been used as a drinking bowl. Stoddert stated he later came

---

54. Minutes of a General Court of Inquiry at the City of Albany, July 18, 1753, 140–41.
55. "Extract of a Letter from Oswego, dated February 22, 1752," *Pennsylvania Gazette*, April 2, 1752, Issue 1216, page 2, (accessed at American Antiquarian Society January 2, 2009) http://infoweb.newsbank.com/com/iw_search/we/HistArchive/?p_product=EANX+p_theme=ahnp+p_nbid=V5
56. Norton, *The Fur Trade in Colonial New York*, 191.

upon an encampment and found Captain Mills's stolen sword, several pistols, a hanger, three shirts, and four muskets. Stoddert also informed Johnson that some Indians on a hunt came across several campsites and found carcasses of other men who had been murdered and cannibalized. The Natives found shirts, muskets, stockings, and a laced waistcoat, all stolen from Captain Mills.[57] It appeared that several of the mutineers got close to reaching their Cataraqui destination before succumbing to the wilderness, starvation, and human cannibalism. But even absent their weakened conditions, the deserters would have experienced great difficulty crossing the swift flowing and hazardous water passages separating New York province from Cataraqui.

Back at Oswego, Nathaniel Downing (the Doctor), had become the "de facto commander" of the garrison following the January 11, 1752, mutiny before the arrival of Benjamin Stoddert and restoration of Captain Mill's command on February 1, 1752. Following Mills's and Stoddert's joint promises of forgiveness to the Doctor and remaining nondeserting soldiers, Downing's three-week "command" unceremoniously ended. Regardless, the situation for the captain remained precarious as he had to command divided garrison in crisis. Mills's and Stoddart's blanket exoneration to nondeserting mutineers was probably a token gesture intended to restore stability to the garrison and return the soldiers to duty. Shortly thereafter, the remaining mutineers recognized their error in supporting the mutiny and turned on the Doctor. Sensing danger from within, Downing moved out of the garrison and sought "sanctuary" in trader William Gough's house in town near the frozen riverbank. Assisting Gough with protecting the Doctor were fellow traders Thomas Davis and Thomas Bearup. Despite his personal assurance of "forgiveness" to Downing, Captain Mills desperately wanted to capture the mutiny's "Judas like" instigator from the traders and detain him for the provincial authorities. Mills tried several times to capture the Doctor but was ultimately unsuccessfully.[58] For example, on March 13, 1752, the Captain ordered the garrison sergeant and a file of soldiers into town and to William Gough's house to arrest the Doctor. Gough informed the sergeant that the Doctor was in the woods. Following a heated exchange, trader Thomas Bearup threatened to use a gun against the soldiers and they withdrew.[59] The next day, Gough, Davis, Bearup, and the Doctor confronted Captain Mills and trader William Rickman at Rickman's house. They profanely warned Mills not to carry arms or send armed soldiers to town. At the same time, Gough and his trader accomplices threatened Rickman with violence if he allowed Captain Mills into his house again.[60] The temerity with which the Doctor, Gough, and other implicated fur traders threatened and intimidated Captain Mills and his loyal soldiers to desist from

---

57. Letter of Benjamin Stoddert to William Johnson et al., March 24, 1752, *Sir William Johnson Papers*, 1: 366–67.
58. Minutes of a General Court of Inquiry at the City of Albany, July 18, 1753, 135.
59. Minutes of a General Court of Inquiry at the City of Albany, July 18, 1753, 137.
60. Minutes of a General Court of Inquiry at the City of Albany, July 18, 1753, 135.

their efforts to arrest Nathaniel Downing is matched only by the captain's timidity and lack of fortitude. A more determined and courageous commander would have managed a way, by dint of surprise and force of arms, to successfully apprehend the Doctor, Gough, and other complicit traders. Perhaps the fact that Captain Mills chose not to do this was one of the very reasons the Doctor, Gough, and other fur traders conspired with impressionable young soldiers to attempt the mutiny in the first place. Indeed, the conspirators may have accurately assessed Mills as too weak, too trusting, and an easy mark to suffer loss of his command and abject humiliation.

A raw power struggle between garrison forces and the fur traders clearly favored Oswego's rogue traders led by a thuggish Mr. Gough. Captain Mills, his armed garrison soldiers, and friendly trader Rickman were undone by Gough's bravado and intimidating verbal warnings. Just two weeks later, on March 29, 1752, Nathaniel Downing (the Doctor) and trader William Gough made their escapes from Oswego. Downing successfully evaded New York's provincial justice system. Ironically, the two made their escape right under the nose of Captain Mills, with direct assistance from unscrupulous members of Oswego's fur business community.[61]

Determined Justice

Under New York's military chain of command, Captain Mills reported to Capt. Hubert Marshall in Albany. After Pvt. Thomas Colson and trader Thomas Davis disclosed the January 11th Oswego mutiny to Marshall at Schenectady in early February 1752, Marshall forwarded news of the event to Governor George Clinton. Clinton immediately recognized his very serious predicament. First, the mutiny and desertion occurred on his watch. Those events represented a major embarrassment to his administration. Clinton's public mortification was exacerbated by a March 23, 1752, article that appeared in the *Pennsylvania Gazette*. The article included excerpts from Pvts. John Dowgan and Michael Finn's account of their month-long northbound desertion into the wilderness, including graphic descriptions of murder and cannibalism.[62] Moreover, Governor Clinton was unable to convene valid general courts-martial trials for the four mutineers because he lacked the requisite thirteen officers, including a presiding field officer, to conduct the proceedings. And only general courts-martial tribunals could impose the death penalty for capital offenses such as mutiny and desertion.[63]

Governor Clinton, recognizing the need for swift action under emergency circumstances, directed that a court of inquiry be held in Albany on July 18, 1752. Capt. Hubert Marshall presided at the inquiry as president. Other members included Capt. Thomas

---

61. Minutes of a General Court of Inquiry at the City of Albany, July 18, 1753, 135.
62. "Extract of a Letter from Oswego, Dated February 22, 1752."
63. Pargellis, "The Four Independent Companies of New York," 116.

Clarke, Lt. William Ogilvie, Lt. John Roseboom, Lt. Lewis Pavy, Lt. Walter Butler, Capt. Simon Soumaien, Lt. Richard Miller, and Lt. William Spearing. The following soldiers charged with mutiny and desertion appeared before the court of inquiry: Pvts. John Colson, John Dowgan, Michael Finn, and John Young. Witnesses testifying at the inquest included Capt. John Mills, fur traders John Ackerman and William Rickman, Schenectady based Sergeant Bayley, and nondeserting mutineers, Pvts. John Bachus, John Phipps, John Gordon, Miles Cahill, John Poulton, and. James Harris.[64]

Sybarnt G. V. Schaick was the court recorder who kept the minutes of the inquiry. Testimony taken at the hearing successfully deconstructed the mutiny. Without doubt, the most arresting revelation came from Oswego fur trader and garrison Pvt. John Ackerman (the former sergeant). On January 12, 1752, the morning after the mutiny, fellow trader William Gough visited Ackerman at his house and discussed the recent uprising. Gough bragged to Ackerman that he was "the whole Creation of it, that is of the mutiny, and that he knew it Twenty Days before it happened."[65] Gough's transparent admission is central to understanding why he engineered the mutiny. Since Mills's arrival at Oswego in the second half of 1751, Gough viewed the captain as his adversary. Recall that Captain Mills did not approve of Ackerman's active involvement in the fur trade while serving as a sergeant, or non-commissioned officer, and that Mills had demoted Ackerman to private. Perhaps Gough's braggadocio was his way of demonstrating to Ackerman he had the guile to pull it off and settle a score with Mills on Ackerman's behalf. Regardless, nothing in the minutes of the Albany inquest implicated Ackerman in the plot. Apparently, Ackerman was not a vengeful sort and did not seek to bring down the captain, despite having plenty of motive for doing so. Quite to the contrary, Ackerman was forthright and told the tribunal that William Gough had persuaded a group of four conspirators: a civilian and three soldiers— the Doctor, the Corporal, the Drummer, and John Colson—to intimidate and bully other garrison soldiers into acquiescing to the uprising. It was William Gough, the vile, unscrupulous, and physically imposing fur trader who covertly schemed with his garrison abettors for twenty days prior to upending Mills's command. Perhaps Gough's unmerciful beating of John Ackerman for questioning Gough's brutal assault on a nondeserting soldier encouraged Ackerman's damaging testimony.[66]

John Ackerman further testified that Gough informed him he had told the men—the Doctor, the Corporal, the Drummer and John Colson to "take the Damn'd Son of a Bitch (Captain Mills), confine him in Irons (exactly what the mutineers did), [and that Gough] would say the same thing to the Damn'd Son of a Bitch's face" (however, Gough never did).[67] Such was the level of animus Gough held for Oswego's new garrison commander

64. Minutes of a General Court of Inquiry at the City of Albany, July 18, 1753, 133–41.
65. Minutes of a General Court of Inquiry at the City of Albany, July 18, 1753, 136.
66. Minutes of a General Court of Inquiry at the City of Albany, July 18, 1753, 138.
67. Minutes of a General Court of Inquiry at the City of Albany, July 18, 1753, 136.

who replaced the more trade-tolerant Lt. John Lindesay. Apparently, Gough's preferred status quo world at the frontier trading post was under direct threat from newcomer Captain Mills. Other witness testimony at the inquiry was damaging to the main conspirators, especially to Pvt. John Colson. Oswego trader William Rickman testified that the Doctor told him he planned to play several "flings," or mean pranks, against Captain Mills. The various "flings" were designed to undermine Mills's command by creating divisions between the captain and the fur traders, garrison soldiers, or Native Americans. Rickman further stated the Doctor described how he (but not Gough) recruited Mills's soldiers to become mutiny conspirators, starting with John Colson. Colson, in turn recruited the Corporall, who later persuaded the Drummer and David Ray to join the revolt. All the ringleaders were recruited and sworn to secrecy around mid to late December 1751, up to the time they ambushed Captain Mills in his garrison quarters on January 11, 1752.[68]

Sergeant Bayley, who was stationed at Schenectady, testified that Private Colson told him Captain Mills did not mistreat his men, but that the Corporal physically assaulted Mills, took his keys, and detained him in handcuffs. Bayley also testified that Colson told him he had recruited Mark Sampson into the mutiny and used rum to facilitate Sampson's "loyalty conversion."[69]

Pvt. John Bachus informed the tribunal that John Colson was one of the conspirators in the mutiny who had "officer status," along with the Doctor, the Drummer, and the Corporal. Bachus also stated the Doctor called William Gough to severely beat him for talking with other nondeserting soldiers regarding how to restore Mills to his command.[70] Mutineer disloyalty among any of the soldiers was not tolerated by the civilian conspirators.

Pvt. John Phipps testified that Captain Mills treated John Colson exceedingly well and that Colson acted as a "Sergeant of the Guard" who watched over the captain while he was detained.[71] In addition, Pvts. John Gordon, Miles Cahill, John Poulton, and James Harris all corroborated that Colson was a mutiny ringleader along with the Doctor, the Corporal, and the Drummer, and that Colson was the main person who watched over Mills.[72] When Private Colson was allowed to speak on his own behalf, he testified that Captain Mills never took provisions from his soldiers and that he had been "forced" into the mutiny.[73]

Pvt. Michael Finn, one of only two survivors of the wilderness desertion along with John Dowgan, testified that all deserters in his party, including the Drummer, Ray, Burns, and Dowgan, declared they "had no reason to Complain for that Captain Mills had been very kind to them."[74] In fact, Finn supposed Ray murdered the Drummer as the Drummer

68. Minutes of a General Court of Inquiry at the City of Albany, July 18, 1753, 139.
69. Minutes of a General Court of Inquiry at the City of Albany, July 18, 1753, 139.
70. Minutes of a General Court of Inquiry at the City of Albany, July 18, 1753, 139.
71. Minutes of a General Court of Inquiry at the City of Albany, July 18, 1753, 139.
72. Minutes of a General Court of Inquiry at the City of Albany, July 18, 1753, 139.
73. Minutes of a General Court of Inquiry at the City of Albany, July 18, 1753, 140.
74. Minutes of a General Court of Inquiry at the City of Albany, July 18, 1753, 141.

accused Ray of taking him from a garrison where he was well treated. Finn added that the deserters often wished they had John Colson so they "might roast him alive as he had been a Chief instrument of all their unhappiness."[75]

Witness testimony at the inquest clearly debunked allegations by the Doctor and other conspirators that Mills had mistreated soldiers at the garrison. To the contrary, the captain treated his men well. The deserters regretted betraying Mills while trudging, cold and starving, through the frozen wilderness.

Mayor Robert Sanders of Albany, who certified the witnesses and evidence at the July 18, 1752, court of inquiry, was heavily involved in the illicit Albany to Montreal fur trade. In addition, Sanders was a close business and political associate of William Johnson, his most important ally in Albany.[76] Mayor Sanders conveyed minutes of the court of inquiry to Governor Clinton. On matters of colonial administration, Clinton reported to the Board of Trade and Plantations in London. Accordingly, in the fall of 1752, John Catherwood, secretary to the New York governor, forwarded Clinton's memorial and minutes of his court of inquiry to the Board of Trade. Clinton did not relish sending these documents to London because they exposed significant failures in his oversight of the important provincial fur trading post and military garrison at Oswego.

Because New York's four Independent companies were not part of the regular British Army, administration of the Independents fell to the governor. In London, Whitehall effectively washed its hands of these troops through chronic neglect. Ironically, Governor Clinton and captains of New York's Independent companies welcomed such neglect because it encouraged them to report inflated muster numbers. The resulting per-capita oversupply of accoutrements and clothing, together with sales of officer commissions, proved rather lucrative to the captains. Also, Clinton basked in colonial prestige as overall commander of provincial New York's Independent companies.[77] The governor surely understood that most perks associated with his laissez-faire oversight of the Independents would likely sunset once news of the Oswego mutiny reached senior ministers and King George II in London.

Upon receipt of Clinton's memorial, the Board of Trade clearly recognized the embarrassing political import of frontier mutiny and desertion and shifted into damage-control mode. The Board swiftly forwarded Clinton's memorial and minutes of the court of inquiry with a cover letter dated January 11, 1753, to Secretary of War Henry Fox. Board member Dunk Halifax specifically asked Fox to present Clinton's memorial and inquiry minutes to George II. In effect, Halifax requested that Fox seek the King's approval of the Board of Trade's recommendation to secure justice for Oswego's four soldier-deserters held in detention at Albany. The Board acknowledged that Governor Clinton had no legal

75. Minutes of a General Court of Inquiry at the City of Albany, July 18, 1753, 141.
76. Norton, *The Fur Trade in Colonial New York*, 190.
77. Pargellis, "The Four Independent Companies," 117.

authority to inflict capital punishment in New York sans a royal warrant authorizing general courts-martial trials. Moreover, Clinton had been unable to muster thirteen British officers, including a presiding field officer, to proceed with the trials.[78]

The Board's plan suggested Governor Clinton send all offenders to Halifax, Nova Scotia, for their trials. The Articles of War specified capital punishment for those found guilty of mutiny and desertion. With the King's consent, the plan could quickly be put into motion via a special warrant authorizing the trials and death sentences. Additionally, the Board considered the mutiny trials of utmost importance to both the Crown and provincial New York. As such, all of Oswego's accused offenders qualified for speedy justice.[79] Firm examples of certain capital punishment needed to be provided to other provincial soldiers across America.

Secretary Fox responded to the Board of Trade's January 11, 1753, letter on February 3, 1753. In his letter, Fox raised the issue of legal jurisdiction for the trials "doubts [have] arisen whether offenders could be legally try'd by a General Court Martial in Nova Scotia, for offenses committed in the Province of New York."[80] Fox mentioned he referred the jurisdiction question to Britain's attorney general for a ruling. Dudley Ryder was the sitting attorney general at the time.[81] In the interest of British justice, the attorney general agreed with the Board of Trade's recommendation that the mutineer deserters be transported from New York Province to Halifax for trial, contingent on securing the King's special warrant. Fox requested that the Board of Trade issue necessary orders to Governor Clinton to send the accused soldiers and witnesses to Halifax forthwith.

Given the high-profile nature of the Oswego mutiny and related desertions as well as the urgency for summary justice, both the Board and Secretary of War Fox acted with atypical dispatch. As their correspondence shows, the Board offered a solution to Governor Clinton's inability to hold courts-martial trials in New York by moving them to Halifax. Similarly, Fox offered a solution to the problem of legal jurisdiction by securing an opinion from the British attorney general.[82]

But the Board's March 16, 1753, letter to Fox raised yet another issue "Difficulty has arisen in what manner the Expense attending the passage of people to and from Halifax is to be defrayed."[83] The Board was unable to order Clinton to send the mutineer deserters and witnesses to Halifax before the issue of travel expenses was resolved. Again, the Board

---

78. Letter of the Board of Trade and Plantations to Henry Fox, Secretary of War, January 11, 1753, CO 5 1128, 30–32, British National Archives.
79. Letter of the Board of Trade and Plantations to Henry Fox, Secretary of War, January 11, 1753.
80. Letter of Henry Fox to the Board of Trade and Plantations, February 3, 1753, CO 5 1064 li 47, 172, British National Archives.
81. "Dudley Ryder (judge)," Wikipedia, accessed April 29, 2022, https://en.wikipedia.org/wiki/Dudley_Ryder_(judge).
82. Letter of Henry Fox to the Board of Trade and Plantations, February 3, 1753, 172.
83. Letter of the Board of Trade and Plantations to Henry Fox, March 16, 1753, CO 5 1128 f30, 35, British National Archives.

offered a solution to the problem. They recommended Governor Clinton request his leg-islative Assembly to defray those expenses, but they also asked Fox for directions to give Clinton if the Assembly refused to pay.[84] It is unclear whether Fox responded directly to the Board regarding their question of travel expenses, but a compromise was reached. Per the Board's initial recommendation, they requested that Clinton ask New York's Assembly to pay the expenses. Should the Assembly decline, Clinton would order the captains of the affected Independent companies to defray the travel expenses. If those costs proved too great, Clinton would then request Secretary of War Henry Fox to cover all expenses the captains were unable to settle.[85]

With time of the essence, the Board of Trade and Henry Fox undertook final mea-sures to bring Oswego's mutineer deserters to military justice in Halifax. Fox handled an important communiqué in his April 2, 1753, letter to Col. Thomas Hopson, governor of Nova Scotia and commander of the King's forces there. Fox's letter contained several key enclosures that apprised Hopson of the Oswego mutiny and authorized him to conduct general courts-martial trials for the mutineer deserters.[86] Enclosed was a copy of New York governor Clinton's memorial and minutes of the court of inquiry. Also enclosed were two special warrants from George II signed, per His Majesty's Command, by Secretary of State the Earl of Holdernesse. The first warrant, dated February 17, 1753, authorized Hopson to appoint general courts-martial trials for punishment of the Oswego offenders—Privates Colson, Dowgan, Finn, and Young.[87] The second warrant authorized Colonel Hopson to confirm and carry out sentences of death, if so decided at the trials.[88] In the first special warrant, Holdernesse mentioned it was His Majesty's Pleasure that upon arrival of the of-fenders in Halifax, Hopson was to proceed forthwith with the trials.[89] Additionally, it is noteworthy this warrant also directed Colonel Hopson to carry out all applicable death sentences at the Halifax garrison "without making any further Report to us."[90] At that point, it appeared the King, Holdernesse, and Fox in London had washed their hands of Oswego's unseemly affair and desired summary closure to it. At the same time, however, the home

84. Letter of the Board of Trade and Plantations to Henry Fox, March 16, 1753, 36.

85. Letter of Thomas Hill, Secretary to the Board of Trade and Plantations to New York Governor George Clinton, April 17, 1753, CO5 1128 f37, 37–38, British National Archives.

86. Letter of Henry Fox to Colonel Hopson, Governor of Nova Scotia, April 2, 1753, WO 4 49, 134–36. British National Archives.

87. King's Special Warrant to Colonel Thomas Hopson, Governor of Nova Scotia, Authorizing General Courts-Marital Trials in Halifax, February 17, 1753, Special Subjects/Royal Warrants, Public Archives of Nova Scotia, Halifax.

88. King's Special Warrant to Colonel Thomas Hopson, Governor of Nova Scotia, Authorizing Carrying Out Death Sentences in Halifax, March 21, 1753, Special Subjects/Royal Warrants, Pub-lic Archives of Nova Scotia, Halifax.

89. King's Special Warrant to Colonel Thomas Hopson, Governor of Nova Scotia, Authorizing Carrying Out Death Sentences in Halifax, March 21, 1753.

90. King's Special Warrant to Colonel Thomas Hopson, Governor of Nova Scotia, Authorizing Carrying Out Death Sentences in Halifax, March 21, 1753.

government was very keen to avoid future mutinies and desertions at other British frontier outposts in North America. Holdernesse inserted appropriate prophylactic language to that effect in the King's second special warrant dated March 21, 1753. Because of their situation and distance from Britain, frontier garrisons like Oswego must have their forces (New York Independent companies) in great readiness, as if always in a state of war. Further, the second warrant added that nothing can keep soldiers diligent to their duties than to bring those guilty of capital crimes, such as mutiny & desertion, to speedy justice with the death penalty.[91] In support of swift action in an otherwise interminably ponderous bureaucracy, the Earl of Holderness signed the King's February 17, 1753, special warrant only a few days after learning from Fox's February 2, 1753, letter to the Board of Trade that the Attorney General ruled Oswego's offenders may be sent legally to Halifax for courts-martial trials. Clearly, George II and his senior ministers wanted the frontier mutineer deserters tried and punished as quickly as possible consistent within prevailing martial protocol.

Similar to Henry Fox's important military communiqué to Colonel Hopson, the Board of Trade sent a vital civil communication in its April 17, 1753, letter to Governor Clinton. Board Secretary Thomas Hill wrote that the Board's Lordships desired Clinton to send the Oswego offenders to Halifax to stand trial. Hill also directed Clinton to request the New York Assembly to pay for all travel expenses. If refused, Clinton would order the captains of the four affected Independent companies to pay, and Secretary of War Henry Fox would defray any applicable shortages as needed.[92] It took some four to five months for Clinton's July 18, 1752, court of inquiry memorial and minutes to reach the Board of Trade and Plantations in London by late fall 1752. Surprisingly, only about the same amount of time was required for the Board, Henry Fox, George II, the Earl of Holdernesse, Governor Clinton, and Colonel Hopson to overcome gnarly legal and fiscal issues in setting up the general courts-martial trials in Halifax.

Despite being ponderously transatlantic, the pathway to justice for Oswego's four mutineer deserters was relentlessly determined. Nevertheless, it fell short of complete justice for the harms suffered. In Halifax, second-tier ringleader Pvt. John Colson, along Pvts. John Dowgan, Michael Finn, and John Young met the firm authority of British military justice and were hanged by summer 1753. Of ten mutineer deserters who left Oswego on January 22, 1752, only two, Dowgan and Finn, survived to tell about it. At least five were brutally murdered and cannibalized, while three others likely died from starvation and hypothermia. Although eight deserters escaped formal military justice, they faced the inexorable certain "justice" of Northern New York's frontier winter landscapes. In a tragic bit of irony, most Oswego deserters regretted betraying a commander who treated them well and felt

---

91. King's Special Warrant to Colonel Thomas Hopson, Governor of Nova Scotia, Authorizing Carrying Out Death Sentences in Halifax, March 21, 1753.

92. Letter of the Board of Trade and Plantations to New York Governor George Clinton, April 17, 1753, CO 5 1128 f37, 38–39, British National Archives.

betrayed themselves by Pvt. John Colson and other conspirators who had pressured them into joining the foolhardy rebellion. Several fur traders, namely William Gough, Thomas Davis, and Thomas Bearup, had secretly conspired with and abetted Oswego's soldiers in their mutiny efforts. Regrettably, these elusive civilians were never held accountable for their actions. With a personal vendetta against Captain Mills, covert strongman William Gough coordinated behind the scenes to enforce the actions of his soldierly accomplices. For weeks, the wily fur trader secretly schemed with Nathaniel Downing, garrison surgeon, to wrest control of the garrison away from Mills. And like Gough, the Doctor cleverly managed to escape Oswego. In doing so, Downing evaded capture by Mills and any provincial criminal charges for the significant role he played in fomenting the uprising.

One my ask what became of Capt. John Mills? Certainly, his hapless performance during the 1752 mutiny might have ended his military career. But like Captain Bligh of the Royal Navy, Mills lived to command another day. With a strong letter of support from trader Benjamin Stoddert, Governor Clinton believed the garrison commander was innocent of any wrongdoing and was allowed to continue at Oswego.[93] Subsequently in 1754, Captain Mills was ordered by New York's new governor, James Delancey, to command a small garrison at Schenectady—but as a lieutenant, not as captain.[94]

Aftermath

The 1752 Oswego mutiny and desertion represented a military and political failure of the first order. For a brief period in January 1752, New York's provincial troops, under weak British command, failed to meet the Crown's firm expectation to protect and maintain its expanding commerce.[95] Nefarious elements within Oswego's fur trading community temporarily usurped those imperial powers. Garrison soldiers fell victim to the subterfuge of lawless fur traders. Nathaniel Downing, William Gough, and other affected traders, civilians all, and most deserving of provincial justice, managed to elude their punishments. By contrast, all remaining garrison soldier-mutineers were executed for their capital offenses under British military law.

Henceforth, Captain Mills was disgraced and humiliated over losing his command that cold January evening. Further, the event embarrassed Governor Clinton who was responsible for administration of the province's four Independent companies. Similarly, the insurrection reflected poorly on William Johnson and his Oswego fur trading enterprise. Anyone with direct military or business connections with either the garrison or trading post desired to quickly distance themselves from the event.

---

93. Letter from John Ayscough to William Johnson, February 26, 1752, *Sir William Johnson Papers*, 9:90.
94. Letter from New York Governor James DeLancey to the Earl of Holdernesse, Secretary of State, April 22, 1754, CO 5 14. 88, British National Archives.
95. Way, "Militarizing the Atlantic World," 360.

In London, King George II took considerable interest in the British army and all things military.[96] How severely disappointed he must have felt at the news of the feckless performance of his New York Independent company "stepchildren" in North America. And too, the Board of Trade, Secretary of War Henry Fox, and the Earl of Holdernesse were all crestfallen by the rebellion, threats to imperial commerce, and loss of British-Colonial martial honor. Collectively, they vowed to prevent similar disorders in the future. To be sure, the King's February 17, 1753, special warrant elevated standards on military leadership, discipline, rule of law, and capital punishment at all frontier garrisons. Importantly, the caliber of officers and soldiers was also upgraded—specifically to prevent ex-convicts and mutiny conspirators, such as William Burchell (the Drummer), and David Ray, from serving in the military in the future.[97] Following 1753, Henry Fox kept his provincial formations on a tighter leash. He required all colonial governors to submit monthly reports on the status of their respective Independent companies. In New York, the Independent companies continued to project imperial power along its borders until the close of the Seven Years' War in 1763. But the martial limbo was short-lived. The Independents were subsequently disbanded as part of Britain's general peacetime drawdown of military forces in North America.[98]

96. Jeremy Black, *George III: America's Last King* (New Haven: Yale University Press, 2006), 366.
97. Minutes of a General Court of Inquiry at the City of Albany, July 18, 1752, 140.
98. Pargellis, "The Four Independent Companies," 121.

When Sunday Baseball Came to Brooklyn

Stuart M. Blumin and Glenn C. Altschuler

On Sunday, May 3, 1874, police in Brooklyn, New York, arrested seventeen boys, ranging in age from ten to seventeen, and hauled them to court where each was fined the nontrivial sum of $2. The boys were not accused of stealing, disturbing the peace, trespassing, interfering with the services of a nearby church, or uttering foul language within earshot of respectable citizens. The "green fields in the suburbs" where they had gathered were remote from stores, churches, homes, and tender ears. Their crime? They were playing a game of baseball. Sunday baseball, it seems, was illegal in Brooklyn, New York.[1]

Sabbatarian laws—"Sunday blue laws" in common parlance—were common in nineteenth-century America, especially in areas dominated by Protestants who maintained religious values and practices inherited from their Calvinist forefathers. Brooklyn's original European settlers were the Dutch, whose Reformed Church sprang from traditions similar to those of English Puritans. But it was New Englanders, direct heirs of those Puritans, who came to dominate this old agricultural community as its East River shoreline began to sprout docks, warehouses, and workshops during the last years of the eighteenth century and when Brooklyn Heights emerged a few decades later as "America's first suburb" on a steeply rising bluff directly across the river from lower Manhattan.[2] The people who pioneered this new form of American community on the Heights were, for the most part, well-to-do merchants, bankers, and brokers who had migrated to New York from Massachusetts, Connecticut, and other New England states. Now they began to make much shorter daily migrations, by steam ferry, to build spacious homes beyond the crowded and noisy city, and to form a pious, well-ordered, and church-oriented community of like-minded believers.

---

1. *Brooklyn Daily Eagle*, May 5, 1874. This essay expands upon our discussion of baseball and Sabbatarianism in Stuart M. Blumin and Glenn C. Altschuler, *The Rise and Fall of Protestant Brooklyn: An American Story* (Ithaca, N.Y.: Cornell University Press, 2022).
2. Robert Furman, *Brooklyn Heights: The Rise, Fall and Rebirth of America's First Suburb* (Charleston, SC: History Press, 2015); Clay Lancaster, *Old Brooklyn Heights: New York's First Suburb* (New York: Dover Publications, Inc., 1979); Kenneth T. Jackson, *Crabgrass Frontier: The Suburbanization of the United States* (New York: Oxford University Press), 25–32.

Figure 1. Large policeman arresting small baseball player. CLIVE WEED, *New York Evening Sun*, FROM *Letters, Comments and Editorials Endorsing Sunday Baseball* (BROOKLYN, N.Y.: N.P., 1918), 51.

Figure 2. "Beautiful Words." NELSON HARDING, *Brooklyn Daily Eagle*, DECEMBER 1, 1920.

When the Village of Brooklyn was incorporated by the State of New York in 1816, among the first acts of its government was a law prohibiting "any work or servile labor on the Lord's day" as well as "shooting, sporting, playing ball, or other unlawful exercises or pastimes on said day."[3] By 1834, when Brooklyn earned a city charter, it was already becoming known as the City of Churches, a sobriquet it would proudly bear through the remainder of the nineteenth century. The charter celebration helped give substance to the name. Citizens assembled before the Dutch Reformed Church and paraded through the downtown and the streets of Brooklyn Heights to the new city's bastion of New England Protestantism, the First Presbyterian Church, where they listened to an ode, an oration, an anthem, and a song praising the Pilgrim Fathers.[4]

Brooklyn was by no means the only American community to claim a Plymouth patrimony or to perpetuate its Puritan lineage by means of laws protecting the sanctity of the Sabbath. But its experience was unique in ways that cast a particularly strong light on both the continuing power of Calvinist and post-Calvinist Protestantism in the United States and various challenges to that power. Brooklyn grew very rapidly during the nineteenth century; by 1860 it was the third largest city in the United States. Accompanying its growth was the appearance of a range of urban secular attractions, some of which were difficult to reconcile with traditional notions of Sunday as a day of church attendance and private prayer. Among those who swelled the local population were foreign immigrants, including Irish Catholics, who brought with them very different forms of religious belief and worship. Even many Protestant immigrants—German Lutherans, among others—saw the American Protestant Sabbath as a dull and needless exercise in self-abnegation. These were general phenomena of the nineteenth and early twentieth centuries; but as a three-year battle over whether horse-drawn trolleys should run on Sundays suggests, Brooklyn experienced them on a larger scale and perhaps with more intensity than most other American communities.[5]

Important aspects of Brooklyn's experience, moreover, were distinctive. It was the largest and most significant American city that was also a suburb of another, even larger city with which it was often at odds. New York had its religious communities and many residents who maintained a quiet and prayerful Sunday. But it was also, and famously, the site of brothels, illicit theatrical performances, and other corrupting institutions—a Sodom just a short ferry ride across the river from the City of Churches. New York loomed over Brooklyn in a way that at once threatened and reinforced the smaller city's values. The *New York Times* expressed this fraught relationship in 1858 when it referred with undisguised sarcasm to "the nice religious feelings of our excellent neighbors across the East

---

3. *Long-Island Star*, July 3, 1816. This ordinance exempted children under fifteen years of age. The City later eliminated this exemption; hence, the arrest of ten-year old boys in 1874.
4. *Star*, April 24, 1834.
5. *Brooklyn Evening Star*, July 6, 1854; October 10, 1854; March 13, 1857; *Eagle*, February 7, 1856; March 14, 1857; April 8, 1857; April 9, 1857; May 13, 1857; May 18, 1857.

River."[6] The sarcasm was undiminished a quarter of a century later when the *Times* termed Brooklyn the "moral suburb" of the great city.[7] Brooklyn was itself a great city by this time, growing more rapidly than New York, but it could not escape the dominance of its larger and more powerful neighbor. "Every other city earns its own way," observed the journalist Julian Ralph in *Harper's New Monthly Magazine* in 1893, "while Brooklyn works for New York, and is paid off like a shop-girl on Saturday nights." When Brooklynites travel, they "write New York opposite their names on hotel registers."[8]

Just as unusual, and as threatening, was Brooklyn's own site of illicit pleasures, the popular seaside resort on Coney Island—a "Sodom by the Sea."[9] Coney Island earned an unsavory reputation as "a haven for gamblers, confidence men, pickpockets, and prostitutes," and though it became more respectable with the construction of large and elegant hotels during the late 1870s, the perceived threat to Brooklyn's moral order was not dispelled.[10] Immense amusement parks built after the turn of the twentieth century attracted their largest crowds of families and young singles on summer Sundays, offering attractions that could not be confused with prayer. Other communities dealt with nearby amusement parks, beaches, or other such distractions from Christian duty, but nothing on the scale of Brooklyn's Coney Island.

And finally, there was Brooklyn's nearly unique relation to baseball. Cooperstown may be the adored, albeit mythical, shrine of baseball's origins, but the game itself developed mainly in the New York metropolitan area, and Brooklyn was an active participant from its earliest days.[11] By 1858 there were at least twenty amateur "base ball" clubs in Brooklyn and an unknowable number of informal "pickup" games on fields and empty lots. The local press embraced the sport, reporting regularly on games and proclaiming baseball to be America's pastime.[12] But some Brooklynites were as deeply committed to Sabbatarianism

---

6. Quoted in *Eagle*, November 5, 1858.

7. David McCullough, *The Great Bridge: The Epic Story of the Building of the Brooklyn Bridge* (New York: Simon and Schuster, 1972), 519.

8. Julian Ralph, "The City of Brooklyn," *Harper's New Monthly Magazine*, 86, no. 515 (April 1893): 652.

9. Oliver Pilat and Jo Ranson, *Sodom by the Sea: An Affectionate History of Coney Island* (Garden City, N.Y.: Garden City Publishing , 1943).

10. John F. Kasson, *Amusing the Million: Coney Island at the Turn of the Century* (New York: McGraw-Hill, 1978), 29.

11. On the early history of baseball see Harold Seymour and Dorothy Seymour Mills, *Baseball: The Early Years* (New York: Oxford University Press, 1960); Peter Levine, *A. G. Spalding and the Rise of Baseball* (New York: Oxford University Press, 1985); Melvin L. Adelman, *A Sporting Time: New York City and the Rise of Modern Athletics, 1820–70* (Urbana: University of Illinois Press, 1986); Warren Goldstein, *Playing for Keeps: A History of Early Baseball* (Ithaca, N.Y.: Cornell University Press, 1989); George B. Kirsch, *The Creation of American Team Sports: Baseball and Cricket, 1838–72* (Urbana: University of Illinois Press, 1989); George B. Kirsch, *Baseball in Blue and Gray: The National Pastime during the Civil War* (Princeton, N.J.: Princeton University Press, 2003); John Thorn, *Baseball in the Garden of Eden: The Secret History of the Early Years* (New York: Simon and Schuster, 2011).

12. *Brooklyn Evening Star*, July 26, 1855; June 18, 1858; October 8, 1858; *Eagle*, September 1, 1858; September 2, 1858; September 4, 1858; September 11, 1858.

as others were to the new game, making Brooklyn, in the estimation of one historian, "the center ring in the battle over Sunday baseball in New York."[13]

During the preprofessional era baseball posed only a limited threat to the traditional Sabbath. Organized amateur leagues and most independent teams did not schedule games or practices on Sundays, and informal Sunday games among boys and young men rarely caught the attention of the Brooklyn police.[14] Amateur baseball, moreover, was easy to defend, except when noise and errant baseballs caused a disturbance. A healthful exercise for youngsters who might otherwise be drawn to Coney Island, local poolrooms, or sidewalk craps games, baseball brought young men who worked indoors all week into the sunshine.[15] Why, some asked, could Brooklyn youth not enjoy an informal Sunday afternoon game after a morning spent in church? Did such games constitute as serious a violation as the taverns and grog shops that kept their side doors open on Sunday while police looked the other way? At least some defenders of the Sabbath agreed that they did not.

Things became more complicated with the development of professional and semi-professional teams and leagues during the latter decades of the nineteenth century. Professional baseball took some time gaining a permanent foothold in Brooklyn. Three Brooklyn teams joined the year-old National Association of Professional Base Ball Players in 1872, but the Association folded in 1875, and the transfer of one of the local teams to the newly formed National League in 1876 lasted only a year.[16] An enduring professional club was founded in 1883, at first as a member of an Inter-State Association of Professional Baseball Clubs, then (from 1884) as a member of the American Association, and finally (from 1890) as a member of the National League, winning the pennant in the club's first year. This team, which cycled over the years through a variety of nicknames—including the Grays, the Atlantics, the Bridegrooms (so called because several of its players married during the 1888 off-season), the Superbas, the Robins (after its longtime manager, Wilbert Robinson), the Trolley Dodgers, and the Dodgers—remained in Brooklyn until its much-mourned removal to Los Angeles in 1957.[17]

---

13. Charles DeMotte, *Bat, Ball and Bible: Baseball and Sunday Observance in New York* (Washington, DC: Potomac Books, 2014), xvi.

14. For one example in which nine boys were arrested see *Eagle*, October 11, 1858.

15. This common argument failed to take into account the time taken from work during the week by players on organized amateur teams, a phenomenon that suggests enthusiasm for the game by various employers, including those who were not organizing company teams. However this may have worked within specific workplaces, it was clearly the case that at least some amateur players did not need Sunday to get their time in the sun.

16. This team was the Mutual Baseball Club of New York, which from 1868 played its home games in Brooklyn.

17. During these early years of professional baseball, club names were usually the inventions of local sportswriters rather than properties of the club itself and could be rather fluid. In one 1906 *Eagle* article, the Brooklyn team was referred to as the Superbas, the Trolley Dodgers, and the Dodgers: *Eagle*, April 14, 1906. The word "Dodgers" did not appear on the uniforms of the Brooklyn Baseball Club until 1932.

At first, the professional teams, including the formidable Bridegrooms, did not challenge Brooklyn's Sabbatarian laws. When the Brooklyn team joined the National League the league itself forbade Sunday games. The issue of organized Sunday baseball arose mainly in response to some of the city's new semiprofessional teams. Semiprofessionals were men who, like most amateurs, held jobs in stores, offices, workshops, and factories. But unlike the amateurs, they supplemented their incomes by charging spectators to watch them play. Amateurs in the early days played mostly on unenclosed fields, where family, friends, and fans were free to gather outside the foul lines and in fair territory behind the outfielders to take in the game. But as the size of crowds was not the amateurs' main concern, they confined their games, with few exceptions, to weekdays and Saturday afternoons. To the semiprofessionals, the lure of large Sunday crowds of paying spectators was irresistible. But when they enclosed their playing fields, scheduled Sunday games, and extracted a fee for passing through the gates, they violated laws of the city and the state.

Brooklyn's ordinances (however erratically enforced) forbade both the playing of games and the conducting of business on the Christian Sabbath. State law added another dimension to the offense. Section 265 of the state penal code, enacted in 1787, long before baseball arrived on the scene, read: "All shooting, hunting, fishing, playing, horse racing, gaming or other public sports, exercise or shows upon the first day of the week, and all noises disturbing the peace of the day are prohibited."[18] Despite Section 265's prohibition of mere "playing," most Sabbatarians were willing to abide pickup games and even the occasional amateur game as private affairs, even if large crowds came to watch. But they seized on the phrase "public sports" to add the power of the state to the defense of the quiet and prayerful Sunday against games for which an admission fee was charged.

Semiprofessional teams adapted to the assault on ticket sales at Sunday games by finding indirect methods of charging admission. They allowed spectators into the stands without a ticket but, before seating them, insisted that they buy a program, or perhaps a bag of candy, at the inflated price of 50 or 75 cents. Or they collected a "voluntary" contribution from each spectator as he or she walked through the gate, with a word of encouragement from a muscular team official to individuals who somehow did not see the collection box. Considerably more subtle was a public declaration that the Sunday game was open only to club members, many of whom were able to enroll at a table just outside the gate, or at a nearby transit stop, by paying a week's dues of 50 or 75 cents. The police were not fooled by these subterfuges and sometimes arrested program and candy sellers, team managers, the leadoff hitter, pitcher, and catcher once the first pitch had been thrown; they even occasionally arrested entire teams.

---

18. The original act included the prohibition of "pastimes," but this was eliminated when this section was amended in 1883, several years before the state's penal code was invoked to prevent Sunday baseball. "AN ACT to amend certain sections of the Penal Code," ch. 358, sec. 2, par. 265, N.Y. Laws 541.

Figure 3. "What did them guys do?" CLIVE WEED, *NEW YORK EVENING SUN*, FROM *LETTERS, COMMENTS AND EDITORIALS ENDORSING SUNDAY BASEBALL* (BROOKLYN, N.Y.: N.P., 1918), 35.

To Brooklyn's Protestant churchmen, Sunday baseball, semiprofessional or otherwise, was at first a manageable problem, handled well enough by the police and magistrates. It grew somewhat more urgent in 1894 when Justice William J. Gaynor decided that games were legal if they were played on private grounds and provoked no complaints of Sabbath disruption. Responding to the arrest of several young men who had traveled to a remote area of Brooklyn to play an informal baseball game, Gaynor clearly intended only to protect amateur Sunday players from what he regarded as overzealous policing. But his ruling alarmed the Sunday Observance Association of Kings County, which had been formed a dozen years earlier by Protestant ministers to deal with the threat of theatrical productions and Coney Island. The Association's counsel, W. T. B. Milliken, contested Gaynor's decision on the grounds that the state's penal code prohibited *any* playing on the Sabbath and called on the police to "enforce the law with the ready zeal of faithful officers of a Christian city."[19] Milliken may have realized that Gaynor's ruling, which did not refer to either direct or indirect admission fees, could be construed as justifying any organized commercial game that did not disrupt the Sabbath. The Sunday Observance Association, in any case, did not pursue Milliken's brief.

By the beginning of the twentieth century the issues posed by baseball to Brooklyn's Sabbatarians became more serious. Many amateur games had shifted to Sunday, semiprofessional teams increased in number, the management of Brooklyn's professional team grew increasingly restive about missing out on the substantial Sunday revenues that were now being collected by National League teams in Midwestern cities, and judicial interpretation of the law regarding Sunday baseball remained unsettled. Arrests and court cases continued and in 1904 reached a frequency and intensity that promised a possible resolution. The focus this time was on professional baseball. That spring, as the 1904 season got underway, Charles H. Ebbets, the president and majority owner of the Brooklyn Baseball Club—now the Superbas—scheduled a series of Sunday games at Washington Park, the Superbas' home field. It was understood that the team would sell programs instead of charging an admission fee.

Ebbets had laid down the gauntlet, and Sabbatarians soon picked it up. The Rev. O. F. Bartholow declared that the Methodist Church was united in opposing commercial Sunday baseball and that the Brooklyn Law Enforcement Society, already known for investigating brothels, gambling dens, and illegal liquor licenses, would file suit. The Rev. J. M. Farrar of the Second Reform Church predicted that moral sentiment in Brooklyn would prevent Ebbets from carrying out his plan.[20] The Brooklyn and Long Island Methodist Preachers Association confirmed Reverend Bartholow's claim of a Methodist Church united against Sunday baseball, and as the season proceeded, the Sabbath Observance Association of Kings County appeared at Washington Park, taking notes alongside police officers from the Sixth Avenue Station.[21]

The Superbas' first Sunday game was played without any intervention, but Police Commissioner William McAdoo decided to make a test case out of the next contest. Before the game started, he had three program sellers arrested, and in the first inning, after

---

19. *Eagle*, August 11, 1894; September 8, 1894.
20. *New-York Tribune*, April 14, 1904.
21. *Eagle*, May 3, 1904; *New York Times*, May 30, 1904.

Figure 4. Charles H. Ebbets. COURTESY LIBRARY OF CONGRESS, PRINTS AND PHOTOGRAPHS DIVISION.

Philadelphia's leadoff hitter, Frank Roth, hit the second pitch, five policemen walked onto the field and arrested him and the Brooklyn battery, pitcher Edward Poole and catcher Frederick Jacklitsch. The game then continued without further interruption, Brooklyn winning 8 to 6. (The box score gave no indication of the initial difficulty—Roth, Poole, and Jacklitsch were simply excluded.)[22] The case was heard by Justice Gaynor, who released the arrestees, ruling as he had done ten years earlier that a Sunday baseball game is illegal only when there is a specific complaint that "the peace and religious liberty of the community has been disturbed." Gaynor once again attacked the police for overzealous enforcement of what he regarded as an obsolete statute, this time going further to criticize "those who control" or "those who rule" the police. Gaynor did not specify who those people were, but he was certainly aware of the involvement of Protestant Sabbatarian groups, one or two of which had openly implored McAdoo to clamp down on the Sunday game and District Attorney John H. Clarke to vigorously prosecute the case.[23]

The Brooklyn team left for a long western road trip, visiting Cincinnati, Chicago, and St. Louis (where Sunday baseball was legal). On the first Sunday after their return, they played their crosstown rival, the New York Giants, and the police brought Brooklyn pitcher

---

22. *New-York Tribune*, April 25, 1904.
23. *Eagle*, May 2, 1904; *New-York Tribune*, May 3, 1904.

and catcher, Ed Poole and Frank Dillon (the Giants' leadoff hitter was spared), to William Gaynor's courtroom. At the arraignment hearing Gaynor asked District Attorney Clarke whether "some people came forward and instigated the police in this matter." "Yes, sir," Clarke responded. "Are none of them willing to swear that the repose of the Sabbath was interfered with?" the judge continued. "Where is their zeal for the Sabbath if they are not willing to do that? It is a very strange thing if they won't." Gaynor continued the case, but not before Clarke raised the issue of an admission fee to the game as a violation of the state's penal code. This in turn provoked Bernard J. York (a former police commissioner, now the attorney for the Brooklyn Baseball Club), to describe Section 265 as "a relic of barbarism," a characterization that seemed to comport with Justice Gaynor's own views.[24]

But when the case returned to Gaynor's court two weeks later, the judge ruled that "a game to which an admission fee is charged—when proposed to be played on Sunday, is prohibited by law." The ruling appeared to be a significant change of mind on Gaynor's part and a great victory for Brooklyn's Sabbatarians. It was not quite either. "In his decision," the *Brooklyn Daily Eagle* explained, "Justice Gaynor is careful to take issue with persons who would make Sunday a day of gloom or of religious ceremony only, that the Ten Commandments only prohibit work, but do not prohibit physical exercise and games and that the New Testament contained no Sunday law at all."[25] Justice Gaynor may have felt compelled to apply the law that prohibited *professional* baseball on the Sabbath once the statute was cited by the District Attorney. But he was willing to do so only as long as the casual, noncommercial pursuit of healthful exercise by ordinary citizens was not compromised. His ruling, moreover, did not settle the status of *commercial* baseball. District Attorney Clarke and Sabbatarian ministers such as the Rev. Arthur W. Byrt of the Warren Street Methodist Episcopal Church, claimed that Gaynor had outlawed Sunday games that charged admission "in any form," including the selling of programs or any other means of gaining revenue from spectators without selling them a ticket.[26] But the judge had mentioned only an "admission fee," which left the issue of indirect charges unresolved. This twentieth-century Battle of Brooklyn had not yet been decided. As for Dillon and Poole, Gaynor released them on their own bond while their case was sent to the Court of Special Sessions.[27]

Two days after Justice Gaynor's decision, the Superbas played another Sunday home game against the Giants, this time without intervention by the police. The game itself, though, was a disastrous 11-0 shellacking by the Giants, and the *Eagle* could not resist

---

24. *Eagle*, May 30, 1904; June 6, 1904; June 7, 1904. York also claimed that by eliminating "pastimes" from Section 265, the state legislature intended to exclude baseball from its restrictions, as baseball "was surely a pastime." The same point was made a year after the 1883 revision by a New York judge, W. H. Kelly. *Eagle*, June 29, 1884.
25. *Eagle*, June 19, 1904.
26. *Eagle*, June 24, 1904; July 26, 1904.
27. *Times*, June 25, 1904.

casting its report in terms of the recent off-the-field proceedings: "If the preparation of a case depended entirely on their batting exhibition the Superbas would hardly be convicted of disturbing anybody's religious repose yesterday afternoon."[28] The police arrested two players and a program seller at the following week's game against the Boston Beaneaters, and the "spectators shouted, hooted and indulged in catcalls when they saw what the police were up to." The *Eagle*'s report the next day hinted at battle fatigue on both sides: "The proceedings in court to-day lacked the spirit characteristic of the crusade when it was begun a few weeks ago, neither the ball playing fraternity nor the church people being so largely represented as they were when the proceedings were more of a novelty than they were to-day."[29] The Superbas' schedule provided a welcome ceasefire, as they went on another road trip after the Boston game. The team returned home in August but played no more Sunday games at Washington Park for the remainder of the 1904 season.

While the Superbas were away, one of the active Brooklyn Sabbatarian ministers, Rev. John Rippere of the Forty-Fourth Street Methodist Episcopal Church, turned his attention to amateur teams that had been playing on Sundays on fields located in sparsely settled areas of the borough, seemingly insulated from claims of illegality by Justice Gaynor's rulings.[30] The results of their Sunday games were reported routinely and without comment in the local press. Early in July, however, Reverend Rippere demanded the arrest of players in three upcoming amateur Sunday games. When Captain Evans of the Fourth Avenue Precinct failed to respond, Rippere warned that ignoring his responsibilities "would bring him into trouble." The arrests were made, and four players from each home team, ranging in age from 15 to 35, were brought before Magistrate James G. Tighe. The case focused on players from the team sponsored by St. Michael's Roman Catholic Church, whose rector, consulted beforehand by Evans, had agreed to the arrests as a test case. Rev. Arthur Byrt, who had earlier challenged the Superbas' Sunday games, joined Reverend Rippere in arguing that the sale of scorecards at the St. Michael's game violated the law as cited by Justice Gaynor. He did not mention that the proceeds from the sale were turned over to the parish relief fund nor that the game was scheduled for 4 o'clock in the afternoon so that it would not coincide with any church service. The players from the other two teams who had not sold anything were dismissed, and the case against the St. Michael's players was carried over until the following Monday.[31]

Magistrate Tighe ruled on Monday that the sale of scorecards at St. Michael's home field, which was not enclosed, was not an admissions fee, and that the players had nothing to do with any Sunday commercial activity. Since no one complained of Sabbath disruption, the magistrate dismissed the players, adding a strong endorsement of amateur Sunday

28. *Eagle*, June 20, 1904.
29. *Eagle*, June 27, 1904.
30. Brooklyn was an independent city only until 1898, when it became one of the five boroughs of a greatly expanded New York City.
31. *Eagle*, July 11, 1904; July 15, 1904.

baseball as a "proper outlet" for youthful energy and as a force for both good citizenship and, borrowing a term from the Sabbatarians, the "repose of the community."[32]

Reverend Rippere, who was not at the courtroom that day, had delivered a sermon at his church the previous evening, wherein, according to the *Eagle*, he gave two reasons for his opposition to amateur Sunday games. One was his suspicion that some two hundred of the seven hundred children enrolled in the church's Sunday school were playing hooky to attend the games. The other was decidedly less relevant to the maintenance of a pious and prayerful Sabbath: that the games "attracted to a respectable neighborhood Italians and negroes. 'Little Italy' and 'Little Africa.' He admits the field is not near the church, but if 'those classes' continue to come to the games they will want to move into the neighborhood, 'and that will drive out the very class of respectable and well-to-do people whom we depend upon to build up our church.'" The *Eagle* noted that "Mr. Rippere had a large and affirming audience to listen to the sermon, and he was encouraged to continue his good work."[33]

Personal bigotries aside, Reverend Rippere's sermon helps us locate the Sabbatarian attack on Sunday baseball within forces that were reshaping the city and borough that Yankee Protestants had dominated for several generations. The Italians he feared were among the latest of Brooklyn's growing ethnic communities—immigrants and their American-born children, differing from the Yankees in their religious and secular lives, asserting their rights as residents and as citizens, and rising collectively to form the majority of Brooklyn's population. Rippere's fear of "negroes" expressed little more than racism: among the still quite small number of African Americans who lived in Brooklyn in 1904 were but a handful whose homes were anywhere near the Sunset Park neighborhood Rippere sought to protect from unwelcome outsiders.

The large-scale immigration of Irish Catholics and German Catholics and Protestants during the 1840s and 1850s had introduced a significant degree of ethnic and religious diversity to Brooklyn. On the eve of the Civil War, these two immigrant communities amounted to nearly 40 percent of the city's population.[34] With some exceptions these were among the poorest and least influential people in the growing city, and if they found ways of resisting the constraints of Yankee Sabbatarianism—the Irish, native Protestant stereotypes maintained, in grog shops, the Germans in beer gardens—they had little power over the law itself or the manner of its enforcement. This imbalance of power began to shift later in the century, with the maturation of the American-born children of the antebellum immigrants, and even more dramatically, with the arrival in the United States of some nine million "New Immigrants" from Eastern and Southern Europe between 1900 and the

32. *Eagle*, July 18, 1904.
33. *Eagle*, July 18, 1904.
34. Bureau of the Census, *Statistics of the United States . . . in 1860* (Washington, D.C.: Government Printing Office, 1866).

beginning of World War I.[35] The majority of these immigrants—Russian, Ukrainian, and other East European Jews; Italian, Polish, and Hungarian Catholics; Greek and Russian Orthodox Christians—arrived through the port of New York, and some found their first American homes on Manhattan's already crowded East Side.

With the opening in 1903 of the Williamsburg Bridge (soon dubbed the Jews' Highway or the Passover Bridge), the 1909 opening of the Manhattan Bridge, and the digging of subway tunnels under the East River, hundreds of thousands of Jews, Italians, and other New Immigrants relocated their homes to Brooklyn. Seemingly overnight, an already shrinking native Protestant minority was reduced to less than 20 percent of Brooklyn's vastly larger population, producing a mosaic of culturally divergent communities sprawling across the whole of Kings County. The largest component of this mosaic, fully a third of Brooklyn's population by 1930, was Jewish, with Italians about half as numerous, the two groups together amounting to half of an "outer borough" that was now more populous than Manhattan.[36]

Brooklyn's Jews had little interest in the Christian Sabbath; indeed, because Saturday was their busiest day of the week, many of the borough's numerous Jewish storekeepers resisted Sabbatarians of their own faith. And Italians bolstered a Catholic community that focused more on attendance at mass and less resolutely on the prayerful private Sabbath that conservative Protestants insisted should follow a morning spent in church. The result was a marked diminution of the reach of Yankee Sabbatarianism. Looking back over the previous generation in 1915, a commentator in *Brooklyn Life*, a self-described journal of Brooklyn's elite, wrote of the diminishing power of the "New England element"; and an *Eagle* report on the 1930 dinner of the New England Society of Brooklyn lamented that this "Gibralter of New England" had crumbled away, while "dominance has passed to racial groups hardly of considerable importance in 1880."[37]

The Brooklyn to which these immigrants were moving (just as the battle over Sunday baseball was heating up), was in other respects different from the place the Irish and Germans had found before the Civil War. Theaters, including at least one devoted to vaudeville, had found a foothold, and were beginning to feel competition from new venues that showed motion pictures. The one moderately sized department store from the antebellum era, Journeay & Burnham, was now dwarfed by Abraham & Straus and one or two other larger emporia in a more imposing—and exciting—downtown Brooklyn. These institutions were not permitted to do business on Sundays, but even those that conformed to the law enhanced a taste for secular amusement and material life that had always competed for the attention and commitment of Brooklyn's churchgoing community.

---

35. Bureau of the Census, *The Statistical History of the United States from Colonial Times to the Present* (Stamford, Conn.: Fairfield Publishers, 1965), 56.
36. Department of Commerce, Bureau of the Census, *Fifteenth Census of the United States: 1930: Population*, vol. 3, part 2 (Washington, D.C.: Government Printing Office, 1932), 279.
37. *Brooklyn Life*, June 1, 1915; *Eagle*, March 2, 1930.

And secular enjoyments were now available on the Sabbath: a large and glorious Prospect Park, designed by Frederick Law Olmsted and Calvert Vaux, replete with woods, gardens, lawns, bandshells, and a lake for summer boating and winter skating; vaudeville and movie theaters that often avoided law enforcement; and, of course, the many commercial amusements on Coney Island, which, as Charles Ebbets never tired of pointing out, operated freely every day of the week without any disturbance from Brooklyn's police.[38] Wealthy Brooklynites joined golf, tennis, and yachting clubs and went for Sunday automobile drives in the Long Island countryside. These, too, attracted the notice of Brooklyn's baseball managers, who argued that ordinary players and fans ought to have affordable Sunday outlets of their own.

None of these secular distractions in modern Brooklyn precluded old-style religious observance in the City of Churches. But simultaneous with their development was what some saw as a decline, or at the very least a significant change, in the religiosity of Protestant Brooklynites. By the 1880s some of Brooklyn's clergy were complaining about preaching to half-empty churches, leading the *Eagle* to reflect on "doubts and questions about the Old Testament, the miracles, plenary inspiration and other dogmas," calling this a "profound change" in Brooklyn's popular culture.[39] Among persisting believers, too, there were shifts in religious practice that de-emphasized the old Sabbatarian ideal. The embrace of the Social Gospel by some local churches elevated Christ's mission to the poor over the duty of private prayer. Brooklyn's most popular preacher, Henry Ward Beecher, who was raised squarely in the New England Calvinist tradition, promoted active engagement with the world and a loving religion that rejected the sternness and gloom of the early Calvinists. "Love, with its freedom," he proclaimed in 1873, "has taken the place of authority, and of obedience to it."[40] Beecher saw himself as a reformer of Calvinism—until he renounced it completely six years before his death.[41]

Brooklyn was home to other eminent Protestant clergymen such as Richard Salter Storrs of the Church of the Pilgrims; Charles H. Hall of Holy Trinity Church; Episcopal Bishop Abram N. Littlejohn (formerly the rector of Holy Trinity); Theodore Cuyler of the Lafayette Avenue Presbyterian Church; Lyman Abbott, who succeeded Beecher at Plymouth Church; and Newell Dwight Hillis, who succeeded Abbott. Some of these men were conservative in their theology, and all ministered to influential congregations heavy in New Englanders (only Cuyler was based outside of Brooklyn Heights, the center of Yankee Protestantism). Yet, none was active in the Sabbatarian movement that took shape in the late nineteenth and early twentieth centuries; nor did important laymen from their

---

38. For evidence that Sunday vaudeville shows and movies were also permitted by the police, see *Eagle*, May 25, 1913.
39. *Eagle*, October 4, 1886.
40. Quoted in Debby Applegate, *The Most Famous Man in America: The Biography of Henry Ward Beecher* (New York: Doubleday, 2006), 355.
41. Applegate, *Most Famous Man*, 462.

Figure 5. Canon William Sheafe Chase. COURTESY HISTORIC IMAGES OUTLET.

churches join in the struggle against Sunday baseball. One of the most important features of this struggle, in fact, was its narrowing to a relatively small number of clergymen and, except for the signing of petitions, still fewer laymen, most of whom served or represented churches that were not the traditional centers of religious influence in Brooklyn. Men from several denominations joined the Methodists we have cited, but it cannot be said that any denomination (despite the claim of a united Methodist Church) brought its full weight to bear in defense of the traditional Sabbath. Rather, a few voices dominated as the struggle went forward. The voice heard most often, sometimes to the exclusion of others, was that of an Episcopalian, Canon William Sheafe Chase, rector of Christ Church on Bedford Avenue in Williamsburg and third vice president of the Sabbath Observance Society of Kings County.

Despite this narrowing of Sabbatarian forces and their relocation outside the old centers of Yankee influence, opposition to Sunday baseball in Brooklyn remained strong enough to continue the dispute over the proper interpretation of the state penal code relating to "playing" and "public games." In September 1904, the Court of Special Sessions released the players arrested earlier that year, and this emboldened Charles Ebbets to schedule Sunday games at Washington Park for the 1905 season. But when a game was announced for April 23—Easter Sunday!—Reverend Byrn and Rev. Daniel H. Overton, chair of the Sunday Observance Association, demanded that Police Commissioner McAdoo enforce the Sunday law.[42] At first McAdoo largely ignored the Sabbatarians' demands. A police captain was sent to Washington Park to gather the names of program sellers and players, and a "big platoon of police was present," but "the bluecoats did nothing but pose," and the game went on with neither arrests nor interruption. For the next month, too, there was little intervention by police in the Superbas' Sunday games, although some arrests of the Brooklyn starting battery were made at the outset before allowing the game to continue. (Anticipating these arrests, Brooklyn's manager paid up to $25 for volunteers from his bench to start the game as pitcher and catcher and serve as "arrestees for hire.")[43] Amateur and semiprofessional games were also allowed to continue in the borough, apparently with no arrests.[44]

But by the end of May, after getting advice from corporation counsel, McAdoo ordered the arrest of those responsible for Sunday games where even an indirect admission fee was charged, and he made it clear that games of this sort would no longer be tolerated. On May 28, seventy amateur players were arrested by Captain Evans in the Fourth District (once again they were members of teams in the Catholic league), and several more were detained in other parts of Brooklyn. The Superbas avoided arrests by canceling that day's game with the Giants, despite the expectation of a huge crowd that had gathered to watch the crosstown rivals.[45] The Superbas then left town on a long road trip, and on the Sunday following their return several hundred hopeful fans found signs on the Washington Park gates that read "No Game To-Day." As in the previous year, that sign forecast the end of

42. *New-York Tribune*, April 22, 1905. The precise meaning of the law was, however, still unclear. In its report of Ebbets' plan the *New-York Tribune* described the right to play Sunday baseball as "a legal enigma."

43. *Eagle*, April 24, 1905; May 1, 1905; May 8, 1905; May 15, 1905; May 22, 1905. On "arrestees for hire," see Charlie Bevis, *Sunday Baseball: The Major Leagues' Struggle to Play Baseball on the Lord's Day, 1876–1934* (Jefferson, N.C.: McFarland, 2003), 9–10.

44. *Eagle*, May 22, 1905, for a report on nine Sunday amateur and semi-pro games played in Brooklyn with no mention of police intervention.

45. *Eagle*, May 24, 1905; May 29, 1905.

major league Sunday baseball in Brooklyn for the remainder of the season.[46] Amateur and semiprofessional teams continued to play on Sunday, however, presumably in the absence of direct or indirect charges for admission.[47]

Commissioner McAdoo's course change in May of 1905 was less than a total victory for Brooklyn's Sabbatarians. Play continued on fields outside of Washington Park, and Ebbets began the 1906 season with renewed dedication to collecting Sunday revenues, resorting this time to "voluntary contribution" boxes rather than to sales of overpriced programs. For two months he succeeded. Deputy Police Commissioner Arthur J. O'Keefe attended the first game of the season, assured himself there was no coercion at the contribution boxes, and announced that the system did not violate the law. It helped, too, that nothing was sold at the ballpark. "The spectator could not buy a programme," the *Eagle* reported, "nor was it possible to buy a peanut."[48]

Deputy Commissioner O'Keefe did warn of possible objections from "the Sabbath Observance people," and when in early June New York City's new police commissioner Theodore Bingham ruled that the Sunday contribution boxes were illegal, an exasperated Ebbets complained of "Sabbatarians who wanted to regulate the morals of everybody."[49] There was no game at Washington Park on June 10, but Ebbets was in no mood to capitulate. He scheduled a game for June 17, and was among thirty-seven team executives, managers, and players, professional and semiprofessional, who were arrested in Brooklyn that day for violating Section 265 of the state penal code. The Superbas game was allowed to continue after the arrests, and the charges against Ebbets and the other arrestees were almost immediately dismissed.[50] And yet, Ebbets capitulated to a force he evidently deemed too strong, or at least too persistent, to defeat with program sales, contribution boxes, or any other subterfuge. Once again, Sunday games were canceled for the rest of the season. But this time the week-to-week battle was not resumed in the following year, nor was it taken up in the years following that. During the next decade and beyond, Brooklyn's major league team played many Sunday exhibition games outside of New York City—in New Jersey, Connecticut, Rhode Island, and upstate New York—where Sunday laws existed but were less likely to be enforced against such popular and occasional barnstormers. But they did not play Sunday ball in Brooklyn.[51]

It was increasingly evident to Brooklyn's baseballers that their problems with Sabbatarians emanated from the law itself, and it is not surprising that the battle over Sunday baseball soon shifted from playing fields, police stations, and courtrooms in Brooklyn to the state legislature in Albany. The initial skirmish was, ostensibly, over the legal exposure of amateur teams and players, who were vulnerable not only because they sometimes raised

46. *Eagle*, June 26, 1905
47. *Eagle* Monday editions, June 5–October 9, 1905.
48. *Eagle*, April 16, 1906.
49. *Eagle*, June 9, 1906.
50. *Eagle*, June 18, 1906; June 19, 1906.
51. Bevis, *Sunday Baseball*, 162–63.

revenue from Sunday games but also because of the very fact that they played on the Sabbath. In 1907, a newly elected Brooklyn assemblyman, William Leo Mooney, introduced a bill that would legalize amateur Sunday baseball by amending Section 265 to exempt players who did not earn their living from the game. This seemed a modest enough proposal, but Mooney was wrong to expect an easy victory. Canon Chase was among several Protestant ministers from Brooklyn and elsewhere in the state who appeared in Albany to oppose a bill that they perceived as a significant threat to Sabbatarianism. Curiously, though, their arguments did not directly challenge the legitimacy of amateur Sunday games. Chase claimed that the real backers of the bill were Brooklyn's trolley companies, which stood to gain from transporting larger crowds to the ball fields, and liquor dealers who would profit from those crowds. Others argued that Mooney's real motive was to protect semiprofessionals, who, like the amateurs, earned their livings from jobs outside of baseball.[52] Mooney had himself been a semiprofessional player and manager in Brooklyn until just before running for the Assembly, and it had already been reported that the semiprofessional Managers Protective Association actively supported the bill.[53] Mooney vehemently objected to Chase's remarks, but he had no answer to the other charge. It is not clear that any of this (or the increasingly cloudy distinction between amateur and semiprofessional teams)[54] was decisive in the face of upstate Protestant Assemblymen who opposed Sunday baseball at any level. The bill ultimately did pass in the Senate (on reconsideration, after an initial defeat), but it did not make it out of the Codes Committee of the Assembly.[55] A slightly amended version of the bill met the same fate during the following year's legislative session.[56]

Over the next several years, amateur baseball continued to be the focus of (or the pretext for) the New York legislature's ongoing combat over Sunday games. During that time Canon Chase emerged as the major nonlegislative opponent of proposed bills, though in the process he shifted his argument to align with those who stressed the hypocrisy of legislators who used amateur players as cover for their support of the semiprofessionals. The result was always the same even after Chase secured an amendment to the 1911 bill that prohibited "admission fees, directly or indirectly," to Sunday games. Upstate opposition remained too strong and pointed to the limits of Chase's influence and that of a borough where the traditional Yankee Sabbath no longer enjoyed broad support.[57]

---

52. *Eagle*, March 14, 1907.
53. *Eagle*, February 9, 1907; February 16, 1907.
54. Amateur teams increasingly resembled the semi-professionals in charging entrance fees or selling programs. The difference, they argued, was that the money they raised was intended only to offset the costs of equipment or the rental of fields, or, as in the case of Catholic teams, to provide funds for their churches' charitable work. Sabbatarians countered that it was the revenue itself, not its disposition, that was at issue. On Brooklyn's "quasi-amateur" baseball teams, see *Eagle*, June 5, 1905.
55. *New York Times*, April 16, 1907; May 17, 1907; *Eagle*, May 16, 1907.
56. *Eagle*, January 9, 1908; February 13, 1908.
57. *New-York Tribune*, April 27, 1910; March 15, 1911; *Eagle*, May 5, 1910; February 2, 1911; February 10, 1911; February 16, 1911; November 8, 1912; February 6, 1913; March 27, 1915. In what may be an urban legend, when William Gaynor, now mayor of New York City, was introduced to Canon

Even while Brooklyn's baseball advocates were failing in Albany, amateurs continued to play Sunday games with at most intermittent interference from the police. They even got a significant boost from city officials. In 1912, after years of closing the parade grounds adjoining Prospect Park, the decision was made to open this large space for Sunday games by amateur players, defying the organized protests of nearby residents (and, according to one interpretation, the state law against "playing").[58] This policy was an immediate success, and the parade grounds were crowded with amateur players on Sundays for years to come. Semiprofessionals, too, continued to play on Sundays across the borough line in Ridgewood, in Queens, and in Red Hook and other Brooklyn working-class neighborhoods where police were less inclined to interfere.[59] The most important practical effects of the failure to change the state's penal code, therefore, were felt by Brooklyn's professional team. In 1907, Charles Ebbets had proposed to the semiprofessionals that the Mooney bill be expanded to include professional baseball, but the Managers Protective Association turned him down not only because they were sure such a move would ensure the bill's defeat but also because they correctly saw the Superbas as a dangerous competitor for Sunday crowds. Ebbets realized he had few allies in Brooklyn's baseball world. And with the defeat of the Mooney bill and its successors over the next few years, he knew that he had little chance of success in Albany.

A new set of possible allies for Ebbets and the Superbas appeared in 1913, when twenty-seven mayors in New York State petitioned the governor to introduce a new law giving each municipality the option of legalizing Sunday baseball within its boundaries.[60] But nothing came of this initiative or of a bill introduced in the Assembly two years later by Arthur G. McElroy of Buffalo (home to a minor league professional team) to legalize Sunday professional baseball in the state. "The up-State won over New York City today," wrote the *New York Times*, "in a contest on the Assembly floor over Sunday baseball." Rural and small-town upstate Assemblymen voted against reporting the bill out of the Rules Committee,

---

Chase, he refused to shake his hand, exclaiming, "Canon? You're no Canon. You're only a popgun." Louis H. Pink, *Gaynor: The Tammany Mayor who Swallowed the Tiger* (New York: International Press, 1931), 77. The broad support for Sunday baseball in Brooklyn, and its much weaker support in upstate New York, helps explain why local Sabbatarian leaders relied on the state's penal code rather than on Brooklyn's Sabbath ordinances to assert their legal claims against Sunday ball in the City of Churches.

58. *Eagle*, May 27, 1912; May 28, 1912; May29, 1912; June 1, 1912; June 3, 1912; May 25, 1914. This new policy did not extend to Prospect Park itself; indeed, during June of the following year, a number of small boys were incarcerated for playing baseball in the park. Mayor Gaynor was infuriated to learn of yet another overzealous police action against mere playing (there was no mention of disturbing the Sabbath or charging fees of any kind) and ordered the prosecution of eighteen policemen who participated in the arrests. See *Eagle*, July 7, 1913.

59. Years earlier, the *Eagle* commented on the games in Red Hook: "There is no church in the vicinity, and most of the residents not being at all Puritanical, there are no complaints." *Eagle*, June 30, 1890.

60. *Eagle*, June 14, 1913; June 29, 1913.

and it never reached the Assembly floor.[61] Ebbets revived the mayors' local option idea for Sunday baseball in 1916, but without effect.[62] In the meantime, he avoided new confrontations with the police or with the courts by scheduling no Sunday games either at Washington Park or, from 1913 onward, at Ebbets Field, his new stadium. As late as 1916, Sunday major league baseball appeared to be a lost cause in New York State.

But a year later, when Brooklyn boys sailed to France to fight in the Great War, Ebbets seized on an opportunity to change the balance of power between professional baseball and the Sabbatarians. On Sunday, July 1, 1917, tickets were sold for a patriotic concert at Ebbets Field "for the benefit of the Naval Militia of Mercy, the Red Cross, and other war relief organizations of this borough." When the concert ended, the stadium gates were opened to all who wished to watch, free of any charge, a baseball game between Brooklyn—now generally known as the Robins—and the Philadelphia Phillies. Neither the concert nor the game was disturbed by the police, but summonses were later issued to Ebbets and field manager Wilbert Robinson for violation of the Sunday laws. After both men were committed to trial at the Court of Special Sessions, a sacred music concert and free game scheduled for the following Sunday were canceled. This was reported by the *Eagle* on Saturday under a large headline: "No Sunday Game Tomorrow; Red Cross Loses about $5,000."[63]

There was already a good deal of support for Sunday baseball in Brooklyn, but this was a public relations triumph for Ebbets and his team. "Sunday Law Agitators Hurt Every Brooklyn Regiment," wrote the *Eagle* on July 17, before listing eleven charitable organizations, along with Brooklyn's hospitals, that stood to lose from the efforts of the Sabbatarians— now labeled "Agitators" against the war effort.[64] Ebbets went on offense, accusing the Albany-based Law and Order Society of orchestrating his summons and arguing for the repeal of "ancient legislation" that "is still invoked by a well-meaning but noisy minority to discredit a perfectly commendable and worthy institution."[65] A month later, his case still pending, he began a newspaper war with Sheriff Edward Reigelmann that culminated in both a large advertisement in the *Eagle* opposing Reigelmann's campaign for borough president and an open letter to legislative candidates asking for their stance on the legalization of Sunday baseball. "The Brooklyn Baseball Club," wrote the *Eagle* shortly before the November election, "is in politics with both feet."[66]

---

61. *New York Times*, April 16, 1916.
62. *Eagle*, June 13, 1916.
63. *Eagle*, July 2, 1917, July 7, 1917. The Yankees held a concert followed by a baseball game at the Polo Grounds two weeks before Ebbets employed the same plan in Brooklyn. The Yankee managers, however, were not arrested. Indeed, they secured the approval of Mayor John Purroy Mitchel before the event. Bevis, *Sunday Baseball*, 186–87.
64. *Eagle*, July 17, 1917.
65. *Eagle*, August 12, 1917.
66. *Eagle*, September 13, 1917; September 14, 1917; September 18, 1917; September 20, 1917; October 24, 1917. On September 24 Ebbets and Robinson were found guilty of violating the Sabbath law and were given suspended sentences. See *Eagle*, September 24, 1917.

Ebbets and his co-owners of the Robins, the brothers E. J. and S. W. McKeever, lined up more than thirty candidates favorable to amending the Sunday laws. New York's American League club, the Yankees, which previously "had not made a yip about the subject," was finally aboard, with Col. Jacob Ruppert announcing that he had enlisted nineteen pro-baseball candidates, mostly in the Bronx.[67] (Giants owner John T. Brush had earlier deferred to Ebbets on the Sunday issue, and his successor, his son-in-law Harry N. Hempstead, stayed out of the fray. Brooklyn really was the "center ring" in the battle for Sunday baseball in New York.) Anticipating yet another difficult fight in the state legislature, Ebbets and E. J. McKeever wrote a conciliatory circular letter to Brooklyn clergy, embracing "the sanctity of the Sabbath," asserting that their opposition to a "blue law" enacted in 1787 reflected the opinions of the vast majority of Brooklyn's "respectable law-abiding church-going citizens," and asking for their views on the subject. Two responses appeared in the *Eagle* the next day. The first, from Rev. T. J. Lacey, rector of the Church of the Redeemer, was entirely favorable to amending the law, the defense of which he considered "utterly senseless, intolerant and antiquated." The second was a much longer letter from Canon Chase, excoriating Ebbets for hypocrisy and assuring him of failure "in every attempt you make to commercialize the Lord's Day." Chase described Ebbets's battle with the sheriff and took obvious pleasure in pointing out that Reigelmann had been elected Brooklyn's borough president despite Ebbets's efforts to defeat him.[68] The coming battle in the state legislature would indeed be a difficult one.

It began on March 5 with the introduction of a bill by Senator Robert R. Lawson, from the Bushwick section of Brooklyn, to legalize Sunday baseball games, whether or not an admission fee was charged. A conference of Lawson's fellow Senate Republicans had refused to back the bill, but Lawson pressed ahead, knowing that the cause was popular among his constituents.[69] The bill was referred to the Codes Committee, where it ran into a second headwind in the person of Canon Chase. In "a verbal war" before the committee, Chase argued that Sunday was "a day for holiness, for the church and for religious instruction," and an exasperated Lawson responded that Chase was "always on the wrong side of every question that ever came up."[70] Fully aware, however, that Chase's defense of the Sabbath would find support among rural upstate legislators, Lawson amended his bill to include the option for localities to reject its terms. "This," according to the *Eagle*, "won the support of quite a number of men from northern cities," several of which had professional minor league teams. In its amended form the committee reported favorably on the bill.[71]

Between the committee report and the floor votes, Lawson worked hard to demonstrate

67. *Eagle*, October 31, 1917, November 3, 1917.
68. *Eagle*, November 23, 1917; November 24, 1917.
69. *Eagle*, March 5, 1918.
70. *Eagle*, March 20, 1918.
71. *Eagle*, March 21, 1918.

that his bill was popular and had the support of the right people in Brooklyn, the state, and across the country. On April 1 he claimed to have a petition signed by some forty thousand people, and submitted to the governor, the New York State Senate, and the Assembly a pamphlet that included favorable testimonials from thirteen Brooklyn clergymen; the New York City Board of Aldermen; the Executive Chairmen of Brooklyn's Republican and Democratic parties; sixteen American mayors from as far away as Butte, Montana; the 1913 pro-baseball resolution of twenty-seven New York State mayors; and dozens of newspaper editors and reporters in New York City.[72] Frank L. Brown, executive secretary of the World's Sunday School Association, responded that the clergymen endorsing Senator Lawson's bill were, with one exception, Catholic, Jewish, Episcopalian, and Lutheran, and hence, the "principal Protestant church membership of the state is not represented at all."[73] He need not have bothered. Lawson's bill passed in the Senate after a "stiff battle," but it never made it to the Assembly floor.[74] The legality of Sunday baseball in Brooklyn, and all over the State of New York, remained in limbo for yet another year.

And that year, 1919, was decisive. Early in March a bill was introduced in the Assembly by Republican John G. Malone of Albany and in the Senate by Democrat James J. ("Gentleman Jimmy") Walker of Manhattan. It was nearly identical to the previous year's bill of Robert Lawson, who was no longer in the Senate, but differed mainly in that the local option required a positive enactment by the municipality rather than the municipality's rejection of the state's legalization of Sunday games.[75] Arguments for and against the bill were much the same as they had been the previous year—and some years before that. This time, however, a few Assembly Republicans, mostly from larger upstate cities, supported the legislation. The Senate passed it on April 3 by a vote of 29 to 21, with 7 Republicans (including one each from the Bronx, Albany, Syracuse, and Rochester) joining all 22 Senate Democrats in favor.[76] In the Assembly, which this time had a floor vote, the result was 82 in favor and 60 opposed. The partisan and geographic patterns were similar to those of the Senate. Fifty-one Democrats (all but one, a Manhattanite) voted for the bill, as did the chamber's two Socialists. Fifty-one of these 53 Assemblymen were from Greater New York City (the other two represented Buffalo and Troy). Among the 29 affirmative Republican votes were only 5 from the predominantly Protestant rural upstate counties that provided 51 of the 59 negative Republican votes. A dozen were from upstate counties with sizable cities—Buffalo,

72. *Letters, Comments and Editorials Endorsing Sunday Baseball* (Brooklyn, N.Y.: n.p., 1918). We cite here the second edition of this pamphlet, which enlarged a first edition published in March.
73. *Eagle*, April 25, 1918.
74. *Eagle*, April 5, 1918; April 12, 1918.
75. *Eagle*, March 5, 1919. A second bill was introduced by Assemblyman Owen M. Kiernan of Manhattan, but it was the Malone-Walker bill that went forward. Malone-Walker also legalized fishing on Sunday.
76. *Journal of the Senate of the State of New York . . .* (New York: E. Holt, Printer to the State, 1919), 866–67.

Figure 6. "The Pied Piper Is Here Today." COURTESY *Brooklyn Daily Eagle*, APRIL 21, 1911.

Rochester, Syracuse, and Albany.[77] Eleven days after the Assembly vote Governor Al Smith signed the baseball bill—and along with it a bill legalizing Sunday movies, which had moved in tandem through the legislature with Malone-Walker.[78]

When the New York City Board of Alderman met on April 22 to consider its new power to authorize Sunday baseball in the boroughs, Canon Chase was prominent among those who appeared in opposition. If the Board approved of commercial baseball, the poor would suffer, he now argued, because all the desirable open lots would be rented by professional teams (he could only have meant fee-charging semiprofessional and amateur teams—the Robins were comfortably at home in Ebbets Field). "All that will be left for the poor," Chase claimed, "will be the privilege of paying 50 cents to see a professional game." He did not carry the day. Only one Alderman, Charles A. Post from Queens, voted

---

77. *Journal of the Assembly of the State of New York . . .* (Albany, N.Y.: J. B. Lyon Company, Printers, 1919), 1701–2. See also *Eagle*, April 8, 1919.

78. *Eagle*, April 19, 1919, *Times*, April 20, 1919. In two states with major league teams, Sunday baseball remained illegal after 1919. Massachusetts legalized Sunday ball in 1928 (to take effect in 1929), and Pennsylvania did the same in 1933 (in time for the 1934 season). Curiously, because of the proximity of Fenway Park to a church, the Boston Red Sox played their Sunday home games at Braves Field until 1932, when someone in the organization finally thought to ask the church's minister if he objected to Sunday games. He did not, and Sunday baseball has been played at Fenway ever since.

to postpone the Board's vote for a week, and that was to enable testimony from others who opposed the measure. By rule, only one negative vote was required for postponement, so there was no vote that day. When the Board reconvened on April 29, representatives of the Baptist Tabernacle Church of Brooklyn, the Methodist Preachers Association, the Presbyterian Ministers Association, the Reformed Church Ministers Association, and the Long Island Ministers Association—but apparently not Canon Chase—spoke in opposition. The Alderman then voted, 64 to 0, to legalize commercial Sunday baseball in the five boroughs of New York City.[79] Mayor John Francis Hylan signed the ordinance almost immediately.[80]

Thus ended decades of conflict over the legal standing of Christian Sabbatarianism and a highly popular form of secular leisure in the place once called the City of Churches. Brooklyn's first indisputably legal Sunday major league baseball game was played on May 4, 1919. The Brooklyn Robins defeated the Boston Braves, 6 to 2.[81] The Giants also played that day at the Polo Grounds, losing to the Phillies, 4 to 3. The *New York Times* reported that sixty thousand spectators attended the two games.[82]

---

79. *Eagle*, April 23, 1919; April 29, 1919; April 30, 1919.
80. *Eagle*, May 2, 1919.
81. *Eagle*, May 4, 1919; May 5, 1919.
82. *New York Times*, May 5, 1919. In 1920 there were twenty Sunday games in Ebbets Field during a twenty-six-week season. This was due in part to the National League's decision to schedule some Sunday games in Brooklyn for both Boston and Philadelphia, which still could not legally play them at home. The establishment of major league Sunday baseball in New York City may have had an indirect effect on the building of Yankee Stadium. The Yankees had been leasing the Polo Grounds for their home games, an arrangement that limited the Giants to thirteen Sunday home games and the Yankees to twelve in 1920, the difference in revenue for the Giants amounting to more than the proceeds of the Yankee lease for the entire year. The *Eagle* speculated that the Giants would not renew the lease for that reason (*Eagle*, February 14, 1920). The lease was renewed, but the relationship between the Giants and the Yankees did not last. Construction of Yankee Stadium began in 1922.

In the Bushes
The Secret History of Anglo-Iroquois Treaty Making

Timothy J. Shannon

The scion of a wealthy family from Maryland's Eastern Shore, Tench Tilghman had no previous experience in Native American diplomacy when the Continental Congress appointed him secretary for a delegation it sent to treat with the Haudenosaunee in 1775. He spent about a month in the Mohawk Valley and Albany on this mission, keeping a journal that detailed his experiences there.[1] Tilghman was much more interested in recording his after-hours social life than anything related to the official proceedings. While much of what he wrote conveyed the snobbery that an eighteenth-century gentleman might have been expected to express about the people and living conditions he encountered in the backcountry, Tilghman also wrote with enthusiasm about some of the experiences associated with treaty making. He admired the manners exhibited by the chiefs he encountered, described in detail an Indian dance, and praised the singing he heard from Native women who had converted to Christianity. Growing frustrated at one point with the slow pace of the diplomatic negotiations that were the raison d'être for his trip, Tilghman wrote, "An Indian Treaty is by the by but dull entertainment owing to the delay and difficulty of getting what you say, delivered properly to the Indians."[2] Yet, the rest of his journal tells a different story: for a novice such as himself, a treaty conference was a singular kind of event that exposed participants to new sights and sounds and to an impressive cross section of Native and early American society.

Treaty making of the kind Tilghman witnessed grew out of the Covenant Chain alliance between the Haudenosaunee (often referred to as the Six Nations or Iroquois in eighteenth-century documents) and the northern British colonies. Treaty conferences brought

I would like to thank Bill Starna for his feedback on an earlier draft of this article, as well as the editors and anonymous readers for *New York History*.
1. Tench Tilghman, *Memoir of Lieut. Col. Tench Tilghman, Secretary and Aid to Washington: Together with an Appendix, Containing Revolutionary Journals and Letters, Hitherto Unpublished*, ed. Samuel Harrison (Albany, N.Y.: J. Munsell, 1876), 79–101.
2. Tilghman, 94.

together delegations representing multiple colonies and Indians numbering in the hundreds, occasionally thousands, for weeks at a time, creating the circumstances in which a system of diplomatic negotiation evolved that combined Native American and European precedents. The publication of some treaties by colonial printers introduced the process and vocabulary of this diplomacy to a broader audience in North America and Britain. Thus, by the time Tilghman journeyed to the Mohawk Valley in 1775, treaty making had become a part of the cultural landscape of British North America, generating a documentary record that scholars have used ever since to recover the form and content of what went on at such meetings.[3]

It is much more difficult, however, to reconstruct how Indians and colonists interacted on such occasions when they were not exchanging speeches around the council fire. In the parlance of Covenant Chain diplomacy, meetings that occurred "in the bushes" were the unrecorded conversations that ran parallel to the public negotiations, enabling the latter to proceed smoothly. Such conversations were often managed by the go-betweens, or brokers, who possessed the language skills and cultural know-how to conduct such business. Some worked primarily as interpreters but others, such as Conrad Weiser and Sir William Johnson, possessed reputations on both sides of the cultural divide that made them particularly influential in treaty proceedings. The archival records left by these figures and others like them have helped historians reconstruct the wheeling and dealing left out of the treaty proceedings.[4] But there was another dimension to what went on in the bushes that was more typically recorded by novices like Tilghman, whose inexperience and peripheral roles kept them out of the negotiations, but whose presence created another vantage point on the treaty making process. Cultural brokers such as Weiser and Johnson did not fill journals

---

3. The best introduction to Anglo-Iroquois diplomacy is Francis Jennings, William N. Fenton, Mary A. Druke, and David R. Miller, eds., *The History and Culture of Iroquois Diplomacy: An Interdisciplinary Guide to the Treaties of the Six Nations and Their League* (Syracuse, N.Y.: Syracuse University Press, 1985). See also William N. Fenton, *The Great Law and the Longhouse: A Political History of the Iroquois Confederacy* (Norman: University of Oklahoma Press, 1998), 363–513; and Francis Jennings, *The Ambiguous Iroquois Empire: The Covenant Chain Confederation of Indian Tribes with English Colonies from Its Beginnings to the Lancaster Treaty of 1744* (New York: W. W. Norton, 1984). The best introduction to the published corpus of Indian treaties from the colonial era remains Lawrence C. Wroth, "The Indian Treaty as Literature," *Yale Review*, n.s. 17 (1927–1928): 749–66. For a comprehensive history of Native treaty making in American history, see Colin G. Calloway, *Pen and Ink Witchcraft: Treaties and Treaty Making in American Indian History* (New York: Oxford University Press, 2013); and Francis Paul Prucha, *American Indian Treaties: The History of a Political Anomaly* (Berkeley: University of California Press, 1994).
4. For the role of cultural brokers and interpreters in treaty making, see James H. Merrell, *Into the American Woods: Negotiators on the Pennsylvania Frontier* (New York: W. W. Norton, 1999); Daniel K. Richter, "Cultural Brokers and Intercultural Politics: New York–Iroquois Relations, 1664–1701," *Journal of American History* 75 (June 1988): 40–67; Nancy L. Hagedorn, "'A Friend to Go between Them': The Interpreter as Cultural Broker during Anglo-Iroquois Councils, 1740–1770," *Ethnohistory* 35 (1988): 60–80; and Nancy Hagedorn, "Brokers of Understanding: Interpreters as Agents of Cultural Exchange in Colonial New York," *New York History* 76 (October 1995): 379–408.

with descriptions of intercultural socializing or Indian dances because they had more important business to transact and record; but for someone like Tilghman, everything at a treaty conference was new and therefore noteworthy.

The number of such sources is small but significant for what we can learn from them about treaty making. Some of these journals were kept by commissioners appointed by colonial governments to attend such meetings. Others came from the pens of figures like Tilghman, who were acting as secretaries or aides to such delegations. Witham Marshe, the secretary of the Maryland delegation to the Lancaster treaty of 1744, authored the most well-known example of this genre. Joseph Bloomfield, a young Continental Army officer from New Jersey, followed in Tilghman's footsteps and wrote about treaty negotiations he observed in the Mohawk Valley in 1776. Griffith Evans served as secretary for the Pennsylvania commissioners who attended the Fort Stanwix treaty in 1784. James Emlen, William Savery, and David Bacon were Philadelphia Quakers who observed a federal Indian treaty in Canandaigua, New York, in 1794.[5] These men and a few others like them recorded personal accounts of treaty making that were not intended to be part of a public or archival record. Their observations were idiosyncratic and anecdotal; but when read collectively, they offer an alternative history of these events in which the official proceedings were, as Tilghman put it, "but dull entertainment." In part, theirs is a sensory history, filled with the unique sights and sounds of intercultural diplomacy. It is also a history of manners, describing how European and Native customs of hospitality merged to create rules of etiquette that introduced novices and strangers to this hybrid statecraft.

If it is true, as James Merrell has argued, that over the course of the eighteenth century both Native and colonial peoples grew contemptuous of treaty making because of its association with land fraud and other abuses, then it is all the more remarkable that these meetings did not devolve into violence.[6] Certainly, the potential was there from the start: Indians arrived to these meetings armed, and the ability of local authorities to police such large gatherings was minimal. Alcohol, a common accelerant of violence on both sides of the cultural divide, was widely available and eagerly consumed by all parties. Grievances expressed around the council fire could easily have led to physical confrontations

---

5. See Witham Marshe, "Journal of the Treaty Held with the Six Nations by the Commissioners of Maryland, and other Provinces, at Lancaster, in Pennsylvania, June, 1744," *Collections of the Massachusetts Historical Society*, Ser. 1, vol. 7 (1792):171–201, https://archive.org/details /collectionsmass05socigoog/page/n190/mode/2up; Mark E. Lender and James Kirby Martin, eds., *Citizen-Soldier: The Revolutionary War Journal of Joseph Bloomfield*, (Newark: New Jersey Historical Society, 1982), 43–99; Hallock F. Raup, ed., "Journal of Griffith Evans, 1784–1785," *Pennsylvania Magazine of History and Biography* 65 (April 1941): 202–33; William N. Fenton, ed., "The Journal of James Emlen Kept on a Trip to Canandaigua, New York," *Ethnohistory* 12 (Autumn 1965): 279–342; William Savery, *A Journal of the Life, Travels, and Religious Labors of William Savery* (Philadelphia: Friends' Book Store, 1861), 88–160; and David Bacon, "Some Account of Our Journey to Canandaigua," in "Diary, Visit to Indians," 1794, Haverford College Library, https:// pennstreaty.haverford.edu/page/hv_bacond_account_1794_001.
6. Merrell, *Into the American Woods*, 253–301.

elsewhere, and yet never appeared to do so. What then was it about the intermingling of Natives and Europeans in these circumstances that enabled peace and order to prevail, if only temporarily?

What follows is an attempt to answer that question. It is not so much a social history of Anglo-Iroquois treaty conferences as a history of being social at them. Filtered through the recollections of elite colonial males, it cannot claim to present fully the Native perspective on such encounters. However, it is possible to cull from these journals insights into what Native men and women expected to happen at treaty conferences and how they interacted with the people they encountered there. In particular, these sources offer us a rare glimpse inside the Indians' camps, where families carried on with their domestic lives and curious visitors had their preconceptions about Native culture challenged. In this manner, treaty conferences extended the opportunities for peaceful face-to-face interactions between Native and European neighbors along the mid-Atlantic frontier, but they also established roles and spaces that kept them apart.[7] In their journals and diaries, Tilghman and his peers give us a fuller picture of how treaty making operated during its heyday in the eighteenth century and what was lost when the locations and purposes of such meetings changed after 1800.

Treaty Places

Most treaty conferences occurred in the backcountry, in towns with commercial connections to the fur trade. Occasionally, parties of Indians traveled to cities like Philadelphia and New York to conduct diplomacy, but it was more common for such meetings to occur at geographic and cultural crossroads like Albany in New York or Lancaster in Pennsylvania. For Indians, such locations were closer to home, more familiar, and less likely to expose them to potentially fatal diseases. As one Onondaga chief explained after receiving an invitation from the governor of Virginia to come to Williamsburg: "We take your invidation kindly and should be very glad to see you but . . . we fear that If we go down to farr as to your Counsel fire we will loose still more [people and chiefs] as there is so many days Journey more to pass through the white people. We desire therefor that you will move your fire

---

7. On the difficulty of trying to "reverse the gaze" in such sources from Europeans' observations of Indians to Indians' observations of Europeans, see Colin G. Calloway, "The Chiefs Now in This City": Indians and the Urban Frontier in Early America (New York: Oxford University Press, 2021), 15–17. On interaction between Native and European communities, see David L. Preston, The Texture of Contact: European and Indian Settler Communities on the Frontiers of Iroquoia, 1667–1783 (Lincoln: University of Nebraska Press, 2009); Gail D. MacLeitch, Imperial Entanglements: Iroquois Change and Persistence on the Frontiers of Empire (Philadelphia: University of Pennsylvania Press, 2011); and Daniel Ingram, Indians and British Outposts in Eighteenth-Century America (Gainesville: University Press of Florida, 2012), 1–26, 59–87.

to Albany."[8] From the Natives' perspective, backcountry towns were also easier to travel to because of their locations along water and land routes that were commonly used for trade and diplomacy. While horses and canoes sometimes figured into this travel, accounts from such meetings usually described the Indians as arriving in large groups on foot, their pace set by the "great many small children and old men" among them.[9] Oftentimes, they arrived considerably later than expected by their colonial hosts and excused their tardiness by noting the need to pause and conduct councils or condolence ceremonies at other Native communities along the way.[10] For Natives then, attendance at a treaty conference was not necessarily a disruption in the normal course of daily or seasonal affairs. Summer, when most such meetings transpired, was the usual time for visiting and trading with neighbors, and they conducted much of this business while traveling to these backcountry locales.

On the other hand, the Anglo-American gentlemen who traveled to these treaty conferences from eastern seaports often described the journey as an arduous and unwelcome undertaking. It took anywhere from three to seven days for a ship to sail the 160 miles upriver from New York City to Albany, but that was easy compared to the overland route from Philadelphia or Boston.[11] Lancaster was only seventy miles from Philadelphia, but it was still a difficult place to reach from just about anywhere else. Marshe and the Maryland commissioners spent four days getting there from Annapolis in 1744. The Virginia commissioners to the same treaty spent several weeks in transit, traveling first by ship from the Potomac River to the mouth of the Susquehanna, and then overland to Philadelphia, where they had a long delay before finally embarking for Lancaster.[12] Other backcountry towns that hosted Anglo-Iroquois treaties included Easton and Carlisle in Pennsylvania. Like Albany and Lancaster, they were frontier communities that served as gateways to Indian country for squatters and fur traders. Their populations were predominantly recent German and Scots-Irish migrants, giving them linguistic and cultural

8. Helga Doblin, trans., and William A. Starna, ed., "The Journals of Christian Daniel Claus and Conrad Weiser: A Journey to Onondaga, 1750," *Transactions of the American Philosophical Society* 84, no. 2 (1994): 19. On the problems Native American diplomats encountered with disease in eastern cities, see also Calloway, "*The Chiefs Now in This City,*" 92–109.
9. See for Marshe, "Journal of the Treaty," 176 (quote), 178.
10. See "[Theodore Atkinson's] Memo Book of my journey as one of the Commissioners on Treaty with the Six nations of Indians, Viz., 1754," in Beverly McAnear, ed., "Personal Accounts of the Albany Congress of 1754," *Mississippi Valley Historical Review* 39 (1953): 731.
11. Tilghman describes a four-day journey up the Hudson River in Tilghman, *Memoir*, 79–80. William Savery describes a difficult ten-day overland journey from Philadelphia to Canandaigua. Savery, *Journal of the Life, Travels, and Religious Labors of William Savery*, 91–93.
12. The route of the Maryland commissioners is described in Marshe, "Journal of the Treaty," 171–75. The route of the Virginia commissioners is detailed in the journal of their secretary William Black, which unfortunately ends before the treaty proceedings began in Lancaster. See R. Alonzo Brock, ed., "Journal of William Black, 1744," *Pennsylvania Magazine of History and Biography* 1 (1877): 117–32, 233–49, 404–19; 2 (1878): 40–49.

characteristics that Anglo visitors from eastern seaports often found unfamiliar. In wartime, Albany and Carlisle became military bases, swelling their populations with soldiers and military contractors, while Easton and Lancaster became crowded with refugees from the countryside.[13]

Genteel travelers uniformly found these towns to be inhospitable places that offered few of the comforts or diversions they enjoyed back home. In their private journals, they gave full vent to their cultural prejudices, more often than not aiming their barbs at the local townsfolk rather than at the visiting Indians. Marshe described Lancaster's population as "chiefly High-Dutch, Scotch-Irish, some few English families, and unbelieving Israelites" who failed miserably to meet his standards of hygiene and hospitality. "The spirit of cleanliness has not yet in the least troubled the major part of the inhabitants," Marshe recorded, "for in general they are very great sluts and slovens." One night during his stay he returned to his room at a local inn to find "three very impudent Indian traders" occupying his bed. After convincing his landlord to evict them, Marshe ordered the room washed out and his bed deloused. Marshe was similarly merciless in his assessment of the town's Scots-Irish and German women, whom he observed "danced wilder time than any Indians."[14]

Marshe's running commentary on what he perceived to be the social ineptitude of Lancaster's residents closely paralleled criticisms levied by visitors to the Mohawk Valley and Albany. When Tilghman traveled to German Flatts to invite Oneidas and Mohawks to treat in Albany, he and his companions took one look at the beds they were given by a local resident and decided to sleep on a threshing room floor instead. Back in Albany, he had little good to say about the locals, except for the family of local magnate Philip Schuyler. For polite conversation, he relied on Schuyler's daughters and "the Carolina ladies," two unnamed women who were also passing through town. When his Carolina friends announced they were leaving, Tilghman despaired and wrote that he would pursue the company of some Native women instead, because he found them in their appearance, cleanliness, and command of English to be "superior to any of the Albanians." Toward the end of his sojourn, Tilghman wrote, "Albany, I care not how soon I bid thee farewell. . . . The town is crowded with Indians and Soldiers, it is hard to say which is the most irregular and Savage."[15] Griffith Evans, who attended the Fort Stanwix treaty in 1784, likewise condemned the Dutch inhabitants of Albany and the Mohawk

---

13. See Judith Ridner, *A Town In-Between: Carlisle, Pennsylvania and the Early Mid-Atlantic Interior* (Philadelphia: University of Pennsylvania Press, 2010), 77–81; Jerome H. Wood Jr., *Conestoga Crossroads: Lancaster, Pennsylvania, 1730–1790* (Harrisburg: Pennsylvania Historical and Museum Commission, 1979), 71–74, 113–18; and Timothy J. Shannon, *Indians and Colonists at the Crossroads of Empire: The Albany Congress of 1754* (Ithaca, N.Y.: Cornell University Press, 2000), 120–27.

14. Marshe, "Journal of the Treaty," 177, 184, 187.

15. Tilghman, *Memoir*, 84, 89, 93, 96–97.

Valley for being "unsociable and disagreeable to strangers" and unfamiliar with the "idea of cleanliness."[16]

By the standards of such eastern elites, towns like Lancaster and Albany failed the test of polite society because they were populated by dirty and ill-mannered bumpkins. The nearly universal concern that these visitors expressed about the cleanliness of their local hosts reflected an emerging genteel aesthetic in the eighteenth century that attached notions of dirtiness and contamination to plebeians and foreigners, thereby doubly damning these communities.[17] It is harder to determine what visiting Indians thought of these towns. These places may have been more familiar to them if they had visited previously to trade or conduct diplomacy, and they may have had acquaintances among their residents. But Albany's fur traders had a reputation for cheating their Native customers, and so familiarity may have bred contempt rather than goodwill. More importantly, during treaty conferences, residents of these backcountry towns did not admit visiting Indians into their homes and public accommodations in the same way that they welcomed European visitors. This may have struck visiting Indians as inhospitable, although Marshe thought the situation reflected Native preferences as much as European prejudices: "They will not, on any occasion whatsoever, dwell or even stay, in houses built by white people."[18] Such was the character of British North America's first intercolonial capitals: backcountry settlements that Natives and eastern elites found either lacking in hospitality or comically inept in the pursuit of it. In this setting, eastern gentlemen like Marshe and Tilghman had their first exposure to Native Americans and found that civility could take an intercultural cast.

Sights and Sounds

At the start of the Lancaster Treaty of 1744, the interpreter Conrad Weiser took Witham Marshe and other visiting gentlemen aside and warned them, "whilst we were here, not to talk much of the Indians, nor laugh at their dress, or make any remarks on their behaviour: if we did, it would be very much resented by them, and might cause differences to arise betwixt the white people and them."[19] Weiser, a veteran of such meetings, apparently anticipated what must have been a common reaction among novices when they attended treaty conferences. Observers were fascinated by the Indians' appearance and deportment, and while Weiser told Marshe and his compatriots not to laugh, another common reaction was rapt attention, as colonial gentlemen used their own standards of behavior to describe and decode the Indians. Their conclusions, not surprisingly, tended to divide Indians according

---

16. Raup, "Journal of Griffith Evans," 205.
17. See Kathleen M. Brown, *Foul Bodies: Cleanliness in Early America* (New Haven: Yale University Press, 2009), 118–58.
18. Marshe, "Journal of the Treaty,"179.
19. Marshe, 180.

to the most significant social divide within colonial America: that between patricians, whose costume and manners defined polite society, and plebeians, whose appearance and comportment did the same for vulgar society.[20]

Eighteenth-century Americans relied on clothing as the most reliable visual indication of a person's social status. The lower sort wore loose-fitting work garments, coarse and dull in feel and color, while the better sort displayed their wealth in well-tailored clothing that featured brighter colors and softer fabrics. Native American dress fell into a category all its own. The "Indian fashion," as colonial observers called it, incorporated cloth and jewelry acquired from Europeans with such Native elements as paint, feathers, and animal pelts. The most distinguishing trait of the Indian fashion was nakedness: time and again, Europeans noted that Indians left uncovered such body parts as legs, arms, and chests.[21] When Marshe watched the Indians arrive in Lancaster, he wrote that they "in general, were poorly dressed, having old match-coats, and those ragged; few, or no shirts, and those they had, as black as . . . that • blot."[22] Joseph Bloomfield, from his vantage in the Mohawk Valley in 1776, noted that the Indians "in general go naked except for a Clout which they wear to cover their Nakedness, Once in a While throwing a Blanket over their Shoulders." Like Marshe, Bloomfield regarded nakedness as the default dress code of the Native male. Native women, on the other hand, covered more of their bodies and exhibited a tremendous variety in their jewelry, which included "wampum, silver, Bead Bracelets . . . Earrings, nose-Jewels, & Pins . . . Necklaces, belts, &c."[23]

When observers did note elaboration in Native American dress, they usually interpreted it as evidence of social distinction, just as they were inclined to do within their own society. Bloomfield, for example, observed that Indian women decorated their blankets with stripes, ribbons, and silver or brass brooches "agreable to their quality in life." At a service for Christian Indians, he admired the "reverence & solemnity [of] the almost naked Savages," noting also that the chiefs and their wives "were elegantly dressed with mockinsens Leggins &c. &c. after their Indian fashion."[24] During his stay in German Flatts, Bloomfield met the clan matron Molly Brant and her daughters, whom he described as "Young

---

20. On the patrician-plebeian divide in colonial society, see Gordon S. Wood, *Radicalism of the American Revolution* (New York: Knopf, 1991), 24–42; and Richard L. Bushman, *The Refinement of America: Persons, Houses, Cities* (New York: Vintage Books, 1993), 3–99. On the tendency of European observers to classify Indians according to the same divide, see Karen Ordahl Kupperman, *Indians and English: Facing Off in Early America* (Ithaca, N.Y.: Cornell University Press, 2000), 41–76; and Nancy Shoemaker, *A Strange Likeness: Becoming Red and White in Eighteenth-Century North America* (New York: Oxford University Press, 2004), 35–60.

21. See Bushman, *Refinement of America*, 69–74; Jonathan Prude, "To Look Upon the 'Lower Sort': Runaway Ads and the Appearance of Unfree Laborers in America, 1750–1800," *Journal of American History* 78 (1991): 124–59; and Laura E. Johnson, "'Goods to clothe themselves': Native Goods and Native Images on the Pennsylvania Trading Frontier, 1712–1760," *Winterthur Portfolio* 43 (Spring 2009): 115–40.

22. Marshe, "Journal of the Treaty," 180.

23. Lender and Martin, *Citizen-Soldier: Journal of Joseph Bloomfield*, 83, 92.

24. Lender and Martin, 72, 83, 90–91.

Ladys . . . richly dressed agreable to the Indian-Fashion." A year earlier, Tench Tilghman had also met Molly Brant and recorded a similar impression: "She was dressed after the Indian Manner, but her linen and other Cloathes [were] the finest of their kind."[25] French diplomat François, Marquis de Barbé-Marbois, who observed the opening speeches of the Fort Stanwix treaty of 1784, was less impressed by the sartorial choices of the Indians but nevertheless associated them with their rank. The warriors, he noted, showed up "armed as if for battle" and therefore "presentable in appearance," but their chiefs were "clothed in the strangest and most ridiculous manner" because of the mishmash of European and Native clothing they wore.[26]

Like dress, comportment helped Europeans at treaty conferences divide their Native counterparts, who could number in the hundreds, into elites and commoners. In general, observers praised the Indians' gravitas in public councils, but disparaged their manners when it came to consuming food and drink. Joseph Bloomfield, for example, voiced a common criticism when he wrote that the Indians "observe no bounds or decency in their eating or drinking."[27] At the Lancaster treaty, Marshe watched two dozen chiefs dine with the colonial commissioners and was surprised to discover that the Indians "made no use of their forks."[28] Such remarks consigned the Indians to vulgar society, although their polite carriage sometimes indicated otherwise. The authors of these journals constantly referred to the Indians' "countenance," using the term to encompass not only facial expressions but also their general physicality in public situations, such as when Marshe described Onondaga chief Canasatego as "a tall, well-made man" with a "very full chest, and brawny limbs . . . a manly countenance, mixed with a good-natured smile."[29] In his 1776 journal, Bloomfield wrote of the Indians' physical appearance, "Their features are regular but their countenances fierce."[30]

Like many of his peers, Bloomfield praised the Indians' demeanor when conducting business, which he thought exhibited a natural affinity to good manners. "They are grave even to sadness, upon any serious Occasion," he wrote, "observant of those in Company, respectful to the old, of a temper cool deliberate." In their councils, "every man there is heard in his turn, According as his Years, Wisdom, or service have ranked him. Not a Word, not a

---

25. Tilghman, *Memoir*, 72.
26. Eugene Parker Chase, ed., *Our Revolutionary Forefathers: The Letters of François, Marquis de Barbé-Marbois, 1775–1785* (New York: Duffield and Company, 1929), 215.
27. Lender and Martin, *Citizen-Soldier: Journal of Joseph Bloomfield*, 83.
28. Marshe, "Journal of the Treaty," 193.
29. Marshe, 179. For more on Canasatego's reputation among Europeans, see William A. Starna, "The Diplomatic Career of Canasatego," in *Friends and Enemies in Penn's Woods: Indians, Colonists, and the Racial Construction of Pennsylvania*, ed. William A. Pencak and Daniel K. Richter (University Park: Pennsylvania State University Press, 2004), 144–63. On the role of "countenance" in eighteenth-century manners, see C. Dallett Hemphill, *Bowing to Necessities: A History of Manners in America, 1620–1860* (New York: Oxford University Press, 1999), 78–80.
30. Lender and Martin, *Citizen-Soldier: Journal of Joseph Bloomfield*, 83.

Wisper, not a murmur is heard from the rest, whilst He speaks; no indecent condemnation, no ill-timed applause." The Indians, in fact, were "put off by our People who interrupt each other, & frequently speak altogether."[31] Tilghman recorded similar impressions in Albany in 1775: "The Behaviour of these poor Savages at a public Meeting ought to put us civilized people to the Blush. The most profound silence is observed, no interruption of a speaker. When any one speaks, all the rest are attentive." Both observers noted that this reserve on the Indians' part extended to the division of diplomatic presents. According to Tilghman, when the commissioners presented the Indians with a large roll of tobacco, "Two of their people cut it into pieces of two or three inches, and then distributed them all around. No man rose from his seat to snatch. When drink was served round it was in the same manner, no Man seemed anxious for the Cup."[32] Griffith Evans recorded the same impressive reserve at Fort Stanwix in 1784: "I took a walk up to the green to view them dividing the goods and observed the greatest decorum and apparent impartiality prevail amongst 'em ... not a word of dispute or dissatisfaction."[33] The consistency in these descriptions indicates a genuine admiration for Native standards of conduct in treaty making and a desire that the factious European delegations at such meetings might learn to imitate them. If the Indians were, as Bloomfield wrote, "put off" by the interruptions and cross-talking among their counterparts, then they certainly set a consistent example for better behavior.

Europeans saved their greatest praise for Indian oratory, especially as it combined speech, gesture, and movement. In their speeches, Indian orators exhibited grace in motion, a mandatory element of what gentlemen considered polite behavior. After listening to Cayuga chief Gachradodon at Lancaster in 1744, Marshe wrote, "His action, when he spoke, was certainly the most graceful, as well as bold, that any person ever saw; without the buffoonery of the French, or over-solemn deportment of the haughty Spaniards."[34] The aural experience of hearing an Indian speaker in a diplomatic council rather than in everyday conversation was evident in an experience recorded by Philadelphia attorney Benjamin Chew at the Easton treaty of 1758. While walking in town, Chew approached a house where "I heard very distinctly the voice of an Indian speaker aloud in the house with the same accent, tone and emphasis as they generally use in public speaking in Treaties." The sound prompted Chew to investigate, and by sticking his head through an open window he discovered "a large assembly of Quakers and Indians sitting around a long table."[35] At

---

31. Lender and Martin, 84.
32. Tilghman, *Memoir*, 86. See also Lender and Martin, *Citizen-Soldier: Journal of Joseph Bloomfield*, 99.
33. Raup, "Journal of Griffith Evans," 215.
34. Marshe, "Journal of the Treaty," 200. Elsewhere in his journal, Marshe praised Canasatego in a similar manner for "a surprising liveliness in his speech" (179). On the importance of grace in speech and carriage to colonial gentlemen, see Bushman, *Refinement of America*, 68–69.
35. "Benamin Chew's Journal of a Journey to Easton, 1758," in Julian P. Boyd, ed., *Indian Treaties Printed by Benjamin Franklin, 1736–1762* (Philadelphia: Historical Society of Pennsylvania, 1938), 313.

Fort Stanwix in 1784, Griffith Evans was taken aback by the oratory he heard from chiefs at the opening of the treaty: "I now for the first time hear men savage in almost every respect harangue on important subjects with eloquence, force and coherence." Fellow auditors more familiar with Indian languages assured Evans that the speeches were even more impressive than what he heard via the interpreter.[36]

When not making speeches at the council fire, Native leaders also exhibited a talent for polite conversation. Bloomfield, upon meeting "the famous Capt. Soloman," a Christian Stockbridge Indian, found his "behaviour is quite different from the rest of the savages being Polite & remarkable free & Easy in conversation." A few days later he shared a "friendly Pipe" with a group of chiefs and found that they "shewed a great deal of Wit & pleasantry" in their conversation.[37] Likewise, at the Canandaigua treaty in 1794, a group of chiefs who joined William Savery for dinner one evening "manifested a high turn for wit and humor" in their private conversation.[38] In his journal, Tilghman noted that when greeting Europeans, Natives "never enter into a controversy," but rather confined their remarks to "indifferent Subjects, such as inquiring after Acquaintances &c." In other words, they knew the art of small talk, another indispensable form of self-presentation in genteel society.[39]

Native music also figured into the distinctive soundscape of a treaty conference. This included songs of greeting when Indians arrived in town, songs of peace when they assembled at the council fire, and songs of mourning when the death of a chief necessitated a funeral.[40] Hymn singing by Christian Indians prompted responses from Europeans who attended religious services conducted by missionaries and their converts. In Albany, Tilghman was not impressed by the "pulpit oratory" of the Reverend Samuel Kirkland, but he thought the Oneida men and women in his congregation "sung one anthem . . . pleasingly enough." Theodore Atkinson, a New Hampshire treaty commissioner in Albany in 1754, attended a Mohawk religious service there and found it "Performed with the utmost Decency." James Emlen, one of the Quaker observers at the Canandaigua treaty in 1794, thought that the singing of Oneida women was better than "anything of the kind that I remember to have heard . . . truly melodious."[41] Such descriptions, while generally positive in regard to the Natives' musical talents, tended to group hymn singing along with other

---

36. Raup, "Journal of Griffith Evans," 208.

37. Lender and Martin, *Citizen-Soldier: Journal of Joseph Bloomfield*, 79, 88.

38. Savery, *Journal of the Life, Travels, and Religious Labors of William Savery*, 117.

39. Tilghman, *Memoir*, 85. On the art of polite conversation, see Bushman, *Refinement of America*, 83–89.

40. For an example of a song of greeting, see Marshe's description of the Indians' arrival in Lancaster. Marshe, "Journal of the Treaty," 178–79. For songs of peace sung at the start of councils, see *An Account of the Treaty between His Excellency Benjamin Fletcher . . . and the Indians of the Five Nations . . . August, 1694* (New York: William Bradford, 1694), 5, 15. For condolence songs, see Conrad Weiser's journal from a treaty conference held in Albany in 1751 in Paul A. W. Wallace, *Conrad Weiser, 1696–1760: Friend of Colonist and Mohawk* (Philadelphia: Sunbury Press, 1945), 329.

41. See Tilghman, *Memoir*, 95; McAnear, "Personal Accounts of the Albany Congress of 1754," 736; and Fenton, "Journal of James Emlen," 299–300.

activities such as dances that European observers described as diversions apart from treaty business, but for Christian Indians such performances had their own diplomatic purposes, introducing converts to the treaty's hosts and distinguishing them from the other Native groups present. Singing of all kinds was a communal exercise among Natives and thus a means of asserting group identity.[42] Other noteworthy aural elements of a treaty conference included the Indians' communal shout of appropriation at the council fire, sometimes transcribed as "Yo-Hah" by listeners, and the drumming and singing that accompanied Indian dances.[43]

When novices like Tilghman and Marshe arrived at treaty conferences, they were greeted by new sights and sounds that quickly challenged whatever preconceptions they may have had about Native Americans. Unaccustomed to the process of intercultural diplomacy, they made sense of their surroundings by assigning new people and experiences to familiar categories. When they encountered Indians with great oratorical skills, polite manners, and beautiful singing voices, the dichotomy between savagery and civility became muddled, but the distinction between patrician and plebeian remained clear. A combination of dress, deportment, and verbal expression defined the Indians' "countenance" on such occasions. Elite Indians, both male and female, exhibited social ease among European audiences. Their posture and carriage conveyed physical self-control and dignity, and their dress indicated elevated social rank among their people. Bloomfield in his journal twice referred to Indian "gentlemen" who "walked [together] in state . . . smoking their Pipes & Looking like Men of great consequence."[44] By their carriage and polite conversation, such Indians distinguished themselves from others who wore ragged clothing (if any at all) and showed no self-restraint in their manners.

Coming Together

"We were busy all the morn[in]g preparing matters for opening the treaty tomorrow," Tench Tilghman wrote in his journal entry for August 24, 1775, "as a vast deal of Ceremony is to be observed."[45] As a novice to such affairs, Tilghman did not realize that he had already been participating in such ceremonies for over a week. Ten days earlier, he had traveled eighty

---

42. On hymn singing among Christian Oneidas, see Karim M. Tiro, *The People of the Standing Stone: The Oneida Nation from the Revolution through the Era of Removal* (Amherst: University of Massachusetts Press, 2011), 15–16. On the diplomatic significance of hymn singing, see also Rachel Wheeler and Sarah Eyerly, "Singing Box 331: Re-sounding Eighteenth-Century Mohican Hymns from the Moravian Archives," *William and Mary Quarterly* 76 (October 2019): 649–96.

43. See Tilghman, *Memoir*, 91–92, for a description of the music and singing that accompanied Indian dances. For the shout of approbation, see Thomas Pownall to Lord Halifax, July 23, 1754, in McAnear, "Personal Accounts of the Albany Congress of 1754," 741; and Richard Cullen Rath, *How Early America Sounded* (Ithaca: Cornell University Press, 2003), 159–68.

44. Lender and Martin, *Citizen-Soldier: Journal of Joseph Bloomfield*, 66, 99.

45. Tilghman, *Memoir*, 92–93.

miles west of Albany with the congressional commissioners to German Flatts to meet with Mohawks and Oneidas who lived nearby. There they encountered several chiefs who inquired as to the cause of their visit. The commissioners explained their intentions, and after two days of speech making, the chiefs presented "what they call a Path Belt, thereby desiring us to make their way clear to Albany."[46]

One week later, Tilghman witnessed "an Assembly of the Indians who were got together to receive the welcome of the people of Albany." That night, the townspeople lit two fires in the streets, and at 8:00 p.m., "the Indians came down, beating their drum, striking sticks together in Exact time and yelling after their Manner." Tilghman described them as "almost intirely naked" as they danced "with the most savage Contortions of Body & limbs." The following day involved more social interaction between the townspeople and their Indian visitors. In the evening Gen. Philip Schuyler hosted an entertainment for visiting gentlemen and gentlewomen at his home. Several Indians visited the party, and after learning that Tilghman did not have "an Indian name," gave him one. An Onondaga chief called him "Teakhokalonde," a name which he told Tilghman meant "having large horns . . . an emblem of strength, Virtue, and Courage." A skeptical Tilghman felt "his Temples every now and then for the sprouting honours." He concluded, "The christening cost a bowl of punch or two which I believe is the chief motive of the institution." The following day, Schuyler opened the conference with a public speech to the Indians.[47]

In his journal Tilghman described all of this eating and drinking as part of his busy, after-hours social life during his stay in Albany. Most of his entries emphasized his enjoyment of Schuyler's hospitality, his attraction to his daughters, and the excursions he made with them. The Indians' presence at some of these activities he attributed to their appetites for food, drink, and tobacco. Veterans of treaty making, however, recognized all this activity as part of a well-established social ritual surrounding intercultural diplomacy, much of it based on the condolence ceremony used by the Haudenosaunee to renew relations within their confederacy and to initiate negotiations with outsiders. Europeans' participation in this ritual altered its material context in some ways: government officials brought with them wampum manufactured with European tools, condolence presents drawn from the fur trader's stock of goods, and hospitality customs of their own, such as toasting the king's health and firing cannon salutes. Nevertheless, the format by which hosts and Indian visitors came together remained essentially Iroquoian in nature.[48]

Tilghman participated in this ritual when he smoked, drank, and talked with the chiefs at German Flatts, when he accepted their wampum belt to clear the path to Albany, and when he received his name from them at the Schuyler mansion. Like many other visitors,

46. Tilghman, 84, 88.
47. Tilghman, 91–93.
48. See William N. Fenton, "Structure, Continuity, and Change in the Process of Iroquois Treaty Making," in Jennings et al., *History and Culture of Iroquois Diplomacy*, 3–36.

he joined in these activities not because he had an anthropologist's interest in understanding Native American customs but because so much of it paralleled the rules of civility that he had internalized as a colonial gentleman. Tilghman valued displays of rank and hierarchy, as well as the roles hospitality and conversation played in mediating social relations.[49] Unwittingly or not, he was learning the ropes of a hybrid social ritual that brought Native and European peoples together at treaty conferences and regulated their interactions there.

In Iroquois diplomacy, councils began with a ceremonial greeting known as "wood's edge," in which outsiders paused before entering a town or village to announce their intentions. Leaders of the host community greeted the visitors, and both sides exchanged wampum while reciting the "three bare words" of condolence to clear eyes, ears, and throats of grief. Hosts then escorted their guests inside and shared refreshments with them before agreeing on a proper time to meet at the council fire.[50] When Tilghman reported on the Indians' arrival in Albany in 1775, he was witnessing one version of the wood's edge. In another variation, the New York governor George Clinton greeted Indians arriving for an Albany treaty conference in 1746 at the city's gates, discharging the fort's cannon in their honor and treating their chiefs to wine afterward.[51] Such encounters were ceremonial and brief. As Tilghman observed at German Flatts, chiefs avoided discussing substantial issues before opening the formal proceedings, for it might disturb the air of amity the wood's edge was supposed to create. Some Europeans, therefore, regarded it as a perfunctory duty. Such was the tone taken by Pennsylvania commissioner Isaac Norris at the outset of another Albany treaty conference in 1745: "In the evening some of the Indians desired to see us. We gave them a dram, and told them we were glad to see them, and then they went away."[52] Nevertheless, treaty commissioners learned to engage in this ritual, and toasting, drinking, and smoking became ubiquitous activities whenever they shared social space with their Native counterparts.[53]

Closely linked to the wood's edge greeting were the processions both Natives and Europeans made into treaty conferences. The use of song by the Iroquois on such occasions, as well as their discharge of firearms created an aural and visual experience that impressed their audiences. Marshe vividly described one such procession when the Indians arrived in Lancaster in 1744. Onondaga chief Canasatego led 252 Indians into town, and as they

---

49. On the code of civility among colonial elites, see David S. Shields, *Civil Tongues and Polite Letters in British America* (Chapel Hill: University of North Carolina Press, 1997), 11–54.
50. See Fenton, "Structure, Continuity, and Change," 18–19, 28.
51. See [New York], *A Treaty between His Excellency ... George Clinton ... and the Six ... Nations ... Albany ... 1746* (New York, 1746), 8.
52. See "The Journal of Isaac Norris, during a Trip to Albany in 1745," *Pennsylvania Magazine of History and Biography* 27 (1903): 23.
53. Other examples of this ritual can be found throughout the journals of Marshe, Tilghman, and Bloomfield. For a discussion of the incorporation of alcohol and toasting into European-Indian diplomacy, see Peter C. Mancall, *Deadly Medicine: Indians and Alcohol in Early America* (Ithaca, N.Y.: Cornell University Press, 1995), 48–49, 72–74.

passed by the courthouse where Marshe and others were dining, he "sung, in the Indian language, a song, inviting us to a renewal of all treaties heretofore made, and that now [are] to be made."[54] At German Flatts in 1776, Bloomfield witnessed the arrival of seventy-two Canajoharie Mohawks, who marched into town "in Indian-file . . . fireing & hallooing & dancing after the Indian-Manner, out of Respect as they said to the General [Schuyler]."[55] William Savery was struck by the arrival of nearly five hundred Senecas in the tiny frontier community of Canandaigua in 1794. After pausing to "paint and ornament themselves before their public entry," they marched into town, where they were greeted by Oneidas, Onondagas, and Cayugas who had arrived ahead of them. As a small number of bystanders looked on, the two groups of Indians exchanged gun salutes, "making a long and loud echo through the woods." They then encircled Timothy Pickering, the federal agent presiding over the treaty, and exchanged speeches and wampum with him before dispersing to set up their camp. Impressed by the sights and sounds of the proceedings, Savery noted that the Indians had made "a truly terrific and warlike appearance."[56]

Native processions into small backcountry towns such as Lancaster and Canandaigua were public spectacles, with the sounds of songs and gun salutes attracting the curious and perhaps sending others scurrying for cover. The visiting Indians included women and children as well as men, but their numbers alone conveyed strength regardless of how many were armed or painted. The 252 Indians that Marshe counted in Lancaster added up to about 50 percent of the town's colonial population at that time.[57] The nearly 1,500 Indians who attended the Canandaigua treaty must have seemed to swallow up the two hundred or so local residents.[58]

Colonial, state, and federal delegations at treaty conferences scrambled to make similarly impressive entrances before their Native audiences. Tilghman noted that in German Flatts in 1775, the patriot commissioners "at the appointed time . . . set out and made as respectable an appearance as we could, having got several of the Neighbouring People to join our Cavalcade."[59] At Albany, the New York governor enlisted redcoats from the town's garrison to give a martial air to his entrances, but these troops were so notoriously ragged

---

54. Marshe, "Journal of the Treaty," 178–79. Conrad Weiser also described two Indian processions with singing at an Albany treaty in 1751; see Wallace, *Conrad Weiser, 1696–1760*, 327, 329.

55. Lender and Martin, *Citizen-Soldier: Journal of Joseph Bloomfield*, 76.

56. Savery, *Journal of the Life, Travels, and Religious Labors of William Savery*, 104.

57. For estimate an estimate of Lancaster's population in the mid-eighteenth century, see J. Wood, *Conestoga Crossroads*, 18.

58. Savery estimated that 1,600 Indians attended the Canandaigua treaty, but his companion David Emlen put the total closer to 1,000. Timothy Pickering, the federal official directing the proceedings, put the total at 1,200 "certain" and "1,500" probable. See Savery, *Journal of the Life, Travels, and Religious Labors of William Savery*, 105; Fenton, "Journal of James Emlen," 289, 291, 301–2; and Fenton, *Great Law and the Longhouse*, 670.

59. Tilghman, *Memoir*, 85.

in appearance that they may have had the opposite effect on Native spectators.[60] In the Quaker colony of Pennsylvania, there were no fortifications or even local militiamen to provide such service. At Lancaster in 1744, the colonial commissioners waited for the Indians to seat themselves "after their own manner" in the courthouse and then marched in together with the Pennsylvania governor at their head.[61]

European observers often expressed impatience with the ceremonies associated with opening a treaty conference. Perturbed by the Indians' delays in arrival, government officials were anxious to get business underway so as to minimize the expense of provisioning their guests; but their counterparts refused to be hurried. After their long journeys to the treaty site, they needed time to rest and consult with each other. Such pauses also established their expectations for hospitable treatment, which would in turn encourage the clear heads and open hearts necessary for successful negotiations. Pipes smoked and drams consumed in brief, polite meetings like the kind Tilghman had in German Flatts and Albany may have struck him as unsubtle efforts by Indian leaders to cadge tobacco, food, and drink; but from the chiefs' perspective, these meetings helped clear the metaphorical brambles and briars accrued en route to the treaty. At Canandaigua in 1794, James Emlen initially expressed frustration with such delays: "We find it requisite to seek for patience to await the arrival of the Indians; they being a people remarkably deliberate in all their proceedings. . . . *Time* the most precious thing in the World, is held with them in little estimation." Later, he came to appreciate the Indians' perspective: "Perhaps no people are greater masters of their time, hence in their public transactions we often complain of their being tedious, not considering that they & we estimate time with very diff[eren]t judgm[en]ts."[62]

The granting of Indian names to newcomers at treaty conferences was another adaptation of Iroquoian ritual. In their diplomacy with colonists, the Haudenosaunee initiated this practice in the seventeenth century by naming governors or agents they negotiated with at the council fire. New York's governors, for example, were called "Corlaer," named after an early Dutch agent. Such names brought colonists into the kin networks of the Haudenosaunee, giving them a place at the council fire and linking them to the metaphorical chains that they constructed between themselves and neighboring peoples.[63] By the mid-eighteenth century, the practice of naming participants in treaty councils had two forms. First, when chiefs encountered a colonial government for the first time or renewed contact with it after a long lapse, they granted it a name. At Lancaster in 1744, Cayuga chief Gachradodon named Maryland "Tocary-ho-gon," a reference to the colony's posi-

60. Thomas Pownall described the Albany soldiers as "bad & useless" and suffering under "a kind of Transportation for Life." See McAnear, "Personal Accounts of the Albany Congress of 1754," 745.
61. Marshe, "Journal of the Treaty," 180–81.
62. Fenton, "Journal of James Emlen," 291, 333.
63. On the names granted to the colonial governments, see the appropriate listings in the "Persons Participating" index in Jennings et al.,, *History and Culture of Iroquois Diplomacy*, 229–55. See also Fenton, *Great Law and the Longhouse*, 199–200.

tion between Virginia and Pennsylvania. At the Albany Congress of 1754, a similar naming occurred on behalf of New Hampshire, which was participating in an intercolonial treaty for the first time. According to Theodore Atkinson, "2 sachems from Each Tribe & Some few others" visited him and another New Hampshire commissioner in their lodgings. After receiving presents from them, the Indians "gave us the name *Sosaquasowane*," and made some polite inquiries about where they were from.[64]

In another variation of this practice, chiefs sometimes granted names to individuals whom they were meeting for the first time. Tilghman, as noted earlier, received his name from an Onondaga chief who visited the Schuyler's mansion the evening before the formal treaty proceedings began. The following day, Tilghman noted in his journal, "When Business was over I was admitted into the Onondago Tribe, in presence of all the six nations, and received by them as an adopted son." In a similar fashion Joseph Bloomfield received an Indian name from several Oneida Indians who visited him in German Flatts. They translated "Bloomfield" to "Field-in-Bloom," which Bloomfield transcribed as "Yo, chee, chiah, raw, raw, gou" in his journal.[65] Observers who recorded such exchanges cynically interpreted them as yet another method the Indians had devised to extract food, drink, and presents from their hosts. In one sense, they were entirely correct, for in all the examples cited here, the recipients of the names responded by treating the Indians to food and drink. Bloomfield's experience was typical. After the Oneidas translated his name for him, "I ordered some Bottles of Porter & drank to them, they in return Calling me by my Indian Name[,] Drank to me, and after learning how to pronounce this long Name by their frequently repeating it to me & makeing them Very merry they parted highly pleased with their Entertainment[,] saying they should esteem me hereafter, as 'Tera otataga neons ol*aa*,' as a 'Brother & a Friend' in English."[66]

The granting of names, therefore, operated on several levels of significance. Tilghman may have dismissed it merely as an honor acquired at the cost of a bowl of punch, but his Native counterparts saw it as a necessary preliminary before starting the negotiations, a way of incorporating Tilghman into their kinship-based diplomacy. The hallmarks of a well-executed naming, such as that described by Bloomfield, were hospitality and reciprocity: each side gave something to the other. The New Hampshire commissioners violated that protocol unwittingly in 1754, when they left the Indians with wine after receiving their name and hurried off to join their colleagues in the Albany courthouse. The next day, the Indians hinted to Atkinson that "*the[y] Expected Some thing as a Treat* when they united & gave a Name," and so the New Hampshire commissioners purchased a cow for them to

---

64. For the Maryland naming at Lancaster, see Marshe, "Journal of the Treaty," 194. For the New Hampshire naming in 1754, see McAnear, "Personal Accounts of the Albany Congress of 1754," 738.
65. See Tilghman, *Memoir*, 92–93; and Lender and Martin, *Citizen-Soldier: Journal of Joseph Bloomfield*, 95–96, respectively.
66. Lender and Martin, *Citizen-Soldier: Journal of Joseph Bloomfield*, 96.

slaughter in their camp; but the New Englanders still flunked the sociability test by failing to partake in the feast.[67]

All the variations of the wood's edge greeting discussed here blended Native custom with the habits of European gentility. What the Indians saw as ceremonies necessary to open treaty negotiations, their counterparts generally interpreted as the rules and rituals of polite society: extending hospitality to guests, engaging them in polite conversation, treating and toasting them as a means of asserting social position and authority. This behavior, of course, did not stop officials from complaining about the number of Indians who attended these treaties, particularly the warriors, women, and children who had to be fed while the chiefs took their time in deliberations and speech making. Governors frequently requested that such negotiations be conducted with only an "executive committee" of chiefs, but the Native model prevailed throughout the colonial and Revolutionary era.[68] And so, Indians arrived en masse and insisted on the rituals of the wood's edge, while officials arranged themselves to exhibit their rank and solidarity. But if business was going to get done in as timely a manner as possible, then treaty ritual also had to preserve peace and public order while the Indians were in town. That happened by assigning treaty participants to certain spaces for the duration of their meeting.

Staying Apart

Treaty conferences typically took place over one to three weeks, depending on the number of delegations and issues involved. That meant there was plenty of time for Indians and Europeans to interact when they were not engaged in the public proceedings. Such encounters had the potential to become disorderly. Indian men arrived armed at treaty conferences and received guns, shot, and gunpowder as part of the diplomatic presents exchanged there. Alcohol flowed freely on both sides, despite the efforts of authorities to curb its consumption. Trade was another potential source of conflict, as merchants sought out and often exploited Native customers. Yet, reports of intercultural violence at treaty conferences were rare. Verbal confrontations evident in the treaty proceedings did not spill over into physical altercations away from the council fire. Treaty participants successfully policed themselves.

How did this come about? From the Native perspective, the wood's edge greeting and condolence ceremony worked to counter potential violence by dispersing feelings of ill will and allowing for clear thinking. Europeans, especially novices like Tilghman, may have found such rituals tedious and unnecessary, but their own self-interest dictated against raising the ire of their numerous and well-armed counterparts. More subtly, the spatial segregation of treaty participants by race, rank, and gender worked to limit or eliminate

---

67. McAnear, "Personal Accounts of the Albany Congress of 1754," 738–39.
68. See Fenton, *Great Law and the Longhouse*, 207.

potential sources of conflict beyond the council fire. The social rituals that evolved out of treaty making regulated where, when, and how Natives and Europeans could come together. These rituals combined traditional elements of Iroquois diplomacy, such as feasting and dancing, with rites of private and public celebration then current in colonial society. On occasions such as royal birthdays and coronation anniversaries, governors and other officials treated the public to food, drink, bonfires, fireworks, and similar forms of communal celebration. In the evening, elites attended dinners and balls in private homes or public buildings, while commoners continued their festivities out-of-doors.[69] This same model prevailed during treaty conferences, only now with visiting officials providing such public entertainments for their Native guests and private gatherings for themselves and occasionally a small number of chiefs. In this manner, they asserted their social and political authority over local residents while also consigning all but a few male leaders among the Indians to the place of plebeians in colonial society.

The spatial segregation of treaty participants began as soon as visitors arrived in town. In Lancaster in 1744, Marshe watched as the Indians moved to "some vacant lots in the back part of town," where they "made *wigwams*, or cabins, wherein they resided during the treaty." In Albany, the Indians encamped on a hill outside of the city's perpetually decrepit walls.[70] Visiting commissioners and other gentlemen, on the other hand, found lodging in inns, taverns, or the homes of local residents.[71] These arrangements created a dichotomy in the experiences of treaty participants. Visiting commissioners usually entertained themselves, local guests, and select Indian leaders behind closed doors. Indians, on the other hand, held their feasts and dances in their camps or in the streets.

Activities within the Indians' camps were not recorded as part of the treaty proceedings, but curious European gentlemen visited them frequently and recorded their experiences in their journals. At Lancaster, Marshe sometimes ended his day with a walk through the Indians' camp. There he distributed small presents, such as tobacco and pipes, and flung handfuls of half-pennies among the children. This last act, he noted, endeared him to Indian parents, who considered it "a mark of friendship" to "make presents to their

---

69. On the emergence of an Anglo-American "imperial rites" of celebration, see Brendan McConville, *The King's Three Faces: The Rise and Fall of Royal America, 1688–1776* (Chapel Hill: University of North Carolina Press, 2006), 49–80, 110–11. On the social divide between private (genteel) and public (vulgar) celebrations, see Serena Zabin, *Dangerous Economies: Status and Commerce in Imperial New York* (Philadelphia: University of Pennsylvania Press, 2009), 87–100.
70. See Marshe, "Journal of the Treaty," 179; McAnear, "Personal Accounts of the Albany Congress of 1754," 733; and "Journal of Conrad Weiser at the Albany Treaty of 1745," in Boyd, *Indian Treaties Printed by Benjamin Franklin*, 309.
71. In Lancaster, Marshe stayed with a local innkeeper named Peter Worrall. See Marshe, "Journal of the Treaty," 175. At Albany in 1745, Isaac Norris stayed at the home of local gentleman Philip Livingston Jr.; and in 1754, Theodore Atkinson stayed at "one Lansighs," the name of another prominent Albany family. See "Journal of Isaac Norris," 22; and McAnear, "Personal Accounts of the Albany Congress of 1754," 730.

children, or treat them with any particular notice."[72] Such glimpses into the Indians' domestic lives left positive impressions on European observers. When William Savery visited the Senecas' encampment at Canandaigua, he was struck by its orderliness and activity. The Indians had quickly assembled "seventy or eighty huts, by far the most commodious and ingeniously made of any that I have seen." Men and women were employed in hunting and butchering the plentiful deer available in the surrounding woods, while their children "in all the activity and buoyancy of health, were diverting themselves according to their fancy." Savery thought that the "ease and cheerfulness of every countenance" meant that Indians must have been "as happy a people as any in the world" before Europeans arrived in America.[73]

The Indians' camps were also where European visitors got a sense of the role Native women played in treaty making. Native women and children attended the public speeches delivered at the council fire, but they sat apart from the chiefs and warriors, much like the local residents and other onlookers who made up the silent audience for a treaty's proceedings.[74] Within the camps, visitors noted the industry of women in domestic tasks such as food preparation and childcare as well as in the production of items such as moccasins and wampum belts for their own use or for sale to others. Women also took the lead in dividing and transporting diplomatic presents.[75] Occasionally, a European visitor conversed with an Indian woman whose reputation for diplomatic prowess or influence preceded her. When Tilghman met Molly Brant in the Mohawk Valley in 1775, he was struck by her "air of ease and politeness" but also feared that "her influence will give us some trouble" because of her sympathies for the British. At Lancaster in 1744, Marshe recorded his encounter in the Indians' camp with "the celebrated Mrs. Montour," a well-known interpreter and go-between whom he described as "a handsome woman, genteel, and of polite address."[76]

Such observers, while aware that individual Native women could have great pull in diplomatic affairs, were typically too inexperienced in such matters to know the degree to which women helped shape the diplomacy conducted around the council fire. That influence, however, was made evident by a peculiar turn of events at Canandaigua in 1794. According to James Emlen, the religious enthusiast Jemima Wilkinson and some of her followers attended a council with the Indians and unexpectedly took the occasion to preach

72. Marshe, "Journal of the Treaty," 189.
73. Savery, *Journal of the Life, Travels, and Religious Labors of William Savery*, 130–31. Savery's companion David Bacon recorded a similar description of an Indian camp he visited at Canandaigua. See Bacon, "Some Account of Our Journey to Canandaigua," 14.
74. See for example Tilghman, *Memoir*, 85.
75. See for example Lender and Martin, *Citizen-Soldier: Journal of Joseph Bloomfield*, 77, 83, 99.
76. Tilghman, *Memoir*, 87; and Marshe, "Journal of the Treaty," 189–91. Isabelle Montour was in fact a métis woman with a long history in European-Indian diplomacy; the "daughters" Marshe met were likely her niece and great-niece. See Alison Duncan Hirsch, "'The Celebrated Madame Montour': 'Interpretress' across Early American Frontiers," *Explorations in Early American Culture* 4 (2000): 81–112.

at length to them about the need to repent for their sins. Two days later, three elderly Native women attended a similar council and asked that "as some white Women had been permitted to speak in council (alluding to Jemina & c.) they also might be allowed the same Liberty." Timothy Pickering, the presiding official, consented. Seneca chief Red Jacket then delivered a speech on the women's behalf, explaining that "it was they who made the Men, [and] that altho' they did not sit in council, yet that they were acquainted from time to time with the transactions at the Treaties." As the "White Woman had told the Indians to repent & turn from their evil Deeds," now then did the Native women "say the same to the White people," and ask that they repent for their own sins by returning land that they had stolen in a previous treaty.[77] Red Jacket's speech was rare for its explicit acknowledgment of the influence Native women had in treaty making. In public proceedings, they may have observed silently while the men exchanged speeches, but consulting about such matters was part of their work in the camp. Europeans were generally oblivious to this dimension of Native diplomacy and tried to limit the attendance of women at treaty conferences because of the provisioning expense, but they never succeeded in doing so because of the important role women played in the bushes.[78]

The spatial segregation at a treaty conference was also evident in the eating that went on there. According to Iroquois custom, a treaty's hosts feasted their guests. Colonial governors understood this duty, as their own culture equated gentility with generous hospitality. When they convened treaty conferences, however, they met this obligation in two distinct ways: first, by grudgingly provisioning the Indians in their camps, and second, by hosting a few private entertainments that brought together smaller numbers of invited guests. Before the American Revolution, the New York governor traditionally paid for such provisions out of his colony's treasury, but the expense could become burdensome if many Indians attended or if they stayed longer than expected. At Albany in 1745, New York governor George Clinton grew weary of his hosting duties and thus spoiled the air of amity that was supposed to prevail at such meetings. According to Conrad Weiser, the Indians asked Clinton for "a Barrel of Beer to drink" after the negotiations ended. Clinton "damn'd them and sayd he gave them some the other day," before relenting. The following day, a group of Mohicans appeared at the governor's door to present a gift of venison and to "shake hands" with him. Clinton refused to see them, and when Weiser pressed the governor's secretary to accept the gift, "He damn'd them & sayd they brought it to get ten times as much as Victuals from the Governor." Weiser was shocked by Clinton's meanness and relieved when the Pennsylvania commissioners acted more generously.[79] While Weiser appreciated the importance of open-handedness, governors and other officials less familiar with Indian diplomacy tended, like Clinton, to complain about what they perceived to be

77. Fenton, "Journal of James Emlen," 304–6.
78. See MacLeitch, *Imperial Entanglements*, 133–45; and Calloway, *Pen and Ink Witchcraft*, 18–19.
79. "Journal of Conrad Weiser at the Albany Treaty of 1745," 311.

the "useless mouths," particularly those of women and children, who showed up on such occasions.[80]

While supplying the Indians in their camps, officials and local elites also hosted numerous social events for themselves. These entertainments took many forms: invitations to dine and take tea with each other, excursions to country estates and local landmarks, and even balls. An intercolonial Indian treaty, despite its backcountry location, was a social occasion of considerable importance. Observers invariably reported the presence of gentlemen and gentlewomen who socialized with the assembled officials. One subset of this polite society consisted of young men—such as Marshe, Tilghman, and Bloomfield—who regarded treaty conferences as an opportunity to rub elbows with potential patrons. Some treaty commissioners brought along their sons to cultivate their social and professional connections. At Lancaster in 1744, these young men formed their own society, dining and visiting the Indians' camp and drinking together after larger social gatherings had ended.[81]

Europeans and Indians converged in one social ritual during treaty conferences that was inclusive to all, locals or visitors, polite or vulgar: Indian dances. Such dances occurred out-of-doors, in the city streets or in Indian camps. In 1776, Bloomfield noted that the Indians twice danced before General Schuyler "for his Entertainment, which was very diverting." Tilghman recorded a similar dance in Albany that "being intirely novel was the more entertaining to the Ladies." During his stay in Lancaster, Marshe described four different Indian dances, the last one given specifically to "entertain the Governour and commissioners."[82] At Canandaigua in 1794, Savery and Emlen recorded separate descriptions of a "brag-dance" in which "whoever deposits a bottle of rum, has the liberty to make a brag of the feats he has performed in war, the number of scalps he has taken, &c."[83] These events attracted large audiences and occasionally participation by non-Indians. Bloomfield estimated that 1,200 Indians attended a Seneca war dance before General Schuyler. Marshe noted that one of the dances he witnessed in the Indians' camp drew "a great number of white people."[84] His failure in this instance to classify the European spectators according to their social rank, as he did whenever discussing private entertainments, suggests that this was likely a mixed audience of common folk and gentlemen like him. Griffith Evans noted the participation of non-Indians in such dances at the Fort Stanwix treaty: "We generally

80. See Rachel Herrmann, *No Useless Mouth: Waging War and Fighting Hunger in the American Revolution* (Ithaca, N.Y.: Cornell University Press, 2019), 21–37.

81. For the social activities of the younger men at Lancaster, see Marshe, "Journal of the Treaty," 188 and 201.

82. See Lender and Martin, *Citizen-Soldier: Journal of Joseph Bloomfield*, 79, 98; Tilghman, *Memoir*, 92; and Marshe, "Journal of the Treaty," 181, 183–84, 189, 198.

83. Savery, *Journal of the Life, Travels, and Religious Labors of William Savery*, 126. Also see also Fenton, "Journal of James Emlen," 297.

84. Lender and Martin, *Citizen-Soldier: Journal of Joseph Bloomfield*, 98, and Marshe, "Journal of the Treaty," 189.

stepped in their [the Indian dancers'] circle when present, which appeared to please them very much. Nay they would think us churlish if we did not."[85]

Similar to dances, sporting events also drew large, mixed crowds at treaty conferences. Typically, local elites or visiting gentlemen sponsored such competitions as another act of noblesse oblige, staking prizes for which the Indians competed. In Albany in 1775, Tilghman and the patriot commissioners sponsored several public games. One evening they "turned out a Bull for the young Indians to hunt and kill after their Manner, with arrows, knives, and hatchets." The commissioners also "put up two laced Hatts and a silver arm band to be run for." These events took place in a field adjacent to Schuyler's mansion, and Tilghman watched them from there, drinking coffee and spending the evening "not in a formal but in the agreeable accidental manner."[86] Bloomfield noted similar Indian races "for sundry Articles" donated by officials a year later.[87] At Fort Stanwix in 1784, Griffith Evans watched a game of lacrosse between Oneidas and Caughnawagas, played for a stake of twenty dollars.[88]

At large outdoor gatherings like dances and races, treaty commissioners and other gentlemen tended to remain aloof from the crowd, observing the action from homes or public buildings. Thus, events that drew mixed audiences of Indians and Europeans re-inforced rather than broke down the social segregation that elites insisted on maintaining between themselves and everyone else. Sometimes, such as when several Indian chiefs took tea with Bloomfield in German Flatts, or when the Maryland delegates hosted two dozen Indian chiefs for dinner at Lancaster, these walls were lowered, but only for the sake of socializing with Indians whom these gentlemen considered their social equals across the cultural divide. More spontaneous socializing across that divide seems to have been the perquisite of young men inclined to join in the Indians' dances and sports. Bloomfield mentioned in several of his entries watching the Indians play a game of ball, which he identified as "what the Scott's call Golf." He was likely witnessing lacrosse matches among Indian men. Over the next month, Bloomfield and his fellow officers picked up the game themselves and played it on at least one occasion with "five Indians from Oneida."[89]

Natives and Europeans alike recognized alcohol as the most likely agent to disrupt the intercultural harmony that was supposed to prevail at treaty conferences, and yet, its presence was ubiquitous. Treaty participants consumed it in toasts when they opened and closed their proceedings and in numerous private councils in between. Europeans consumed it copiously in their private entertainments. Natives sought it out and traded for it with private parties while they were in town. At Albany treaties, the New York governor usually banned local merchants from selling alcohol to Natives during the proceedings and

85. Raup, "Journal of Griffith Evans," 214.
86. Tilghman, *Memoir*, 94–95.
87. Lender and Martin, *Citizen-Soldier: Journal of Joseph Bloomfield*, 95.
88. Raup, "Journal of Griffith Evans," 213.
89. Lender and Martin, *Citizen-Soldier: Journal of Joseph Bloomfield*, 91–92, 101, 109.

withheld rum from diplomatic presents until their guests were leaving town, but the latter tactic enabled binges that could lead to intercultural violence on the road home.[90] Observing Indians at the Albany Congress of 1754, British visitor Thomas Pownall wrote: "But Rum they will have, so ye Traders & People bye [buy] their presents all the way as they pass for Rum. . . . The People bye out of their very mouths the Provisions that are given them & You see them dead drunk, in the Face of Day, at their Doors."[91] Chiefs expressed as much interest in proscribing alcohol sales and consumption as their European counterparts. Tilghman heard a speech by a chief who "desired that the White people might not have liberty to sell rum to their Young Men" while they were in town. Marshe observed at Lancaster that chiefs maintained their sobriety because they did not wish to be "over-reached" in their negotiations. Savery, by contrast, recorded several points in the Canandaigua treaty when the proceedings needed to be paused because drinking binges had disabled Native leaders.[92]

In retrospect, it is surprising that the alcohol consumed at treaty conferences did not lead to intercultural violence, as it often seemed to do in other contexts.[93] One factor at play here may have been the cooperative regulation of firearms. While visiting the Indians in Lancaster one evening, Marshe observed that they became uneasy when some local German residents "brought their guns with them to the camp." Canasatego asked Marshe and his companions to "tell the Germans to withdraw, and leave their musquets out of their sight, otherwise some bad consequences might ensue." Marshe intervened as requested and the Germans departed.[94] Paradoxically, the constant toasting and treating of Indians by their European hosts may also have helped preserve peace. Bloomfield wryly noted that the chiefs he met were "Very artful & always speak in such A manner as to insinuate a little Liquor would be agreable," but these frequent occasions for moderate drinking gave treaty hosts the opportunity to exhibit their hospitality, thus reinforcing feelings of goodwill and fellowship without the disruptions caused by intoxication.[95] Excessive drinking that occurred outside of such gatherings had much greater potential to lead to violence, but Natives engaged in that activity in their spaces, apart from Europeans. This segregation likely explains why, despite the great deal of excessive drinking at Canandaigua, Emlen reported

---

90. See Preston, *Texture of Contact*, 162–63.

91. McAnear, "Personal Accounts of the Albany Congress of 1754," 743.

92. Marshe, "Journal of the Treaty," 183; Tilghman, *Memoir*, 86; and Savery, *Journal of the Life, Travels, and Religious Labors of William Savery*, 136, 142, 147.

93. See Mancall, *Deadly Medicine*, 79–84. For Native drinking patterns, see Maia Conrad, "Disorderly Drinking: Reconsidering Seventeenth-Century Iroquois Alcohol Abuse," *American Indian Quarterly* 23 (Summer–Autumn 1999): 1–11. For an instance of intercultural homicide related to drinking, see Nicole Eustace, *Covered with Night: A Story of Murder and Indigenous Justice in Early America* (New York: W. W. Norton, 2021).

94. Marshe, "Journal of the Treaty," 182.

95. Lender and Martin, *Citizen-Soldier: Journal of Joseph Bloomfield*, 98.

only one incident of intercultural violence: a tavern brawl between intoxicated Indians and an intoxicated Irishman.[96]

Treaty conferences provided plenty of opportunities for eating, drinking, and other kinds of socializing between Europeans and Indians, but as the above analysis indicates, such interaction could be as highly ritualized as that which took place around the council fire. These encounters were a hybrid of Native and European precedents, evolving out of each side's emphasis on distinguishing between hosts and guests and from the importance in each culture of exhibiting hospitality. Even in situations involving large and potentially raucous crowds, such as at dances and athletic competitions, the European elites present insisted on maintaining their status by keeping their distance from everyone else. Natives mixed with local residents on some celebratory occasions but also maintained their own social and physical distance, and for the most part, what went on in their camps stayed in their camps.

Conclusion

Tilghman's journal and others like it provide us with a much fuller version of what went on "in the bushes" at treaty conferences than other records produced at such meetings. The expectations that each side had for the other in regard to hospitality and reciprocity meant that food and drink were as much a part of these meetings as words and wampum. It also meant that social distinctions within and between groups were enforced and maintained by rituals designed to delineate hosts from guests and elites from commoners. Treaty conferences did not devolve into violence, but neither were they love feasts in which Europeans and Indians mixed freely. Successful diplomacy required participants to mingle at some times and to remain apart at others, and the social life they experienced beyond the council fire helped establish these boundaries.

This kind of treaty making declined in the early national era for several reasons. After the ratification of the Constitution, the new federal government asserted its monopoly power over the nation's Indian relations. Several states, including New York, continued to insist on the power to treat with Indians within their borders, but the days of multilateral treaty making between the Haudenosaunee and several different colonies or states were over. Also, as the focus of the nation's Indian affairs shifted to the trans-Appalachian frontier, treaty making moved westward. Towns like Albany and Lancaster were no longer backcountry crossroads, and treaty conferences became militarized, convened by army officers at isolated western military outposts. By 1800 the influence of the Haudenosaunee in U.S. Indian affairs had been eclipsed by other Native peoples, and diplomacy became a

---

96. See Fenton, "Journal of James Emlen," 296.

matter of dispossession. Starting in the 1780s, federal and state agents worked to dispense with treaty rituals they considered unnecessary, time-consuming, or expensive and became increasingly dictatorial in their treatment of their Native counterparts. In such circumstances, chicanery, bribery, and deception flourished, and pretensions to intercultural civility in treaty making evaporated.[97] What was lost as federal and state governments moved toward embracing the removal policies of the Jacksonian era was not just a system of diplomatic negotiation but a wider social milieu created by that system that enabled Natives and non-Natives to come together peaceably and in good faith.

---

97. On treaty making in the federal era, see Leonard Sadolsky, *Revolutionary Negotiations: Indians, Empires, and Diplomats in the Founding of America* (Charlottesville: University of Virginia Press, 2009); and Calloway, *Pen and Ink Witchcraft*, 96–120. For Iroquois negotiations with the federal government and New York, see Fenton, *Great Law and the Longhouse*, 601–706; Michael Leroy Oberg, *Peacemakers: The Iroquois, the United States, and the Treaty of Canandaigua, 1794* (New York: Oxford University Press, 2016); and Laurence M. Hauptman, *Conspiracy of Interests: Iroquois Dispossession and the Rise of New York State* (Syracuse, N.Y.: Syracuse University Press, 1999).

The Great Haudenosaunee-Lenape Peace of 1669

Oral Traditions, Colonial Records, and the Origin of the Delaware's Status as "Women"

Evan Haefeli

The Delaware Indians, known in their language as the Lenape, have a unique reputation as the only nation in the Americas—and perhaps the entire world—accorded the status of "women." This unusual designation entered the surviving documentary record in notorious fashion at a conference held in Pennsylvania in 1742 between representatives of the Iroquois Confederacy (known in their language as the Haudenosaunee), the Lenape, and Pennsylvania to discuss the "Walking Purchase" that had recently deprived the Lenape of virtually all their remaining traditional territory. When the Lenape complained that they had been defrauded, an Onondaga spokesman for the Haudenosaunee by the name of Canasatego berated them into accepting the deal, saying, "We conquered you; we made Women of you"; and therefore the Lenape deferred to the decision of the Haudenosaunee.[1] Ever since then, the Lenape's designation as "women" (we do not know what the original Indigenous word was) has been a subject of fierce debate among both the Indigenous nations involved and their Anglo-American colonizers. Eighteenth-century sources indicate that the status had been conferred in the seventeenth century at a peace conference where the Haudenosaunee had symbolically wrapped the Lenape in a "petticoat," conferring to them the status as "women."

From the outbreak of the Seven Years War to the conclusion of the Northwest Indian War in 1795, the Haudenosaunee made various efforts to remove that "petticoat," but the Lenape resisted, proudly clinging to their symbolic female garment. The resulting debates

---

1. Susan Kalter, ed., *Benjamin Franklin, Pennsylvania, and the First Nations: The Treaties of 1736–62* (Urbana, 2006), 80; William A. Starna, "The Diplomatic Career of Canasatego," in *Friends and Enemies in Penn's Woods: Indians, Colonists, and the Racial Construction of Pennsylvania,* ed. William A. Pencak and Daniel K. Richter (University Park: The Pennsylvania State University Press, 2004), 144–63.

New York History, 104.1, Summer 2023

constitute most of the sources that scholars have used to evaluate just what this unusual status meant. Since the Lenape were being steadily pushed ever farther west from their ancestral Mid-Atlantic homelands during the time these discussions took place, many see it as a gendered reflection of defeat, subordination, and dispossession. Bolstered by the pioneering anthropologist Lewis Henry Morgan, who drew on Seneca oral tradition to argue that the designation meant "the Delaware had been subdued" and that they "never emancipated themselves, after this act of denationalization," this interpretation prevailed until the second half of the twentieth century.[2] Since then, scholars have increasingly endorsed the Lenape argument that the status was a mark of honor and respect, reflecting in part the important role of women in these largely matrilineal societies.[3] To this day, leading scholars remain uncertain about its meaning and purpose.[4]

The "Delaware as women" phenomenon presents a complicated historiographical puzzle with a number of interrelated elements that cannot all be resolved within a single article. Here, with the aid of new sources—colonial documents and oral traditions—two elements are addressed that so far have largely been ignored in the debate. The first element is the odd fact that the modern Lenape almost completely ignore scholars' long-standing fascination with their ancestors' distinctive status as "women." It is at best incidental to their

---

2. Lewis Henry Morgan, *League of the Ho-de-no-sau-nee or Iroquois* (Rochester, 1851), 338; C. A. Weslager, "The Delaware as Women," *Journal of the Washington Academy of Sciences* 34 (December 1944): 381–88; C. A. Weslager, "Further Light on the Delaware Indians as Women," *Journal of the Washington Academy of Sciences* 37 (September 1947): 298–304; Roger Carpenter, "From Indian Women to English Children: The Lenni-Lenape and the Attempt to Create a New Diplomatic Identity," *Pennsylvania History* 74 (Winter 2007): 1–20; Richard S. Grimes, *The Western Delaware Indian Nation, 1730–1795: Warriors and Diplomats* (Bethlehem, Pa.: Lehigh University Press, 2017), esp. xix, 13, 55, 85.

3. Daniel G. Brinton, *The Lenape and Their Legends* (Philadelphia D. G. Brinton, 1885), 109–22, reviewed this nineteenth-century consensus before arguing for a more nuanced interpretation of the "Lenape as 'women.'" But that trend did not gain steam until Frank Speck published "The Delaware Indians as Women: Were the Original Pennsylvanians Politically Emasculated?," *The Pennsylvania Magazine of History and Biography* 70 (October 1946), 377–89. Notably, most of the scholars developing this argument have been anthropologists and/or women: Anthony F. C. Wallace, "Women, Land, and Society: Three Aspects of Aboriginal Delaware Life," *Pennsylvania Archaeologist* 17 (1947): 1–35, esp. 20–32; Jay Miller, "The Delaware as Women: A Symbolic Solution," *American Ethnologist*, 1 (August 1974): 507–14; Vicki Camerino, "The Delaware Indians as Women: An Alternative Approach," *American Indian Journal* 4 (April 1978), 2–11; Gunlög Fur, *A Nation of Women: Gender and Colonial Encounters among the Delaware Indians* (Philadelphia: University of Pennsylvania Press, 2009).

4. Eric Hinderaker, *The Two Hendricks: Unraveling a Mohawk Mystery* (Cambridge, Mass.: Harvard University Press, 2010), 167; Daniel K. Richter, "'No Savage Should Inherit': Native Peoples, Pennsylvanians, and the Origins and Legacies of the Seven Years War," in *Trade, Land, Power: The Struggle for Eastern North America* (Philadelphia: University of Pennsylvania Press, 2013), 163, 167–72. Neal Salisbury concludes that the "relationship of the Delawares to the Covenant Chain was ambiguous and contested, and cannot be ascertained definitively from documentary evidence alone." See Neal Salisbury, "The Atlantic Northeast," in *The Oxford Handbook of American Indian History*, ed. Frederick E. Hoxie (Oxford: Oxford University Press, 2016), 347, 357n6.

understanding of their own history. For example, the official history of the Delaware Tribe of Western Oklahoma (now known as the Delaware Nation), *Peacemakers on the Frontier*, mentions the designation only once, on page one.[5] As the title suggests, the rest of the book insists that what mattered most was their special status as "peacemakers" and diplomats. Lenape oral histories and newspaper articles from the twentieth and twenty-first centuries agree. Pointing to their ancestors' negotiations with William Penn as well as to their being the first Indigenous nation to sign a treaty with the United States (the 1778 Treaty of Fort Pitt), present-day Delaware people proudly call themselves America's "first treaty tribe." The Delaware Nation claims their ancestors had carefully handed down an original copy of Penn's treaty for generations until Confederates burned it during the Civil War (rebels torched their leader Black Beaver's house after the Delaware sided with the Union).[6]

The second element is that no one has yet figured out exactly when the treaty that made the Lenape the "women" of the Haudenosaunee took place. Determining this date could help resolve some of the confusion, but it is not a simple task. There is no known documentary record of the treaty, and the surviving oral traditions are rather vague about such details. Nevertheless, a careful calibration of the existing oral traditions with the documentary record indicates that this decisive treaty took place in the spring of 1669. It proved to be the first of a long series of peace treaties between the Haudenosaunee and their Indigenous neighbors, many of which were mediated by the Lenape. The Great Peace of 1669 does not yet figure in histories of New York, the Iroquois Confederacy, or the Lenape but it

---

5. Duane Kendall Hale, *Peacemakers on the Frontier: A History of the Delaware Tribe of Western Oklahoma* (Anadarko: Delaware Tribe of Western Oklahoma Press, 1987), 1.

6. Duane Kendall Hale, *Turtle Tales: Oral Traditions of the Delaware Tribe of Western Oklahoma* (Anadarko: Delaware Tribe of Western Oklahoma Press, 1984), 3, 45; *Delaware Indian News*, April 2000, 14; Ruth Parks, interview, June 24, 1937, Indian-Pioneer History, Oklahoma Historical Society (hereafter OHS), S-149. Ruth, apparently the first in her family to become fluent in English, was recounting this history as her mother, born in Indian Territory in 1880, told it. See also Mary Crow, interview, February 3, 1984, Oral History Collection, OHS, 1984.005.01. These references to American history are reminiscent of the political nature of Indigenous oral records. Since much of what survives comes to us through a colonial context dominated by Western, document-based forms of understanding history and is often preoccupied with Indigenous struggles for land and survival, Indigenous historical memory is no more a purely objective record of the past than the colonial documents with which they are often in dialogue. As Claudio Saunt argues, Indigenous historical memory often had deliberate goals and strategies and could adapt in order to achieve them, not least by deliberately engaging with the historical expectations of colonists. By "borrowing the narrative categories of their antagonists [Europeans and Euro-Americans]," they "creatively used history and myth to defend their nations' land titles and sovereignty," mixing "elements from Indian and European traditions" to find "common ground with" colonists and U.S. citizens accustomed to "linear narratives with source citations and calendrical dates." Claudio Saunt, "Telling Stories: The Political Uses of Myth and History in the Cherokee and Creek Nations," *Journal of American History* 93 no. 3 (December 2006): 673–97, esp. 674. For a similarly relevant study of Indigenous people's use of "emotionally infused, politically potent places" to contest historical memory, see Christine DeLucia, "The Memory Frontier: Uncommon Pursuits of Past and Place in the Northeast after King Philip's War," *Journal of American History* 98, no. 4 (March 2012): 975–97, esp. 977.

should. It was a major turning point in the history of both Indigenous nations as well as the English colonies, inaugurating an inter-Indigenous peace that survives to this day. Situated in the context of the 1660s, the status as "women" clearly appears as integral to Lenape's role as "peacemakers." In 1669, they not only became the first Indigenous nation to make a lasting peace with the Haudenosaunee but also accepted the task of spreading that peace across the Eastern Woodlands. It is to this "diplomatic" action, even more than to their treaties with William Penn or the United States, that the modern Delaware can trace their reputation as "first treaty tribe." Reconstructing the origins of this crucial peace treaty thus not only recovers an important event of great significance to the history of colonial and Indigenous America it also helps resolve some (but not all) of the uncertainty surrounding the unusual phenomenon that has long (and, as we shall see, somewhat misleadingly) been referred to as "the Delaware as women."

Although the existence of the 1669 treaty council can be detected in colonial records, one would never guess its significance from the surviving evidence. Since this treaty largely took place out of sight of the colonists, scholars have overlooked it favor of the much better documented Covenant Chain alliance established between the Iroquois Confederacy and the English at Albany, New York, in 1677. So far, the negotiations surrounding the Covenant Chain has seemed like the most likely source of the peculiar relationship between the Haudenosaunee and the Lenape.[7] The emphasis on the Covenant Chain is characteristic not only of historians' reliance on written records but also of their tendency to focus more on Haudenosaunee relations with Europeans rather than with their Indigenous neighbors. The existence of a Great Peace in 1669 has also been obscured by the fact that when scholars focus on Haudenosaunee relations with other Indigenous nations, they look primarily at those involving the western or southern nations rather than those to the east like the Lenape.[8]

---

7. Francis Jennings makes this case in various places including in "Iroquois Alliances in American History," in *The History and Culture of Iroquois Diplomacy: An Interdisciplinary Guide to the Treaties of the Six Nations and Their League*, ed. Francis Jennings et al. (Syracuse: Syracuse University Press, 1985), 37–65; Francis Jennings, "The Delaware Indians in the Covenant Chain," in *A Delaware Indian Symposium*, ed. Herbert C. Kraft (Harrisburg: Pennsylvania Historical and Museum Commission, 1974), 89–101; Francis Jennings, *The Ambiguous Iroquois Empire: The Covenant Chain Confederation of Indian Tribes with English Colonies* (New York: W. W. Norton, 1984), 159–62, 262–64. So far, his conclusions have remained unchallenged.
8. Robert S. Grumet, *The Munsee Indians: A History* (Norman: University of Oklahoma Press, 2009), 112–15, discusses the events surrounding the treaty, but it figures hardly at all in the important studies of Iroquois diplomacy. See Jennings, *Ambiguous Iroquois Empire*; Francis Jennings, William N. Fenton, Mary A. Druke, and David R. Miller, eds. *The History and Culture of Iroquois Diplomacy: An Interdisciplinary Guide to the Treaties of the Six Nations and Their League* (Syracuse, N.Y.: Syracuse University Press, 1985); Daniel K. Richter, *The Ordeal of the Longhouse: The Peoples of the Iroquois League in the Era of European Colonization* (Chapel Hill: University of North Carolina Press, 1992); Daniel P. Barr, *Unconquered: The Iroquois League at War in Colonial America* (Westport, Conn.: Praeger, 2006); Jon Parmenter, *The Edge of the Woods: Iroquoia, 1534–1701* (East Lansing: Michigan State University Press, 2010).

By drawing in a mix Haudenosaunee and Lenape oral traditions, however, the significance of the documentary scraps that survive from 1669 becomes clear. Since the 1980s, scholars have increasingly argued for using Indigenous oral traditions when reconstructing the past. Those working on the Indigenous history of the colonial northeast, especially on the Haudenosaunee, have been prominent among these voices, although some have pointed to the challenges of using oral traditions as primary sources. For example, if a tradition claims to remember a particular incident but its details cannot be reconciled with the existing documentary record, some have suggested that the tradition should be deemed dubious if not fraudulent.[9] Others suggest that oral traditions should be considered less "a chronicle of past events" than a "cultural charter, situating the group and its activities in a knowable and continually evolving social environment." In short, oral tradition is better treated as an interpretation of the past rather than as a record of it.[10] However, as many others believe, oral traditions can provide access to events barely visible, if at all, in the documentary record, and thus allow Indigenous people to weigh in on their own history, illuminating not only Indigenous experience but also causes, concepts, and motives that existed outside of European cultural priorities or understanding.[11]

Obviously, if oral traditions are to be integrated with the wider historical record, they require at least as much critical handling as primary documents. So far, scholars have developed several different methods to do so. For specific events documented by colonists, scholars have searched through oral traditions for congruencies and overlapping details that correspond with the documentary and archaeological record, "complementing" them

---

9. See the discussion of the Mohawk "Story of the Bell," in Evan Haefeli and Kevin Sweeney, eds., *Captive Histories: English, French, and Native Narratives of the 1704 Deerfield Raid.* (Amherst: University of Massachusetts Press, 2006), 213–52. This particular tradition is especially fraught because of its association with a Mohawk man of dubious veracity, whose life and motives are sensitively treated in Michael Leroy Oberg, *Professional Indian: The American Odyssey of Eleazer Williams* (Philadelphia: University of Pennsylvania Press, 2015).

10. William A. Starna, "Retrospecting the Origins of the League of the Iroquois," *Proceedings of the American Philosophical Society* 152, no. 3 (September 2008): 319–20. See also Anthony F. C. Wallace, "The Dekanawideh Myth Analyzed as the Record of a Revitalization Movement," *Ethnohistory* 5 (April 1958): 118–30, who argues that the structural theory of revitalization movements can prove that the seemingly mythological event of the founding of the Iroquois League must actually have happened.

11. Among other works, see Raymond D. Fogelson, "The Ethnohistory of Events and Nonevents," *Ethnohistory* 36, no. 2 (Spring 1989): 133–47; Raymond J. DeMallie, "'These Have No Ears:' Narrative and the Ethnohistorical Method," *Ethnohistory,* 40, no. 4 (October 1993): 515–38; Evan Haefeli, "On First Contact and Apotheosis: Manitou and Men in North America," *Ethnohistory* 54, no. 3 (June 2007): 407–43; Julie Cruikshank, "Oral History, Narrative Strategies, and Native American Historiography: Perspectives from the Yukon Territory, Canada," in *Clearing a Path: Theorizing the Past in Native American Studies,* ed. Nancy Shoemaker (New York: Routledge, 2002), 3–27; Patricia Galloway, *Practicing Ethnohistory: Mining Archives, Hearing Testimony, Constructing Narrative* (Lincoln: University of Nebraska Press, 2006); Donald Fixico, "Oral Tradition and Language," in *Call for Change: The Medicine Way of American Indian History, Ethos, and Reality* (Lincoln: University of Nebraska Press, 2013), 129–48.

with details and perspectives from the Indigenous side of the story.[12] Oral traditions have also been used to affirm the existence of otherwise poorly documented interactions with colonists. Operating under the assumption that oral traditions are more reliable the closer in time they are to the events they purport to discuss, scholars have traced traditions back in time to confirm the substance of more recent Indigenous claims, sometimes reinforcing their findings with material evidence like wampum belts.[13]

This method of tracing traditions back in time, and of trusting earlier versions somewhat more than later versions, is most relevant for reconstructing the Great Peace of 1669; but in this instance there is an additional challenge: reconciling contradictory oral traditions from different Indigenous nations. Usually when scholars rely on oral traditions, they are drawing on those coming from one group that are of relevance primarily to that group. The treaty of 1669 was important to both the Lenape and the Haudenosaunee, and their traditions have been disputing its meaning since at least the mid-eighteenth century. Hitherto, scholars using Indigenous tradition to interpret "the Delaware as women" have privileged just one group's tradition, effectively repackaging the Haudenosaunee-Lenape debate in new historiographic clothing. The goal here is to strive for a new synthesis acceptable to both.

In addition to not agreeing on all the details, the connection between the Haudenosaunee and Lenape traditions and the seventeenth century origins of the "Delaware as women" has become increasingly tenuous over time, as the memory of the treaty has been adapted to account for the evolving geopolitical contexts in which the descendants of the diplomats of 1669 found themselves. One can trace references to the treaty up through the twentieth century, but generally the accounts that entered the documentary record in the eighteenth and early nineteenth centuries are more informative and reliable than later versions. Throughout, the oral traditions primarily discuss the peace treaty in terms of the contemporary consequences of the Lenape's status as "women" rather than in terms of the context of the 1660s. Here I follow an approach similar to that of Carla Gerona in her study of Caddo "sun accounts," looking "at multiple historical points out of order" to avoid "privileging one account over another." Following Gerona's "nonlinear approach" to the

---

12. Gordon Day, "Oral Tradition as Complement," in *In Search of New England's Native Past: Selected Essays by Gordon M. Day*, ed. Michael K. Foster and William Cowan (Amherst: University of Massachusetts Press, 1998), 127–35; Andrew Newman, *On Records: Delaware Indians, Colonists, and the Media of History and Memory* (Lincoln: University of Nebraska Press, 2012), ch. 2.

13. Jon Parmenter, "The Meaning of *Kaswentha* and the Two Row Wampum Belt in Haudenosaunee (Iroquois) History: Can Indigenous Oral Tradition be reconciled with the Documentary Record?" *Journal of Early American History* 3, no. 1 (2013): 82–109; and Paul Otto, "Wampum, Tawagonishi, and the Two Row Belt," *Journal of Early American History* 3, no. 1 (2013): 110–25. One of the bizarre aspects of this particular controversy is that a document did surface in the mid-twentieth century, purportedly depicting the treaty in question, but it was eventually proven to be a fraud. Consequently, some assume the oral tradition cannot be trusted either.

"different and unique information" each account offers, I agree that "none and all" is the most "authentic" version of what happened.[14]

Unfortunately, none of these oral traditions is available in its original language. Each was mediated in different ways before entering the documentary record, usually by being translated by a colonist. The principal source for the Lenape tradition is in the writings of Moravian missionaries, especially David Zeisberger and John Heckewelder. Zeisberger, who began working as a missionary among the Lenape and Haudenosaunee in 1745, recorded the earliest and most extensive account of the treaty in a manuscript history he composed in German in 1779–80. This manuscript remained in the archives until translated and published in 1910, and it served as the basis for several influential Moravian histories published in the late eighteenth and early nineteenth century, including that of John Heckewelder, who was a missionary with the Lenape between 1771 and 1786. For some of that time he worked alongside Zeisberger before becoming a translator and negotiator at various Lenape treaty councils. Although he drew on Zeisberger's manuscript when he published his own history of the Lenape, Heckewelder also took many notes of his own. His unpublished manuscripts contain much additional material of value that has been underutilized in the debate on "the Delaware as women."[15]

While the Moravian sources have been the primary reference point for those invoking the Lenape perspective on this debate, two additional versions emerged in the Michigan Territory in the 1820s that have not received much attention. General Lewis Cass, the territory's governor, desiring to learn more about the people he was governing, sent around a questionnaire on "The History, Traditions, Languages, Manners, Customs, Religion, etc. of the Indians, Living within the United States." In 1821, one of his Indian agents interviewed a group of Lenape living on the Ohio River. Two years later his secretary, a young man from Albany named Charles Trowbridge, interviewed two other individuals, the elderly Delaware leader Captain Pipe and an American who had married a Delaware woman and was fluent in the language. The manuscripts of these interviews sat in archives until they were

---

14. Carla Gerona, "Caddo Sun Accounts across Time and Place," *American Indian Quarterly* 36, no. 3 (Summer 2012): 348–76, esp. 349, 373.

15. David Zeisberger, *History of the Northern American Indians*, ed. Archer Butler Hulbert, trans. William Nathaniel Schwarze (Columbus: Ohio State Archaeological and Historical Society, 1910); Georg Heinrich Loskiel, *Geschichte der Mission der evangelischen Brüder under den Indianern in Nordamerika* (Leipzig, 1789); George Henry Loskiel, *History of the Mission of the United Brethren among the Indians in North America* (London, 1794), 124–27; John Heckewelder, *History, Manners, and Customs of the Indian Nations*, ed. William C. Reichel (Philadelphia: Historical Society of Pennsylvania, 1876); John Heckewelder, "Communications made to the Historical and Literary Committee & to Members of the American Philosophical Society, on the Subject of the History, Manners & Languages of the American Indians" (1821), Mss.970.1.H35c, American Philosophical Society, Philadelphia, Pa. (hereafter Heckewelder, "Communications").

published by historian Clinton Alfred Weslager in 1978. They have not yet figured much in accounts of "the Delaware as women."[16]

Another overlooked source is the Mohawk tradition, most importantly a brief account written down in English by Joseph Brant that is the only source that comes directly from an Indigenous individual. The bilingual and bicultural Brant was actively involved in Haudenosaunee-Lenape diplomacy in the second half of the eighteenth century. In 1795 he even staged a diplomatic deconstruction of the 1669 treaty. Using his knowledge of what the treaty meant in practice, he presented his understanding of the Mohawk tradition in an English language note he wrote to the Reverend Elkanah Holmes in 1801. Holmes was a Baptist minister sent by the New York Missionary Society to work among the Seneca and Tuscarora. Brant's recounting of the Mohawk tradition was part of a broader discussion the two had over Haudenosaunee history in response to a questionnaire about the history and culture of the Six Nations that the Presbyterian minister Samuel Miller, actively involved with the Missionary Society since its establishment in 1796, had likely given to Holmes in a quest for material for his proposed history of New York. Holmes's transcription of Brant's answers to these questions eventually made its way into the New York Historical Society and have since been published. Brant's note, penned in his own hand, was pasted into Miller's notes and then forgotten. Apart from a few small differences, it is essentially the same as Holmes's transcription, but since it is our only account of the 1669 treaty that comes directly from an Indigenous source, and as it is one directly connected to the relationship defined by that treaty, it is of tremendous value.[17]

Perhaps Brant had told Miller that he planned to write a history of the Iroquois Confederacy when he visited with Miller in New York in 1797 (Miller described Brant as "a remarkable man"). Unfortunately, Brant, like Miller, never managed to finish his history, but John Norton, who served as Brant's secretary from 1795 to 1804, did write a history of the Eastern Woodlands nations in which he included an account of the 1669 treaty. Norton, a former British soldier of Scottish and Cherokee ancestry, had also participated in Holmes's interviews with Brant. His history, part of a manuscript journal of his adventures, remained largely hidden away in a British aristocrat's library until it was discovered and published in 1970.[18]

---

16. C. A. Weslager, *The Delaware Indian Westward Migration* (Wallingford, Pa.: Middle Atlantic Press, 1978), 85–87, 125–26; C. A. Weslager, *The Delaware Indians: A History* (New Brunswick, N.J.: Rutgers University Press, 1972), 481.

17. Col. Brant to Rev. Eleazer Holmes, January 1801, Miller Papers, volume, I:6, New York Historical Society, New York, N.Y. (hereafter NYHS); Douglas W. Bryce, ed., "A Glimpse of Iroquois Culture through the Eyes of Joseph Brant and John Norton," *Proceedings of the American Philosophical Society* 117, no. 4 (August 1973): 286–94.

18. Isabel Thompson Kelsay, *Joseph Brant, 1743–1807: Man of Two Worlds* (Syracuse, N.Y.: Syracuse University Press, 1984), 534, 579–80, 714n42; Carl Benn, "Norton, John [called Teyoninhokarawen] (1770–1831?)," *Oxford Dictionary of National Biography*, September 23, 2004, http://www.oxforddnb.com/view/article/68142; John Norton, *The Journal of Major John Norton, 1816*, ed. Carl F. Klinck and James J. Talman (Toronto: Champlain Society, 1970), xiii–xv, xxxvi–xli.

Together, these sources offer a more comprehensive basis for identifying the origin and meaning of "the Delaware as women" than what scholars have relied on thus far. However, before going any further, we need to clarify who the "Delaware" were, because they did not actually exist as a recognizable group before the eighteenth century; even then the term did not always refer to all Lenape people. At the time of European arrival, the Lenape had evolved into two broad ethnolinguistic groups, the Munsee and the Unami, who lived around two different river valleys: the Munsee in the lower reaches of the Hudson Valley (today's southern New York, western Connecticut, northern New Jersey and northeastern Pennsylvania); the Unami in the southern half of the Delaware Valley (today's southern New Jersey, southeastern Pennsylvania, and northern Delaware). They spoke slightly different dialects of the same language, and their territory, "Lenapehoking," was divided into about forty independent village-based groups whose names, as recorded by the early colonists, included Esopus, Hackensack, Weckquasgeck, Mantaes, and Okehocking. The Lenape were not then, nor have they ever been, united into a single political entity. However, over time, as they suffered from depopulation and other pressures of colonialism, colonists began lumping them into larger categories. The colonists initially grouped them with the Mohicans inhabiting the northern half of the Hudson River valley into the generic category of "River Indians," sometimes dividing them into separate "North" and "South" River Indians, using the seventeenth century terms for the Hudson and Delaware. After Pennsylvania was founded, "Delaware" became the term to describe the "River Indians" of the Delaware Valley. By the mid-eighteenth century, as most of the Lenape were being forced west, away from those river valleys, diplomats described them with different labels that divided them into two or sometimes three distinct groups. A typical example from 1760 referred to them as "Menissings, Delawares, & Unamoas." Modernized into Munsee, Northern Unami, and Southern Unami, these terms map onto those used in scholarly studies of the Lenape. The Northern Unami, as evident from other names applied to them like "Jersey Indians" and Unalachtigo (meaning "those who were detached from where there are waves"), were associated with New Jersey. The Southern Unami, meanwhile, were associated with Pennsylvania.[19]

These historical differences are neatly reflected in the ultimate fate of the Lenape. With few exceptions, today's Unami communities are in Oklahoma, while the Munsee

---

19. Robert S. Grumet, ed., *Journey on the Forbidden Path: Chronicles of a Diplomatic Mission to the Allegheny Country, March–September, 1760* (Philadelphia: American Philosophical Society, 1999), 80; Ives Goddard, "Delaware," in *Handbook of North American Indians*, vol. 15: *Northeast*, ed. Bruce G. Trigger (Washington D.C.: Smithsonian Institution, 1978), 213–239; Jay Miller, "The Unalachtigo?," *Pennsylvania Archaeologist* 44 (1974): 7–8; William A. Hunter, "A Note on the Unalachtigo," in Kraft, *Delaware Indian Symposium*, 147–152; Marshall Becker, "Teedyuscung's Youth and Hereditary Land Rights in New Jersey: The Identification of the Unalachtigo," *Bulletin of the Archaeological Society of New Jersey* 47 (1992), 37–60; Robert S. Grumet, "Zeisberger's *Diaries* as a Source for Studying Delaware Sociopolitical Organization," in *Ethnographies and Exchanges: Native Americans, Moravians, and Catholics in Early North America*, ed. A. G. Roeber (University Park: Pennsylvania State University Press, 2008), 49–63.

communities are far to the north, mostly in Ontario but also in Wisconsin, where some live alongside their ancient Mohican neighbors. Most scholarly accounts of "the Delaware Indians" focus on the Unami, not the Munsee, and on the Delaware's relationship with Pennsylvania. That tendency has confused the debate about "the Delaware as Women," because both the Mohawk oral tradition and contemporary documents focus primarily on the Munsee, not the Unami, and their relationship with New York.[20]

The Mohawk oral tradition, more attuned to the original Hudson Valley context of the treaty of 1669, also differs from that of the Lenape in its emphasis on political geography rather than on generic ethnicity. Joseph Brant, for example, claimed that the "people that were overcome by the Mohawks were not really the Delawares; but those Indians living on the North River between Albany and New York." John Norton claimed the Mohawks only defeated the "Mohikanok" (Mohicans). In other words, not "all the Delaware race," just "those who inhabited the banks of the Hudson River." Blurring modern ethnolinguistic categories while recognizing the importance of contemporary political affiliations, Norton explained that the "Mohikanok" were but one of "the most numerous remnants" of the Delaware. The others included the "Enomie" (Unami) and the "Minseok" (Munsee).[21]

In the end, none of the oral traditions is entirely correct in the sense that none can be taken fully at face value, but none is completely wrong either. Each contains vital clues about what happened. When carefully weighed against each other and the surviving documentary sources, they allow us to date the Great Peace forged between the Haudenosaunee and Lenape back to the spring of 1669 and to reconstruct what happened to better appreciate its contemporary significance. For example, although none of the traditions gives a specific date for when the Great Peace happened, they all point in the same general direction. The Lenape tradition transmitted by the Moravians claimed that the "Confederation" with the Iroquois took place "some time after the European had been in this Country," or "soon after Pennsylvania had been settled by the whites." The Iroquois Confederacy and the Lenape had been involved in "continual Wars" since "before the coming of the white man." The Lenape accounts from the Ohio Country agree that the peace ended "a former war between the Monsies[,] Delaware and the Wyindots and Senekies." Joseph Brant's note provides the crucial detail that allows us to trace the event back to a specific date. Claiming the Lenape "had the worst of a war which had subsisted between them some time to the great detriment of both," he says the "peace was concluded" after the

20. For example, Weslager, *The Delaware Indians: A History*; Jean R. Soderlund, *Lenape Country: Delaware Valley Society before William Penn* (Philadelphia: University of Pennsylvania Press, 2015). Amy C. Schutt, *Peoples of the River Valleys: The Odyssey of the Delaware Indians* (Philadelphia: University of Pennsylvania Press, 2007), includes some discussion of the Munsee, but is primarily about the Unami. Grumet, *Munsee Indians*, is the exception.

21. Brant to Holmes, January 1801, NYHS; Norton, *Journal of Major John Norton, 1816*, 83–84.

Lenape and their allies "received a severe defeat a little above Schenectady on the Mohawk River."[22]

The battle Brant mentions took place in August 1669. It marked the culmination of a massive war that raged from the 1660s to the 1670s, pitting virtually all of the coastal nations from today's Maine to Pennsylvania against the Haudenosaunee. This conflict was itself the culmination of a series of smaller wars dating back to before the dawn of European colonization. The full history of these wars has yet to be written. The few existing studies focus primarily on its New England dimensions, but the involvement of the Lenape and their close neighbors the Mohicans is evident in various sources.[23]

By 1669, the Lenape, Mohicans, and Haudenosaunee, who had been engaged in decades of on-and-off-again warfare and peacemaking, were ready to secure a lasting peace. The oral traditions differ on who initiated the negotiations. Norton claims the "Mohikanok . . . who inhabited the banks of the Hudson River . . . sued for Peace." Brant claims the treaty took place when "the River Indians came to the Mohawk village." Reflecting the Lenape view, Zeisberger claims it was "the Six Nations" who "sent an embassy to the Delaware." They were eager to negotiate because the Lenape "were always too powerful for the Six Nations," who became "convinced that if they continued the wars, their total extirpation would be inevitable" (Brant meanwhile claimed that "the Mohawks had taken some towns from the others; but these never succeeded in taking any from the Mohawks."). The Ohio Delaware of 1821 agreed that their ancestors had "whipped the others in every engagement till the Wyandots and Senekies became very afraid of them and sued for peace."[24]

The first hint of these negotiations in contemporary colonial records comes from early February 1669, when a group of Unami and Munsee delegates arrived at the Munsee town of Esopus. Esopus is midway up the Hudson River valley, near today's Kingston in Ulster County. Through the Ulster magistrates, these men solicited the support of the English governor of New York, Francis Lovelace, before heading north to negotiate with the Haudenosaunee. Lovelace responded approvingly. He agreed with the proposals of the

---

22. John Heckewelder, "Answers to Queries respecting Indian Tribes," in Heckewelder, "Communications," fol. 1; Zeisberger, *History*, 34; Weslager, *Delaware Indian Westward Migration*, 85–87, 125–26; Brant to Holmes, January 1801, NYHS.

23. Gordon M. Day, "The Ouragie War: A Case History in Iroquois–New England Indian Relations," in *Extending the Rafters: Interdisciplinary Approaches to Iroquoian Studies*, ed. Michael K. Foster, Jack Campisi, and Marianne Mithun (Albany: State University of New York Press, 1984), 35–50; Neal Salisbury, "Toward the Covenant Chain: Iroquois and Southern New England Algonquians, 1637–1684," in *Beyond the Covenant Chain: The Iroquois and Their Neighbors in Indian North America, 1600–1800*, ed. Daniel K. Richter and James H. Merrell (Syracuse: Syracuse University Press, 1987), 66–70; and Francis Jennings, "'Pennsylvania Indians' and the Iroquois," in Richter et al., *Beyond the Covenant Chain*, 77–80; Patrick Frazier, *The Mohicans of Stockbridge* (Lincoln: University of Nebraska Press, 1992), 4–9.

24. Brant to Holmes, January 1801, NYHS; Norton, *Journal of Major John Norton*, 83–84; Zeisberger, *History of the Northern American Indians*, 34; Weslager, *Delaware Indian Westward Migration*, 85–87, 125–26.

"Esopys Indians . . . Joyned wth the South Indians [i.e., those from the Delaware Valley] & those of Nevisans [in today's northern New Jersey] to make a firme peace wth the Maquas and Synnekes [the Mohawks and the rest of the Haudenosaunee]." Lovelace requested the magistrates of Ulster County send a colonist "to be a witness of what shall be done" who could then send him a full report "at his & the Indians returne back." Once he received that report, Lovelace would "Ratify and Confirme, what they shall agree & Conclude upon tending to peace and unity."[25]

The Lenape "Plenipotentiarys" represented a variety of Unami and Munsee groups "united in peace." Lovelace initially characterized them as "from the Sout Rivir, Neves-inghs, Hakkinsack and the Sopus in fine all the nations," but there were more groups whose participation is evident from later documents.[26] The South Indians, or those from the "Sout Rivir" were Unami. The rest were Munsee. The Navesinks (Nevesinghs, Nevisans) lived near its mouth in today's northeastern New Jersey. The Hackensacks were from north-western New Jersey. The Tappans lived just north of the Hackensacks. The Esopus, the northernmost Munsee, lived just north of the Tappan. All these groups lived west of the Hudson River, as did the Catskills, the Mohican group that was also included in the 1669 peace. They lived just north of Esopus and likely joined the delegates on their way into the Haudenosaunee country, as their participation in the treaty is not revealed until a later remark by Lovelace. He worried that the 1669 peace would fail because it included only the nations from the west bank of the Hudson River and left out their kinsmen on the east-ern bank. Without them, the peace would be incomplete because, "there being so great a Correspondence with them of the Esopus, Cattskile, etc. that hee that attack the one, must needs injure the other, since in all extremityes they will recourse one to the other." The peoples on both sides of the river shared a "great affinity" that came from their being "so nearly seated and relatd to the rest."[27]

We do not know exactly when the delegates entered Haudenosaunee territory, but the peace negotiations took place sometime in the spring of 1669. That July, one of the Ulster County magistrates wrote to Lovelace to confirm that a peace had been settled.[28] Then in August 1669, around the time of the disastrous battle near Schenectady that Joseph Brant refers to, the sachem of the "Hackensack, Toppan & Staten Island Indians" (the "Staten Island Indians" also being Munsee) appeared before the governor and council of New York to confirm his peoples' recent peace with the "Maquess & Synakers." He displayed "a band of Seawant" that "he said they received from ye Maquaesses upon concluding ye peace

25. Edmund B. O'Callaghan and Berthold Fernow, eds. *Documents Relative to the Colonial History of the State of New York*, 15 vols. (Albany: Statue University of New York Press, 1853–1887), 13:423 (hereafter *DRCHNY*).
26. Francis Lovelace to John Winthrop, Fort James, February 25, 1668–69, Winthrop Family Papers [transcripts], 1630–1741, Massachusetts Historical Society, Boston, Mass. (hereafter WFP).
27. O'Callaghan and Fernow, *DRCHNY*, 13:427, 428, 440; Francis Lovelace to John Winthrop, Fort James, August 3, 1669, WFP.
28. O'Callaghan and Fernow, *DRCHNY*, 13:427.

wth them." He then asked the governor to hold on to the wampum belt, "that if ye Maques should fall out wth them that band of Seawant might remaine as Testimony of their former agreement." Peacemaking efforts between these nations had failed in the past. Determined it would last this time, they invited in the neutral help of the English to secure it. Lovelace accordingly "ordered that a Letter should be wrytt to ye Commissioners of Albany to signi-fye to ye Maquess & Synakers that ye Sachem of theise Nations hath declared ye peace they made wth them & are resolved to keep it inviolably."[29]

Contemporary records regarding the Mohawks confirm the existence and timing of this treaty council, which Joseph Brant claims took place at a "Mohawk village." This is the only mention I have found as to where the treaty took place, but it seems plausible as the Mohawks were still in the process of making Albany the center of Haudenosaunee diplomacy. On September 19, 1669, just a few weeks after they had beaten back the invasion of their country by the Lenape's allies, Mohawk spokesmen approached the Albany magis-trates to propose a more comprehensive peace. Claiming they had been waiting for Gover-nor Lovelace to expand the peace "from the Last Spring," they seemed to be "so farre from beeing elated by their sucesse" in defeating the recent invasion that, in Lovelace's words, "they proffer after this victory (which is very Considerable) such termes and of so much moderation and Condesention as was more reasonable for the Conquered to sue for, then the victorious to proffer." Lovelace explained to Connecticut Governor John Winthrop Jr. that he wanted to "improove this accidentell oportunety toward the establishment of an universall peace" more effective than the one just forged between the Mohawks and "all the nations on the Westward of Hudsons Rivier."[30]

As for the details of the treaty council, we are forced to rely entirely on Indigenous oral traditions. No contemporary record survives. The report of the colonist who accom-panied the Lenape delegates has never been found. Still, we know it was an important event because of all the wampum that figures prominently in both the seventeenth century sources and the later oral traditions. No diplomatic transaction in the Eastern Woodlands was complete without a mutual exchange of wampum. In the spring of 1669, the Lenape delegates carried "sumptuous presents" of "78 large belts of Seawant" (wampum). And, as the Hackensack sachem's conference with Lovelace reveals, they in return received wam-pum from the Mohawks.[31]

Wampum figured centrally in what was for all the participants the most memorable moment of the treaty: the designation of the Lenape as "women." Brant claims that when

---

29. Victor Hugo Paltsits, ed., *Minutes of the Executive Council of the Province of New York: Admin-istration of Francis Lovelace, 1668–1673*, 2 vols. (Albany: State University of New York Press, 1910), 1:35–36.
30. Brant to Holmes, January 1801, NYHS; Francis Lovelace to John Winthrop, Fort James, September 22, 1669, WFP; Propositions of the Mohawkes, September 19, 1669, WFP; Salisbury, "Toward the Covenant Chain," 68–69; Holly A. Rine, "Mohawk Reinvention of the Fort Orange and Albany Courthouses, 1652–77," *Journal of Early American History* 2, no. 1 (2012): 3–31.
31. Francis Lovelace to John Winthrop, Fort James, February 25, 1668–69, WFP.

"the River Indians came to the Mohawk village and made piece," they went "through a long ceremony of having women's apparel put on—and were adopted as nieces and gave a great quantity of wampum." Norton agrees that the Mohawks "put on them the garb of females, and gave them implements of agriculture and those for pounding corn, stiling them their Niece, and imposing on them a tribute of wampum."[32]

From the distance of a century and a half, the Ohio Delaware remembered how "a great council was held and conditions of peace [were] agreed upon," although they had forgotten the Mohawks' role and instead attributed it to the "Wyandots and Senekies" who were currently their primary intermediaries with the Haudenosaunee. The Haudenosaunee representatives "made a petticoat of wampum and put it on their conquerors" (i.e., the Lenape) "saying that it was not fit that such great warriers should fight any more but that they should remain like women who were not considered warriers." They also insisted that the "treaty is held sacred all this time and they say it will until the party that put the coat onto them shall take it off, or break the treaty," something they obviously felt had not yet happened, notwithstanding various previous efforts to do so, including, as we shall see, one by Joseph Brant in 1795.[33]

Zeisberger's account offers the most detailed version of what happened. The Mohawks "opened negotiations and said: It is not profitable that all the nations should be at war with each other, for this would at length ruin the whole Indian race." To prevent "this evil" they proposed "one nation should be the woman. She should be placed in the midst, while the other nations, who make war, should be the man and live around the woman." Doubtless this reference to warring masculine nations refers to the Lenape's allies who at that very moment were preparing to invade the Mohawk country in August. The remark highlights the central position that the Lenape occupied within this anti-Mohawk coalition, which stretched from the Susquehannock in today's central Pennsylvania to the Abenaki in northern New England.[34]

No doubt some of those allies saw the Lenape's separate peace with the Mohawks as a betrayal. Consequently, the Haudenosaunee wisely offered them protection as well as peace. They told the Lenape that "no one should touch or hurt the woman, and if any one did so, they would immediately say to him, 'Why do you beat the woman?' Then all the men should fall upon him who has beaten her." Moreover, by designating the Lenape as a "woman," the Haudenosaunee relieved them of the awkward responsibility of going to war against their former allies subsequent to their new alliance with the Haudenosaunee. The Lenape and Mohican delegates agreed that the "woman should not go to war but endeavor to keep the peace with all." If "the men" surrounding "her" (in other words the Lenape's old Susquehannock and Algonquian allies as well as their new Haudenosaunee allies) "should

32. Brant to Holmes, January 1801, NYHS; Norton, *Journal of Major John Norton*, 83–84.
33. Weslager, *Delaware Indian Westward Migration*, 85–87, 125–26.
34. Zeisberger, *History of the Northern American Indians*, 34.

beat each other and the war be carried on with violence, the woman should have the right of addressing them, 'Ye men, what are ye about; why do you beat each other? We are almost afraid. Consider that your wives and children must perish unless you desist. Do you mean to destroy yourselves from the face of the earth?' The men should then hear and obey the woman."[35]

The Lenape were "declared . . . to be the woman" upon terms of peace, protection, and the freedom from any obligation to fight their allies who were still waging war against the Haudenosaunee. This designation also represented their promise to try to bring their former allies into Great Peace with the Haudenosaunee. The Mohawks then confirmed the agreement with wampum, symbolically dressing the Lenape "in a woman's long habit, reaching down to the feet." Zeisberger suggested that this was an exaggerated gesture designed to serve as a lasting mnemonic device, because in reality "Indian women wear only short garments that reach but little below the knee." The lengthy dress was then "fastened . . . about their bodies with a great, large belt of wampum. They adorned them with earrings, such as their women were accustomed to wear. Further, they hung a calabash filled with oil and beson [*mpisun*, a Lenape word for medicine[36]] on their arms, therewith to anoint themselves and other nations. They also gave them a corn-pestle and a hoe." As Zeisberger explained, each of these steps "was confirmed by delivering a belt of wampum and the whole ceremony observed with the greatest solemnity." Zeisberger also clarified that "the woman's garment signified that they should not engage in war, for the Delaware were great and brave warriors, feared by the other nations; the corn-pestle and hoe that they should engage in agriculture. The calabash with oil was to be used to cleanse the ears of the other nations, that they might attend to good and not to evil counsel. With the medicine or beson they were to heal those who were walking in foolish ways that they might come to their senses and incline their hearts to peace."[37]

The ceremony firmly imprinted this important—and complex—diplomatic agreement on the memories of the Lenape and Mohawk delegates in a way that could easily and effectively be transmitted to their descendants for generations to come. That was very important, for within a generation, the geopolitical context of 1669 had changed. A series of events over the next two decades, including the establishment of the Covenant Chain, the foundation of Pennsylvania, and the beginning of the long series of imperial wars with France, created a drastically different diplomatic scene. It was in the shadow of this altered context that the eighteenth-century descendants of the treaty delegates of 1669 disputed the significance of the designation as "women," even as they continued to agree on the essentials of what had happened and sustain the peace it had produced. A sense of the

35. Zeisberger, *History of the Northern American Indians*, 34.
36. "Lenape Talking Dictionary," Delaware Tribe of Indians, accessed May 23, 2022, https://www .talk-lenape.org/results?query=medicine&lang=english&type=dictionary_entry.
37. Zeisberger, *History of the Northern American Indians*, 35.

kind of performance that had made this Great Peace of 1669 so compelling and memorable can be gained from Joseph Brant's June 1795 effort to reverse the status of "women" it had conferred.

The meeting in June 1795 took place about a month and a half before the signing of the treaty of Greenville that ceded most of Ohio to the United States. Heckewelder, who recorded the story in the early nineteenth century, heard about it from Zeisberger, who had heard it in 1796 from some of the Lenape present at the ceremony. The Lenape met the Mohawks and the rest of the Haudenosaunee on the shores of Lake Erie, at "the Miami of the Lake." The "Mohack Nation from Col. Brandts town on Grand River in Upper Canada, being appointed to officiate for & in behalf of the whole of the 6 Nations, performed the Ceremony" intended to restore "the Lenni Lennape [Delawares] to their former & original Character; namely that of being Men." First the Mohawks selected a Lenape "Man suitable for the occasion." Then they took him aside and "stripped all the Cloaths off from his body except the cloth covering his nakedness. After shaving all the hair off of his head, except that on the crown (and which no Warrior ever cuts off) they painted his whole body, head & face, red" and "bedaubed the standing hair on the Crown of the head with tallow, pressing the white plume of the Bald Eagle" (an emblem meant "to endow the warrior with courage") into his hair. They then put "a War billet or Club into his right hand," and "brought him forward to where the Delaware Chiefs & Council were assembled." Brant then addressed the Lenape, saying "Cousin! A long time ago I adopted you after the manner of a Woman, putting a Petticoat on you! I also at the time hung a Callabasch [gourd] filled with Oil [Bear fat] at your side, wherewith you were to anoint your Head. I also put a Hoe & Corn Pounder into your hands, that you might be enabled to plant Corn & till the Ground; & pound the Corn you raised for Bread. Cousin!" He continued, "I now have thought proper to change your situation, to relieve you from the inconvenience of the Petticoat, which obstructs you when walking! See! I take the Petticoat off of your body, & throw the same in yon thicket." Turning back to the assembled Lenape, Brant cried "Cousin! You are now again transformed into a Man! Into such a Man, as the one is, now brought before you! Cousin! Let your actions in future be such, as is required of the Man." Having made his point through performance and rhetoric, Brant then confirmed it with a gift of wampum. While such political theater was essential to the diplomacy of these societies that still relied on oral tradition, in this case Brant failed to overturn the results of the 1669 treaty.[38]

Much has been made of the gendered significance of "the Delaware as women," more than can be addressed here. However, by tracing it back to its source we can see that it began with a very specific set of diplomatic meanings, some of which survived in the Lenape oral tradition long after the immediate circumstances of 1669 were largely forgotten. As

---

38. "Concerning the reinstating of the Lenni Lenape as Men, by the Six Nations," in Heckewelder, "Communications," fol. 1.

Zeisberger explained, ever since this treaty, "the Delaware nation" has been "looked to for the preservation of peace and entrusted with the charge of the great belt of peace and the chain of friendship which they must take care to preserve inviolate and which they bear on their shoulders at its middle, the other nations and the Europeans holding the ends." This last sentence uses imagery typically associated with the Covenant Chain to highlight the intermediary role (that some but not all) the Lenape acquired in 1669. By applying a similar blend of oral traditions and contemporary documents to those used to reconstruct this treaty, we find that the Lenape "women" began fulfilling their role as peacemakers in 1675, when they facilitated the peace between the Haudenosaunee and their Mohican and Munsee kin living east of the Hudson River.[39]

Additional evidence indicates the Lenape and Mohicans exercised this role as peacemakers between Indigenous nations up through the eighteenth century. Zeisberger notes that they adopted the Shawnees as "grandchildren, even as had been done with the Mahikanders," which benefited the Shawnee tremendously, for "having been adopted by the Delawares," they "are so secure that no nation will venture to attach them, even though they are a cruel, warlike people." The Cherokees, too, "sought the friendship of the Delawares," who made peace with them, "and the Cherokees recognized the Delawares as their grandfathers. Through intervention of the Delawares the Cherokees secured peace also with the Six Nations and others, which was established in 1768."[40]

By the eighteenth century, when the existence of this status as women was revealed to colonists, and when all the sources scholars have used to debate the issue so far were produced, the original significance of the 1669 peace treaty had become blurred by subsequent events. While recovering the original context of the 1660s helps understand the origins of "the Delaware as women" phenomenon, it cannot explain its full significance. Attentive readers will have noted the use of kinship language in these sources—nieces, cousins, grandfathers—as well as the involvement of the Wyandot (Wendat), an Iroquoian people who were not Haudenosaunee but instead, originally, one of its greatest enemies. These and other issues (like how this treaty was transmitted to the rest of the Haudenosaunee) still need to be clarified before we can fully understand what was going on, both in the seventeenth century and subsequently. However, for now we can do so with the knowledge that whatever became of "the Delaware as women," it all started in the spring of 1669 in today's New York State.

---

39. Zeisberger, *History of the Northern American Indians*, 35; Evan Haefeli, "Becoming a 'Nation of Statesmen': The Mohicans' Incorporation into the Iroquois League, 1671–1675," *New England Quarterly* 93, no. 3 (September 2020): 1–48.
40. Zeisberger, *History of the Northern American Indians*, 34, 109; Haefeli, "Becoming a 'Nation of Statesmen.'"

The Arrival of Enslaved Africans in New Amsterdam

Jaap Jacobs

The introduction of the institution of slavery in New Amsterdam and New Netherland—and by extension in its successors, New York City and State—has long been assumed to have taken place in 1625 or 1626.[1'] E. B. O'Callaghan was the first historian to date the first arrival of enslaved Africans in his seminal *Voyages of the Slavers St. John and Arms of Amsterdam*, published in 1867, a few years after the Civil War. An Irish-born, anti-British journalist deeply involved in the social issues of his time, O'Callaghan had fled south from Canada in the late 1830s when riots threatened his home and livelihood. His political engagement is evident in the historical publications he subsequently produced in New York.[2] While O'Callaghan presents his view on the "introduction of slavery into New Netherland" as an established historical fact, his evidence is tenuous. He based the timing on a request submitted to Director and Council of New Netherland dated February 25, 1644, that is, a considerable number of years after the first arrival was assumed to have taken place. The document contains the names of a group of enslaved Africans, "who have served the Company for eighteen to nineteen years," and thus O'Callaghan concluded they first set foot on

1'. This article evolved out of a series of conversations with the congregation of St-Mark's-Church-in-the-Bowery in New York City in 2021. I thank Rev. Anne Sawyer, Nicole Maskiell, Andrea Mosterman, Dennis Maika, Jeroen Dewulf, Rik Grandia, Russell Shorto, Lou Roper, and Julie van den Hout for their contributions, advice, support, and assistance. I also thank the anonymous reviewers of *New York History*, whose critical reading helped to present the arguments in this article in a convincing manner.
2. A. P. G. J. van der Linde, "De 'Remonstrantie van Nieu-Nederlandt' (1649) en haar bijzondere betekenis voor Edmund Bailey O'Callaghan," in *Klassiek Amerikaans: opstellen voor A. Lammers*, ed. E. F. van de Bilt and H. W. van den Doel (Leiden, 2002), 92–102; E. B. O'Callaghan, trans. and ed., *Voyages of the Slavers St. John and Arms of Amsterdam, 1659, 1663* (Albany: J. Munsell, 1867), xiii–xiv, xxii. O'Callaghan was not aware of the existence of Juan Rodriguez, a free mulatto from Santo Domingo who in 1613 briefly stayed in the area later called New Netherland. See Anthony Stevens-Acevedo, Tom Weterings and Leonor Alvarez Francés, "Juan Rodriguez and the Beginnings of New York City" (2013), CUNY Academic Works, http://academicworks.cuny.edu/dsi_pubs/17.

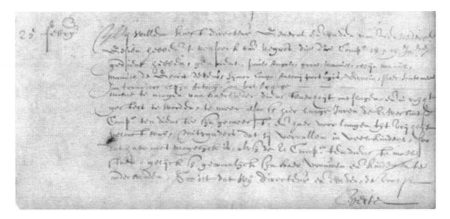

Figure 1. First part of the apostil on the request of enslaved Africans to be released from their servitude, February 25, 1644, with the insertion of names in a slightly smaller hand with reduced line spacing on the third, fourth and fifth lines. "Dutch Colonial Council Minutes, 1638–1665," ser. A1809–78, vol. 4, 183–84. NEW YORK STATE ARCHIVES, NEW NETHERLAND COUNCIL, , NYSA_A1809-78_V04_P183-184, HTTPS://DIGITALCOLLECTIONS .ARCHIVES.NYSED.GOV/INDEX.PHP/DETAIL/OBJECTS/11580.

Manhattan in 1625 or 1626.[3] However, O'Callaghan did not provide firm evidence of how this may have happened. Taking his lead from the arrival of the first Africans in Virginia in 1619 via a Dutch ship, O'Callaghan suggests that those who arrived first at New Amsterdam were "probably captured at sea." He points out that "during the War with Spain," Dutch privateers took many prizes "among the Caribbean Islands and along the Spanish Main." While, as we will see later, the first point is a correct assumption and the second point is corroborated by the historical record, neither actually supports his conclusion that the first arrival took place in 1625 or 1626. Working with the records available to him at the time, O'Callaghan was unable to pinpoint exactly *when* or *how* the first arrival had taken place. Nevertheless, for more than a century many historians have adopted his interpretation almost unquestioningly.[4]

---

3. New York State Archives (hereinafter NYSA), A1809, 4: 183–84 (25 February 1644; Arnold J. F. van Laer, trans. and ed., *Council Minutes, 1638–1649* (Baltimore, Md.: Genealogical Publishing Co., Inc., 1974), 212–13; E. B. O'Callaghan, trans., *Laws and Ordinances of New Netherland, 1636–1674* (Albany: Weed, Parsons and Company, 1868), 36–37). When revising the translation by O'Callaghan, Van Laer changed O'Callaghan's translation of "18 a 19 Ja[ren]" from "18 *a* 19 years" into "18 or 19 years."

4. Edgar J. McManus, *A History of Negro Slavery in New York* (Syracuse: Syracuse University Press, 1966), 4; P. C. Emmer, "De slavenhandel van en naar Nieuw-Nederland," *Economisch-Historisch Jaarboek* 35 (1972): 94–148, herein 105; Joyce D. Goodfriend, "Burghers and Blacks: the Evolution of a Slave Society at New Amsterdam," *New York History* 59 (1978): 125–44, herein 125; Thomas J. Davis, "New York's Long Black Line: A Note on the Growing Slave Population, 1626–1790," *Afro-Americans in New York Life and History* 2 (1978): 41–59, herein 41; Morton Wagman, "Corporate Slavery in New Netherland," *Journal of Negro History* 65 (1980): 34–42, herein 34; Joyce D. Goodfriend, "Black Families in New Netherland," *Journal of Afro-American Historical and Genealogical Society* 5 (1984): 95–108, herein 95; Henry B. Hoff, "A Colonial Black Family in New York

In 1993 Robert Swan challenged O'Callaghan's interpretation in a critical essay. As he pointed out, there are at least three issues with the document: "its originator, its intent, and the names and numbers involved." First, the Dutch colony's Director Willem Kieft had no first-hand knowledge of the arrival. Second, as Swan phrases it, "the intent of the ordinance has no direct relationship in determining a date of origin," and the phrase from the 1644 document should therefore not be taken literally. Third, the various places of origin of the Africans mentioned in the 1644 document, according to Swan, cast doubt on whether the enslaved Africans arrived as a single group.[5] While Swan's 1993 article leaves a few loose ends, he concluded that "a 1625 or 1626 date is not supported" by the 1644 document nor by evidence which had subsequently come to light. Swan also concluded that the exact year was moot in some respect, as it made "no difference in mitigating the harsh reality of slavery," nor did it have "intrinsic value in understanding the economic, political, and social implications of a slave system." Even so, he insisted that "in historiography . . . a few years makes a significant difference," and he urged historians to be more critical of the meager data at hand." In the wake of Swan's article, many (but not all) scholars have distanced themselves from the chronological part of O'Callaghan's interpretation, sometimes avoiding a specific reference to 1625/1626, at other times employing imprecise time indications or ignoring the issue all together. Thus Swan's "significant difference of a few years" has not been subjected to research.[6]

---

and New Jersey: Peter Santomee and His Descendants," *Journal of the Afro-American Historical and Genealogical Society* 9 (1988): 101–34, herein 101.

5. Robert J. Swan, "First Africans into New Netherland, 1625 or 1626?," *de Halve Maen* 66 (1993): 75–82, herein 77; Robert J. Swan, *New Amsterdam Gehenna: Segregated Death in New York City, 1630–1801* (Brooklyn: Noir Verite Press, 2008), 79–80, 143.

6. Willie F. Page, *The Dutch Triangle: The Netherlands and the Atlantic Slave Trade, 1621–1664* (New York: Garland Publishing, 1997), 189; Willie F. Page, "'By Reason of Their Colour': Africans in New Netherland, 1626–1674," *de Halve Maen* 71 (1998): 75–84, herein 80; Graham Russell Hodges, *Root and Branch: African Americans in New York and East Jersey, 1613–1863* (Chapel Hill: University of North Carolina Press, 1999), 7–8; Dennis J. Maika, "Slavery, Race and Culture in Early New York," *de Halve Maen* 73 (2000): 27–33, herein 28; Leslie M. Harris, *In the Shadow of Slavery: African Americans in New York City, 1626–1863* (Chicago: University of Chicago Press, 2003), 14; Leslie M. Harris, "Slavery, Emancipation, and Class Formation in Colonial and Early National New York," *Journal of Urban History* 30–33 (March 2004): 339–59; Thelma Wills Foote, *Black and White Manhattan: The History of Racial Formation in New York City, 1624–1783* (Oxford: Oxford University Press, 2004), 36; Linda M. Heywood and John K. Thornton, *Central Africans, Atlantic Creoles, and the Foundation of the Americas, 1585–1660* (Cambridge: Cambridge University Press, 2007), 36–37; Linda Heywood and John Thornton, "Intercultural Relations between Europeans and Blacks in New Netherland," in *Four Centuries of Dutch-American Relations*, ed. Cornelis A. van Minnen, Hans Krabbendam, and Giles Scott-Smith (Amsterdam: Boom Publishers, 2009), 192–203, herein 196; Henry B. Hoff, "Researching African-American Families in New Netherland and Colonial New York and New Jersey," in *A Beautiful and Fruitful Place: Selected Rensselaerswijck Papers, Volume 3*, ed. Margriet Lacy (Albany: New Netherland Institute, 2013), 109–16, herein 109; Susanah Shaw Romney, *New Netherland Connections: Intimate Networks and Atlantic Ties in Seventeenth-Century America* (Chapel Hill: University of North Carolina Press, 2014), 195, 198–200 (esp. 198n8, where Romney makes the point that there is no reason to equate the eleven petitioners of 1644 with the first arrivals in New Netherland);

This lack of further scrutiny is remarkable, especially compared with the scholarly attention devoted to the first arrival of enslaved Africans in Virginia in 1619, which constitutes the introduction of slavery into North America. In 2019, the four-hundredth anniversary of the delivery of "20. and Odd Negroes," in which a Dutch privateer was instrumental, was publicly commemorated as a seminal event for the United States. Regardless of the controversy of the *New York Times* 1619 Project, commemorations still serve a purpose in heightening public awareness of history in general and neglected facets of the past in particular.[7] For New York City and New York State, the exact timing and circumstances of the introduction of its system of slavery warrants further investigation, first because of the

---

Anne-Marie Cantwell and Diana diZerega Wall, "Looking for Africans in Seventeenth-Century New Amsterdam," in *The Archaeology of Race in the Northeast*, ed. Christopher N. Matthews and Allison Manfra McGovern (Gainesville: University Press of Florida, 2015), 29–55, herein 32; Patricia U. Bonomi, "'Swarms of Negroes Comeing about My Door': Black Christianity in Early Dutch and English North America," *Journal of American History* 103, no. 1 (June 2016): 34–58, herein 40; Jeroen Dewulf, *The Pinkster King and the King of Kongo: The Forgotten History of America's Dutch-owned Slaves* (Jackson: University Press of Mississipi, 2017), 24, 36–37; Jeroen Dewulf, "Iberian Linguistic Elements among the Black Population in New Netherland (1614–1664)," *Journal of Pidgin and Creole Languages* 34, no. 1 (2019): 49–82, herein 50–51; Dennis J. Maika, "To 'experiment with a parcel of negros': Incentive, Collaboration, and Competition in New Amsterdam's Slave Trade," *Journal of Early American History* 10 (2020): 33–69, herein 41; Susanah Shaw Romney, "Reytory Angola, Seventeenth-Century Manhattan," in *As If She Were Free: A Collective Biography of Women and Emancipation in the Americas*, ed. Erica L. Ball, Tatiana Seijas, and Terri L Snyder (Cambridge: Cambridge University Press, 2020), 58–78, herein 58–59; Anne-Claire Faucquez, "Corporate Slavery in Seventeenth-Century New York," in *The Many Faces of Slavery: New Perspectives on Slave Ownership and Experiences in the Americas*, ed. Lawrence Aje and Catherine Armstrong (London: Bloomsbury Academic, 2020), 89–100, herein 90–91, 97n15; Andrea Mosterman, "Nieuwer-Amstel, stadskolonie aan de Delaware," in *De Slavernij in Oost en West: Het Amsterdam Onderzoek*, ed. Pepijn Brandon, Guno Jones, Nancy Jouwe, and Matthias van Rossum (Amsterdam: Spectrum, 2020), 164–71, herein 164; Anne-Claire Faucquez, *De la Nouvelle-Néerlande à New York: La naissance d'une société esclavagiste (1624–1712)* (Paris: Les Indes savantes, 2021), 62–63; Henk den Heijer, *Nederlands slavernijverleden: Historische inzichten en het debat nu* (Zutphen: Walburg Pers, 2021), 109; Andrea Mosterman, *Spaces of Enslavement: A History of Slavery and Resistance in Dutch New York* (Ithaca, N.Y.: Cornell University Press, 2021), 154n114; Nicole Saffold Maskiell, *Bound by Bondage: Slavery and the Creation of a Northern Gentry* (Ithaca, N.Y.: Cornell University Press, 2022), 28.

7. From a plethora of publications on 1619 and the 1619 Project, see Engel Sluiter, "New Light on the '20. and Odd Negroes' Arriving in Virginia, August 1619," *William and Mary Quarterly*, 3rd. ser., vol. 54 (1997): 395–98; John Thorton, "The African Experience of the '20. and Odd Negroes' Arriving in Virginia in 1619," *William and Mary Quarterly*, 3rd ser., vol. 55, no. 3 (July 1998): 421–34; Victor Enthoven, "De Witte Leeuw en de '20. and Odd Negroes,'" in *Alle streken van het kompas: Maritieme geschiedenis in Nederland. Opstellen over maritieme geschiedenis in Nederland aangeboden aan Femme S. Gaastra bij zijn afscheid als hoogleraar zeegeschiedenis aan de Universiteit Leiden*, ed. Maurits Ebben, Henk den Heijer, and Joost Schokkenbroek (Zutphen: Walburg Pers, 2010), 233–47; *New York Times Magazine*, August 14, 2019, https://www.nytimes.com/interactive/2019/08/14/magazine/1619-america-slavery.html; Alex Lichtenstein, "From the Editor's Desk: 1619 and All That," *American Historical Review* 125, no. 1 (February 2020): xv–xxi. For attention to '1619' in the Netherlands, see, for instance, Leendert van der Valk, "De eerste Afrikaanse Amerikanen werden verhandeld onder de Nederlandse vlag" *NRC*, January 1, 2021, https://www.nrc.nl/nieuws/2021/01/01/de-eerste-afrikaanse-amerikanen-werden-verhandeld-onder-de-nederlandse-vlag-a4025588.

public importance attached to chronologically pinpointing seminal events, and second, because establishing a sequence of events leading up to the first arrival of enslaved Africans in New Amsterdam may help historical researchers shed light on the characteristics of its slavery system in its earliest phase.

This article will answer the intertwined questions of *when* and *how* the arrival of the first enslaved Africans in New Amsterdam took place. The first three sections will analyze the historical context. First, we will look at shipping patterns. How did the arrival of captives taken during privateering raids fit into the shipping patterns of voyages to New Netherland by ships from the Dutch West India Company (WIC)? Was there any non-WIC privateering or shipping that might have provided a means? Second, when did the WIC begin to actively engage in slave trade? Third, what was the situation in New Netherland at this early stage? Was it a feasible destination for enslaved Africans, and when and how was this communicated to the Dutch Republic? The combined contextual evidence as presented below rules out the arrival of enslaved Africans prior to 1627. The final section of this article will show that the yacht *Bruynvisch*, which arrived at New Amsterdam on August 29, 1627, delivered the first enslaved Africans to Manhattan.

Shipping Patterns and Privateering

From the outset of the Dutch Revolt, the Dutch employed privateering, piracy legalized by a letter of marque, as a means to inflict damage on its enemy, the combined monarchies of Spain and Portugal. Dutch privateering in the Atlantic increased in the late sixteenth century and the first decade of the seventeenth century, particularly in the Caribbean; but it came to an almost complete standstill during the Twelve Years' Truce (1609–21). The example of the Zeeland ship *Witte Leeuw*, which captured the Portuguese slave ship *São João Bautista* and then sailed to Virginia, shows that at least some privateering with a Dutch letter of marque took place, even though the *Witte Leeuw*'s captain was an Englishman. The 1619 voyage of the *Witte Leeuw* led O'Callaghan to believe that the arrival of the first enslaved Africans on Manhattan in 1625 or 1626 occurred in a similar fashion. Yet in doing so he ignored the significant changes that had subsequently taken place. When the Dutch West India Company was founded in 1621, it received a monopoly that combined all private shipping and privateering in the Atlantic into one organization. During the few years that the WIC required to assemble its starting capital, a few private ships may have been sent out on expeditions to the Caribbean or to the Wild Coast. Similarly, Dutch merchants continued to engage in the fur trade on the Hudson River and in the acquisition of salt from the South American coast. As their journeys contravened the WIC's state-granted monopoly, private merchants had to obtain exemptions through a resolution of the States General, a process that provided historians with a reliable series of extant records. By late 1623, the records show that no further exemptions were granted to private merchants. On the contrary, as the 1624 example of David Pietersz de Vries shows, the WIC protected its monopoly with all possible means. In January 1624, the WIC, now in full control, initiated its first privateering expedition. All privateering in the Caribbean was carried out exclusively by the WIC for a number of years. The adoption of patroonship systems de facto, private colonies under the jurisdiction of the WIC from 1627 onward created a small loophole for non-WIC privateering, as it provided the patroons with a limited right to send out ships of their own, with permission to engage in privateering. The Company's own privateering efforts began to wane in the mid-1630s and petered out when peace agreements with Spain and Portugal were reached in subsequent decades.[8]

The privateering expeditions of the WIC in the 1620s are well documented through Johannes de Laet's 1644 compendium and have been analyzed by Cornelis Goslinga, Henk den Heijer, Linda Heywood and John Thornton, among others. The general mode of operation was for the WIC Chambers of Amsterdam and Zeeland to send out flotillas separately in the early months of the year. These flotillas sailed into the South Atlantic and then tried to join forces in Caribbean waters. They consisted of a combination of fast yachts and heavily armed and larger but slower ships. The WIC ships were usually ordered to visit little-known islands and other places to obtain relevant geographical information. They also captured merchant ships and raided coastal settlements in a general effort to harass the Iberian enemy, to obtain plunder, and to acquire information about the main target: the annual fleets of richly laden galleons that transported silver and other precious cargoes to Spain. The general route of the Dutch flotillas was set by the prevailing currents and winds: first south from Europe to cross the Atlantic and reach the South American coast, then west along the Wild Coast to enter the Caribbean and gradually progress toward the western point of Cuba and lie in wait north of Havana in the summer months. Before the start of the hurricane season, the Dutch ships set course for the Northern Atlantic for their return to Europe. The usual route for privateering ships did not include a stopover at New Amsterdam.[9]

---

8. Cornelis Ch. Goslinga, *The Dutch in the Caribbean and on the Wild Coast 1580–1680* (Gainesville: University of Florida Press, 1971), 82–83; Jaap Jacobs, *New Netherland: A Dutch Colony in Seventeenth-Century America* (Leiden: Brill Academic Publishers, 2005), 40–41; Jaap Jacobs, "Dutch Proprietary Manors in America: The Patroonships in New Netherland," in *Constructing Early Modern Empires: Proprietary Ventures in the Atlantic World*, ed. L. H. Roper and Bertrand Van Ruymbeke (Leiden: Brill Academic Publishers, 2007), 301–26; L. A. H. Hulsman, "Nederlands Amazonia. Handel met indianen tussen 1580 en 1680" (Ph.D. dissertation, University of Amsterdam, 2009), 104n10. For the resolutions of the States General and the States of Holland, see "N. Japikse, H. H. P. Rijperman, A. Th. van Deursen, J. G. Smit, and J. Roelevink ed., "Resolutien der Staten-Generaal 1576–1625," Huygens Instituut, accessed December 9, 2022, https://www.huygens.knaw.nl/resources/resolutien-der-staten-generaal-1576-1625/; and E. C. M. Huysman, A. Langeveld-Kleijn, J. C. Stok, and J. W. Veenendaal-Barth, "Notulen van de vergaderingen der Staten van Holland 1620–1640 door N. Stellingwerff en S. Schot," Huygens Instituut, accessed December 9, 2022, https://www.huygens.knaw.nl/resources/notulen-van-de-vergaderingen-der-staten-van-holland-1620-1640-door-n-stellingwerff-en-s-schot/.
9. Johannes de Laet, *Historie ofte Iaerlijck verhael van de verrichtinghen der geoctroyeerde West-Indische Compagnie* (Leiden: Bonaventuer ende Abraham Elsevier, 1644), appendix; Goslinga, *The Dutch in the Caribbean*; Henk den Heijer, *De geschiedenis van de WIC* (Zutphen: Walburg Pers, 1994); Heywood and Thornton, *Central Africans.*

Shipping to New Netherland followed a different pattern, as the Voyages of New Netherland database shows. Ships destined for New Amsterdam did not enter Caribbean waters; instead, after crossing the Atlantic, they headed northwest to cross over to the North American mainland, following the coastline to reach the Hudson River. This route made sense as the ships sailing to New Netherland from 1623 to the early 1630s were supply ships, carrying colonists, cattle, and provisions for a nascent colony. These ships were generally not as heavily armed as vessels specifically equipped for privateering. Entering the Caribbean to engage in hostilities would have jeopardized passengers and supplies and wasted valuable time; in addition, the New Netherland–bound ships did not have spare cargo space to take in prize goods. The three ships that set out in 1623 and 1624 transported the bulk of the Walloon colonists, while the six supply ships of 1625 (of which two fell prey to enemy privateers in European waters) carried cattle, forage, and provisions. Subsequently, the shipping frequency dropped to one or two vessels per year until it began to rise again in the late 1630s. By that time, the WIC had captured Curaçao, which became an occasional port of call for ships bound for New Netherland. The return route from New Netherland to the Dutch Republic was a straight crossing of the North Atlantic.[10]

On the whole, the presumed arrival of African captives in New Amsterdam in 1625 or 1626 (or 1623–24) does not fit with the routes of the WIC ships destined for New Netherland or for those engaged in privateering in the Caribbean. None of the WIC ships arriving in New Netherland before 1627 captured an Iberian prize. In those years there was no non-WIC shipping to New Netherland, as there had been up to 1623. Nor did any foreign ships arrive in New Amsterdam in those years. The shipping patterns thus rule out the possibility that enslaved Africans, captured through privateering, arrived on Manhattan in 1625 or 1626.[11]

The West India Company's Entry into the Slave Trade

By the turn of the sixteenth century, the Dutch had acquired a superficial knowledge of the Iberian slave trade, both through the publications of, for instance, Jan Huygen van Linschoten, a Dutchman who had served in the Portuguese empire, as well as through Dutch skippers in Portuguese service who transported enslaved Africans to Brazil. Yet such voyages were extremely rare and did not involve Dutch colonies which, for a long time,

10. Julie van den Hout, "Voyages of New Netherland," New Netherland Institute, accessed December 8, 2022, https://www.newnetherlandinstitute.org/history-and-heritage/digital-exhibitions/voyages-of-new-netherland/. The database has been compiled from various primary sources and is complete and reliable for the 1620s.
11. If there had been a foreign arrival, there would doubtlessly have been a considerable fracas, with complaints and recriminations leaving traces in diplomatic sources in England and the Dutch Republic, as happened when the English ship *William* attempted to trade on the Hudson in 1633. See National Archives of the Netherlands (hereafter Nat. Arch.), Archive States General (1.01.02) (hereafter SG), inv. nr. 5893, I 70–77 (November 1, 1633; rec. June 13, 1634).

remained very few in number. In the 1610s, merchants from Zeeland had planted a few, mostly short-lived, outposts in the Amazon region, with the aim of obtaining indigo and other plantation products. In the same decade Dutch merchants set up a small number of trading posts in West Africa to facilitate the trade in gold and ivory. None of these minor ventures are known to have employed enslaved labor or to have been involved in the transatlantic slave trade. By 1617, most of the Dutch trading posts in South America were abandoned following hostilities with the Natives or attacks by Spanish forces.[12]

The founding of the WIC marked a transition from small private ventures to large-scale corporate activities. It also initiated a protracted process in which the WIC's role in the slave trade gradually moved from an inconceivable notion to a stark reality. Once the WIC became operational, the directors set their sights not on New Netherland, which had hitherto supplied a minor stream of furs to a small group of merchants, but instead on initiating major expeditions against Iberian colonies, in particular the Portuguese holdings in South America and Africa. The prize coveted by the WIC directors was Brazil, the major sugar colony of the Atlantic world, where plantations used enslaved labor from Africa to produce a steady stream of molasses for European consumers. In late 1623, the WIC drew up a "Grand Design," which involved a two-pronged attack: on Salvador da Bahia, the capital of Portuguese Brazil, and on the city of Luanda in Angola, the main supplier of enslaved labor, with a follow-up expedition to capture the Portuguese stronghold of Elmina. Soldiers were recruited, ships were fitted out, and in December 1623 and January 1624, a fleet of twenty-six vessels set sail from the Dutch Republic. In this, as well as in other cases, the course of the expeditions as they unfolded demonstrate that Dutch plans were inspired by bellicose audacity rather than founded on a thorough knowledge of local circumstances, geographical information, and detailed anticipatory planning. The attack on Salvador initially appeared to succeed when the city was conquered in May 1624. The Portuguese fled into the hinterland and started a form of guerrilla warfare which, together with tropical diseases and a lack of victuals, weakened the Dutch occupation force. When news of the victory arrived in the Dutch Republic, plans to send out reinforcements were put into action, but the preparations took more time than was available. Eventually, the Portuguese sent out a powerful fleet that retook Salvador in April 1625. Meanwhile, the planned attack on Luanda was called off when the city turned out to be much more heavily fortified than expected. A subsequent attack on Elmina in 1625 ended in a disaster, with numerous Dutch casualties. By the summer of 1626, this series of failures left the WIC's coffers empty with very little to show for it.[13]

---

12. Wim Klooster, "Het begin van de Nederlandse slavenhandel in het Atlantisch gebied," in Ebben et al., *Alle streken van het kompas*, 249–62; Hulsman, *Nederlands Amazonia*, ch. 2.

13. Den Heijer, *Geschiedenis van de WIC*, 35–39; Henk den Heijer, ed., *Expeditie naar de Goudkust: Het journaal van Jan Dircksz Lam over de Nederlandse aanval op Elmina, 1624–1626* (Zutphen. Walburg Pers, 2006), 30–39; Wim Klooster, *The Dutch Moment: War, Trade, and Settlement in the Seventeenth-Century Atlantic World* (Ithaca, N.Y.: Cornell University Press, 2016), 39–43.

The Grand Design shows that the WIC was from the outset aware of the economic importance of enslaved labor to the Portuguese plantations in Brazil and thus to the Dutch, too, provided their attempted expeditions would be successful. This awareness raised the crucial question that the Company directors now faced: Was their involvement in the institution of slavery justifiable overseas, even if it was not allowed in the Dutch Republic itself? Slavery could include actively enslaving people, using enslaved labor, and even "the trading of Christians" (as many captured Angolans, for instance, had been baptized). It was an issue with wide-ranging ramifications, economic, legal, and religious but also existential, both to the Company and the Dutch Republic. Could they succeed without it? And if it were decided that they could not, what would the effect be on the Dutch war effort in its struggle with Spain? For such weighty questions, the WIC turned to a traditional Dutch solution: they appointed a committee to look into it.[14]

While these matters were under consideration in the Dutch Republic, the WIC did not yet engage in the transatlantic slave trade. Nor did it use or acquire enslaved labor in its few overseas factories and conquests.[15] Wim Klooster points out that even during the

---

14. Nat. Arch., Archive Old WIC (1.05.01.01) (hereafter OWIC), inv. nr. 1, fol. 2–2v, 8–8v (July–August 1623): "behalven dat het schijnt dat den handel der Christenen niet geoorlooft en is, welcks aengaende eenige naerder onderrichtinge soude dienen gedaen." There is an extensive literature on early Dutch views on slavery, for instance D. L. Noorlander, *Heaven's Wrath: The Protestant Reformation and the Dutch West India Company in the Atlantic World* (Ithaca, N.Y.: Cornell University Press, 2019), 166–73; Dienke Hondius, "Afrikanen in Zeeland, Moren in Middelburg," *Zeeland* 14 (2005): 13–24; Willem Frijhoff, *Fulfilling God's Mission: The Two Worlds of Dominie Everardus Bogardus, 1607–1647* (Leiden: Brill, 2007), 530–37; Den Heijer, *Nederlands slavernijverleden*, passim; Janny Venema, *Kiliaen van Rensselaer (1586–1643): Designing a New World* (Hilversum: Verloren, 2010), 281–83; Goslinga, *The Dutch in the Caribbean*, 340–42; Emmer, "De slavenhandel van en naar Nieuw-Nederland," 98–103; P. C. Emmer, *De Nederlandse slavenhandel 1500–1800* (Amsterdam: Arbeiderspers, 2000), 30, 34–39; W. S. Unger, "Bijdragen tot de geschiedenis van de Nederlandsche slavenhandel," *Economisch-Historisch Jaarboek* 26 (1956): 133–74, herein 138.

15. Susanah Shaw Romney, *New Netherland Connections*, 198–99. Romney suggests that in the early period enslaved Africans arrived in New Netherland in an unknown ship through Dutch ports in Africa. This is remotely conceivable for the late 1630s and 1640s, but not for the 1620s. Gorée Island, off Dakar, was the only Dutch presence on the western coast of West Africa in 1623–26. From 1621 onward, the Dutch maintained a small presence on the island, first run by the Admiralty of Amsterdam, subsequently by the WIC. The island served as a refreshing post for ships sailing south and facilitated some trade in ivory, wax, gum, sugar, and hides. After 1630, it also supplied enslaved labor for Pernambuco. Fort Nassau in Moree on the southern coast of West Africa was, after an earlier stint, occupied by the Dutch from 1623 onwards and facilitated trade in gold, ivory, pepper, and camlet. There is no indication that slave trade involving Gorée or Fort Nassau occurred from 1623 to 1626, which would have been a remarkable breach of WIC policy at that time. The Slave Voyages database does not contain any Dutch slaveships for these years. Neither is there evidence that enslaved labor was employed on these outposts. On the whole, Romney's uncorroborated suggestion does not align with the scholarly consensus on the Dutch entry into the Atlantic slave trade. See Filipa Ribeiro da Silva, "African Islands and the Formation of the Dutch Atlantic Economy: Arguin, Gorée, Cape Verde and São Tomé, 1590–1670," *International Journal of Maritime History* 26 (2014): 549–67; Den Heijer, *Expeditie naar de Goudkust*, 63; Klooster, "Het begin van de Nederlandse slavenhandel"; Den Heijer, *Nederlands slavernijverleden*, chs. 2–3; Johannes Menne Postma, *The Dutch in the Atlantic Slave Trade, 1600–1815* (Cambridge: Cambridge

short-lived occupation of Salvador, the Dutch commanders had no idea what to do with the enslaved Africans that they encountered in the city. Their instructions did not contain a single reference to enslaved labor. Neither did they know what to do with Africans on the slave ships that they captured. Joannes de Laet remarked on this with hindsight twenty years after-the-fact: while sailing to Salvador, the fleet captured "a ship coming from Angola to Bahìa with 250 Blacks" (*swarten*). They allowed the ship to sail on, "not aware how suitable and useful these could be to them." From 1624 and 1626, there were four similar occurrences, all in Brazilian waters, in which Dutch privateers had no use for slave ships and their Black captives and thus allowed them to sail on after taking plunder or putting them ashore at a convenient spot.[16]

Meanwhile in the Dutch Republic, the WIC slowly moved toward a decision. The committee, composed of delegates of the States General, the General Board of the WIC, and the Amsterdam chamber, most likely solicited advice from the religious authorities in Amsterdam and elsewhere. Regarding the legal issues, it may have been influenced by the publication in 1625 of Hugo Grotius's *De Jure Belli ac Pacis*. Grotius's reasoning provided a legal framework that legitimized slavery to some extent, but it suggested limitations as well. These related to the application of the right of booty to enslaved people captured on prize ships as opposed to actively trading in human beings. This would allow the WIC to use captured Africans as forced laborers, but not to purchase or sell them. This distinction would obviously not change the dire condition of the enslaved, nor does it seem that the WIC directors were of one mind. The WIC held its general meeting in Amsterdam in November 1626, and a month later, on December 21, 1626, the Zeeland chamber, one of the five regional chambers of the WIC, decided to send a yacht to Angola specifically to acquire "a few Blacks" through trade and to take these people to the Amazon, "or to such a place where the Company might have settled its people." This is the first reference to the intention of some within the WIC's leadership to use enslaved labor and even to acquire such laborers through trade, despite Grotius's considerations. It was quickly followed up by Company servants overseas. In March 1627, captain Jan van Ryen, the leader of an expedition to the Oyapoc River, asked his superiors in Zeeland to send additional manpower, "and I request Blacks rather than Dutch, for the Blacks are more inclined to work than

University Press, 1990), ch. 1; Pieter Emmer and Ernst van den Boogart, "The Dutch Participation in the Atlantic Slave Trade, 1596–1650," in Pieter C. Emmer, *The Dutch in the Atlantic Economy, 1580–1880* (Ashgate: Aldershot, 1998), 33–63. The first direct slave voyage from Africa to New Netherland took place in 1654, see Maika, "To 'experiment with a parcel of negros.'"

16. Klooster, "Het begin van de Nederlandse slavenhandel," 150; De Laet, *Historie ofte Iaerlyck Verhael*, appendix, 10, and main text, 17, "niet wetende hoe dienstigh ende nut deselve haer konden wesen." Den Heijer, *Geschiedenis van de WIC*, 55–68; Klooster, *Dutch Moment*, 43–46; Goslinga, *The Dutch in the Caribbean*, 141–46, 158–72, 339–42; Emmer, *Nederlandse slavenhandel*, 34; Nat. Arch, SG, inv. nr. 5751A, "Ordre van Regieringe," two drafts, October–November 1624. See also G. J. van Grol, *De grondpolitiek in het West-Indisch domein der Generaliteit. Een historische studie*, 2 vols. ('s-Gravenhage: Algemeene Landsdrukkerij, 1934–1937; 2nd ed., Amsterdam: S. Emmering, 1980), 2:22–23.

the Dutch." By 1627, the Dutch WIC was about to condone the use of enslaved labor, but it would not engage in "the trade of Christians" until the 1630s.[17]

Prior to 1620, the Dutch were only to a very limited extent involved in the slave trade, which was carried out by private merchants on an incidental basis. The creation of the Dutch West India Company in 1621 was a watershed. Private ventures were quickly phased out between 1621 and 1623. The Company was initially reluctant to enter into the slave trade, and during its early forays in South America and the Caribbean, it did not have a use for Africans captured on prize ships. Only in late 1626 did the WIC decide to enter into the slave trade. Thus, a presumed first arrival of enslaved Africans at New Amsterdam in 1625 or 1626 is not compatible with the policy and practice of the WIC regarding slavery and slave trade as it developed between 1623 and the 1630s.

The Early Development of New Netherland

The benefit of hindsight sometimes slants the historians' view of the past, focusing on what happened rather than on what contemporaries thought might happen. We know that the Dutch attempt to settle on Manhattan met with success, but it was not a foregone conclusion from the beginning. Contemporaries were very much aware of the dangers that could bring ruin to a new, vulnerable settlement in its first years; failed harvests, extreme weather events, the interruption of supplies from Europe, and attacks by European competitors or hostile Indigenous peoples could wipe out the colonists completely. It would be months or years before news arrived back in Europe that an attempted colony had failed miserably.

In the years preceding the settling of Manhattan, news of deadly incidents in America had regularly reached Amsterdam. Such information permeated the decision-making processes. For instance, the death of skipper Hendrick Christiaensz and several of the crew members of the *Swarte Beer* near Governors Island in early 1619 reached Amsterdam later the same year. In April 1620, when the States General asked the Amsterdam Admiralty Board for advice, the fear of Indigenous attacks was a contributing factor in the decision to turn down the proposal to use the Leiden Brownists as colonists for their ventures along the Hudson River. The subsequent travails of the Pilgrims, including the death of half of their group

---

17. Nat. Arch., OWIC, inv. Nr. 20, fol. 27 (December 21, 1626): "Is goetgevonden het jacht out Vlissinghe toe te maken naer Angola om eenighe swarten aldaer tehandelen ende die te brenghen inde Amazones ofte op zoodanige plaetse daer de Comp. haer volck zoude mogen hebben leggen." A. J. F. van Laer, trans. and ed., *Documents Relating to New Netherland, 1624–1626, in the Henry E. Huntington Library* (San Marino: Henry E. Huntington Library and Art Gallery, 1924), 22–31: "ende versoucke ook liever swarte dan Nederlanders, want de swarte meer tot den arbeyt genegen sijn dan de Nederlanders." See also Hulsman, *Nederlands Amazonia*, 101–6; Den Heijer, *Nederlands slavernijverleden*, 35; Michiel van Groesen, *Imagining the Americas in Print: Books, Maps, and Encounters in the Atlantic World* (Leiden: Brill, 2019), 156; Postma, *The Dutch in the Atlantic Slave Trade*, 10–18.

over the winter, were communicated to those who had remained in Leiden and reached the ears of WIC director Johannes de Laet. Likewise, news of the attack by Native Americans on Virginia in March 1622 soon became known in Leiden and Amsterdam.[18]

Despite these incidents, the WIC in late 1623 decided to send a number of Walloon families to New Netherland. In order to expand the Dutch territorial claim vis-à-vis the English, the colonists were distributed across four sites, including Governors Island and Fort Orange, on the upper reaches of the Hudson River. The group that had settled on Governors Island received the order to relocate to the southern tip of Manhattan, which they obeyed in 1625, or more likely, or in the following year. Yet in 1626, an incident occurred at Fort Orange, resulting in the death of Daniel van Krieckenbeek and a small number of soldiers. The colonial authorities quickly decided to concentrate all colonists on Manhattan in order to reduce their vulnerability as well as to enhance their defense. News of the precarious state of New Netherland reached the Dutch Republic when the ship *Meeuwken* returned to Amsterdam in the course of 1626. There was a sigh of relief when in November the latest news from New Amsterdam arrived: the people were safe, children had been born, the harvest was good, a number of peltries had been shipped over, and the island of Manhattan had been acquired. As the news arrived in November, during the general meeting of the WIC, held in Amsterdam, one of the representatives of the States General quickly sent a letter to inform his colleagues in The Hague. Its writer was the Alkmaar burgomaster and member of the States General Committee on West Indian affairs, Pieter Jansz Schagen, and the letter named after him is often called the "birth certificate" of New York City, as it contains a reference to the "purchase," as Schagen put it, of Manhattan. Yet within the context of contemporary events, the news that New Netherland and its people were safe was much more important. Ironically the birth certificate served as a crucial link in the chain of events that led to the introduction of slavery on Manhattan.[19]

By November 1626, after a nervous few months, the WIC authorities in the Dutch Republic knew that the future of New Amsterdam was secure, at least in the short term. The danger of the outbreak of hostilities with the Native Americans receded. Now the colony could be strengthened. As we have seen, at about the same time, the WIC had made the

---

18. Jaap Jacobs, *The Colony of New Netherland: A Dutch Settlement in Seventeenth-Century America* (Ithaca, N.Y.: Cornell University Press, 2009), 28–31; Nat. Arch., SG, inv. nr. 3179, fol. 45; inv. nr. 3181, fol. 91 and 150; inv. nr. 5484; J. G. Smit and J. Roelevink, eds., *Resolutiën der Staten-Generaal, Nieuwe Reeks, 1610–1670, vierde deel, 1619–1620* ('s-Gravenhage: Martinus Nijhoff, 1983), no. 2655; Johannes de Laet, *Nieuvve wereldt: Ofte Beschrijvinghe van West-Indien wt veelderhande schriften ende aen-teeckeninghen van verscheyden natien by een versamelt* (Leiden: Elzevier, 1625), book 3, chs. 5, 6, 21; Alison Games, "Violence on the Fringes: The *Virginia* (1622) and *Amboyna* (1623) Massacres," *History* 99, no. 3 (July 2014): 505–29, herein 525.
19. Jaap Jacobs, "'Discoverers and First Finders': Anglo-Dutch Rivalry in Early Seventeenth-Century North America," forthcoming; Charles T. Gehring, "New Netherland: The Formative Years, 1609–1632," in Van Minnen et al., *Four Centuries of Dutch-American Relations*, 74–84; Jacobs, *The Colony of New Netherland*, 28–31.

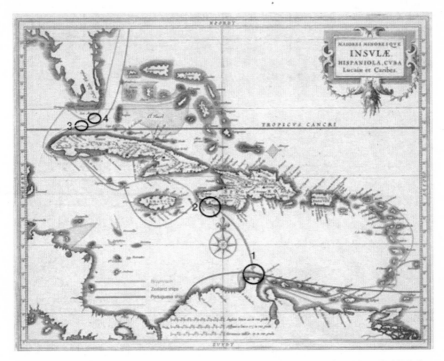

Figure 2. Map of the Caribbean, ca. 1640. "Maiores minoresque Insulæ. Hispaniola, Cuba, Lucaiæ et Caribes," from Jean de Laet, *L'Histoire du Nouveau Monde ou description des Indes Occidentales* (Leyde: Chez Bonaventure and Abraham Elseviers, 1640). The routes of Dutch, Portuguese, and Spanish ships in 1627 are indicated by colored lines. The black circles indicate the locations of (1) the capture of the Portuguese ship en route from São Tomé to (presumably) Cartagena; (2) the roadsteads at Île-à-Vache, where the captured Africans were transferred to the *Bruynvisch*; (3) the battle between the Zeeland flotilla and the two Spanish galleons arriving from Trujillo in Honduras; and (4) the area where the *Bruynvisch* and the *Vlieghenden Draeck* lost contact.

decision to use the labor of enslaved Africans captured from Iberian ships in its colonies and had started including it as an option in the extensive instructions to its officials. Up to 1626, New Netherland, located at the far end of the standard shipping routes, had not been a potential destination for enslaved labor. But by early 1627 it was. All that was now required was for motive and means to come together with opportunity. This happened in 1627 during the voyage of the Amsterdam yacht *Bruynvisch*.

The Voyage of the *Bruynvisch*

The 1627 voyages of the *Bruynvisch* and the other ships in its fleet highlight many of the standard operating procedures used by the Dutch West India Company in its privateering campaigns of the 1620s.[20] In late 1626 and early 1627, the Zeeland chamber and the Amsterdam chamber prepared to send out several ships. The Zeeland chamber equipped three ships, the *Ter Veere*, skippered by admiral Hendrick Jacobsz Lucifer; the *Leeuwinne*, under vice admiral Jan Pietersz; and the yacht *Vlieghenden Draeck*, captained by Galeyn van Stapels. The first task of this flotilla was to transport a group of colonists to the Oyapock River to renew attempts to start a colony there after earlier failures on the Amazon. They landed the group in March. The assistant commissary on the expedition, Marijn Adriaensz van Veere, did not stay on the Oyapoc but boarded the Zeeland ships when they departed for the Caribbean. The planned rendezvous with two Amsterdam yachts, the *Kater* and the *Bruynvisch*, eventually took place north of the Guajira Peninsula on the Venezuelan coast on May 4, 1627.[21]

---

20. The reconstruction of the 1627 voyages presented here required combining information from several sources, mainly De Laet's *Historie ofte Iaerlyck Verhael* but also several others not previously used in the historiography. The *Bruynvisch* is mentioned in Edna Green Medford, *The New York African Burial Ground History Final Report* (2004), 12, 32, https://core.tdar.org/document/4868 /new-york-african-burial-ground-history-final-report; Heywood and Thornton, *Central Africans*, 36–37; Heywood and Thornton, "Intercultural Relations," 196; Faucquez, *De la Nouvelle-Néerlande à New York*, 62–63; Van den Hout, "Voyages of New Netherland," no. v_047. Medford as well as Heywood and Thornton mention the 1627 voyage but do not rule out an earlier arrival, without providing solid corroboration. In contrast to what is asserted in some of the literature, the 1627 voyage was the only time that the yacht *Bruynvisch* stopped at New Amsterdam. See I. N. Phelps Stokes, *The Iconography of Manhattan Island 1498–1909*, 6 vols. (New York: Robert H. Dodd, 1915–28), 4:944; followed by Swan, "First Africans," 82; Medford, *The New York African Burial Ground*, 13; Heywood and Thornton, *Central Africans*, 41; and the Intra-American Slave Trade Database (Voyage ID 107994), accessed October 13, 2022, https://www.slavevoyages.org /american/database, for the suggestion that the *Bruynvisch* arrived in New Amsterdam in 1630 with a cargo of enslaved Africans destined for New Jersey. This is based on a mistaken identification of Michiel Pauw's patroonship named *Pavonia*. There were two patroonships with this name, one in New Jersey and the other on Fernão de Noronho. In 1630, the *Bruynvisch* sailed to the latter. See Nat. Arch, OWIC, inv. Nr. 49, doc. 24 (September 25, 1630); A. J. F. van Laer, trans. and ed., *Van Rensselaer Bowier Manuscripts, being the Letters of Kiliaen van Rensselaer, 1630–1643, and Other Documents Relating to the Colony of Rensselaerswyck* (Albany: University of the State of New York, 1908), 155; S. P. l'Honoré Naber, ed., *Reisebeschreibungen von Deutschen Beamten und Kriegsleuten im Dienst der Niederländischen West- und Ost. Indischen Kompagnien 1602 – 1797*, 13 vols. (Den Haag: Nijhoff, 1930–1932), 1: 63: "Den 10. [August 10, 1630] hat der Hr. Admiral, die Jacht den Braunfisch, von hier nacher der Insul de Vernando gesandt, darauff etliche Morianen gesetzt worden, welche neben den Holländischen Völckern, so daselbsten ligen vnd zwey Stuck Geschütz bey sich hatten, das Land sollen bawen helffen." See Klooster, "Het begin van de Nederlandse slavenhandel," 250, 259n8; De Laet, *Historie ofte Iaerlyck Verhael*, 198, 228–29.

21. For Marijn Adriaensz, see Book of "commissions, instructions and conditions for colonists," 1626–71, conditions for the colonists destined for the Oyapoc River, with list of signatories, January 6, 1627, Nat. Arch., OWIC, inv. nr. 42, p. 18; P. M. Netscher, *Geschiedenis van de koloniën Essequebo, Demerary en Berbice* ('s-Gravenhage: Martinus Nijhoff, 1888), 54; Nat. Arch., OWIC, inv. Nr. 20, fol. 61v (December 9, 1627); and Arnold J. F. van Laer, trans. and ed., *Register of the Provincial Secretary, 1638–1642* (Baltimore: Genealogical Publishing Co., 1974), 101–2. For the most recent treatment of Dutch attempts to found colonies on the Amazon and adjacent rivers, see Hulsman, *Nederlands Amazonia*. For the rendez-vous, see De Laet, *Historie ofte Iaerlyck Verhael*, 111–20. See also Goslinga, *The Dutch in the Caribbean*; and Nicolaes van Wassenaer, *Historisch*

The *Bruynvisch* was a yacht of sixty lasts, nine guns, and a crew of thirty-seven, commanded by captain Jan Reyersz Swart. It had sailed from Texel on January 4, 1627, in the company of two other yachts, the *Kater* and the *Otter*. On the journey south, the *Bruynvisch* and the *Kater* lost contact with the *Otter*, which proceeded on to Pernambuco and out of this story. The *Bruynvisch* and the *Kater* then joined up with the Zeeland ships off the Guajira Peninsula. The Zeeland ships had been instructed to cruise between the Cabo de la Vela and the Cabo de Coquibocoa (the western and eastern points of the Guajira Peninsula). After a conference had taken place, the Amsterdam yachts decided to sail westward to cruise between the Cabo de la Vela and Santa Martha, about two hundred kilometers west. The Zeeland and Amsterdam ships planned to meet again four weeks later at Cabo de la Vela. Over the following days, the Amsterdam ships sailed along the coast, spotting the sails of what they presumed were pearl fishers' boats, passing the village of Riohacha, and scouting out a potential landing place outside of the range of the fort. Subsequently they turned back to Cabo de la Vela and met up with the Zeeland ships. As Johannes de Laet informs us: "These had in the meantime captured a Portuguese ship, coming from São Tomé with 225 Blacks, and as the ship was very leaky and they did not know what to do with the Blacks, they took only twenty-two of the healthiest Blacks and what else they could use, and let the ship with the others sail on."[22]

The aim of taking "only twenty-two of the healthiest Blacks" was to provide the Oyapoc colony with enslaved labor. So, the Dutch ships tried to sail east; but after ten days of tacking against the strong Caribbean current, they had not progressed farther than Cabo Coquibocoa. Therefore, the fleet decided to cross over to Hispaniola to prepare for the next phase in the plan outlined in their instructions: attacking richly laden Spanish ships on route from Honduras or Mexico to Europe through the Straits of Florida, between the Florida Keys and Cuba. By 1627, previous years of privateering had supplied the Dutch with good intelligence as to the routes and seasons best suited to intercept such transports. The two large Zeeland ships were better equipped to engage large Spanish galleons than the smaller yachts, which were mostly used for reconnoitering, communications, and capturing small enemy ships. In the case of a major sea battle, the presence of captives would be a hindrance to the two large

---

verhael alder ghedenck-weerdichste geschiedenisse, die hier en daer in Europa, als in Duijtsch-lant, Vranckrijck, Enghelant, Spaengien, Hungarijen, Polen, Sevenberghen, Wallachien, Moldavien, Turckijen en Neder-Lant, van den beginne des jaers 1621 . . . tot octobri, des jaers 1632, voorgevallen syn, 21 vols. (Amstelredam: Ian Evertss Cloppenburgh en Jan Janssen, 1622–35), vol. 13, July 1627, fol. 60v–62. Van Wassenaer mentions the *Bruynvisch* but does not include events prior to the rendezvous at Cabo de Corrientes and the battle with the two Honduras ships. Instead, he focuses on the aftermath. Admiral Pieter Ghysen received a golden chain worth three hundred guilders in the plenary meeting of the West India Company. The crews of the victorious ships received thirteen months salary as bonus. The crews of the yachts *Bruynvisch* and the *Vlieghenden Draeck* which had split off from the main fleet well before the battle each received twelve months salary as bonus.
22. De Laet, *Historie ofte Iaerlyck Verhael*, 117: "de welcke ondertusschen ghenomen hadden een Portuges schip kommende van St Thome, met twee hondert ende vijf-en-twintich swarten, namen daer maer tween-en-twintich vande kloeckste swarten uyt ende wat haer voorts dienstich was, ende lieten het schip met de reste varen."

Zeeland ships and there would not be time to move them from one ship to another. And if a battle resulted in a rich booty, it would be imperative to leave the Caribbean waters as quickly as possible and return to the Dutch Republic, leaving little opportunity to offload the enslaved "cargo." During their eleven days' stay at the roadsteads between Île-à-Vache and Hispaniola—a long time to stay in one location during operations in enemy waters—the ships took on fresh water and prepared for what was to come. The long stay gave the captains time to discuss plans and transfer cargo and people from one ship to another. At least one crew member of the Zeeland ships, Marijn Adriaensz van Veere, transferred with the twenty-two African captives to the yacht *Bruynvisch*, one of the smallest ships in the fleet. Moving the enslaved Africans from the Zeeland ships to an Amsterdam yacht indicates that the decision had been made to send them to New Netherland, a colony supervised by the Amsterdam chamber, rather than to the colony on the Oyapoc, run by the Zeeland chamber. The role of Marijn Adriaensz was to act as a supercargo and to supervise the transferal of the "prize cargo" captured by Zeeland ships to Company servants belonging to the Amsterdam chamber. It is likely that the small *Bruynvisch*, of only sixty lasts and with a crew originally of just thirty-seven, also received additional supplies to feed the extra mouths.[23]

Sailing on westward, the ships anchored at Cabo Corrientes on the south coast of Cuba. Subsequently two of the Zeeland ships and the Amsterdam yacht *Kater* sailed to Cabo San Antonio, the western-most point of Cuba, leaving the two yachts, *Bruynvisch* and *Vlieghende Draeck*, behind at Cabo Corrientes. This was part of a preconceived tactical plan, which involved the major ships laying in wait north of Havana and the two yachts acting as scouts to cover the Florida Straits. Their task would be to alert the main force when an important target was sighted. Yet proceedings did not go according to plan. The Zeeland ships rounded Cabo San Antonio and cruised in the waters west of Havana. On the morning of July 8, they spotted two large Spanish ships to the south and prepared to engage. A fierce and bloody battle ensued, in which one of the Spanish ships, the *San Antonio*, was captured. Taking their Spanish prize north to the passage east of Florida—the agreed-upon place of rendezvous—the victors transferred its rich cargo of 1,404 chests with indigo, 4,280 hides, and 32 vessels of balm oil to their own ships. They sent the surviving Spaniards south to Havana with a frigate captured earlier. Keen to avoid Spanish counterattacks, the Zeeland ships then quickly sailed for home, arriving back on September 5, 1627.[24]

23. Nat. Arch., OWIC, inv. Nr. 20, fol. 61v (December 9, 1627): "Is goet gevonden aen de camer van Amstredam te schrijven om te weten de gel[eg]entheyt van Marijnus Adriaenss uuijtgevaren met schip Veere ende met jacht den bruijnvisch in nieu nederlant aen landt gelaten."
24. See also Goslinga, *The Dutch in the Caribbean*, 170–72; N. Stellingwerff and S. Schot, *Particuliere notulen van de vergaderingen der Staten van Holland 1620–1640 door N. Stellingwerff en S. Schot*, Vol. 3: *July 1625–April 1628*, ed. J. W. Veenendaal-Barth ('s-Gravenhage: Instituut voor Nederlandse Geschiedenis, 1992), 401. On the Spanish reaction to this battle, see Irene A Wright, ed., *Nederlandsche zeevaarders op de eilanden in de Caraïbische Zee en aan de kust van Columbia en Venezuela gedurende de jaren 1621–1648(9): Documenten hoofdzakelijk uit het Archivo General de Indias te Sevilla* 2 vols (Utrecht: Kemink, 1934), 1:170–73.

Meanwhile, the Amsterdam yacht *Bruynvisch* and the Zeeland yacht *Vlieghenden Draeck* had stayed on at Cabo Corrientes on the south side of Cuba and remained unaware for several weeks of the great victory that their compatriots had achieved north of Cuba. Departing from Cabo Corrientes and rounding the western point of Cuba, the two ships arrived off Havana on July 28 and spotted three Spanish galleons and a smaller ship. Clearly, capturing a galleon was beyond their powers. The captains of the two Dutch yachts agreed to proceed farther south, probably to keep an eye on the Spanish ships with the intention of alerting the larger Zeeland ships which, unbeknownst to them, were by this time well on their way back to Europe. During the night, the yachts lost contact with each other. Thereupon the *Bruynvisch* turned north and sailed to the agreed-upon point of rendezvous off the Florida coast. But the *Vlieghenden Draeck* did not turn up and, after some days, captain Jan Reyersz Swart decided that he could not hang around any longer.[25] The only option left to him was to sail to New Amsterdam and deliver his "cargo." Johannes de Laet informs us of the subsequent route of the *Bruynvisch*: "Finally, this yacht sailed along the coast of Florida to New Netherland and anchored in the mouth of the North River on the 29th of August. Departing from there on the last of September, it returned to Texel on the 25th of October."[26]

Conclusion

The first group of Black Africans arrived at Manhattan with the *Bruynvisch* on August 29, 1627. The historical context, consisting of shipping patterns, privateering practices, the decision-making process of the WIC, and the development of New Netherland in its earliest years, rules out an arrival in 1624–26, as previously presumed. An arrival in 1627 dovetails with the decision of the WIC in late 1626 to become actively involved in the slave trade. The *Bruynvisch* is the only known ship that both had access to enslaved people through its collaboration with the Zeeland ships and also arrived in New Netherland. In addition, both the origin and number of the African Blacks are consistent with later sources, including the 1644 document granting conditional freedom.

The importance of establishing that the first arrival took place on August 29, 1627, is not just that it provides a firm date and dispels the vagueness that has surrounded the start of slavery in New York. It also allows us to define the role of enslaved labor in the initial phase of the colonization of New Netherland. By the time that the first enslaved Africans

---

25. Stadsarchief Amsterdam, Notarial Archives (5075), inv. nr. 441, fol. 267 (December 15, 1627).
26. De Laet, *Historie ofte Iaerlyck Verhael*, 119: "Eyndelijck soo zeylden dese Jacht langhs de Custe van Florida naer Nieuw-Nederlandt, ende anckerde inde mondt van de Noordt-Rievier den neghen-en-twintighsten Augusti; ende den lesten September weder van daer ghescheyden zijnde, keerde den vijf-en-twintighsten October in Texel." The twentieth-century edition of De Laet contains an unfortunate typo: 20 instead of 29. Johannes De Laet, *Iaerlyck Verhael van de verrichtingen der Geoctroyeerde West-Indische Compagnie (1644)*, ed. S. P. l'Honoré Naber and J. C. M. Warnsinck, 4 vols. ('s-Gravenhage: Martinus Nijhoff, 1931–1937), 2:30.

arrived, New Netherland had weathered its first precarious years and had achieved the stability that allowed it to expand further, at least for the time being. Although slavery was not a feature of New Netherland from its inception, the enslaved labor that the first African Americans provided would nevertheless play an important role in the colony's development into the 1630s and 1640s. And their role became more important in the 1650s and 1660s, when slave imports directly from Africa increased their numbers even further.

Of course, the story of the first arrival as presented here corroborates many of the features of slavery in New Amsterdam and New Netherland that have long been a staple of the colony's historiography: the geographic origin of the first arrivals, their capture on board of a Portuguese ship, and the corporate nature of enslavement, by the Dutch West India Company. As the first arrivals constituted a legitimate capture of enemy property during wartime, their labor could be used, but they could not be transferred to another owner. In a legal sense, this set them apart from most of the later arrivals. Beyond New Netherland, the story is also of importance to the development of the Dutch West India Company as a slave trader and owner. The capture of the twenty-two enslaved Africans by Zeeland ships off the Venezuelan coast is the first time that enslaved people were taken with the intent to use their forced labor in a Dutch colony. The destination of choice was the Oyapoc River, but when this turned out to be impossible, New Amsterdam was chosen instead. While the destination changed, the intention to enslave remained the same. All in all, the voyage of the *Bruynvisch* was the first slaving voyage of the WIC, in this case confined to an Intra-American trip. For all practical purposes, the WIC's activity as a slave-holding institution started when the *Bruynvisch* arrived off Manhattan in 1627, not when the Company was founded in 1621.

As is so often the case, the few extant sources shed almost no light on the lived experience of the group. Presumably enslaved in Central Africa, most likely in Angola, the Africans probably left through Luanda and must have spend several weeks at sea after making a stop at São Tomé, possibly in March. The ship's intended destination may have been Cartagena, a usual destination for Portuguese ships taking enslaved Africans to Spanish colonies. While its capture off the coast of Venezuela in early May does not appear to have been accompanied by much fighting, it is likely that the Africans below deck experienced the boarding of the ship only through the sounds coming from above. It must have been harrowing. The subsequent transportation of the selected twenty-two on sloops to another ship cannot have eased their anxiety. And they had to endure a similar operation about four weeks later, when the Dutch ships stayed at the roadsteads at Île-à-Vache. On board the *Bruynvisch,* their ordeal continued for many weeks. It was not until late August, after an estimated total of five months at sea, that the group of captives finally reached Manhattan. Many of them very likely spent the rest of their lives there.

In his conclusion, Swan posited that it was "moot to debate whether Africans arrived in New Netherland in 1625, 1626, 1628, or 1630," as it did not mitigate "the harsh reality of slavery."[27] Clearly it does not. Yet, as the 1619 Project and numerous other anniversaries have shown, exact years and dates of historical events have a powerful effect on the public's perception of history. Establishing that the first enslaved Africans arrived on the *Bruynvisch* allows us to pinpoint exactly when the institution of slavery was introduced into New Amsterdam and New Netherland and thus into what later became New York City and State. It is also the first occasion of a Dutch ship with enslaved Africans arriving in a Dutch colony in the Americas. Whether and in what way August 29, 1627, should be remembered or commemorated is beyond the purview of historical scholarship, but those to whom this history has significance—in New York as well as in the Netherlands—may find appropriate ways to do so.

---

27. Swan, "First Africans," 82.

Community-Building in the History and Memory of Slavery in Dutch New York

Anne-Claire Faucquez

Looking at slavery from the perspective of the community breaks the representation of the enslaved as victims of a harsh system. Northern slavery especially has traditionally been depicted as a world in which the enslaved were totally isolated, rarely being more than two or three per household, with limited possibilities of contact with other individuals of the same culture.[1] Focusing on the community thus immediately restores enslaved people's humanity and agency. One can see them as a group in which they are unfortunately seen as anonymous, except for those individuals who occasionally stand out in archival records, but in which they are willing to associate themselves and interact with one another. They can find comfort and relief despite their predicament. The existence of slave communities has been recognized since the 1970s and the publication of John Blassingame's *The Slave Community: Plantation Life in the Antebellum South* (1979) in which he advanced that the enslaved were able to maintain cultural traditions and used them as a form of passive resistance to slavery.[2] As Dylan Penningroth puts it, "Slave communities and families were tough, resilient havens that helped Black people survive the oppression of slavery and Reconstruction."[3] If the concept has widely been studied for the Southern region, where enslaved people lived on plantations and were necessarily brought together, communities in the North

---

1. For such conclusions on Northern slavery see Melville Herskovits, *The Myth of the Negro Past* (New York: Harper and Brothers, 1941), 123; John F. Watson, *Annals and Occurrences of New York City and State, in the Olden Time: Being a Collection of Memoirs, Anecdotes, and Incidents Concerning the City, Country, and Inhabitants, from the Days of the Founders . . . Embellished with Pictorial Illustrations* (Philadelphia: H. F. Anners, 1846), 18.
2. See also George P. Rawick, *From Sundown to Sunup: The Making of the Black Community* (Westport, Conn.: Greenwood, 1972); and Charles W. Joyner, *Down by the Riverside: A South Carolina Slave Community* (Urbana: University of Illinois Press, 1984). The concept of community was also developed about enslaved people's religion in Albert J. Raboteau, *Slave Religion: The "Invisible Institution" in the Antebellum South* (New York : New York University Press 1978; Oxford: Oxford University Press, 2004).
3. Dylan Penningroth, "My People, My People: The Dynamics of Community on Southern Slavery," in *New Studies in the History of American Slavery*, ed. Edward E. Baptist, Stephanie M. H. Camp (Athens: University of Georgia Press, 2006), 166.

have widely been ignored in favor of studies on free Black citizens. Gary Nash, for instance, made a compelling study of the community of free Black people in Philadelphia who were able to build social institutions such as charity organizations, churches, and schools to help free African Americans to assert themselves as citizens. The community was seen not only as "a geographic clustering" but as "a community of feeling and consciousness."[4] Graham Russell Hodges extended the work on enslaved communities to the populations in New York and New Jersey. Having been partly emancipated by the Dutch West India Company, the first generation of Africans in New Amsterdam were able to create a "community based on personal freedom, land ownership, religion and local institutions."[5]

We intend here to broaden the study of the efforts made by Africans, both free and enslaved, at building a community in Dutch New York. To understand the concept of community, we will follow the definition given by the *Encyclopedia of Race, Ethnicity, and Society* used in the contemporary concept of "community empowerment." The community can refer to a "geographic community," a "community of common interests," or a "community of ascribed characteristics."[6] Indeed, the African community in Dutch New York was geographically delimited to the Southern tip of the island of Manhattan and displayed common characteristics, as most were Atlantic Creoles who came from regions under Iberian influence; shared common Yoruba, Akan, and Kongo cultures; and demonstrated common interests in fashioning kinship and friendship ties to alleviate their daily suffering.[7] This community will have to be looked at not as "a fixed entity, but a dynamic process," as Leslie Harris puts it. It was a group in which individuals constantly adapted "to the exigencies of the times and the needs of the people involved."[8]

This article will thus consider the way the building of a community was both a survival strategy during the times of slavery and a mode of action that was used by African-descended people to have the New York African Burial Ground recognized as a site of memory in the 1990s. I will try to show how history and memory are brought together

---

4. Gary B. Nash, *Forging Freedom: The Formation of Philadelphia's Black Community, 1720–1840* (Cambridge, Mass: Harvard University Press, 1988), 7. See also Harry Reed, *Platform for Change: The Foundations of the Northern Free Black Community, 1775–1865* (East Lansing: Michigan State University Press, 1994); James, O. Horton, *Free People of Color, Inside the African American Community* (Washington, D.C.: Smithsonian Institution Press, 1993); James O. and Lois E. Horton, *In Hope of Liberty, Culture, Community, and Protest Among Northern Free Blacks, 1700–1860* (New York: Oxford University Press, 1997).
5. Graham Russell Hodges, *Root and Branch: African Americans in New York and East Jersey, 1613–1863* (Chapel Hill: University of North Carolina Press, 1999), 12.
6. Richard T. Schaefer, ed., *Encyclopedia of Race, Ethnicity, and Society*, 3 vols. (Los Angeles: Sage Publications, 2008), 1:326; Raphael Lambert, *Narrating the Slave Trade, Theorizing Community* (Leiden; Boston: Brill Rodopi, 2019), describes the notion of "all in the same boat," analyzing fiction about the slave trade through the lens of community.
7. Ira Berlin, *Generations of Captivity: A History of African–American Slaves* (Cambridge, Mass.: Belknap Press of Harvard University Press, 2003), 6.
8. Leslie Harris, *In the Shadow of Slavery: African-Americans in New York City, 1626–1863* (Chicago: University of Chicago Press, 2003), 8–9.

around the notion of community. How does the idea of community connect both past and present generations in the way they define themselves and try to fight for social and political inclusion? If the creation of a community has long been seen as a way for enslaved people to gain a sense of identity, it also highlights their will to be part of a larger group. As Rodolfo Rosales puts it in *Community as the Material Basis of Citizenship* (2019), based on Tocqueville's conception of associations as the basis of democracy, the community is the locus of social participation where one expresses one's rights as a citizen.[9] For Kathleen Wilson, in *A New Imperial History: Culture, Identity and Modernity in Britain and the Empire 1669–1840* (2004), African Americans would "publicly mimic the behaviors of citizenry 'in the public spheres of association.'"[10] It was via the community or the group that they could assert themselves politically, forming what Ana Lucia Araujo calls a public memory, which is when collective memory "is transformed into a political instrument to build, assert, and reinforce identities."[11]

Starting with the Dutch period (1626–64), I will look at the specificity of this small and concentrated enslaved population, to understand how they built a community through land ownership to compensate the lack of families and how they used the church and baptism to expand kinship networks beyond blood ties. This Black community also found expression in the funerary rites practiced around the burial ground. These rites that were forged around common cultural traits fashioned both by their African ancestries and the many European influences they encountered created an African American identity. Finally, this community feeling that had emerged in colonial America reappeared when the New York African Burial Ground was rediscovered in 1991. The decade-long fight led by the African-descended people to have the site recognized and memorialized brought a community together and helped refashion what French sociologist Maurice Halbwachs has defined as "collective memory": the construction of a social group's identity—be it a small cohesive unit or an Andersonian "imagined community"—with narratives and traditions that give its members a sense of community.[12] Through this collective action, turning collective memory into public memory, this heterogeneous group fashioned a new, imagined, "African" identity that traced its supposed lineage to the ancestral remains that were buried in the ground. This is indeed this African identity that is memorialized in the heritage site composed of the African Burial Ground Monument and interpretive center.

---

9. Rodolfo Rosales, *Community as the Material Basis of Citizenship* (New York: Routledge, 2018).
10. Quoted in Helena Woodard, *Slave Sites on Display: Reflecting Slavery's Legacy through Contemporary "Flash" Moments* (Jackson: University Press of Mississippi), 9.
11. Ana Lucia Araujo, *Politics of Memory: Making Slavery Visible in the Public Space* (New York: Routledge, 2012), 1; Ana Lucia Araujo, *Slavery in the Age of Memory: Engaging the Past* (London: Bloomsbury Academic, 2021), 69.
12. Maurice Halbwachs, *Collective Memory* (New York: Harper and Row, 1980); Benedict Anderson, *Imagined Communities: Reflections on the Origin and Spread of Nationalism*, (London: Verso, 1983).

Community-Building in Dutch New York

A Small and Concentrated Enslaved Population

Two years after its foundation in 1624, New Amsterdam welcomed a small group of eleven enslaved African men, followed two years later by three women "for the comfort of the Company's Negro men."[13] As early as 1640, about one hundred Black people made up 16.7 percent of the village's population.[14] By the time of the English conquest in 1664, the Black population had tripled, reaching 375 individuals (300 enslaved and 75 free) out of 1,875 inhabitants, representing 20 percent of the total population and spread over about 39 slave-owners (12.5 percent of households).[15] This rate is far from negligible because the population of New Amsterdam was extremely small; the concentration of Black people thus seems all the more important.

The peculiarity of this first group of enslaved people lies in the fact that they belonged to the Dutch West India Company.[16] The Company housed, fed, and clothed them and even allotted them a 50-by-100-foot garden that they were allowed to cultivate when they were done with their daily chores.[17] Beginning in 1633, they were housed in the old Reformed Church that was located in a grain mill above which a large room had been built.[18] They were later accommodated outside the city in what became the *Out Ward*. This was a "Negro neighborhood" that was located on the eastern shore of Manhattan Island, near the present 77th Street, and it was called "'t Quartier van de swarten de Comp Slaven."[19]

On February 25, 1644, Governor Willem Kieft emancipated ten enslaved men (Paul Angola, Big Manuel, Manuel de Gerrit de Reus, Simon Congo, Anthony Portugis, Gracia, Pieter Santomee, Jan Fransisco, Little Anthony, and Jan Fort Orange) with their wives.[20]

---

13. Robert J. Swan, "First Africans into New Netherland, 1625 or 1626?," *de Halve Maen* 66, no. 4 (1993): 79.
14. Robert J. Swan, "Slaves and Slaveholding in Dutch New York, 1628–1664," *Journal of the Afro-American Historical and Genealogical Society* 17 (1998): 63, 67.
15. Evarts B. Greene, Virginia D. Harrington, *American Population before the Federal Census of 1790* (New York: Columbia University Press, 1932), 92–93.
16. Anne-Claire Faucquez, "Corporate Slavery in New Netherland," *The Many Faces of Slavery. New Perspectives on Slave Ownership and Experiences in the Americas*, ed. in Lawrence Aje, Catherine Armstrong (London: Bloomsbury, 2019), 89–101.
17. Robert J. Swan, *New Amsterdam Gehenna: Segregated Death in New York City, 1630–1801* (Brooklyn, N.Y.: Noir Verite Press, 2006), 230; Phelps Stokes, *The Iconography of Manhattan Island, 1498–1909, Compiled from Original Sources and Illustrated by Photo-Intaglio Reproductions of Important Maps, Plans, Views, and Documents in Public and Private Collections*, 6 vols. (New York: Robert H. Dodd, 1915–1928), 2: plate 82, 297.
18. Swan, *New Amsterdam Gehenna*, 164; Stokes, *Iconography*, 4:96, 99; 2:97.
19. Stokes, *Iconography*, 1:76; 2:183; 4:88.
20. E. B. O'Callaghan, ed. and trans., *Documents Relative to the Colonial History of the State of New York*, 15 vols. (Albany: Weed, Parsons, 1865–1887), 1:425; Stokes, *Iconography*, 4:101; "Act of the Director and Council of New Netherland Emancipating Certain Negro the Enslaved Therein Mentioned" (February 25, 1644), in E. B. O'Callaghan, *Laws and Ordinances of New Netherland, 1638–1674* (Albany: Weed, Parsons, 1868), 36–37.

The Company thus allocated plots of cultivable land, of about 5 to 10 acres each, to these freed Africans.[21] These were concentrated around the Fresh Water Pond, or *Kolch*, west of the Bowery[22] (located in the current district of China Town) and were called "Negroes Land."[23] Between 1643 and 1664, twenty-eight Africans were emancipated and were offered parcels of land by governors Willem Kieft and Petrus Stuyvesant; all the parcels were located near the Bowery.[24] In 1659–60, when the colony feared a potential Native American attack, Stuyvesant relocated a group of Black farmers for safety. Nine of them received land along the Bowery Road, alongside the Director General's land.[25] In 1664, New Amsterdam had a population of 75 free Blacks and 300 enslaved Blacks out of a total of 1,500 inhabitants.[26] The Black community was thus reinforced through the process of land ownership. Even if owning land is an individual deed—the land is given to one individual—land ownership was experienced collectively as these emancipated Blacks people received their plots of land almost simultaneously and in the same geographic zone.

This geographical proximity facilitated the tying of bonds between the enslaved and free Black populations. Having worked together for the Company or on Petrus Stuyvesant's

---

21. Richard B. Dickenson, "Abstracts of Early Black Manhattanites," *New York Historical and Biographical Review* 116, no. 2 (April 1985): 101–4, 169–73.

22. Stokes, *Iconography*, 1:76; 4:97; 6:3–76, 123–24; Edmund Bailey O'Callaghan, *Calendar of Historical Manuscripts in the Office of the Secretary of State, Albany, N.Y., Part I Dutch Manuscripts, 1630–1664* (Albany, Weed, Parsons, 1865–66), 368, 369, 370, 372, 374. (Hereafter CHMD).

23. It is probable that the Black community had already settled in this area since 1639 because we learn from the sources that Thomas Valaren had been condemned for having deteriorated the houses of the Blacks (*Swarte huysen*) for which he had to pay twelve florins, Stokes, *Iconography*, vol.1, 76; vol. 4, 97; CHMD, 368, 369, 370, 372, 374. In 1696, Wolfert Webber owned a group of lands that he designated as the "farm of the Negroes" in his will dated April 15, 1715, Stokes, *Iconography*, 6:73–76.

24. The twenty-eight freed Blacks people were Catalina Anthony (Jochem's widow), on July 13, 1643; Domingo Anthony, on July 13, 1643; Cleijn Manuel, in December 1643; Manuel Gerrit de Reus, in December 1643; Manuel Trumpeter, on December 12, 1643; Marycke (Lawrence's widow), on December 12, 1643; Gracia d'Angola, on December 15, 1644; Simon Congo, on December 15, 1644; Jan Francisco, on December 15, 1644; Pieter Santomee, on December 15, 1644; Manuel Groot (Large Manual), on December 21, 1644; Klijn (Small) Anthony, on December 30, 1644; Paulo d'Angola, on December 30, 1644; Anthony Portuguese, on September 5, 1645; Anna d'Angola (Andries's widow), on February 8, 1647; Francisco d'Angola, on March 25, 1647; Anthony Congo, on March 26, 1647; Bastian Negro, on March 26, 1647; Jan Negro, on March 26, 1647; Manuel the Spanish, on January 18, 1651; Mathias Anthony, on December 1, 1655; Domingo Angola, on December 2, 1658; Claes Negro, on December 2, 1658; Assent Angola, on December 2, 1658; Francisco Cartagena, on December 2, 1658; Anthony du Bowery, in 1658; Anthony "the blind Negro," in 1658; and Manuel Sanders, in 1662. Stokes, *Iconography*, 6:123–24; Dickenson, "Abstracts of Early Black Manhattanites," 101–04, 169–73.

25. The nine Black farmers were Christoffel Santomean, Solomon Pieters, Francisco Cartagena, Assent, Willem Antonys, Groot Manuel, Manuel Sanders, Claes the Negro, and Pieter Tambour. Stokes, *Iconography*, 6:73–76, 123–24; New York Colonial Manuscripts, vol. 10, 329, New York State Archives, Albany.

26. Joyce D. Goodfriend, *Before the Melting Pot: Society and Culture in Colonial New York City, 1664–1730* (Princeton: N.J., Princeton University Press, 1992), 13.

farm, they had been able to keep their spirit of camaraderie after their emancipation.[27] Some Africans like Anthony Domingo, John Fortune, Emmanuel Pietersen, or Peter Porter even became slave-owners themselves after their own emancipation.[28] Even though surprising at first sight, this practice could be a way for free Black people to integrate into white society and to increase their personal wealth and status, or it could be a manifestation of what Carter Woodson has called "benevolent slavery," which is the redemption of family members, wives, children, godchildren, or mere acquaintances in order to give them better treatment and access to freedom.[29]

Andrea Mosterman highlights the many interactions enslaved and free persons could have in the public spaces in New Amsterdam, whether in taverns or at the market.[30] The market was indeed a key location in the life of the African community. Enslaved and free Black people mingled with Dutch, English and Native American people to trade, drink, and enjoy various games of skill.[31] According to Ira Berlin and Philip D. Morgan, the market functioned as a safety valve that was crucial to the physical and psychological survival of the Black community: "By producing food for themselves and for others, tending cash crops, raising livestock, manufacturing finished goods, marketing their own products, consuming and saving the proceeds, and bequeathing property to their descendants, enslaved people took control of a large part of their lives. In many ways, the independent economic endeavors offered a foundation for their domestic and community life, shaping the social structure of the slave society and providing a material basis for the slaves' distinctive culture."[32]

Community-Building to Compensate for the Lack of Families

The small size of New Amsterdam households and the fortuitous distribution of enslaved people among owners limited the possibility of enslaved people forming families in the traditional sense of the term (a couple with one or more children); this was the case, too, as Wilma Dunaway has shown, for small plantations in Virginia. In the same way, the imbalanced sex ratio in the New Amsterdam urban environment made it difficult for couples to form. According to Leslie Harris, between 1626 and 1664, "the sex ratio among slaves was 131 males to 100 females."[33] Moreover, enslaved people suffered from the lack of concern of their masters, who did not hesitate to sell them multiple times, or whenever they needed to. Director Gen-

---

27. Goodfriend, *Before the Melting Pot*, 120.
28. CHMD, 269.
29. Calvin Wilson, "Black Masters: A Side Light on Slavery" (1905) unpublished paper, quoted in Sherill D. Wilson, *New York City's African Slaveowners: A Social and Material Culture History* (New York: Garland Pub., 1994), 6, 10.
30. Andrea Mosterman, *Spaces of Enslavement: A History of Slavery and Resistance in Dutch New York* (Ithaca, N.Y.:, Cornell University Press, 2021), 37–38.
31. Hodges, *Root and Branch*, 15.
32. Ira Berlin, Philip D. Morgan, *The Slaves' Economy: Independent Production by Slaves in the Americas* (Portland, Or.: Frank Cass, 1991), 1.
33. Harris, *In the Shadow of Slavery*, 21.

eral Peter Stuyvesant mentioned in his correspondence a group of enslaved people who had within four years "two, three, or more times [been] re-sold and [had] changed masters."[34]

However, in spite of these strenuous circumstances, human bonding remained a natural reaction to enslavement, and community-building was a way to both compensate for the lack of family and adapt to a new environment.[35] According to the records of the Dutch Reformed Church of New Amsterdam, 27 Black couples got married between 1639 and 1664, out of 441 marriages (representing 2.8 percent% of the total number).[36] The first registered marriage took place in May 1641 between the widow Lucia of Angola (previously married to Laurens of Angola) and the widower Anthony van Angola (Klein or Little Antonio, also known as Anthony the Blind Negro), immediately after the death of his first wife, Catalina van Angola.[37] The presence of these widows and widowers from the early years of the colony confirms the fact that some marriages were celebrated before 1639. On February 26, 1642, Emmanuel van Angola married Phizithaen d'Angool, the widow of Leen Laurens. Ten days later, Francisco van Angola married Palassa van Angola, the widow of Francisco d'Angola. Finally, on September 28, 1642, Andries van Angola married Anna van Angola, the widow of Francisco van Capo Verde.[38] This "serial monogamy" can be seen as a form of African cultural retention, an adaptation of polygamous practices that Africans could no longer maintain once in the New World. Yet, it would be a mistake to see this practice as a single act of cultural resistance and to forget that it was, above all, a human reaction, a desire to recreate a family circle in this hostile and foreign environment. Historian Philip D. Morgan prefers to speak of it as "co-residential union" or "serial polyandry" rather than as widowhood or separation.[39]

Getting married could also be a way to be protected from potential separation. On October 4, 1659, Franciscus Neger and Catharina Negrinne, two enslaved people belonging to the same owner got married, recorded as "Slaven Van Cornelis de Potter" in the register, but this is the only case we have encountered.[40] In 1664, an enslaved couple working for the

---

34. Quoted in Harris, 21.
35. On the survival of the family among enslaved people, see Herbert Gutman, *The Black Family in Slavery and Freedom: 1750–1925* (New York: Pantheon Books, 1977); or Ann Patton Malone, *Sweet Chariot, Slave Family and Household Structure in Nineteenth-Century Louisiana*, (Chapel Hill: University of North Carolina Press, 1992). On the other hand, Brenda E. Stevenson, *Life in Black and White: Family and Community in the Slave South* (New York: Oxford University Press, 1996); and Wilma Dunaway, *The African-American Family in Slavery and Emancipation* (Cambridge: Cambridge University Press, 2003).
36. Samuel S. Purple, ed., *Collections of the New York Genealogical and Biographical Society*, vol. 1: *Records of the Reformed Dutch Church in New Amsterdam and New York: Marriages from 11 December, 1639, to 26 August, 1801*, (New York: New York Genealogical and Biographical society, 1890), 33–130 (hereafter RRDC, Marriages).
37. Stokes, *Iconography*, 4:93.
38. RRDC, Marriages, 1:32.
39. Philip D. Morgan, *Slave Counterpoint: Black Culture in the Eighteenth-Century Chesapeake and Low Country* (Chapel Hill, University of North Carolina Press, 1998), 499.
40. RRDC, Marriages, 1:24.

Company asked Director General Petrus Stuyvesant to intervene to prevent the husband from being sold to Jeremias Van Rensselaer. Stuyvesant managed to convince Rensselaer to buy the couple and not only the man.[41] On February 9, 1664, Christina Emanuels and Swan van Loange were able to marry in the Dutch Reformed Church because Christina had been emancipated. A few months earlier, on December 6, 1663, the free Black man Domingo Angola, applied to the Company to free Christina because she had been baptized. The Company accepted, but only on the condition that it obtained either another enslaved worker or the sum of 300 florins. The owner of Swan, Govert Loockermans, a wealthy merchant of the city, agreed to pay to emancipate Christina and allow their marriage.[42]

Enslaved people also acted as surrogate parents, taking care of children, or assisting the elderly as if they were their parents or grandparents, respectively. Ties of fraternity and solidarity developed to make daily life more bearable. Community-building was also reinforced via the church and the practice of baptism. The children of enslaved people held by the members of the Dutch Reformed Church of New Amsterdam were baptized as early as 1639, even if no Black people were members of the church. Between 1639 and 1656, 61 Black children were baptized out of 879 children.[43] African parents may have wanted to baptize their children in the hope this might secure them emancipation which was not restricted until the passage of the 1706 law[44], or because they themselves had married in church and wished to include their children in the Christian community, either for religious or social reasons. The importance of the family unit is emphasized in the baptismal records in which children are systematically listed with their parents and not as the property of the master. Fathers played a dominant role, and only their names appeared in the registers (except for two women). This may be explained by the fact that men were considered heads of the family or perhaps because they were emancipated or semi-emancipated while their wives were enslaved. Mothers were sometimes listed as godparents.[45]

---

41. Jeremias Van Rensselaer, *Correspondence of Jeremias Van Rensselaer, 1651–1674* (Albany: University of the State of New York, 1932), 364–65.

42. Henry B. Hoff, "Swan Janse van Luane: A Free Black in 17th Century Kings County," *New York Genealogical and Biographical Record*, no. 125 (1994): 74–77.

43. *Collections of the New York Genealogical and Biographical Society*, vol. 2: *Baptisms from 1639 to 1730 in the Reformed Dutch Church, New York*, ed. Thomas Grier Evans (New York: New York Genealogical and Biographical Society, 1901), 10–39 (hereafter RRDC, Baptisms). The figures vary from Jaap Jacobs who counted fifty-six children from mixed marriages, Joyce Goodfriend who found at least sixty-one, and Peter C. Christoph who found fifty-eight. See Jaap Jacobs, *The Colony of New Netherland: A Dutch Settlement in Seventeenth-Century America* (Ithaca, N.Y.: Cornell University Press, 2009), 282n81; J. Goodfriend, "Black Families in New Netherland," in *A Beautiful and Fruitful Place*, ed Nancy McClure Zeller (Albany: New Netherland Project, 1991), 151; Peter C. Christoph, "The Freedmen of New Amsterdam," *Journal of the Afro-American Historical and Genealogical Society* 3–4 (1984): 60. Robert J. Swan states that between 1639 and 1646, 77 slaves (32 men, 19 women and 26 children) were baptized. Robert Swan, "Slaves and Slaveholding in Dutch New York," 46–81.

44. *Colonial Laws of New York*, vol.1, 597-98.

45. Anne-Claire Faucquez, *De la Nouvelle-Néerlande à New York: la naissance d'une société esclavagiste 1624–1664* (Paris: Les Indes savantes, 2021), 306–11.

The role of godparents was central to strengthening community ties. Bastiaen, or Sebastiaen, the Black overseer, was chosen three times as a witness. Peter St. Anthony had Barent Jan baptized on October 2, 1639, and took Dominico Anthony, Jan Francoys, Trijntje van Camp, and Susanna of Angola as witnesses. Trijntie Jans (van Camp) and Susanna van Angola were probably midwives as they often appear as witnesses at baptisms (even once for a white child, Jan Suyderken Gerrit's son).[46]

The study of the second- and third-generation baptisms proves how entrenched the Black community was under English rule. Among the first enslaved Africans to arrive in New Amsterdam was Pieter Tamboer (also called Pieter van Campen) who, on June 21, 1665, became godfather to the grandson of Pieter Santomee, who had also landed in the 1630s and was emancipated by the Company in 1644. It was no doubt out of friendship that he accepted this role of "spiritual father" for the grandson of his old friend. He was also godfather to the grandson of Emmanuel van Angola in 1683.[47] On August 14, 1667, Manuel Sanders was godfather to Isabel, the daughter of François d'Angola and Barbara Manuels.[48] Thus, by participating in the baptisms of the second and third generations of Africans, Pieter Trompetter and Manuel Sanders guaranteed the cohesion of the African community in New York.

Members of the African community also understood that colonial authorities were willing to release orphaned enslaved children if they agreed to take on the role of surrogate parents. On March 21, 1661, a free Black couple, Emanuel Petrussen and Dorothy Angola, were granted emancipation by the Company for their adopted son, Anthony Angola, whom they had raised and educated as their own son.[49] Another similar case was that of an enslaved man, Cleijn Antony, who married Lucie of Angola on May 5, 1641. Their son, Anthony, was baptized on July 30, 1643, but his mother died four weeks later. Cleijn Antony, who was unable to take care of his son alone (or whose master refused to take the son in), entrusted him to Dorothy Angola, his godmother. In 1648, Cleijn Antony died in turn, leaving his son to Dorothy. In 1661, Dorothy, who had married to Emmanuel Pietersen (also called Little Manuel or Manuel Minuit), sent a request to the Director General and his council that Anthony be emancipated because she and her husband had raised him with love and affection without ever asking for financial help from the authorities and now wanted him to inherit the property of his adoptive parents. The authorities agreed, and Anthony joined the list of free Black landowners.[50]

The Dutch Reformed Church was a pillar in the formation of New Amsterdam's African American community. Baptisms and marriages did not signify the actual conversion of

---

46. Karen Sivertsen, "Babel on the Hudson: Community Formation in Dutch Manhattan" (MA thesis, Duke University, 2007), mentions Trijntie Jans (Van Camp) as a midwife.
47. RRDC, Baptisms, 2:191, 238.
48. RRDC, Baptisms, 2:79, 88.
49. CHMD, 22.
50. CHMD, 222; Christoph, "The Freedmen of New Amsterdam," 114; Dickenson, "Abstracts of Early Manhattanites," 140–41.

Africans to Calvinism, a fact that pastors have consistently deplored. What Africans sought in joining the church was a home that could welcome them, distract them from their daily work, and provide a particular locus where they could build and strengthen their families and social bonds. Severed from their birth families and African identities since their arrival in the New World, Black people were able to recreate new community ties, a feature that was typical of New Amsterdam and the Dutch Reformed Church, as Andrea Mosterman shows in *Spaces of Enslavement: A History of Slavery and Resistance in Dutch New York* (2021).[51] If creating a feeling of community was a real survival strategy for enslaved people that were denied any humanity by their enslavers, they nevertheless needed to adapt to the circumstances by creating a dual African American identity.

Community-Building in the Burial Ground: The Creation of a Dual Cultural Identity

Cultural Cohesion

The building of a community spirit was facilitated by the cultivation of common cultural practices and beliefs from the different African regions enslaved people came from. Indeed, most of the captives arriving in New Netherland had been seized by privateers from enemy Portuguese or Spanish vessels.[52] The first generation of enslaved people belonged to what historian Ira Berlin called "Atlantic Creoles" who were distinguished by their cultural homogeneity. They all came primarily from African Iberian colonies, such as the port of El Mina (on the Gold Coast) or Luanda and Benguela (Angola), and had then been transported to São Tomé, Cape Verde, and Brazil before arriving in North America. Most were multiracial, multilingual, and familiar with some aspects of European culture; some had been converted to Catholicism. Many bore the name of their region of origin such as Simon Congo, Christoffel Santomee, Anthony of Angola, Anna van Capo Verde, Francisco Capo Verde, Francisco Cartagena or Sebastian de Britto van St Domingo, regions of the former Portuguese colonies.[53] Some bore the names of the imperial powers such as Pieter Portugies or Emanuel van Spangien. Others had generic designations of their African origin such as Clara Criolo, Jan Creoly, Hilary Criolyo, Anna Negerinne, Pedro Negretto, Sebastiaen Neger, or Philippe Swartinne van Angola. Even though some may have felt proud to bear

---

51. "Simply being a worshipper in the church could enhance one's social status." Mosterman, *Spaces of Enslavement*, 107, 39–43.

52. Between 1623 and 1636, the Dutch captured about 2,356 slaves from the Spanish. Susannah Shaw Romney, *New Netherland Connections: Intimate Networks and Atlantic Ties in Seventeenth-Century America* (Chapel Hill: University of North Carolina Press, 2014), 199.

53. Linda M. Heywood and John K. Thornton, *Central Africans, Atlantic Creoles, and the Making of the Foundation of the Americas, 1585–1660* (New York: Cambridge University Press, 2007), 277–79, 346–52.

names that highlighted their African identity, these geographical designations were necessarily reductive, approximate, or even completely erroneous.[54]

These common geographical origins facilitated the formation of connections between the newly arrived enslaved people. Indeed, forming a community must have come naturally as it was at the center of the African way of life. As French theologian Bruno Chenu states, "Without the community, the individual is lost, confused, and powerless. In the community, he finds the framework of his being and his action. His cogito is the family and the community. I participate, therefore, I am."[55] For these enslaved Africans, the community was understood in a global sense, including the living and the dead. The study of the cosmologies of the Yoruba, Akan, and Kongo peoples reveals a similarity between different concepts such as the recognition of the spirit world, the mutual relationship between human beings and spirits, and death as a stage in the circle of life, not as an end. For the Yoruba, *ayé* is the visible and physical world, and *órun* is the invisible world of spirits, ancestors, and deities. The orishas can be either divinized ancestors or natural forces. *Olódùmarè* (or *Olórun*) is the Supreme Being and creator of both worlds. Among the Akan, the Supreme Being is called *Nyame* and is the creator of heaven, earth, spirits, and order. *Nyame* is related to the wind, a power that is invisible and intangible but whose actions are perceptible. The spirit world, nature, and society are intrinsically linked and permeated with *sunsum*, the spiritual energy that flows through both animate and inanimate things. For the Kongo people, the Supreme Being is called *Nzambi*. Their world is divided in two between the world of the living and the dead. Cosmological time is cyclical, and death is only a transition in a process of growth, maturity, death, and rebirth.[56] Based on these beliefs, the worst disgrace that could be inflicted on the family was not being able to organize adequate ceremonies upon the death of one of its members, a notion that is understandable when one knows how dependent the soul is on the care provided by the community. The funerary rite was a pivotal moment when the living and the dead were reunited.

We can thus assume the importance of funerary practices for the first generation of enslaved Africans who had to find their own places to bury their dead as traditional Calvinist denominations forbade the presence of enslaved people in their churchyards.[57] The

---

54. Mosterman, *Spaces of Enslavement*, 13, 26, 43, 45, 48.

55. Bruno Chenu, *Dieu est noir: Histoire, religion et théologie des Noirs Américains* (Paris: Le Centurion, 1977), 84.

56. Andrea E. Frohne, *The African Burial Ground in New York City: Memory, Spirituality, and Space* (Syracuse, N.Y.: Syracuse University Press, 2015), 103–23.

57. Mosterman, *Spaces of Enslavement*, 125–27. In New Netherland, Black people had access to few places to bury their dead. The enslaved working on Stuyvesant's *Bouwerij* certainly used this site on which a chapel was erected between 1660 and 1687. Others were probably buried near the "Negro Quarters," where the Company housed enslaved people who worked at the mill on the *Sawkill*. A third possible location was the municipal cemetery situated west of Broadway which was used from 1649 to 1676. After this date, the cemetery was moved north of the town palisades and was later incorporated into the *Trinity Church Cemetery*. However, on October 25, 1697, a municipal ordinance forbade the use of the cemetery by the African population. This chapel

African Burial Ground that was discovered in 1991 in downtown Manhattan is said to have been in use starting in 1697, when Trinity Church excluded free and enslaved Africans from their cemetery.[58] The burial ground was in an area extending west to Broadway and east to the Collect Pond. To the south was the *Vlacht*, or Common, which was common land used for pasture that became the place of executions and public demonstrations like parades or bonfires.[59] As it was located between the city and the parcels of land that were allocated to free Blacks people in the 1640s, we can assume that the Black community chose this site to bury their dead because it was close to their farms and a place where they could escape white surveillance. Andrea Frohne also points to the fact that it was situated "next to a large body of water that could have held spiritual significance."[60] Similarly, the absence of a common grave also proves that the enslaved took care of their burials themselves. In 1713, the Anglican reverend, John Sharpe stated that the enslaved "were buried in the common ground by their compatriots and those of the same skin color without office, on the contrary, the pagan rites are practiced in front of the graves by their compatriots."[61] The reference to the "pagan rites" clearly points to African traditions of dancing, singing, and shouting that were despised by the Anglican community. David Valentine, a New York City official commissioned to write a history of the city in 1860, explained that the enslaved maintained their African customs "among which was the custom of burying their dead at night, accompanied by various mummies and screams."[62] What Europeans feared most in these celebrations were physical or emotional exuberance and the practice of sacrifices. All religions, Calvinists, Jews and Muslims condemned the shedding of blood in cemeteries because, according to certain ancestral beliefs, the soul was in the blood which could pollute the sanctity of churches and cemeteries.[63] In 1722, the city council passed a law to regulate the burial practices of African and Native American enslaved workers, prohibiting night ceremonies and limiting the number of individuals allowed to attend, as well as their use of coffins and burial cloths, under penalty of a 10-shilling fine.[64] The existence of this

---

would be located at the corner of 2nd Avenue and 10th Street, in the cemetery of St. Mark's Church. Stokes, *Iconography*, 4:202.

58. Anne-Marie Cantwell and Diana diZerega Wall, "'We Were Here': The African Presence in Colonial New York," in *Unearthing Gotham: The Archaeology of New York City* (New Haven: Yale University Press, 2003), 279.

59. Edna Greene Medford, *New York African Burial Ground History Final Report* (Washington, D.C.: Howard University), 2004, 7, https://doi.org/10.6067/XCV8VM49FN.

60. Frohne, *The African Burial Ground*, 72.

61. John Sharpe, "Proposals for Erecting a School, Library and Chapel at New York City [1712/13]," *New York Historical Society Collections* 13 (1880): 355.

62. David T. Valentine, ed., *Manual of the Corporation of the City of New York* (New York: J. W. Bell, 1853), 567.

63. Swan, *New Amsterdam Gehenna*, 187.

64. Herbert Levi Osgood, ed., *Minutes of the Common Council of the City of New York, 1675–1776*, 12 vols. (Albany: Weed Parsons, 1901), 3:296.

law informs us that these rites actually took place and strengthened the Black community in New York.[65]

Cultural Syncretism and the Formation of an African American Community

By analyzing the remains in the African Burial Ground, archaeologists, bioanthropologists, and historians were able to reveal many cultural practices through funeral rites.[66] What is interesting is that despite a wide variety of regions and diverse European influences, their practices were relatively homogeneous and helped frame a new creole African American identity.

The typical burial consisted of a coffin large enough to hold one body lying on its back, wrapped in a shroud, with its head facing west. From the late seventeenth century, the use of coffins was indeed common throughout Europe, Africa, and the Americas.[67] Coffins were also filled with ornaments. The most striking decoration was a heart shaped by fifty-one nails driven into the coffin lid. A team of archaeologists recognized this *Sankofa* symbol from Ghana, representing the link between the dead and the living, the past, the present and the future,[68] even though scholars like Erik Seeman have asserted that such decorations were frequent on Anglo-American coffins.[69] Whether it was African or European, or if it derived from a syncretism of the two traditions, this ornament reflects both the significance of the deceased and the freedom African Americans enjoyed in practicing their funerary rites. Choosing the decoration of their coffins allowed them to recover their dignity and restored their humanity.

Inside the coffins, the skeletons were all covered by shrouds, a custom that also has its origins both in Europe and Africa. In the report on the cemetery, Edna Green Medford states that many accounts by travelers to Africa in the eighteenth century testify to the use of shrouds. In New York City, this practice is attested to by the presence of copper pin

---

65. Jean Howson, Barbara A. Bianco, and Steven Barto, "Chapter 2: Documentary Evidence on the Origin and use of the African Burial Ground," in *New York African Burial Ground Archaeology Final Report* (Washington, D.C.: Howard University, 2006), 51.-
66. The conclusions here are drawn from the analysis of the first group, which was buried from the early years of the cemetery until the 1730s. Frohne, *The African Burial Ground*, 92.
67. Julien Litten, *The English Way of Death: The Common Funeral since 1450* (London: Hale, 1991); Alice Morse Earle, *Costume of Colonial Times* (New York: Scribner and Sons, 1894); Alice Morse Earle, *Colonial Days in Old New York* (New York: Charles Scribner's Sons, 1896); Wilfred Talman, "Death Customs among the Colonial Dutch," *de Halve Maen,* 43, no 1 (1968) 13–14; Medford, *New York African Burial Ground History Final Report*, 174–79.
68. The meaning of this symbol is: *"se wo were fi na wo sankofa a yenkyi en Twi,"* meaning "look at the past to understand the present." See Michael L. Blakey, "The New York African Burial Ground Project: An Examination of Enslaved Lives, A Construction of Ancestral Ties," *Transforming Anthropology* 7, no. 1 (1998): 53–58.
69. Erik R. Seeman, " Reassessing the 'Sankofa Symbol' in New York's African Burial Ground," *William and Mary Quarterly* 67, no. 1 (2010): 101–22.

fragments found in coffins.[70] Yet, contrary to what was practiced in Europe, hands and feet were not tied under the shroud.[71]

Africans in New York seem to have followed the European custom of burying their dead with their heads facing west.[72] This Christian tradition was intended to prepare the body for Christ's return on Earth, and thus shows a certain degree of assimilation among these Atlantic Creoles, because in most African American communities in the United States, the bodies were buried with their heads pointing eastward, toward Africa.[73] Only two coffins were positioned with their heads facing south. The archaeologists could not find a plausible explanation for it and noticed only that these two coffins were put aside, marking their ostracism from the rest of the group.[74] This might have been part of a ritual, as Ruth Annette Mathis describes from Barbados in 1788, in which the enslaved asked the deceased where he wanted to be buried: "Burials among the Negroes took place in their gardens, preceded by wakes, and animated by strange and fantastic ceremonies. If the body was that of an adult, they would consult with the deceased to determine where he or she wished to be taken, trying out different directions before the correct location was finally revealed."[75]

The enslaved in New York seemed to follow the custom common among African American communities in the New World of placing various objects in coffins or on graves. This tradition is typically African, because the Dutch and English preferred to bequeath their possessions to their heirs rather than to bury them. Among these objects were glass beads, rings, metal jewelry, coins, shells, pewter button, or pipes. The skeleton of a fifty-two-year-old woman who was found with beads around the waist and wrist had hourglass-shaped teeth, which proves that she was born in Africa.[76] The wearing of beads around the waist

---

70. Ruth Annette Mathis, "From Infancy to Death? An Examination of the African Burial Ground in Relation to Christian Eighteenth Century Beliefs," PhD diss., University of Massachusetts Amherst, 2008, 135.

71. Medford, *New York African Burial Ground History Final Report*, 174–79.

72. Ross Jamieson, "Material Culture and Social Death: African-American Burial Practices," *Historical Archaeology* 29, no. 4 (1985): 39–58; Erik R. Seeman, "Reassessing the 'Sankofa Symbol' in New York's African Burial Ground," *William and Mary Quarterly* 67, no. 1 (2010): 101–22.

73. Warren R. Perry, Jean Howson, "Chapter 5: Overview of Mortuary Population, Burial Practices, and Spatial Distribution," in *New York African Burial Ground Archaeology Final Report*, vol. 1 (Washington, D.C.: Howard University, 2006), 134–39, https://doi.org/ 10.6067 /XCV8CJ8CDR.

74. Warren R. Perry, Jean Howson, Augustin F. C. Holl, "Chapter 6: The Early Group," in *New York African Burial Ground Archaeology Final Report*, vol. 1 (Washington, D.C.: Howard University, 2006),, 176, https://doi.org/ 10.6067/XCV8736PX2.

75. Frank Wesley Pittman, "Fetishism, Witchcraft, and Christianity Among the Enslaved," *Journal of Negro History* 11, no. 4 (1926): 650–68, quoted in Mathis, "From Infancy to Death?," 140.

76. Jerome S. Handler, "Determining African Birth from Skeleton Remains: A Note on Tooth Mutilation," *Historical Archaeology* 28, no. 3 (1994): 114, 118. The wearing of beads around the waist and the filing of teeth is a common tradition in West Africa but no accounts of such practices have been recorded in America, which proves that these people were born in Africa. See Cantwell and Wall, "'We Were Here'", 277-297.

could have an aesthetic, erotic, or spiritual function of protection against the evil eye. The tradition of placing coins in the coffin was found in both European and African countries. This Christian custom made it easier for the deceased to cross over into the afterlife, whereas the Yoruba and Akan peoples used copper and other metals to pay homage to their ancestors and to protect the living from possible scourges. The presence of oyster shells, which were abundant on the New York shores, had the same function of aiding transition from one world to the next. According to African beliefs, burying the deceased with their possessions prevented them from coming back to haunt the living.[77] The objects that were last touched by the deceased represented the link between the living and the dead.[78]

The burial ground in New York testifies to the importance of the funeral rites for the enslaved African community, which found a place to express themselves freely, far from the supervision of their masters. They were able to maintain and mix some of their ancestral customs, while adopting many European influences, thus forging their own African American identity. Leslie Harris explains how this dual culture was materialized in the African Burial Ground, which holds at the same time "cowrie shells and brass buttons, Christian crosses and West African *sankofa* and *akoma*."[79] This mixed heritage that formed a new African American culture was transmitted to contemporary generations who, interestingly, associated in the name a new imagined global African identity that African-descended people then used to claim the preservation of what they consider their ancestral remains in the burial ground.

Commemorating the Enslaved Community in the African Burial Ground Monument and Interpretive Center

The Monument and Interpretive Center

Designed by Haitian American architect Rodney Leon and erected in 2007, the African Burial Ground Monument is a two-piece structure of black granite, coming from both South Africa and North America, symbolizing the two worlds coming together. It has been conceived as a counter-monument, inviting the visitor not to passively observe but to become active and embark on a journey through time and space.[80] When walking from

---

77. "Unless you bury a person's things with him, he will come back after them." See Newbell N. Puckett, *Folk Beliefs of the Southern Negro* (Chapel Hill: University of North Carolina Press, 1926), 103, https://archive.org/details/folkbeliefsofsou00puck.
78. Robert Farris Thompson, *Flash of the Spirit: African and Afro-American Art and Philosophy* (New York, Vintage Books, 1983); Elliot J. Gorn, "Black Spirits: The Ghostlore of Afro-American Slaves," *American Quarterly* 36 (1984): 549–65; Paul Finkelman, ed., *The Culture and Community of Slaver* (New York: Garland Publishing Company), 1989, 113–29.
79. Harris, *In the Shadow of Slavery*, 9.
80. James E Young, "The Counter-Monument: Memory against Itself in Germany Today," *Critical Inquiry* 18, no. 2 (1992): 267–96.

the street up the alley leading to the monument, one notices on the right, seven mounds of grass that lay bare, with no sign or indication of what they are. Underneath are seven large crypts that were reburied on October 4, 2003, containing sixty coffins each, in which the remains of the 419 exhumed graves were placed. The last coffin contains offerings left by participants at the excavation ceremony. Turning around, the visitor then faces a high structure with two outside walls and an entry into a small room called the Ancestral Chamber. The wall on the left, the Memorial Wall, is marked with the West African *Sankofa*, a symbol associated with learning from the past. An epitaph reads, "For all those who were lost / For all those who were stolen / For all those who were left behind / For all those who were not forgotten." The wall on the right is called the Wall of Remembrance and displays a map showing the location of the African Burial Ground in the city. The visitor is then invited to enter into the Ancestral Chamber, a tiny, cramped room with an open triangular roof. The Chamber is twenty-four feet high—the walls are twenty feet high, and the chamber sits four feet above the circular lower court—as the remains lie twenty-four feet underneath the city surface. Its tininess provides a place for individual contemplation and prayer but also likens the visitors' experience to that of a slave ship, whereas its triangular roof recalls the Triangular Slave Trade. It then leads to a narrow "door of return" that takes visitors four feet down, into a circular lower part, the Ancestral Libation Court, surrounded by the Spiral Procession Ramp. All along the ramp is a circular wall called "The Circle of Diaspora," adorned with carvings of religious and cultural symbols used by members of the African Diaspora, mixing West and Central African cosmologies with Muslim, Christian, and Native American icons. Inscribed on the surface of the Ancestral Libation Court is a world map with Africa at its center, showing the migration of African people and cultures to North, South and Central America and the Caribbean.[81]

Adjacent to the monument is the interpretive center, which opened in February 2010, in the Ted Weiss Federal Building at 290 Broadway. It is built over part of the archaeological site. This small slavery museum with a circular shape houses various historic and artistic panels detailing the history of slavery in seventeenth and eighteenth century New York, the history of the cemetery, and the unfolding of the struggles faced by the African American community to have the sacredness of the burial ground recognized and memorialized. There is also a cinema and a souvenir shop. A permanent contemporary art exhibition is to be found on the ground floor of the Ted Weiss building as part of the Federal Art in Architecture Program. The diversity of shapes and themes that are exhibited enlarge

81. Frohne, *The African Burial Ground*, 308–17; Joyce Hansen and Gary Mcgowan, *Breaking Ground Breaking Silence: The Story of New York's African Burial Ground* (New York: Henry Holt, 1998); Cantwell and Wall, "'We Were Here'", 277-297; *Unearthing Gotham: The Archaeology of New York City* (New Haven, Conn.: Yale University Press, 2001), 277–94; Marc H. Ross, *Slavery in the North: Forgetting History and Recovering Memory* (Philadelphia: University of Pennsylvania Press, 2018), 22–31; Araujo, *Slavery in the Age of Memory*, 41–44; Woodard, *Slave Sites on Display*, 47–68.

our understanding of the African American community: *Unearthed*, a bronze sculpture by Frank Bender, reproduces the faces of three enslaved people buried in the cemetery holding hands; *Untitled*, a glass mosaic, depicts a pile of more or less gaunt faces buried under the city and represents enslaved people and AIDS patients; *Renewal*, a silkscreen print by Tomei Arai, displays a collage of symbols and references connected to slavery in New York City; *The New Ring Shout*, by sculptor Houston Conwill, architect Joseph DePace, and poet Estella Conwill Mojozo, is a polished brass work inlaid in the ground that represents a circular cosmogram showing the diversity of African American cultures against the background of a map of New York; and *Africa Rising*, a bronze sculpture by Barbara Chase-Riboud, portrays a goddess on an African stool.[82]

Celebrating the Activism of the African-descended Community

The celebration of the community materialized with the activism of the people of African descent and their fight to have the sacredness of the site recognized and memorialized. Here the definition of community becomes political, and collective memory becomes public memory. This is, as Rodolfo Rosales puts it in *Community as the Material Basis of Citizenship* (2019), a way for African Americans to affirm their desire to be included in American society at large, to be part of the larger group. Associating and petitioning is indeed what the First Amendment to the Constitution is about and is thus at the basis of the functioning of the democracy. Making the memory of slavery visible in the public space is for the African-descendant community a way to fight "the structures of white supremacy" and restore the balance between "the public memory of pro-slavery historical actors" and the public memory of the enslaved.[83]

Tensions emerged immediately after the discovery of the cemetery between the General Services Administration in charge of the excavations of the site, civic government agencies, and New York City African Americans. Local community activists quickly protested the disrespectful treatment and poor storage of the bones. Sensitive to complaints from his Black constituency about persistent racial injustice, New York City's African American mayor at the time, David Dinkins, called for a suspension of the excavations and for proper treatment of the exhumed remains. In 1992, Dinkins was eventually received with members of the Black Caucus in a public hearing before a Congressional committee convened by African American Illinois representative Gus Savage and managed to get an allocation of

---

82. "African Burial Ground Commissioned Artwork," U.S. General services Administration, accessed July 17, 2022 https://www.gsa.gov/about-us/regions/welcome-to-the-northeast-caribbean -region-2/about-region-2/african-burial-ground/african-burial-ground-commissioned-artwork; Frohne, *The African Burial Ground*, 228–317; see also Anne-Claire Faucquez, "Commémorer l'esclavage par l'art: le cas de l'African Burial Ground Memorial à New York," in *La mémoire de l'esclavage: Traces mémorielles de l'esclavage et des traites dans l'espace atlantique*, ed. Lawrence Aje and Nicolas Gachon (Paris: l'Harmattan, 2018), 231-252.
83. Araujo, *Slavery in the Age of Memory*, 94.

$3 million for the scientific study of the exhumed human remains and artifacts as well as the construction of a memorial and interpretive center at the site.[84] Andrea Frohne explains that "African Americans (were) reclaiming a history and identity of the space through an African-based perspective"; they voiced an "African-based discourse of spirituality in which a demand for respectful treatment was wrapped up in honoring the ancestors, calling on the spirit world, writing messages to the dead, and leaving offerings."[85]

First, the scientific study of the bones was entrusted to a team of African American researchers from the historically Black Howard University, led by anthropologist Michael Blakey. Pride emerged that the past was in the hands of the Black community. Anthropologist Sherill Wilson declared that "taking the remains from a white archaeological firm and putting them in the hands of a Black institution had never been done before."[86] The bones were thus well taken care of by the descendants who even organized a spiritual departure ceremony that was a mixture of Christian, Islamic and Yoruba practices before they were taken to Washington. Similarly, the Pan-African activist Sybil Williams Clarke declared that the memorial and interpretive center that the African American community should "record and tell our story—our story, told by us: not by the enslavers or the children of the enslavers."[87]

During the reburial ceremony, which took place between October 1 and 5, 2003, the local community also became involved. A total of 419 coffins traveled from Howard University to Broadway, New York, some by train and others by boat, and they were welcomed by a cheering crowd of thousands of people. Frohne recalls how involved the local community was: "On 3–4 October 2003, visitors could move in, out, and around the GSA property at any time of day and night; they could leave any object as an actual offering that would not be discarded; and they could even sleep in sleeping bags during an all-night vigil prior to the funerary ceremony the next day."[88] The ceremony then celebrated through songs, poems, speeches, display of cultural artifacts, and performances, which Andrea Frohne has called a "Burial Ground diaspora."[89] This engagement of the African American community has been commemorated in the interpretive center where a third of the exhibition is dedicated to it. In this way, a new community was born, one that identified as the "descendant community," but that was, according to Ana Lucia Araujo, a "rhetorical and political designation embraced by individuals who in the New York City's context saw themselves as symbolic heirs of the men and women interred in the burial ground."[90] Indeed, all members

84. Woodard, *Slave Sites on Display*, 50–53.
85. Frohne, *The African Burial Ground*, 175, 187, 193, 196.
86. Quoted in Frohne, *The African Burial Ground*, 197; Terrence W. Epperson, "The Politics of 'Race' and Cultural Identity at the African Burial Ground, New York City," *World Archaeological Bulletin* 7 (1996): 108–17.
87. Frohne, *The African Burial Ground*, 218.
88. Frohne, 222.
89. Frohne, 224.
90. Araujo, *Slavery in the Age of Memory*, 42.

of the diaspora claimed their belonging to this imagined community, as no individuals could be identified among the remains and as few African-descendant people could trace their lineage to the enslaved African population that lived in New York in the seventeenth and eighteenth centuries.[91] This imagined community was represented by a group of New Yorkers who called themselves "the Committee of the Descendants of the African Ancestral Burial Ground."[92] The memorialization of the burial ground, promoted by the collective action of the African-descendant population, helped thus to "stabilize collective memory" and served to sustain the "community's efforts to maintain solidarity in the formation of a conceptual identity."[93] This is indeed this imagined identity that was chosen to be portrayed in the commemorative complex.

Celebrating an Imagined African Identity

The scenography of this commemorative complex chose to honor the lives of the enslaved population of New York by centering their efforts at building a community while reinforcing the bonds of the African-descendant population. In the center of the circular space of the interpretive center is a life-sized scene, entitled "Reclaiming Our History," representing the burial of an African adult and a child, placed in two wooden coffins, surrounded by mourners, with funeral chants audible in the background. This key moment in the lives of the enslaved can thus be experienced through several senses (sight, touch, and hearing) and recreates a moment of intimacy that helped unite the enslaved African community around common practices and beliefs. Visitors are involved in the scene as they are invited to pay their respects to the deceased. This feeling is enhanced with the projection of the documentary film *Our Time at Last*, which uses many visual strategies to enable the visitor to identify with the victims of slavery and to experience empathy: footage from the 1990s discovery of the cemetery is interspersed with the fictionalized story of a young enslaved girl in the 1700s in New York whose family came to bury her father. The narration through an enslaved child, a symbol of innocence, and the reference to her mother's death by the quote "some of those bones were my mother's bones" inscribed above the funeral scene amplify the compassion.[94] In this way, the visitor may engage by "metonymic transference" or what in psychoanalysis is called "melancholic identification," by asking "What would I

---

91. Many Africans had left the city after the Draft Riots in 1863 and a new African population came to settle in the city at the turn of the twentieth century, fleeing the Jim Crow South or immigrating from the West Indies. See Harris, *In the Shadow of Slavery*, 280–86. In 1900, New York's African population only totaled 2 percent. See Edwin G Burrows and Mike Wallace, *Gotham: A History of New York City to 1898* (New York: Oxford University Press, 1999), 1112.

92. Ross, *Slavery in the North*, 260n18.

93. Paul Connerton, *How Societies Remember* (Cambridge: Cambridge University Press, 1989), 35; Woodard, *Slave Sites on Display*, 63.

94. Anne-Claire Faucquez, "Esclavage et tourisme mémoriel à New York : expérience d'apprentissage ou quête identitaire ?," *Revue française d'études américaines* 168, no. 3 (November 2021): 30–46.

have done if it had been me in the place of the oppressed . . . or the oppressor?"[95] As Silke Arnold-de Simine explains, "In the tradition of Aristotle, Gotthold Ephraim Lessing and Friedrich Schiller, the catharsis experienced in the theatre [here, the cinema] is thought to convert an excess of emotions like terror and pity into virtuous dispositions and virtues."[96]

Similarly, after entering the tiny Ancestral Chamber of the monument, with its twenty-foot-high walls, the visitor descends the four-foot-high stairs, bonding physically and spiritually to the ancestors whose remains lie just twenty-four feet below the street level. The second part of the monument, the Spiral Procession Ramp, descends another six feet below street level, taking the visitor even closer to the burials. The ramp and stairs serve as bridges between the world of the living and the spirit world, and they symbolize the process of transcendence from the physical to the spiritual world, from the profane to the sacred.[97] This proximity with the past generations is expressed in the testimony of one visitor, Mary Palmer, an African American woman from Harlem, who was deeply touched by her experience in the Ancestral Chamber: "When I entered, I felt my heart begin to beat because I felt the souls coming to me. Like your cousin or someone you never saw coming to you? And then say, 'Hey, hello.' They're touching you . . . you can feel it. That's what it felt like. Someone who was part of my family, they touched me deep down and made me shake a little bit. I had to lean back and wait. It's a heartbreaking feeling, a little scary."[98]

This monument to an enlarged community connecting past and present generations refers to a generalized idea of Africa that does not evoke any historical reality but that addresses instead the whole African diaspora. The contemporary African-descendant population recreated their stolen past by referring to a fantasy African heritage. As New York City mayor David Dinkins declared, "The African Burial Ground may be a small piece of Manhattan-but it links us directly to the great continent of Africa."[99] This artistic ensemble presented there has therefore chosen to celebrate a Pan-African identity, to emphasize the cultural diversity of the diaspora and the international dimension of this Africanness. The memorial highlights this diversity of African American culture in the Circle of the Diaspora, while the artwork *The New Ring Shout* celebrates the tradition of ground markings made during African American ritual ceremonies as practiced throughout North America and the West Indies but very little in New York in the absence of large plantations. The bronze statue *Africa Rising*, by Barbara Chase-Riboud, celebrates this African diversity by representing a wide range of famous African American figures and members of the diaspora

95. Fabrice Folio, "*Dark tourism* ou tourisme mémoriel symbolique?," *Téoros* 35, no. 1 (2016), http://journals.openedition.org/teoros/2862.
96. Silke Arnold-de Simine, *Mediating Memory in the Museum: Trauma, Empathy, Nostalgia*, (New York: Palgrave MacMillan, 2013), 119–21.
97. "African Burial Ground Exterior Monument," U.S. General Services Administration, https://www.gsa.gov/portal/content/113743, accessed July 17, 2022.
98. Adam Phillips, "NYC Slave Cemetery Is Now Hallowed Ground," Voice of America, accessed July 12, 2017, http://www.voanews.com/a/ny_africa-burial-ground-6aug15/2904083.html.
99. Frohne, *The African Burial Ground*, 276.

such as W. E. B. Dubois, Marcus Garvey, Malcolm X, Josephine Baker, Alexander Pushkin, or Alexander Dumas. The depiction of the goddess both inspired by the *Victory of Samothrace*, and by the story of Sarah Baartman, the Venus Hottentot, thus bestows a universal significance every visitor, descending from the New York enslaved or not, can connect to.[100]

Conclusion

Community-building is a very instructive lens through which to look at the history and memory of slavery in New York. Indeed, ever since the Dutch period, enslaved people have been able to break with isolation, a typical characteristic of slavery. They managed to form personal ties in the small cluster of New Amsterdam, recreating family bonds and using the Dutch Reformed Church and baptisms to incorporate new members to their community. They were also connected culturally by their common geographical origin. In their funeral practices, they managed to preserve spiritual ties inherited from Africa as well as to design new syncretized practices that were common to most African American communities. Community-building is also at the core of the commemoration of this past, as reflected in the African Burial Ground Monument and interpretive center, which revolve around the need to connect the present and past generations, giving birth to a new type of community, what Frohne has called a "Burial Ground diaspora."

The commemorative act is indeed a collective undertaking, the aim of which is to bind members of the community. As the French philosopher Joëlle Zask explains, "To objectify a memory presupposes that the group has given its agreement, accepted a consensus around the object, thus making the commemoration a fundamental act, repairing the social fabric."[101] It is therefore a political act, which presupposes the acceptance of common values and the recognition of a collective identity, indispensable to the construction of a new public memory shared by all. Yet, we can wonder to what extent the celebration of this "Burial Ground diaspora" helps repair the social fabric by limiting its membership to the descendants of the enslaved. As enlarged as this community is, it is still exclusive as it rejects the descendants of the enslavers. The tragedy of slavery is as much African as it is human. At this point, we all feel appalled by this history, and it is about time we enlarge the community of penitents and fashion a broader global community that will carry together this collective memory of slavery and help heal the scars that still injure our contemporary societies.

100. Barbara Chase-Riboud, *Barbara Chase-Riboud: Africa Rising* (Paris: Mullen Books, 1998).
101. Joëlle Zask, "Pourquoi fait-on appel à l'art (le plus souvent) pour procéder à une commémoration?," *Le blog de Joëlle Zask* (blog), March 2007, http://joelle.zask.over-blog.com /article-31847400.html.

The Eagle, the Bell, and other Fragments from the Intersecting Stories of Queen Anne's Chapel and Fort Hunter

James W. Bradley and James B. Richardson III

Background

Although established for fundamentally varied reasons, the stories of Queen Anne's Chapel and Fort Hunter have been intertwined from the beginning. In June 1701, William III, the Protestant King of England, established by Royal Charter a new organization, the Society for the Propagation of the Gospel in Foreign Parts (hereafter SPG). The new society had two main aims: to strengthen Christian ministry among English people overseas and to evangelize of the non-Christian peoples of the world, especially in North America. In part, this was a response to the remarkable success French Jesuits had had among Indian peoples. It was also part of a broader plan to bring English manners and customs to the wayward colonies in America.[1]

This fit well with plans of the governor of New York at the time. Richard Coote, First Earl of Bellomont, was a devoted Anglican and a strong advocate for a missionary presence among the neighboring Mohawks, the easternmost of the Five Nations. He was also a good imperial agent. The primary purpose of Coote's 1700 plan was to build an English fort in Indian country, one with "100 Souldiers constantly in Garison . . . employed in making tar and pitch during peace time." Hopefully, Coote continued, "this would draw some English families thither and maybe a minister as well." Although Coote's's plan was derailed by New York's chaotic politics during the first decade of the eighteenth century, everyone agreed on the need to have a fort somewhere in Mohawk territory. Especially as renewed hostilities with the French began in 1702 (Queen Anne's War), it was vital to have a marker of English imperial claims to the Mohawk Valley.[2]

---

1. "United Society Partners in the Gospel," Wikipedia, accessed February 26, 2021, https://en.wikipedia.org/wiki/United_Society_Partners_in_the_Gospel.
2. James W. Bradley, *Onondaga and Empire: An Iroquoian People in an Imperial Era*, New York State Museum Bulletin 514 (Albany: State University of New York, State Education Department, 2020), 498. (Hereafter *Onondaga and Empire*).

After William III's death, his successor Queen Anne continued to support the SPG, sponsoring the publication of *An Account of the Society* in 1706 and encouraging Anglican priests to relocate to New York. The Reverend Thomas Barclay, "a priest of greater vision" than his predecessors, arrived in Albany in 1708 and began to visit the eastern Mohawk town known as Tionontogue. At this time the Anglican Church did not exist beyond New York City. Although a few priests had begun missionary efforts in Albany, there was no established Anglican Church, and there was little support for one. Most of the Anglo-Dutch inhabitants remained strongly tied to their Dutch Reformed heritage. The first Anglian Church, St. Peter's in Albany, would not be established until 1715, and its building was not completed two years after that. [3]

A pivotal event occurred in the spring of 1710 when the visit to London of the renowned "Four Indian Kings" took place. Engineered by Peter Schuyler, mayor of Albany, and Col. Francis Nicholson (an active member of the Society), the real goal of the visit was to raise interest in another invasion of Canada after the embarrassing failure of the previous attempt in 1709.[4] As a public relations event, the trip was successful and raised significant public and royal support. In their address to Queen Anne on April 19, the four representatives followed Schuyler's script and asked for military assistance as well as Anglican missionaries. The Queen was deeply moved by these exotic and dignified men and, although the documentary trail is thin in terms of written instructions, several follow-up commands were issued. On May 2, the "Indian Sachems" sent a reply, undoubtedly drafted by Schuyler and Nicolson, expressing their "great satisfaction" in accepting the proposals prepared for the Queen. As John Lydekker reports, "The Queen supported the Society's proposals and gave orders for the erection of a fort in Mohawk country" but does not cite a specific reference for this in the SPG archives.[5]

When Schuyler and his delegation returned from London in May, they found a new political landscape. Three years earlier, England and Scotland had merged to become Great Britain through the Acts of Union signed in May 1707. In June 1710, the newly appointed

---

3. Tionontogue, the Mohawk lower castle, was established around 1690 by Protestant Mohawks. It became one of the two major Mohawk towns after the French destroyed several of the other Mohawk towns during the raid of February 1693. Eric Hinderaker, *The Two Hendricks. Unraveling a Mohawk Mystery* (Cambridge, Mass.: Harvard University Press, 2010), 48. For St. Peter's, Reverend Joseph Hooper, *A History of Saint Peter's Church in the City of Albany* (Albany: Fort Orange Press, 1900), 61.

4. Richard P. Bond, *Queen Anne's American Kings* (Oxford: Clarendon Press, 1952). Prominent among these four was Hendrick Tejonihokarawa, a tribal leader from the lower castle who had been baptized in 1690. Hinderaker, *The Two Hendricks*, 15. All four, the three Mohawks and one from Schaghticoke, had long standing ties with Schuyler. Hinderaker, 84.

5. Lydekker reprinted this address based on the copy in the SPG Archives. John W. Lydekker, *The Faithful Mohawks* (Cambridge, UK: Cambridge University Press, 1938), 27–28. The Queen's reply, drafted by the Society, observed that any missionaries will want "a house to live in and a Chapel" and requested these "should be built within an Indian Fort for their security & defense." Lydekker, 29, 31. "great satisfaction," Lydekker, 30–31. Bond states that Schuyler's 1710 request included a parsonage. Bond, *Queen Anne's American Kings*, 15.

governor-general Robert Hunter arrived to oversee his imperial charges. Since Queen Anne's War continued to ravage the frontier, Hunter was careful to hold his first Indian conference with Five Nations that summer. Hunter needed the Five Nations as allies and took the opportunity to ask if they really did approve of having resident missionaries and "a Garrison Planted in one or more of your Castles, and a Chapel or Chapells built there." Speaking on behalf of the Five Nations, the Onondaga spokesman Kaquendaro [Aqeendaro] replied yes, they "approve it very well."[6]

As hostilities between France and Great Britain intensified during the rest of 1710 and into the following year, Hunter's priorities were increasingly military, not spiritual. Another two-pronged invasion of Canada was proposed, one by sea against Quebec and another by land against Montreal. After months of preparation and cajoling by Schuyler and Nicholson, the Montreal expedition of 1711 finally departed in early August, only to return a few weeks later. Once again, the promised naval assault on Quebec did not happen, and Schuyler's men, colonial and Indian alike, returned to Albany frustrated and angry.[7]

The Indian conference held in October 1711 was a somber affair. The Five Nations, especially the Mohawks, felt betrayed by another military failure. Decisive action was needed to restore their confidence, and Hunter responded by agreeing to build the long-promised Mohawk fort and chapel immediately. Two days later, contracts were signed with five carpenters from Schenectady to build "a ffort, Chaple, [and] Block houses" at the confluence of Schohaire Creek and the Mohawk River. The contract was quite specific and required that the fort be 150 feet square with curtain walls made of logs, a foot square laid upon one another, and pinned in place to a height of twelve feet. There would also be a blockhouse at each corner twenty-four feet square, built of logs nine inches square; each blockhouse was to be two stories high, with a roof of boards and shingles, and a chimney on an inside wall. The contract also specified that at least one blockhouse would be completed before winter and that a second fort of the same description would be built in Onondaga after the Mohawk fort was completed. There is nothing in the contract that describes the fort's function as a mission other than the presence of a chapel. There is no indication that a parsonage was planned. [8]

Back in England in March 1712, the SPG finally settled on the Reverend William Andrews as its new missionary to the Mohawks at Fort Hunter. Andrews departed for New York in August and arrived in early October. Work on "the Queen's Fort" was completed by the time he arrived. During the first week of October 1712, Reverend Thomas Barclay, as the resident clergyman, visited the fort and formally dedicated the chapel.[9]

---

6. E. B. O'Callaghan and B. Fernow, eds., *Documents Relative to the Colonial History of the State of New York*, 15 vols. (Albany, N.Y.: Weed, Parsons, 1856–1887), 5:220–21 (hereafter *DRCHSNY*); "approve it very well," O'Callaghan and Fernow., 223–25; also Bradley, *Onondaga and Empire*, 603–6.
7. Bradley, *Onondaga and Empire*, 604–5; Lydekker, *The Faithful Mohawks*, 32.
8. O'Callaghan and Fernow, *DRCHSNY*, 5:279–81. The contract is also preserved in the Society archives along with Colonel John Redknap's surviving drawing. Lydekker, *The Faithful Mohawks*, 32n1, Plate V. For political context, Bradley, *Onondaga and Empire*, 603–6.
9. Lydekker, *The Faithful Mohawks*, 33–34.

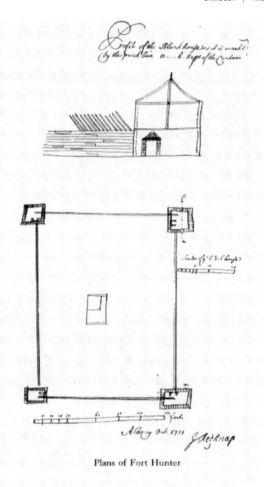

Figure 1. Col. John Redknap's Plans for Fort Hunter, October 1711. From James W. Bradley, "Onondaga and Empire," *New York State Museum Bulletin* 514 (2020): 606. COURTESY OF NEW YORK STATE MUSEUM, ALBANY, N.Y.

Plans of Fort Hunter

Reverend Andrews finally arrived in Albany on November 13, and two days later met with Commissioners of the Indian Affairs and a small Mohawk delegation. He presented a letter from the archbishop of Canterbury (head of the Anglican Church) on behalf of the Queen and the Society and introduced himself as the "Missionary to the Mohawk Indians" they had requested, "to Instruct them in ye principals of the Christian Religion for the Good of their Souls Salvation." In turn, he was welcomed by the Mohawk delegation, and the missionary work of Queen Anne's Chapel began.[10]

To summarize, by the end of 1712 both the fort and the chapel had been completed. The construction contract specified that a wooden "Chaple" would be built in the middle of the fort. It would also be made from squared timbers and would be twenty-four feet square, one story, ten feet high with a garret over it, roofed with boards and singles. Little is

---

10. E. B. O'Callaghan, ed., *Documentary History of the State of New-York*, 4 vols. (Albany, N.Y.: Weed, Parsons, 1849–51), 3:542–43.

OLD FORT HUNTER AND QUEEN ANNE CHAPEL

Drawn from the Original Contract Specifications of
October 11, 1711.

Figure 2. Reconstruction of "Old Fort Hunter and Queen Anne Chapel." From James W. Bradley, "Onondaga and Empire," *New York State Museum Bulletin* 514 (2020): 606. COURTESY OF NEW YORK STATE MUSEUM, ALBANY, NY.

known about what was built. While there has been much speculation, one frequently used depiction shows a stone chapel within the fort although there is no evidence to confirm such a reconstruction.[11]

In addition to the chapel, the Queen in "her Royal munificence and Christian Piety" also bestowed upon the Mohawk "the Furniture of the Chapel," which arrived safely with Reverend Andrews. The best known of these gifts were the two engraved sets of silver communion vessels, one set for "her Indian Chappel of the Mohawks" and the other for "her Indian Chappel of the Onondagwus." Each set consisted of "1 Large Silver Salver, 1 Ditto Small, 2 Large Silver Flaggons, 1 Silver dish, 1 Silver Chalice." The Mohawk set reached its destination and was used in the chapel as intended for the next sixty years. The Onondaga set met a vastly different fate. [12]

---

11. Richard Berleth, *Bloody Mohawk: The French and Indian War and American Revolution on New York's Frontier* (Hensonville, N.Y., Black Dome Press 2009), 22. Bradley, *Onondaga and Empire,* 606, figure 12.10. Hanson claims that "the parsonage, still standing, was [also] erected" at this time. Willis T. Hanson, Jr., *A History of St. George's Church in the City of Schenectady* 2 vols. (Schenectady, N.Y.: privately printed, 1919), 20.
12. "the Furniture of the Chapel," Reverend Joseph Hooper, *A History of St. Peter's Church in the City Albany* (Albany, Fort Orange Press, 1900) 53–54. "The Mohawk set," Lydekker, *The Faithful*

While many sources mention other items sent as gifts, the most reliable list comes from the SPG's Annual Report. To impress the Indians and make a "more decent performance of Divine Worship" in her chapel, the Queen also sent:

> 1 Communion Tablecloth, 2 Damask napkins, 1 carpet for the Communion Table, 1 Alter cloth, 1 pulpit cloth, 1 large cushion with Tassels for the Pulpit, 1 small ditto for the Desk, 1 Holland Surplus, a Large Bible, 2 Common Prayer Books, one wholly for the clerk, 1 book of Homilies . . . [and] 4 of her Majesty's Imperial Arms painted on Canvass, 1 for the Chappel, and 3 for so many Castles [Indian towns].

A few additional gifts were sent by the archbishop of Canterbury and the Society. Neither a brass lectern nor a bell is specifically mentioned in the Society's records although it is unclear how comprehensive the list of gifts was. [13] Whatever the actual complement of gifts, these were grand furnishings, ones appropriate for a royal chapel. As such, it is a little difficult to visualize such elegant and valuable objects housed and used within a timber structure at the edge of the frontier. This, however, appears to have been the case.

Intersecting Histories

By the end of 1712, both Queen Ann's Chapel and Fort Hunter had been built, whatever the motivations were for their construction. Governor-General Hunter had stationed a garrison of "20 private men and an officer" at the fort in October, while Reverend Thomas Barclay had traveled from Albany to dedicate the chapel about the same time. Still, based on the documentary record, it remains unclear where these structures were located and how they were related to one another. [14]

By March 1713, Reverend Andrews had settled into "the Queens ffort near the Mohawks Castle" and wrote long, gossipy letters back to the SPG. In addition to the complaints about drinking, unruly behavior by the soldiers assigned to the fort, and his difficulty with the language, Andrews also provided valuable information about his new neighbors. As he noted, "Their chief town or [lower] castle as it is called, stands by the ffort, consisting of 40 or 50 Wigwams or houses pallizadoed Round. Another of their Chief Towns between

---

Mohawks, 31n2, Plate IV. The communion set, intended for Onondaga —two large flagons, one large and one small patten, one chalice, and an alms basin—was committed to the custody of St. Peter's Church, Albany. Hooper *History of St. Peter's Church*, 55. Since the Onondaga chapel was never built, these pieces stayed there. William M. Beauchamp, *History of the New York Iroquois, Now Commonly Called the Six Nations*, New York State Museum Bulletin 78 (Albany: New York State Education Department, 1905), 422, Plate 14. Nearly fifteen years later, Hanson observed: "An effort is now being made under the leadership of the Onondaga Indian Welfare Society to induce the authorities at St. Peter's Church to turn over the communion set to the Onondaga "o be'used In the chapel on their reservation," Hanson, *History of St. George's*, 26n300. This effort was not successful.

13. Hooper *History of St. Peter's Church*, 53–54.
14. Bond, *Queen Anne's American Kings*, 128n.

20 & 30 houses is three or four & twenty Miles distant from here [the upper castle at Canajohaire]." Fort Hunter also appears to have quickly become a convenient stopping place between Schenectady and Albany to the east, and Five Nations towns to the west. On September 12, 1713, for example, an important delegation, including "de Cannasora" [Tegannisoren] the Onondaga leader, Hendrick Hansen, Capt. John Bleeker, and Laurens Classen, stopped at the fort on their way to a Grand Council meeting at Onondaga.[15]

In a September follow-up letter, Andrews continued to catalog the difficulties of "being here" while expressing his desire to do "some good among these poor dark ignorant Creatures." Andrews was also concerned about his safety. Should there again be Indian trouble, he fretted, this fort "could not defend it self, it is so weakly mann'd." Fortunately, that would not matter. By spring 1714, Queen Anne's War was effectively over, and stability began to return to the northern frontier. By August, the Queen herself was dead. At the Indian conference, a year later, the Speaker [Tegannisoren] offered condolence on the Queen's death and Andrews now sent his reports from "the Kings ffort by the Mohawk Castle."[16]

With things quiet on the military side, Reverend Andrews continued to toil on, attempting to teach English to Mohawk children while continuing to struggle with the Mohawk language on one hand and the lax discipline of the garrison on the other. "The Mohocks Language is extream hard to be learnt," he confided to the Society. There was always "Trouble with the Indians, who are Constant Visitors for their Bellies," not to mention his "ffear of Receiving Mischief" from them. Nor was there much other choice. The only alternatives were the drunkards of the garrison and the "Wicked Traders" who were always ready to provide rum. By October 1718, Andrews, finally worn down by the lack of success and intense loneliness, requested reassignment. Before leaving he arranged to have Captain John Scott, the commander of the fort, take charge of the furniture, plate, and fittings of the chapel. It would eight years before another minister was sent.[17]

Although missionary work was on hold, Fort Hunter continued to be manned by a small garrison. The fort itself, however, was not holding up well. In August 1720, Hunter described the colonies defenses—the forts at Albany, Schenectady, and Fort Hunter—as" barely Palisadoed" and not "place[s] of defense." His successor, William Burnet, wrote to his masters, the Lords of Trade, that these same fortifications were "quite decayed" and requested funds to renew them. Neither the funds nor needed repairs were made available.[18]

Fifteen years after establishing the chapel, the SPG finally appointed another minister

---

15. Andrews letter, Lydekker, *The Faithful Mohawks*, 34–38. "Tegannisoren and others stop," O'Callaghan and Fernow, *DRCHSNY*, 5:372.

16. Andrews follow-up letter, Lydekker, *The Faithful Mohawks*, 39. "offered condolence," O'Callaghan and Fernow, *DRCHSNY*, 5:438. "the Kings ffort by the Mohawk Castle," O'Callaghan and Fernow, 49.

17. "The Mohocks Language is extream hard," Lydekker, *The Faithful Mohawks*, 45. "Trouble with the Indians," Lydekker, 39. "Wicked Traders," Lydekker ,47. "Before leaving," Lydekker, 51.

18. "barely Palisadoed," O'Callaghan and Fernow, *DRCHSNY*, 5:556. "quite decayed," O'Callaghan and Fernow, *DRCHSNY*, 5:557.

to serve both at St. Peter's in Albany and at the Indian mission at Fort Hunter. The Reverend John Miln arrived in December 1727 and, although he spent most of his time in Albany, he did make a practice of visiting the mission at least four times a year. Miln continued to serve both congregations for the next four years until his health gave out; he returned to England in 1731. His efforts were appreciated by the colonial government. Before he left, he received a certificate from Lt. Walter Butler, commandant of Fort Hunter, recognizing his efforts that had "greatly civilized" the Mohawks. [19]

Among the issues that continued to plague the Mohawks of the Lower Castle was the constant pressure to sell their land. The presence of Fort Hunter had encouraged European settlers, especially newly arrived German Palatines who began to homestead along Schoharie Creek. There were other claimants, too. In November 1733, thirteen men apparently "in behalf of the rest of our Nation" signed a deed for the land "commonly called the Mohock flatts . . . being near Fort Hunter" to His Majesty King George II. This transfer took place at the fort and was "Sealed and delivered" by Walter Butler and another trader. This was the start of a dispute between the city of Albany and the colonial government over who owned this piece of land, a dispute that would not be resolved for another thirty years. [20]

In April 1735, the SPG, again under pressure to renew the mission, appointed Henry Barclay as the catechist at Fort Hunter. Barclay was a suitable candidate. He had been born in Albany and was the son of Reverend Thomas Barclay. He was, however, too young to be ordained a priest. Nonetheless, he moved to Fort Hunter and restarted the previous efforts to educate Mohawk children. Being from the area, Barclay was also more comfortable with the Mohawks than his predecessors had been. In addition to shepherding his congregation at the Lower Castle, Barclay also made a practice of visiting the Upper Castle, some twenty miles away, by horse. Barclay's dedication was noticed by the acting governor George Clarke who authorized a payment of 60 pounds to Mr. Barclay to encourage him in missionary work. With such assistance, Barclay returned to England late in 1737 where he was ordained a priest in January 1738. He arrived back in Albany in April with the same charge Andrews had been given—to serve as a missionary in Albany as well as at Fort Hunter. [21]

The year 1738 began uneventfully. Walter Butler, now captain, was still in command of the Fort Hunter garrison, while services and even weddings were conducted by Reverend Barclay in the chapel. In May, a young Irishman named William Johnson arrived. As agent for his uncle, Sir Peter Warren, Johnson visited the fort located at the westernmost boundary of Warren's estate. Johnson quickly became friends with Butler and Barclay

---

19. "Reverend John Miln," Lydekker *The Faithful Mohawks*, 52. "Lt. Walter Butler, commandant of Fort Hunter," Lydekker, 53. This was Walter Butler, the father of John and grandfather of his son (young) Walter Butler.

20. "in behalf of the rest of our Nation," O'Callaghan and Fernow, *DRCHSNY*, 6:15–16. For other examples, see Hinderaker, *Two Hendricks*, 49–51, 110–11.

21. "payment of 60 pounds," O'Callaghan and Fernow, *DRCHSNY*, 6:88. "Barclay's return," O'Callaghan and Fernow, 4:88. Lydekker, *The Faithful Mohawks*, 54.

and began to absorb important, if quite different, lessons from each. From Butler, Johnson learned how to work with the Mohawks, especially in terms of buying land. From Barclay, he gained an appreciation of the spiritual quality of Native life. Both would help shape Johnson's future.

A year later, Johnson abandoned working for his uncle, bought land on the north side of the Mohawk, downriver from Fort Hunter, and built his own home (Mount Johnson). Even though Johnson chose to live on the other side of the Mohawk River, he maintained a special relationship with Fort Hunter and its chapel. In June 1740, Barclay baptized Ann, daughter of William Johnson and Catharine Weisenberg, as is recorded in the official register of baptisms. Two years later, Barclay baptized the couple's second child, Johnson's son and heir, John.[22]

Meanwhile, Barclay was successful on other fronts. At the Albany Indian conference in August 1740, he was asked to preach and did so, in Mohawk. The Five Nations' representatives were impressed, as was acting governor George Clarke. As a result, Clarke sponsored a special recommendation to the New York Assembly to rebuild the Fort Hunter chapel that had "fallen into great disrepair." By November of 1741, Barclay reported that the new building, "a neat Stone Church," was nearly complete. Unfortunately, few details are available. Kevin Moody and Charles Fisher argue that, since the original timber structure was not demolished until 1742, these two chapels must have been located on different sites. They also provide evidence from the 1750s indicating that the new stone church was built between Fort Hunter and the Mohawk Lower Castle.[23]

Another notable change occurred at this time. According to Max Reid, in November of 1741, King George II conveyed three hundred acres of Crown land on the south side of the Mohawk River to the Reverend Henry Barclay. Known as the Barclay's Patent, the intent was to provide a "glebe," or lands whose revenue would support the chapel and its mission. It seems likely that the parsonage, located a mile east of the fort and chapel, was built at this time.[24]

---

22. Timothy Shannon "The World That Made Johnson," *New York History* 89 (2008): 111–26. Captain Walter Butler, Milton W. Hamilton et al., eds., *The Papers of Sir William Johnson*, 14 vols. (Albany, University of the State of New York, 1921–65), 1:1–3 (hereafter *SWJP*). "Johnson's new friends," Butler, Hamilton, et al., *SWJP*, 1:7–8. Fintan O'Toole, *White Savage: William Johnson and the Invention of America* (New York, Farrer, Straus and Giroux, 2009), 22; Lydekker, *The Faithful Mohawks*, 62. "Baptisms," O'Toole, *White Savage*, 44–45, 105.

23. "a neat Stone Church," Lydekker, *The Faithful Mohawks*, 55. "not demolished until 1742," Kevin Moody and Charles L. Fisher "Archaeological Evidence of the Colonial Occupation at Schoharie Crossing State Historic Park, Montgomery County, New York" *Bulletin: Journal of the New York State Archaeological Association* 99 (1989):1–13.

24. Max W. Reid, Esq., *The Mohawk Valley: Its Legends and Its History* (New York and London, G. P. Putnam's Sons, 1901), 85–86 (hereafter *The Mohawk Valley*). Max W. Reid, Esq., *Ye History of St. Anne's Church in ye city of Amsterdam N.Y. and its Original Queen Anne's Chapel at Fort Hunter in ye Mohawk Country* (Amsterdam, NY: Fegel Brothers, 1897), 6:15–16, citing Library of Patents 12, page 140 (hereafter *History of St. Anne's*). The exact terms of this land transfer seem murky at best, Butler, Hamilton, et al., *SWJP*, 3:589. The parsonage still stands.

While these events would have important local repercussions, so too would events far away in Europe. In 1744, a feud over the Austrian Succession spilled over into North America where it became known as King George's War. Although not as destructive as earlier border wars had been, the frontier was again awash with "rumors and counter-rumors." The following year, given fears of a French raid, Barclay decided to leave his Fort Hunter and Albany parishes for the greener fields of Trinity Church on Wall Street in New York City. A new minister would not arrive until March 1750. [25]

With Barclay gone, Fort Hunter reverted to its role as a military post established primarily to protect the Mohawk Lower Castle. Fulfilling this mandate now fell to Col. William Johnson, who had the authority to "remove" any officer who disobeyed instructions to provide this support. With the end of the war in October 1748, the frontier again stabilized in terms of Anglo-French hostilities. Tensions remained high, however, over the expansion of colonial settlement and the insatiable desire for Indian land even though, by this time, the Mohawks of Tiononderoge had sold off all that they owned.[26]

By midcentury, Fort Hunter and its chapel continued to serve the Protestant Mohawks of the Lower Castle as both a physical and a spiritual refuge. Even without a resident missionary, Queen Anne's Chapel continued to be the focal point for the Protestant Mohawk community. In March 1750, a replacement finally arrived. As with his predecessors, Reverend John Ogilvie was charged with serving both the congregation of St. Peter's in Albany and the mission at Fort Hunter. Ogilvie was enthusiastic and soon set about reviving his disparate congregations and teaching English to Mohawks at Fort Hunter. Although there were still problems with rum, Ogilvie found himself "quite pleased with their behavior." In July 1754, the Mohawks of the Upper Castle requested a church and a bell for their town, which suggests that perhaps Queen Anne's Chapel in the Lower Castle already had one.[27]

Beyond the Mohawk Valley, the world was changing in significant ways. As hostilities between French and British interests again edged toward open conflict, Fort Hunter had become a minor player on the imperial game board. Troops were still garrisoned there. A full complement of twenty-five soldiers under a lieutenant was reported in December 1754. Once a strategic location, however, Fort Hunter was viewed increasingly as a backwater as imperial concerns moved west into the Ohio Valley.[28]

What changed this and put Fort Hunter and its chapel back on the imperial map was William Johnson's plan to bring British civility and culture to his growing domain. In 1749, Johnson had moved to a new stone house he called Fort Johnson. This quickly became his

---

25. "rumors and counter-rumors," Lydekker, *The Faithful Mohawks*, 56–57. "Barclay's departure," Lydekker, 59.
26. "authority to 'remove,'" Butler, Hamilton, et al., *SWJP*, 1:61–62; 1:175–76. "insatiable desire for Indian Land," Hinderaker, *Two Hendricks*, 128–33.
27. "quite pleased with their behavior," Lydekker, *The Faithful Mohawks*, 65–68. "requested a church and a bell," O'Callaghan and Fernow, *DRCHSNY*, 6:877.
28. "A full complement," O'Callaghan and Fernow, *DRCHSNY*, 6:924

operational base on the north side of the Mohawk River, while Queen Anne's Chapel and Fort Hunter as well as the adjacent Mohawk towns played a comparable role on the south side of the river.

For Johnson, the protection of his Mohawk communities was a priority. After visiting the Lower Castle in 1755, he proposed a new fortification, recommending "it to be on a line with Fort Hunter, to take in the church as a bastion and to have a communication pallisado between the two forts." Although Johnson contracted to build this fort in 1755 and submitted receipts for having paid the builders in August 1756, it remains unclear what was built, or even where. The real problem was maintaining an adequate garrison, especially after Montcalm's capture of Fort Oswego, a defeat that threatened Mohawk and British settlements across the western frontier. As Johnson reported, there were only thirty men under Lt. William Williams at "the King's Fort" in the Lower Castle and one officer and twenty-five militiamen in Fort Hendrick at Canajoharie. [29]

Unfortunately, the presence of troops did not always mean a good relationship with the adjacent Mohawk community. Language continued to be a problem between the garrison and the town. Another complaint from the Mohawks was the need for someone, preferably an officer who was familiar with "their ways & manners" to be assigned to Fort Hunter. With the shocking defeat of General Braddock's expeditionary force, a month later, in July 1755, it became even more important to keep the Mohawks happy.[30]

The most accessible route for invasion between French Canada and British New York was the Champlain Valley. Even before Braddock's defeat, Col. William Johnson had started to muster provincial troops to move against new French fortifications along the Champlain corridor. By mid-September 1755, Johnson's force had reached the southern end of Lac du Saint-Sacrament, which he promptly renamed Lake George. In the bloody fighting that followed, Johnson's Mohawks played a crucial role in the victory.

Reverend Ogilvie had hoped to accompany Johnson's force to Lake George, but the demands of his two congregations had grown. In addition to St. Peter's, Ogilvie also served as the chaplain to the growing number of British troops stationed in Albany. The situation was similar at Fort Hunter where many of the Mohawk had suddenly developed "a serious & habitual sense of Religion." Once again, Fort Hunter was in an important location, and Ogilvie was asked by the newly ennobled Sir William Johnson to take care of "all ye War-parties of Indians" that constantly were passing through. The friendship that grew up between Johnson and Ogilvie would last throughout the war.[31]

Although the renewed conflict may have brought new life to Fort Hunter, it did not

29. "proposed a new fortification," O'Callaghan and Fernow, *DRCHSNY*, 2:657. "contracted to build," Butler, Hamilton, et al., *SWJP*, 1:605. "submitted receipts" Butler, Hamilton, et al., 13:90. "maintaining an adequate garrison," Butler, Hamilton, et al., 9:509.

30. "their ways & manners," Butler, Hamilton, et al., *SWJP*, 1:603–4.

31. "a serious & habitual sense of Religion," Lydekker, *The Faithful Mohawks*, 82–84. "all ye War-parties of Indians," Lydekker, 82–84.

solve the fundamental problem of cross-cultural relationships. In May 1756, a Mohawk dele-gation from the Lower Castle again complained to Johnson. "It is true we have a Garrison of regulars but on them we can't depend . . . as they don't understand us, nor would be willing to help us." A year later, the problem was even more serious. In January 1757, Johnson wrote to Gen. James Abercromby to report "an unhappy Affair between Soldiers of Fort Hunter Garrison & some of the Mohawks . . . wherein several of the latter were wounded." How ironic that the facility built to protect the Mohawks had now become a threat to their safety.[32]

Ogilvie remained active, tending to his beleaguered Mohawk as well as he could. He helped to establish a schoolmaster at Fort Hunter, continued to serve at St. Peter's in Al-bany, and even assisted at "the Grand Hospital of the Army" established nearby. In recog-nition of his dedication, Ogilvie was offered a commission as Chaplain to the Royal Amer-ican Regiment, an offer that, with the Society's approval, he accepted. Ogilvie continued his missionary work under harsh conditions, spending two months during the winter at the mission at Fort Hunter Mission. He also visited the neighboring settlements, as far west as German Flats, and was present at Canajoharie when a surprise attack by French and Indian raiders struck the community. [33]

In July 1759, Ogilvie finally was able to join Sir William Johnson's expedition against the French fortification at Niagara. Now, with the SPG's approval, he could accompany his friend and his Mohawk warriors on campaign. Army life agreed with him, and he wrote to the SPG enthusiastically about serving both his regimental and Mohawk congregations. Ogilvie's zeal was noticed and, after the capture of Niagara, the British commander, Maj.-Gen. Jeffery Amherst, recruited him as an army chaplain. [34]

While Ogilvie may have believed that his missionary service was "intirely compatible" with his army chaplaincy, the realities were soon apparent. Conditions at the Lower Cas-tle were not good. In February 1760, Ogilvie reported, "my Indian Congregation is much decreased by the late Mortality that prevailed amongst the Mohawks." There were also re-ports of famine around Fort Hunter that fall. Ogilvie was about to learn that, as an army chaplain, he no longer had control over his choices. As he wrote to the SPG in October, he would not be returning to Ft. Hunter or Albany since "by express Order from General Amherst," he would spend the winter with the army in Montreal. He remained there for the next four years, never returning to Fort Hunter.[35]

---

32. "they don't understand us," O'Callaghan and Fernow, *DRCHSNY*, 7:105. "an unhappy Affair," Butler, Hamilton, et al., *SWJP*, 2:772–73.

33. "Grand Hospital of the Army," Lydekker, *The Faithful Mohawks*, 85–86. "commission as Chaplain," Lydekker, 87. "Surprise attack by French and Indian raiders," Lydekker, 90.

34. "Johnson's expedition against the French," Lydekker, 92.

35. "intirely compatible," Lydekker, *The Faithful Mohawks*, 98. "the late Mortality," Lydekker, 99. "reports of famine," Butler, Hamilton, et al., *SWJP*, 3:218–19. "express Order from General Amherst," Lydekker, *The Faithful Mohawks*, 104–5. After his regiment was disbanded in 1763, Ogilvie chose to stay in Montreal, where he served a considerable congregation of British merchants and occupying soldiers. Lydekker, 113–14.

Fortunately, the Lower Castle Mohawks still had a faithful friend in Sir William Johnson. Even though most of Johnson's concerns focused north of the Mohawk River, he continued to keep a watchful eye on his friends and allies. In September 1763, Johnson stepped into the old land dispute between the Lower Castle Mohawks and "the Claim of the Corporation of Albany to their dwelling place at Fort Hunter." Sir William's advocacy was powerful and a year later the Lords of Trade in London directed Lt. Governor Colden to vacate the Corporation of Albany's Patent.[36]

Johnson also helped to revive the mission. Through his SPG connections, he learned about a young minister, Reverend Henry Munro, formerly a Presbyterian chaplain for a Highland Regiment, who recently had taken Anglican orders. Johnson invited him to Johnson Hall, where they discussed the future of the Mohawk Mission and the "scattered and reduced" condition of the Anglican Church. Johnson's concerns were driven by several issues. One was certainly the well-being of his Mohawk communities. Another was the growing influence of "Dissenting missionaries" over Indian people as well as over British colonists. As others have pointed out, Johnson was not a particularly religious man. He did not marry his long-term lovers, nor did he worry much about sin. What he did understand was that religion was a powerful cultural tool, one that shaped loyalties in the temporal as well as the spiritual realms.[37]

In 1763, Sir William moved from Fort Johnson to a grand new house, Johnson Hall, located in the newly established community of Johnstown. By establishing public institutions, including a courthouse and jail, Johnson took one more step in his plan to establish the social values of British imperial society—order, hierarchy, and control—within his dominion. To achieve this, he focused on two key objectives: establishing a new county where he would have greater political control and encouraging the appointment of an Anglican bishop, one with the authority to ordain new clergy and strengthen the colony's growing Anglican network.

In April 1766, Sir William was elected as a member of SPG, and he quickly began to devote more time and resources to these goals. He established his own Anglican Church, St. John's in Johnstown, sometime after 1760, completing a small building by 1766. That April, he ordered "One bell for church" although it is unclear which church was to receive it. Johnson also assisted with the effort to build an Anglican church in Schenectady, a project that began in 1758 but was not completed until a decade later.[38]

---

36. "Claim of the Corporation of Albany," O'Callaghan and Fernow, *DRCHSNY*, 7:562, 577. "vacate the . . . Patent," O'Callaghan and Fernow, 7:633.

37. "scattered and reduced," Lydekker, *The Faithful Mohawks*, 114. "nor did he worry much about sin," O'Toole, *White Savage*, 310.

38. member of Society," Butler, Hamilton, et al., *SWJP*, 5:156. "One bell for church," Butler, Hamilton, et al., 5:157–58, 195. "One bell for church," Butler, Hamilton, et al., 5:211. Please combine the two per suggestion "Anglican church in Schenectady," Hanson, *St. George's Church*, 1:37–44.

Building churches was one thing; finding good clergy to serve in them was a different challenge. As Johnson wrote to his friend Reverend Samuel Auchmuty, the rector at Trinity Church in New York, "I have the Establishment amongst the Lower Mohocks Much at heart and earnestly wish for a Good Resident Missionary & School Master." He went on to observe that there were now "Four Good Churches Viz. Albany, Schenectady, the Mohocks & mine at Johnstown," all of which needed reliable ministers.[39]

Johnson also wrote to Daniel Burton, secretary for the SPG in London in December 1767, laying out both concerns and the opportunities. Once again, he observed there were "Good Churches of Stone erected at Albany, Schenectady, My Village of Johnstown, and that of the Mohocks [at Fort Hunter]." Johnson all but begged the SPG to help recruit clergy. He was even willing to obtain the land necessary for their support. It was "The Church of the Mohawks" that concerned Johnson in particular. This was "the Door to the Six Nations," yet it had "always been a Mission, being united to Albany from whence it is distant 40 miles." As a result, they got minimal service and, "at present, they have none at all." Johnson floated one more idea—why not establish a new Episcopate for the colonies, one with its own bishop? This would make it easier to ordain new clergy. It also paralleled Johnson's plan to have a new county designated, one that separated his lands from Albany and Schenectady. Johnstown would be its center. Burton replied that he understood Johnson's concerns but did nothing. [40]

The following summer, in 1768, Johnson wrote to Reverend Auchmuty again expressing his frustration. Now was the time to show Indian people what the British had to offer. The upcoming treaty conference at Fort Stanwix offered a unique opportunity to address a large and diverse Indian audience. It will be "the absolute necessity," he continued, "for Seizing upon the Flying Moment, the only one which may ever offer." Not willing to wait any longer, Johnson decided to act on his own. He assisted the small Anglican congregation in nearby Schenectady in finishing their church building (St. George's) and began to solicit funds for a church for "the Indians of Conajoharee" (Upper Castle).[41]

By February 1769, the church in Canajoharie was well underway, a wooden structure 50 feet long by 32 wide. Pleased with the progress, Johnson ordered "a Ball made and gilt & also a weathercock" for the roof, plus all the mounting hardware. He also asked his supplier for an update on "A bell which I wrote about some time ago." By May, Johnson was pleased to report to a donor that, thanks to his help, "The Church at Canajoharie is in a fair way of being soon finished." There was progress on other fronts as well. Johnson obtained the deeds for the late Dr. Barclay's house and lands [the parsonage and glebe] at the Lower Castle and would make them available if a new missionary were found.[42]

39. "Four Good Churches," Butler, Hamilton, et al., *SWJP*, 6:12–13.
40. "the Door to the Six Nations, . . . none at all" Butler, Hamilton, et al., *SWJP*, 6:27–30.
41. "the absolute necessity," Butler, Hamilton, et al., 6:292. "the Indians of Conajoharee" Butler, Hamilton, et al., 6:464–65, 563.
42. chapel fittings, Butler, Hamilton, et al., 6:639. "soon finished," Butler, Hamilton, et al., 6:745. "deeds for the late Dr. Barclay's house and lands," Butler, Hamilton, et al., 7:114–15.

In April 1770, Johnson wrote to the SPG expressing his approval of Mr. John Stuart as a missionary for the "Mohock Mission." Although not yet ordained, Stuart seemed "very hearty in the undertaking I have pointed out—the Mohock Mission," and Johnson sent him off to England with a strong recommendation. Meanwhile, the church in Canajoharie was nearly finished and Johnson continued to urge for support of Stuart and the Mohawk communities. The Mohawks, "our faithful allies who have been greatly reduced in our Cause, are now in point of Numbers, few, but from their Authority & Situation are of much Consequence." At Fort Hunter there were now "32 Houses & about 160 people." Before the end of the year, the Reverend John Stuart was back as the Society's approved missionary for service at Queen Anne's Chapel.[43]

Stuart's arrival marked a major turning point in the story of Queen Anne's Chapel, or the Mohawk Mission at Fort Hunter, as it was usually called. In his first letter back to the SPG in January 1771, Stuart reported he held two services every Sunday, one for the Indian converts and another for the European residents, numbering approximately two hundred. Johnson was pleased with the new missionary's work. A few months later, Stuart wrote that Sir William Johnson had repaired the chapel at Fort Hunter, providing it with a "new floor, pulpit, desk, Communion Table, windows, belfry and bell." By now, it was no longer Queen Anne's Chapel, it was Sir William's.[44]

Meanwhile, Johnson continued his personal quest to bring Anglican values and British culture to the Mohawk Valley. His correspondence marks his efforts and successes. In February 1771, he reported to the SPG that he had built a church at Canajoharie and projected the need for a new one at Johnstown. To another friend, Johnson observed with pride, "I find it necessary to rebuild the Church [in Johnstown] . . . a much larger Plan to accommodate the increased Number of Neighboring Inhabitants." By January 1772, he noted that "a Large Stone Church" had just been finished in Johnstown. It was a grand structure for a frontier town. As he later reported to the SPG, "I built . . . a handsome stone building near 90 feet in length with the Steeple and Chancel, to which I have lately added an . . . Organ." Church records also note that a "wonderfully toned bell" hung in the belfry, another gift from Sir William. In March, Johnson finally achieved one of his key political objectives—a formation of a new county, separate from the Anglo-Dutch of Albany and Schenectady and named for Governor William Tryon. Not surprisingly, Johnstown was named the county seat.[45]

---

43. "Mohock Mission," Butler, Hamilton, et al., 7:543–44. "church in Canajoharie was nearly finished," Butler, Hamilton, et al., 7:666–68. "Description of Lower Castle," Butler, Hamilton, et al., 7:875–76. "Reverent John Stuart was back," Butler, Hamilton, et al., 7:841.
44. "in January 1771, Stuart reported," Lydekker, The Faithful Mohawks, 130. "belfry and bell," Lydekker, 130.
45. "a church at Cananjohaire," Butler, Hamilton, et al., SWJP, 7:1160. "rebuild the Church [in Johnstown]," Butler, Hamilton, et al., 12:893. "a Large Stone Church" Butler, Hamilton, et al., 8:357. "added an . . . Organ," Butler, Hamilton, et al., 8:927. "wonderfully toned bell," "History of

Not all Anglican churches fared as well. That same January, the vestry of St. George's in Schenectady wrote to the SPG asking for financial assistance. They were already in debt, without "Steeple, Bell, Communion plate, or any sort of church furniture," and now they could not even pay their rector, Reverend William Andrews. Schenectady, however, was not a town Sir William considered within his realm and no financial support was offered to the beleaguered congregation. In August 1773, Andrews left Schenectady for both financial and health reasons.[46]

The situation continued to change at Fort Hunter as well. Although Johnson had underwritten a major renovation of the chapel in 1771, the fort itself was a disaster. In April 1773, Johnson wrote to Gen. Thomas Gage that an accidental fire had reduced "one of the Block houses and two of the curtain [walls] . . . to Ashes." Unfortunately, two "good framed Houses belonging to the Indians" had also been destroyed. Since the remainder of the fort was "in a very Ruinous state," the Mohawk had asked for permission to use any of the serviceable timber left for rebuilding.[47]

While Johnson continued to do his best to support both his Mohawk communities, the Mohawk Mission and Lower Castle always seemed special. He encouraged Stuart's work with Joseph Brant to translate the Gospel of Mark into Mohawk and was pleased that "The Indian school goes on as usual." Meanwhile, Reverend Stuart had finally learned Mohawk well enough to conduct services in that language. In November 1773, Johnson wrote to the SPG again stressing the need to support the clergy. This time he could not resist observing, "I lately had the Church [of the Reverend Mr. Stuart at Fort Hunter] repaired at my own Expense." In December Johnson provided a final service to his friends in the Lower Castle by fending off one more attempt by the Albany Common Council to take control of the "Meadowland at Tionnondorogoe."[48]

Johnson's time was nearly over, however, and with it, his ability to protect his Mohawks. On July 12, 1774, Sir William Johnson died during an Indian conference at Johnson Hall. The next day, Reverend John Stuart from the Mohawk Mission at Fort Hunter

---

St. John's," St. John's Episcopal Church, Johnstown, N.Y. accessed February 14, 2021, https://www .stjohnsjohnstown.org/history_of_st_johns. A bell was more than ornamental. It embodied a community's identity. A bell called the faithful to church, warned residents of a fire or impending raid, and expressed community feelings at wedding, funerals, and other significant events. Johnson's effort to provide bells for the churches he built was an indication of how seriously he took his civic obligation, whether the community was British or Mohawk.
46. "without Steeple, Bell, Communion plate," Hanson, *St. George's Church*, 1:68. The arrival of Mr. John Doty filled the vacancy left by Williams' departure. Although not ordained, Doty was willing to take responsibility for St. George's and the vestry wrote to the Society in London for confirmation in December 1773. The Society, however, was "not well pleased" and, after Johnson's death in 1774, Doty and St. George's were left to fend for themselves. Hanson, 1:78.
47. "an accidental fire," Butler, Hamilton, et al., *SWJP*, 8:753.
48. "The Indian school," Butler, Hamilton, et al., 8:928. "repaired at my own Expense," Butler, Hamilton, et al., 8:928. "Meadowland at Tionnondorogoe," Butler, Hamilton, et al., 8:955–68.

conducted the burial service at St. John's Church in Johnstown. Along with many others, Fort Hunter and its chapel had lost their primary benefactor. Initially, little seemed to change. At an Indian conference held in mid-December that year, a Mohawk delegation addressed Col. Guy Johnson and promised their continued loyalty to the British. The reason was simple—"bad white people" had tried to take their land at Fort Hunter, and "our late Brother Sir William Johnson" had protected them.[49]

With Sir William gone, everything began to change in the Mohawk Valley. Long before the armed conflict known as the American Revolution began, the script for the last chapter of Queen Anne's Chapel and Fort Hunter had already been written. Although well behind the edge of colonial settlement, Fort Hunter was again a location of secondary importance. What was left of old Fort Hunter was torn down in 1775, and the stone chapel was enclosed by a new palisade. This new fortification was also called Fort Hunter. Although little information is available, it was garrisoned during the latter years of the war, although no hostilities took place there.[50]

As sides became increasingly polarized during 1775, Loyalist (or Tory) sentiments organized around the Johnsons, while most of the people in Albany and Schenectady supported reform and eventually independence. There was little room in between. Shortly after the Battle of Bunker Hill in June 1775, Col. Guy Johnson, Capt. John Butler, and Joseph Brant left for Canada to organize loyalist forces to suppress the rebels who threatened their homes. Sir John Johnson did not depart until the following year. Although he did not take a political stance, Stuart was increasingly looked upon with suspicion by his patriot neighbors. Nonetheless, he decided to remain in his post at Fort Hunter. He had married the year before and saw his first son born in June 1776. Just as he vowed to stay and serve his congregations, the Mohawks also "publically declared that they would support and defend him."[51]

Stuart remained at Fort Hunter through challenging times. His last letter to the SPG was dated October 1775. Although mentioned briefly in June 1777, when Brant reputedly asked Gen. Nicholas Herkimer if Stuart "might be allowed to retire to Canada," little more is known. It was not until May 1778, when the Reverend John Doty, the former rector of St. George's church Schenectady who had fled to Canada, reported: "The situation of Mr. Stuart at Fort Hunter was very disagreeable when I took my flight. He had been frequently threatened and was obliged to be retired. A great part of his flock having joined the Royal Army, are now in this Province." As Stuart would later relate, "the faithful Mohawk" of the Lower Castle "chose to abandon their Dwellings & Property" rather than break their oath of allegiance. Most had left to join Burgoyne in 1777, then went on to Canada after his defeat. Stuart was arrested as a suspected Tory shortly thereafter. He admitted to being a

49. "[Johnson's] burial service" Butler, Hamilton, et al., 12:1184n3, 1195–96. "bad white people," O'Callaghan and Fernow, *DRCHSNY*, 8:522.
50. "Simms 1845," Jeptha R. Simms, "History of Schoharie County" (1845), Schoharie County NYGenWeb Site, accessed February 16, 2021, http://sites.rootsweb.com/~nyschoha/simms4.html.
51. "they would support and defend him," Lydekker, *The Faithful Mohawks* 148.

loyal subject of the King and was confined to the limits of Schenectady, on parole, where he spent the next three years. He and his family were finally allowed to leave for Canada in September 1781. Here Stuart was welcomed by his former Mohawk congregants and was offered a position as Chaplain in the King's Royal Regiment of New York by Sir John Johnson. [52]

Fort Hunter and its chapel did not fare well either. As Stuart later reported, "My Church was plundered by the rebels & the Pulpit Cloth taken away . . . it was afterwards imployed as a tavern, the Barrel of Rum placed on the Reading Desk. The succeeding Season it was used for a Stable, and now serves as a Fort to protect a Set of as great Villains as ever disgraced Humanity."[53] Sir William had hoped that the Anglican Church would serve as an essential bond, one that along with the army and the provincial government could keep the structure of New York's imperial society together. Instead, the Church became one of the clearest demarcation points between those who supported independence and those who opposed it.

One of the best-known stories concerning the dismantling of the Mohawk Mission is how Queen Anne's silver survived the war. There are several romantic and apocryphal versions of this story. According to Reid:

> It is said that at the beginning of the Revolution the silver service, curtains, fringes, gold lace, and other fixtures of the chapel were put in a hogshead by the Mohawks and buried on the side of the hill south of the Boyd Hudson Place near Auriesville, N.Y. At the end of the war, when found by sounding with iron rods, it was discovered that the silver service had been removed and the cask reburied. . . . Most of the articles remaining were so damaged by moisture as to be unfit for use.

The presumption was that the Mohawks had recovered their silver during a wartime raid. According to Stuart, however, he was the one who removed the communion set and left it with a "Friend in Schenectady" for safekeeping. Whatever the real story, the silver did survive the war. After the Mohawks had settled on their new lands near Brantford in 1785, on the Bay of Quinte, a party was sent back to retrieve the silver. It was then divided between the two Mohawk communities, where it remains today.[54]

In whatever ways it was used, or misused, during the Revolution, the stone building and erstwhile chapel known as Fort Hunter was left derelict and abandoned after the war. After preaching there in June 1790, the Reverend Thomas Ellison, the new rector of St. Peter's in Albany, observed: "The church is in a wretched condition, the pulpit, reading desk,

---

52. "allowed to retire to Canada," Lydekker, *The Faithful Mohawks*, 148–49. "the situation of Mr. Stuart at Fort Hunter," Lydekker, 152–53. "the faithful Mohawk," Lydekker, 164–65.
53. "My Church was plundered," Lydekker, 164–65.
54. "Mohawk silver," Reid, *The Mohawk Valley*, 91. Berleth suggests the silver was hidden beneath the chapel's dirt floor. Berleth, *Bloody Mohawk*, 243. "Friend in Schenectady," Lydekker, *The Faithful Mohawks*, 165. Reid, *History of St. Ann's*, 32; Reid, *The Mohawk Valley*, 94.

and two of the pews only being left, the windows being broken, the floor demolished, and the walls, cracked." Even in this state of disrepair, the chapel remained a point of local interest. It was described as a one-story structure built of limestone, twenty-four feet square, with a pyramidal roof with a belfry. This description closely matches Rufus Grider's drawing based in part on "recollection of persons who had seen the Chapel and who attested to the correctness of the drawing."[55]

The whole Fort Hunter–Lower Castle area recovered slowly after the war. It was not until 1797, when Issac Dupey, a local entrepreneur, built a bridge across Schoharie Creek, that these lands became more accessible. According to Reid, the building itself was destroyed in 1820 to facilitate use of Dupey's bridge for towing canal boats across the Schoharie. As another witness observed, "The roof had been burned off to get at its stone walls" which were then used in the construction of the adjacent guard lock. As the walls were cannibalized for this purpose, one other component of the chapel was salvaged. This was the chapel bell, described by Jeptha R. Simms as "a small bell which was of a very dark green color." The bell itself was taken across the Mohawk River to Johnstown, where it graced the roof of the new Johnstown Academy. Here it served for many years until the building was destroyed by fire late in the nineteenth century; the bell was broken, and a few fragments were saved as souvenirs. Even with the building gone, the land was still referred to as "the site of Queen Anne's Chapel." In 1823, the vestry finally sold the glebe property and, with the assistance of Trinity Church on Wall Street, a new Episcopal Church was built in Port Jackson (now Amsterdam). It was, appropriately, named St. Ann Church.[56]

The Eagle and the Bell

At some point during the 1860s, Boyd R. Hudson, a farmer whose property overlooked the confluence of the Mohawk River and Schoharie Creek, made an unusual discovery—a small brass eagle, apparently from a church Bible stand or lectern. This exotic item attracted attention at a time when artifacts and antiquities from the Colonial and Revolutionary War periods were being rediscovered and recorded. One such recorder was Rufus Grider, who had come to the Mohawk Valley in 1883 at the age of sixty-six and served as an amateur historian and art teacher at the Canajoharie Academy. Grider drew the brass eagle

---

55. "a wretched condition," Reid, *The Mohawk Valley*, 91. "one-story structure built of limestone," Reid, *The Mohawk Valley*, 86). "Grider's drawing," Reverend Edward T. Carroll, *Service for the Two Hundredth Anniversary of the founding of Saint Ann's Church, Amsterdam, New York* (1912), cover.
56. "The roof had been burned off," Reid *History of St. Ann's*, 13; Reid, *The Mohawk Valley*, 91. Reid also stated that while the cut stone facing used in the 1820 east side guard lock were made on site during construction, the roughly dressed stone in the lock walls were from "the walls of Queen Anne's Chapel which stood about twenty feet from the east end of the right side of the lock and about the same distance south of the canal," Reid, *History of St. Ann's*, 28. "bell itself was taken across the Mohawk River to Johnstown," Reid, *The Mohawk Valley*, 87. "the site of Queen Anne's Chapel," Reid, *History of St. Ann's*, 16. "St. Ann's Church," Reid, *The Mohawk Valley*, 92.

Figure 3. Rufus Grider's undated drawing of the brass eagle. RICHARDSON ARCHIVE, SECTION OF ANTHROPOLOGY, CARNEGIE MUSEUM OF NATURAL HISTORY.

at least twice—once with other artifacts (notebooks, volume 1 #39) and a second time in greater detail (figure 3).

In addition to drawing this piece, Grider speculated that it might have been part of the lectern from which scripture lessons were read during services. The eagle, the symbol of St. John the Evangelist, was often used for lecterns, its spread wings supporting the Bible. Similar lecterns had been used in Catholic churches since the Middle Ages, a tradition that continued under the Anglican Church. Grider went on to note, "It possibly belonged to the Alter Furnishings [of] Queen Anne's Chapel, Fort Hunter, built in 1712." Nearly one hundred years after it was found, the brass eagle, long presumed lost, surfaced in Longmeadow, Massachusetts, and caught the eye of a young teenager while visiting family friends. Since first seeing this unusual object, author James B. Richardson has tried to reconstruct its history, discover where it originated, and why it survived.[57]

_____

57. The visit was with Virginia Alstom, who had been one of Richardson's mother's bridesmaids in 1935. During the visit, ca. 1955, Virginia's mother, Dorothy Devendorf, showed Richardson the Indian artifacts collected by her father, DeWitt Devendorf, including the brass eagle. DeWitt, a broom manufacturer in Fort Hunter, was an avid Indian artifact collector. His 1899 obituary stated, "He was an extensive collector of Indian relics, and as an antiquarian, ranked second in the state at the time of his death." The brass eagle had been given to him by Boyd R. Hudson, in whose

Figure 4. Brass lectern in the form an eagle, attributed to Jehan Aert van Tricht, ca. 1500. COURTESY METROPOLITAN MUSEUM OF ART, THE CLOISTERS COLLECTION, 68.8. HTTPS:// WWW.METMUSEUM.ORG/ART /COLLECTION/SEARCH/471867.

Even a cursory look indicates this eagle was well made and part of a larger object. Stylistically, it is most like brass lecterns of the sixteenth and seventeenth centuries. Although there are some casting flaws, there is also careful detailing such as the five rows of feathers that cover the body between the head and tail. The vertical perforation that runs through the body was part of its mounting. The presence of other perforations and tenons indicates where the wings and other features had been attached. The legs have been broken off and there is evidence of wear, especially on the head and tail.

Brass eagle lecterns were popular in East Anglian churches as well in as those in the Low Countries during the fifteenth and sixteenth centuries, but they fell out of favor with the rise of Puritan sentiments in the early seventeenth century. At the time of the English Civil War, many were destroyed, along with other "monuments to idolatry and superstition," while others were hidden. After the Restoration of the monarchy in 1660, several were

---

home DeWitt and his first wife, Agnes (Hudson's daughter), were married in 1887. DeWitt Devendorf also owned the Queen Anne Parsonage where Dorothy was born in 1894 and where he died five years later. Dorothy later married Harvey Alstrom of Longmeadow and, although she sold her father's collection in the 1950s, she kept the brass eagle. Upon Dorothy's death in 1993, Richardson contacted her son as to the whereabouts of the eagle. Unfortunately, its location then and now is not known. Fortunately, Richardson had photographed, measured, and drawn the eagle during the 1960s. It measures 6 ½" in length, 2" at its widest, and is 6 ⁶/₁₆" in circumference just below the wing attachments.

Figure 5. Brass eagle from the lectern: (a) Proximal view. (b) Ventral view.
PHOTOGRAPH BY JAMES B. RICHARDSON III.

A

B

retrieved and placed back in their parish churches and cathedrals. Whatever the story of this Tudor-style eagle, it came from someplace special. [58]

The bell fragment has a similar story. In 1959, Richardson, then a junior at St. Lawrence University, had the opportunity to participate in an excavation at Johnston Hall, Sir William Johnson's final home. Renovation work on the building was also taking place. This included the removal of miscellaneous rubbish from the basement. Amid this trash, Richardson spotted a fragment from a large bronze bell along with a label "Piece of Bell Sent by Queen Ann and Hung in Queen Ann Chapel, Fort Hunter in 1714. Later it was Hung in Johnstown Academy." He asked if he could have it, and the site manager said, "help yourself."[59]

---

58. Marcus van der Meulen, ed., *The Brass Eagle Lecterns of England* (Stroud, UK: Amberley Publishing, 2017), 21, and *passim*

59. The excavation was directed by Dr. Paul Ducey. Robert McMeekin, the manager of Johnson Hall, told us to help ourselves to anything in the basement rooms. As he explained, the Johnstown Historical Society had left that material behind. Founded in 1892, the Historical Society had used Johnson Hall since 1906 and stored their collections there. When they moved into their own building in 1944, they left behind the material they did not want. McMeekin said he had tried repeatedly to get the Society to take the remaining items; however, the reply was they did not want items that did not fit their mission —the Johnstown area and its history. Queen Ann's Chapel was built on the other side of the Mohawk River.

5 inches

Figure 6. Bell fragment, reputedly from Queen Anne's Chapel. PHOTOGRAPH BY JAMES B. RICHARDSON III.

The bell fragment appears to have come from a medium-size, high-quality bell. The fragment is approximately 8″ (20 cm) across, 5 1/4 ″ (13.1 cm) high, and weighs 7.6 lb. (3.4 kg). It has a maximum thickness of 1 1/8 ″ (3 cm) at the sound bow, the thickest portion of the bell where it would have been struck. It is undecorated except for integral raised rings on the exterior. There is evidence of lathe marks on the interior, indicating that the bell had been tuned. Based on the arc of the remaining lip, the original bell appears to have been approximately 19 1/4 ″ (48.1 cm) in diameter. A complete bell this size would weigh in the range of 140 to 150 lbs. (63 to 67.5 kg). Bells this size were usually called chapel or cupola bells and commonly ranged in size from 17″ to 24″ in diameter with a weight between 100 and 250 lbs. Church bells were considerably larger, a minimum of 28″ in diameter. Like most bells of this period, they were cast bronze, usually 80 percent copper and 20 percent tin. Bells this size were expensive, luxury items. While there are no identifying marks on the fragment, bells this large were cast only in a limited number of places. If this bell was made for Queen Anne's Chapel, it may have been cast in the well-known Whitechapel Bell Foundry, London.[60]

---

60. "Church Bells," Brosamer's Bells, Inc., accessed March 13, 2021, http://www.brosamersbells .com/church/index.html; "Whitechapel Bell Foundry," Wikipedia, accessed March 13, 2021, https://en.wikipedia.org/wiki/Whitechapel_Bell_Foundry.

Taken together, these two unusual objects provide a window into one of the more complex stories of early eighteenth-century New York—the construction of Queen Anne's Chapel in 1712 and its relationship to Fort Hunter completed that same year. These are two distinct, if contemporaneous, stories where the histories and motivations for each were quite different. The story of Queen Anne's Chapel is a demonstration of royal piety and the use of religion as an agent of cultural expansion. The story of Fort Hunter is one of political and military expediency and the need to keep a critically important ally happy.

Adding Archaeology

While the historical documents provide a basis for reconstructing why these structures were built and how their roles changed over six decades, they tell us little about the people who occupied and used them—colonial militia, traders, and the Mohawk people of the Lower Castle. To date, archaeology has not been able to contribute significantly because the actual sites were not known and so few material culture objects, other than the communion silver, have survived.

This changed in the spring of 1987, when a parking lot was planned for the new Visitors' Center at the Schoharie Crossing State Historic Site. Although this parking area did not require excavation, archaeologists from the Bureau of Historic Sites monitored the project. During the removal of topsoil, a portion of a well-laid drystone wall was observed, and additional investigation was undertaken for its identification. Subsequent testing revealed more sections of stone wall as well as diagnostic mid-eighteenth-century artifacts. Since raising the level of the parking lot would protect this stonework, no further excavation was conducted. Even with this limited information, the excavators concluded that these stone features were components of what had been Fort Hunter. [61]

In August 2011, when Hurricane Irene passed through New York State, the historically high floodwaters of Schohaire Creek destroyed the Visitors Center parking lot. As the water receded, several sections of stone wall were exposed along with a thick layer of flood deposits consisting of asphalt, river cobbles, gravel, and more eighteenth-century artifacts. Once the flood deposits were removed, more walls were exposed. Numerous test units excavated in November and December 2011 revealed that these foundations were from a twenty-four-foot square blockhouse and section of the curtain wall.

The discovery of fort's location opens the possibility of clarifying some of the outstanding questions related to these institutions and how they were connected. At present it appears that some of the stone footings were part of the original Fort Hunter. With additional remote sensing and testing, it would be possible to confirm this or identify that more than one iteration of the fort was built over the six decades of its use. The chapel's location

61. Moody and Fisher, "Archaeological Evidence," 1–13. The site was acquired by the State of New York in 1966 in order to preserve and interpret the remains of the Erie Canal.

Figure 7. Holmes Hutchinson Map of 1834 in relation to the Visitors Center. IMAGE COURTESY OF MICHAEL ROETS.

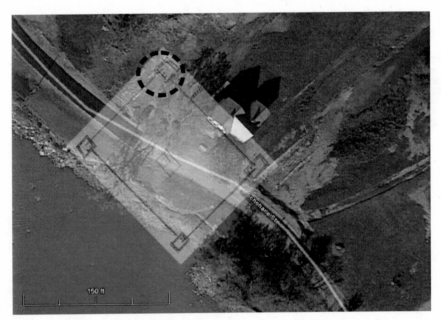

Figure 8. Redknap plan and archaeological results superimposed on the current site, December 2011. IMAGE COURTESY OF MICHAEL ROETS.

poses a similar problem. If this is the site of the 1711 fort, the cellar of the original log chapel may still survive. When the chapel was rebuilt in stone, in 1741 and again in 1771, did it remain on the same spot? Or was it moved to a different location outside the fort? Additional testing, especially in the area south of the guard lock, may indicate whether any evidence of this later stone structure, one that served as both a chapel and a fort, has survived.

Analysis of the materials recovered offers a unique way to look at these sites and those who lived there. In terms of the fort, the recovered objects included building materials, food refuse, ceramic fragments, and a series of personal items such as a clothing buckle and pieces of smoking pipes. In general, the materials from Feature 1 date from the first half to the middle of the eighteenth century. Tin-glazed earthenware vessels were most common, followed by those of buff earthenware, porcelain, and stoneware. The mean occupation date for this assemblage was 1758. One surprise was the predominance of tea-related vessels, primarily cups, saucers, and teapots. Hardly what one would expect in a rough and tumble frontier fort. Smoking pipes were also plentiful and produced a mean occupation date of 1758. Several of these pipes bore the mark of Bristol pipe maker Robert Tippet. Other objects recovered were three British coins, two halfpennies from William II and one from George II, and items related to trade, an iron Jew's harp, and a folding iron knife. Interestingly, no gun parts or other military items were included in this sample. A more precise interpretation of these materials may be possible if more systematic excavation clarifies how many discrete levels this site has.[62]

In addition to the materials at the fort site, a series of exploratory test squares were excavated in the Lower Castle area south of the old Erie Canal bed. Although limited, the results indicate that significant deposits from this Mohawk community have survived. These items document the continuation of traditional practices—the making of red slate objects, the use of wampum and bear canines—along with the use of trade silver, glass beads, and other European materials. Further archaeological work has the potential to document the Mohawk side of the Queen Anne's Chapel and Fort Hunter story more fully.

Taken together, the historical record and the potential for additional archaeological work provide a unique opportunity to examine in detail the changing relationships between the Protestant Mohawks of the Lower Castle and their colonial neighbors at Fort Hunter during the decades between 1711 and the American Revolution.[63]

---

62. Moody and Fisher, 6–11).
63. The authors would like to thank Michael Roets, Historic Site Regional Supervisor, New York State Parks, Recreation, and Historic Preservation, for his generous assistance and permission to use his images. We also thank Paul Huey, Wayne Lenig, and William Starna for their observations and comments.

Memorial Day's Interracial Legacy in Brooklyn, New York, 1878–1897

Lawrence J. King

> The citizens are ... approaching the fulfillment of the martyred Lincoln's dream and
> prophecy of one brotherhood and one citizenship this broad land over.
> —Gen. Stewart L. Woodford quoted in *The Brooklyn Daily Eagle*, May 28, 1888

Wednesday, May 30, 1883, exhibited all the characteristics of a beautiful spring day in
Brooklyn, New York. Under blue skies, its residents, along with scores of Americans across
the United States, interrupted their daily regimens in dutiful fashion and took to the streets
and cemeteries "with enthusiasm and spirit" to honor their Union war dead. It was Memorial Day. Along Bedford Avenue, where the annual parade started, "flags fluttered, stream-
ers waved, and bunting added its adornment." Businesses near Third Street and Broadway
vied with one another in honoring the occasion. Even passing carriages "bore evidences of
patriotism" as the heads of the horses drawing them displayed "splendid plumes" to cor-
roborate the sentiments of those on the road. A multiracial sea of well-dressed passengers
disembarking from the ferries and pedestrians walking across the Brooklyn Bridge carried
bouquets of fresh spring flowers. Brooklynites and visitors to the city—male and female,
representing multiple ages, classes, races, and creeds—hurried to witness the morning's
parade and then make the solemn trek to "the grave of some fallen though, perhaps, unrecorded hero—husband, father, brother, relative or friend." Leading them in this respected
holiday was the Grand Army of the Republic (GAR).[1]

Black and white members of Brooklyn's GAR, a diverse group now in their forties and

Disclaimer: The views expressed in this article are those of the author and do not reflect the
official policy or position of the United States Air Force, Department of Defense, or the U.S.
Government.
1. Scenes from "At the Graves," *Brooklyn Daily Eagle*, May 30, 1883. Hereafter referred to as the
Eagle.

fifties, donned their "simple but handsome" dark blue, army-styled uniforms.[2] In prompt fashion, they formed up to kick off their public memorial. Hours later, the martial display, complete with locally based armed forces and divisions of GAR posts, dismissed to the city's expansive cemeteries with heavy hearts and flowers in tow to honor the dead. At the graves, distinguished orators reminded the vast crowds that without the sacrifice of white and Black men such as these, the Union would have faced certain demolition and slavery indefinite perpetuation. Brooklyn's patriotic observance on May 30, 1883, deviated in look and feel from national holidays observed during the early republic and antebellum periods. Having won an equal stake in American patriotism, Black citizens now stood next to their white compatriots. Subsumed by the GAR in Brooklyn and other unionist cities, towns, and villages after the Civil War, Decoration Day, the remembrance's original name given by the public before the GAR's 'Memorial Day,' served as an adhesive, historicizing a distinct Union cause and infusing patriotism into a Gilded Age of capitalist expansion. To comprehend this shared devotion on a localized scale, I argue that ritualized interracial participation, buoyed by the GAR's integrated mission and by a growing African American patriotic consciousness, defined Memorial Day's postbellum legacy in Brooklyn, New York, during the Gilded Age (1878 to 1897), eroding racial divides and championing emancipation over reconciliation in the public sphere.[3]

Proper examination of the May holiday's origins and purposes rests on an intimate knowledge of the blue and the gray veterans. In what has become a budding subgroup of Civil War era studies, scholars of the nineteenth-century United States continue to historicize Union and Confederate troops within the larger scope of their postwar experiences, examining their efforts to cement their struggles within the rebellion's legacy.[4] Societies and their rituals act as one lens through which to study the war's memorization, as seen in the GAR and numerous other associations.[5] When compared to recent advancements in Lost

---

2. "At the Graves," *Eagle*, May 30, 1883; per organizational requirements, all GAR members had to have served in some honorable capacity during the Civil War.

3. The author selected the period from 1878 to 1897 for two reasons. First, it aligns with established historical demarcations of the Gilded Age. Second, the City of Brooklyn ceased to be an independent municipality beginning in 1898, when its corresponding county (Kings) joined New York, Richmond, Queens, and Bronx Counties to form the modern City of New York.

4. For greater context on postwar veterans—Union and Confederate, see Matthew Brian Jordan, *Marching Home: Union Veterans and Their Unending Civil War* (New York: Liveright Publishing Corporation, 2014); and James Marten, *Sing Not War: The Lives of Union and Confederate Veterans in the Gilded Age* (Chapel Hill: University of North Carolina Press, 2011).

5. After the official end of the rebellion in 1865, Union veterans formed dozens of societies throughout the Northern and border states. They acted as oases for those struggling to transition from war to peace and from slavery to emancipation as well as rallying points for bonding and sharing battlefield memories. Outside the GAR, separate groups included the Military Order of the Loyal Legion of the United States, the Society of the Army of the Potomac, and the Union Veteran Legion, among others. The Grand Army was the most popular and well-known of these groups in Brooklyn. See Marten, *Sing Not War*; James Marten, *America's Corporal: James Tanner in War and Peace* (Athens: University of Georgia Press, 2014).

Cause studies, and considering its oversized impact on the nation's politics, economics, culture, and social scene, the GAR remains understudied in Reconstruction, Gilded Age, and Progressive Era histories, outside the efforts of a handful of historians.[6]

Founded in 1866 to be a national safe haven for boys-in-blue, the GAR suffered from partisan behavior within its ranks soon after its inception.[7] As a result, the fraternity's first iteration dissolved by the early 1870s. However, by the beginning of the Gilded Age, the apolitical pillars of fraternity, charity, and loyalty had rejuvenated the GAR. The Union veterans' group flourished in ways unseen before and became a prominent national powerhouse for veterans and their needs.[8] The GAR's controversial beginnings informed nineteenth-century perceptions of the society but also played a large part in its self-rebranding. Additionally, it gained distinction as one of the nation's earliest integrated social organizations, in which Black veterans and their families found comradeship and equality that was far from widespread.[9]

The core of this argument responds to two schools of thought and their interpretations of Memorial Day's racial legacy in the Northern United States. On one side, scholars like Cecilia Elizabeth O'Leary, Matthew Dennis, and James Marten contend that nationwide Memorial Day observances further detached the Civil War's meaning from emancipation and marginalized African American participation in patriotic exercises.[10] Their works, along with David Blight's, paint a national picture of white reconciliation and white supremacism that overpowered emancipationist views and Black agency after the Civil War officially ended in 1865.[11] They offer a convincing depiction of Memorial Days in the

---

6. Mary R. Dearing, *Veterans in Politics: The Story of the G. A. R* (Baton Rouge: Louisiana State University Press, 1952); Stuart McConnell, *Glorious Contentment* (Chapel Hill: University of North Carolina Press, 1992); Barbara Gannon, *The Won Cause: Black and White Comradeship in the Grand Army of the Republic* (Chapel Hill: University of North Carolina Press, 2011); Marten, *Sing Not War*. Authors David Blight, Caroline Janney, and Matthew Brian Jordan also incorporate frequent GAR references in their works.

7. The GAR's widespread association with and support of the Republican Party during Reconstruction alienated inducted and prospective Democratic-affiliated members, causing a steep decline in membership. McConnell, *Glorious Contentment*, xiv; Gannon, *The Won Cause*, 20–21; Marten, *Sing Not War*, 12.

8. In addition to promulgating its own innovative brand of patriotism, which emphasized the sacrifices of fallen service members, shared military service, and the flag, the GAR lobbied for pensions and other veteran welfare benefits on the state and federal levels of government. See Cecilia Elizabeth O'Leary, *To Die For: The Paradox of American Patriotism* (Princeton, N.J.: Princeton University Press, 2000), 30; Marten, *Sing Not War*.

9. Gannon, *The Won Cause*, 3–6.

10. O'Leary, *To Die For*, 134–35; Matthew Dennis, *Red, White, and Blue Letter Days: An American Calendar* (Ithaca, N.Y.: Cornell University Press, 2005), 226.

11. In *Race and Reunion*, Blight labels and compares three sects of postwar remembrance: reconciliationists or reunionists, who sought to bridge the divide between North and South at the expense of African Americans; white supremacists, who were predominantly Southern and perpetuated the Lost Cause; and emancipationists, who fought to keep slavery and emancipation centered in postbellum remembrance. David Blight, *Race and Reunion: The Civil War in American Memory* (Cambridge, Mass.: Belknap Press of Harvard University Press, 2003).

South, in former border states, and in parts of the West. However, that argument, as it applies to the North, especially in urban centers, warrants additional scrutiny. Meanwhile, the second body of work, led by Barbara Gannon and Caroline Janney, attests to the holiday's interracial foundations among Union veterans in the North but stops short of interpreting them in light of broader public participation and perceptions of remembrance.[12] Supported by substantial newspaper and archival findings, this article situates Brooklyn's Memorial Day exercises during the Gilded Age within the crosshairs of race and national identity, and it centers emancipation within veteran and nonveteran postwar remembrance in the public domain.

Memorial Day in Reconstruction and the Gilded Age

Yours has the suffering been / The memory shall be ours
—Henry Wadsworth Longfellow, "Decoration Day" (1882)

In the twenty-first-century United States, the average citizen recognizes the purpose and ambiance of Memorial Day as a federal holiday, complete with parades and perhaps wreath-laying, along with summer cookouts and commercial sales gaining equal attention. These scenes and the overall national sentiment associated with the last Monday of May, however, diverge in clear ways from the holiday's post-Reconstruction and Gilded Age origins. Remembrance and execution of the holiday has changed over time, but its roots remain the same. In the historiography, Memorial Day, or Decoration Day, falls under the purview of Memory studies in conjunction with studies of the Civil War Era. Memory, capitalized in this instance and for the purpose of this study, refers to the manner in which a nation collectively remembers its past, which differs from personal memory, its lowercase cousin.[13] Only in the last few decades has Memory become a major lens or approach of interest for historians of the Civil War Era. Since then, a canon of seminal works has established itself.[14] The reason for this uptick stems from the Nation's perceptions of the American Civil War and its enduring and ongoing consequences. It is impossible for any scholar to write about America's bloodiest conflict without paying due diligence to Memory.

While Memorial Day's legacy is steeped in ritual, its obscure evolution requires an examination of post–Civil War Memory in order to situate and investigate interracial participation. The holiday's origins are muddled across sectional and racial lines, with formal acts of mourning being the one constant.[15] Both Unionists and former Confederates portrayed

---

12. Gannon, *The Won Cause*; Janney, *Remembering the Civil War*, 8, 75, 119.
13. Gannon, *The Won Cause*, 3.
14. Three of those scholarly works, which figure prominently in the following pages, include Blight, *Race and Reunion*; Janney, *Remembering the Civil War*; and Barbara Gannon, *Americans Remember Their Civil War* (Santa Barbara, Calif.: Praeger, 2017).
15. Dennis, *Red, White, and Blue Letter Days*, 221; Blight, *Race and Reunion*, 65.

themselves as the ritual's originators. Victorious postrebellion celebrations in the North allotted time to recognize the Union dead—local and distant.[16] Tied to a distinct Union cause, remembrance took place in Northern streets and graveyards, where the living came together to pay homage to the dead.[17] According to federal decree, the town of Waterloo, New York, holds distinction for being the birthplace of Memorial Day due to its well-chronicled memorial remembrances in May of 1866.[18] At the same time, white ex-Confederates, asserted their ownership of the day's heritage, citing Southern women's practice of placing flowers on their beloveds' graves.[19] Still, there was a racial element to Memorial Day outside of sectional conflict. David Blight claims emancipated Black South Carolinians and their white Northern abolitionist allies founded the observance when an interracial crowd held a parade and decorated the graves of the Union fallen in Charleston on May 1, 1865.[20] Over time, as Reconstruction ended and the Gilded Age commenced, it would become clear that Memorial Day and patriotism provided cause for all to rally around the flag.

Not everyone was in favor of the observance and some thought it best to dismiss Memorial Day for various reasons. One *New York Times* journalist claimed that the holiday would serve only to stoke the "smouldering [*sic*] flames that are almost extinguished in the breasts of the people of the two sections."[21] When recalling the rationale of those Northerners, Hosea W. Rood, a Union veteran, GAR member, and historian, wrote: "They feared it would tend to keep alive the memories of the war, and foster animosities that would better be forgotten; some also objected to the expense that might be incurred for music and flowers."[22] Overall, those in favor of erasing it from the calendar were more prevalent in Northern states, where some reviled the idea of celebrating what they saw as a Confederate-derived day of remembrance.[23] Another group, the Anti-Masonic Party, criticized the decoration of graves as a pagan, masonic practice.[24] However, the collective voice of those who supported Decoration Day stifled the outcry of those against.

Beginning in 1868 with Maj. Gen. John A. Logan's "General Order Number 11," the GAR began a gradual campaign to lead public commemorative efforts and subsumed Decoration Day into its organizational mission. Logan, who also led the GAR early in its life and who backed its racial integration, designated May 30 a national holy day *"for the purpose of strewing with flowers or otherwise decorating the graves of comrades who died in defense*

---

16. Barbara Gannon, conversations with author, September 2021.
17. Gannon, *Americans Remember Their Civil War*, 21.
18. U.S. Department of Veterans Affairs, Office of Public and Intergovernmental Affairs, *The Origins of Memorial Day*, May 23, 2018.
19. Janney, *Remembering the Civil War*, 99; Dennis, *Red, White, and Blue Letter Days*, 221.
20. Blight, *Race and Reunion*, 65; see also Dennis, *Red, White, and Blue Letter Days*, 221.
21. *New York Times*, quoted in *New York Soldier's Friend*, June 27, 1868.
22. Hosea W. Rood, "The Grand Army of the Republic," *Wisconsin Magazine of History* 6, no. 4 (June 1923): 406, http://www.jstor.org/stable/4630452.
23. Janney, *Remembering the Civil War*, 99.
24. John W. Phelps, "Decoration Day," John Wolcott Phelps Papers, Series V, Box 3, Folder 12, Manuscripts and Archives Division, New York Public Library (NYPL).

of their country during the late rebellion."[25] *Per Logan, the "country" mentioned included only those states and territories loyal to the Union.*[26] *His request to Congress to make Memorial Day a national day of commemoration was designed not only to recognize service but to counter Southern ideology.*[27] *Only one side had defended the Union.*[28] *As a result, a* new pillar was added to enhance the society's mission: to honor the Union's heroic dead.[29] Accordingly, chapter 1, article 1 of the GAR's Rules and Regulations obligated all members "to perpetuate the memory and history of the dead and maintain allegiance to the United States of America."[30] In this respect and others, the GAR afforded Black and white veterans a venue through which to build on their wartime sacrifices, counter Lost Cause ideologies, and showcase their patriotic zeal during Reconstruction and the Gilded Age.

From 1868 onward, especially following the fraternity's resurrection in the late 1870s, Memorial Day gained popularity on the national stage and contributed to the GAR's resurgence.[31] New York was no different. The state's GAR department succeeded in pushing the state's legislature and governor to pass and sign an act on Memorial Day. Passed on May 22, 1873, it declared May 30 a state holiday, making New York State the first in the nation to officially do so.[32] The campaign testified to the strength of the GAR's combined lobbying power. Within Brooklyn, starting in 1881, local Black and white posts paraded together annually in front of thousands, including honored guests, such as the president and the governor of New York.[33] Comrades placed such importance on memorialization

25. John A. Logan, "General Orders, No. 11," Headquarters Grand Army of the Republic, Washington, D.C., May 5, 1868, in Grand Army of the Republic Brooklyn City Post 233, minutes, Manuscripts and Archives Division, NYPL.
26. Decorating Confederate graves, those bearing the names of traitors, became a contested topic among GAR posts. While Logan and many veterans were not in favor of recognizing Confederate service and sacrifice on the battlefield, others disagreed and asserted that their bravery in the heat of battle deserved recognition; M. Keith Harris, *Across the Bloody Chasm: The Culture of Commemoration among Civil War Veterans* (Baton Rouge: Louisiana State University Press, 2014), 50–51, 105–6.
27. Dennis, *Red, White, and Blue Letter Days*, 224–25.
28. Dennis, 245.
29. Rood, "The Grand Army of the Republic," 403.
30. Albert C. Leonard, *Grand Army of the Republic Hand Book* (Lancaster, Pa.: A.C. Leonard, 1884), 8, https://hdl.handle.net/2027/loc.ark:/13960/t44q80v51.
31. Grand Army of the Republic, Department of New York, *Proceedings of the Twelfth Annual Encampment of the Grand Army of the Republic Department of New York, Held at Utica, January 23d and 24th, 1878* (Buffalo, N.Y.: Young, Lockwood & Co's Steam Press, 1878), 21 (all New York Department encampments hereafter will be cited as *[Numbered] Encampment*); Dearing, *Veterans in Politics*, 214.
32. Robert Burns Beath, *History of the Grand Army of the Republic* (New York: Bryan, Taylor and Co., 1889), 453; James D. Bell and W. Burt Cook Jr., *Appendix No. 1: Chronological List of the Laws of New York Relating to the War of the Rebellion and Veterans of the War, 1861–1910* (Albany, N.Y.: J. B. Lyon & Co., State Printers, 1910), 60a, https://archive.org/details/chronologicallis00bell/page/n1/mode/2up.
33. Henry W. B. Howard, ed., *The Eagle and Brooklyn: The Record of the Progress of the Brooklyn Daily Eagle Issued in Commemoration of its Semicentennial and Occupancy of its New Building; Together with the History of the City of Brooklyn from its Settlement to the Present Time,* Proof

that in 1884 they formed the Memorial and Executive Committee for Kings County, whose founding purpose was "to secure a better observance of Memorial Day."[34] By 1895, May 30 had fully transformed into the "Sabbath of the Grand Army of the Republic."[35] Decoration Day's popularity blossomed in the City of Brooklyn and countless other towns where the GAR existed and veterans roamed, welcoming the participation of citizens, regardless of race, and encouraging solidarity.

Applying the GAR's Integrated Mission to Memorial Day

"To let all men know that the ties of brotherhood, wedded at the camp-fires still bind together the members of the Grand Army"
—Comrade Jas. Duncan, Greenwood Cemetery (1879)

Predicating the holiday and informing its origins, the American Civil War (1861–65) left a tremendous imprint on the City of Brooklyn.[36] The city had sent some 28,000 to 30,000 men, just under 10 percent of its overall population, to fight in the Union armies and state militias, along with an untold number of noncombatants.[37] Moreover, Brooklyn's role in preserving the Union stayed fresh in the minds of GAR men and residents beyond 1865. Addressing the city at-large in 1880, Cdr. L. Coe Young of the New York Department proclaimed, "We remember well the glorious achievements of your illustrious sons and how well they maintained your reputation for devotion and loyalty to the flag."[38] "We remember that many of the best regiments of the army . . . came from Brooklyn."[39] Locals served in prominent units, such as the 48th, 84th, and 87th New York Infantry Regiments, in addition to the 20th U.S. Colored Infantry Regiment.[40] Moreover, the ethnic and cultural melting pot of these battlefield-bound Brooklynites was mirrored in the city's postbellum GAR,

ed. (Brooklyn, N.Y.: Brooklyn Daily Eagle, 1893), 959; Beath, *History of the Grand Army of the Republic*, 445; Dennis, *Red, White, and Blue Letter Days*, 223.

34. Beath, *History of the Grand Army of the Republic*, 448; per societal regulations and tradition, GAR members referred to one another as "comrades."

35. Department of New York, GAR, *Memorial Day, May 30th, 1895* (Albany, N.Y.: 1895), https://hdl.handle.net/2027/loc.ark:/13960/t9w09g94h.

36. Epigraph above, from "Oration by Comrade Jas. Duncan [at Greenwood Cemetery]," in GAR, New York City, *Decoration Day, [Report and proceedings], May 30th, 1879* (New York: John Polhemus, printer, 1879), 86, Microfilm ZH-IK, p.v. 51, no. 2, NYPL.

37. William C. DeWitt, Corporation Counsel, quoted in GAR, Department of New York, *Fifteenth and Sixteenth Encampments, 1880–81* (Nyack, N.Y.: Rockland County Journal Print, 1881), 21, Center for Brooklyn History, Brooklyn Public Library; Stephen M. Ostrander, *A History of the City of Brooklyn and Kings County*, ed. Alexander Black, 2 vols. (Brooklyn: n.p., 1894), 127; percentage calculation is based on Brooklyn's population as reflected in the 1860 federal census. The modern-day equivalent to this statistic, as of 2020, stands at over 270,000 men.

38. GAR, Department of New York, *Fifteenth and Sixteenth Encampments, 1880–81*, 22.

39. GAR, Department of New York, *Fifteenth and Sixteenth Encampments, 1880–81*, 22.

40. The 84th and 87th N.Y. Volunteer Infantry Regiments were both state militia units.

with native-born, Irish, German, and African American predominant posts abounding. After the disbanding of the federal armies, Brooklyn's streets overflowed with Union veterans, some returning home and others looking to make new lives for themselves. For whatever reason, each member found renewed purpose, an oasis of some sort, in the GAR. For African Americans, this feeling derived from the bona fide social and political equality that did not readily exist outside the group.[41]

In the case of Brooklyn and other northern centers, the cultural richness of urban living propelled that sense of purpose as well. Before and after losing its independent status in 1898, when it was folded into the City of New York, Brooklyn boasted an increasingly diverse population and growing economic footprint.[42] The populace of its county, the County of Kings, which rose by over half a million people from 1860 to 1890, reflected its place as a national crossroads of race and class.[43] Newly arrived immigrants from Western and Eastern Europe lived near established Irish-Catholic families, down the hill from nativist WASPs, and across town from emancipated and freeborn African Americans.[44] Democrats worked and fraternized with their Republican neighbors. Moreover, their candidates took turns occupying city hall, as Democrats held only a slight margin over Grand Old Party voters. Brooklyn's budding diversity also manifested in other ways, namely, through celebration of Black and white service that contributed to emancipation and the Union's preservation but fell short of full integration.

Alongside the metropolis's racial and ethnic make-up, the war itself played a role in bringing Brooklyn's blue veterans together. Many white Union veterans, who served in units organized from the city's population, had fought alongside U.S. Colored Troops in battle, many of whom hailed from the same city.[45] After the rebellion ended, shared service on the battlefield translated into shared remembrance. It is important to note that such camaraderie did not yield full integration, as interracial GAR posts never materialized within the confines of Kings County or its neighbors. Locally, the organization was integrated in some ways but still segregated in others. It is possible that many resident white veterans viewed

---

41. The GAR's integrated policies thrived in the Northern states. Outside of staunch unionist territory, the GAR's referendum on racial inclusion stood tall, but met opposition from some in the South and border states.

42. Prior to 1898, when state legislation combined the five boroughs into the City of New York, Brooklyn was independent from New York and one of the fastest growing cities in the nation.

43. While class serves as an important lens of analysis, especially in urban centers, it will not be thoroughly discussed in this examination nor is it the main subject of this work; the city of Brooklyn fell within the confines of Kings County and, by Reconstruction and the Gilded Age, its cultural composition rivaled that of New York. See Campbell Gibson, *Population of the 100 Largest Cities and Other Urban Places in the United States: 1790 to 1990*, ed. U.S. Bureau of the Census, Population Division (Washington, D.C., 1998), tables 9 and 12.

44. WASPs stands for White Anglo-Saxon Protestants.

45. Per the American Battlefield Trust and N.Y. State Military Museum, the 48th N.Y. Infantry Regiment served alongside USCT units at the following engagements: Olustee (February 20, 1864) and the Crater (July 30, 1864). The 84th N.Y. Infantry fought with USCT members at the Wilderness (May 5–7, 1864), Spotsylvania Court House (May 8–21, 1864), and the Crater.

the body in the same light as their wartime service, and so interpreted the society's integration differently: segregated in organization but united in allegiance to the Constitution and each other as well as to the mission. Differing from Gannon's work, which focuses on the GAR's proceedings behind closed doors, this article concentrates on the GAR's public practices and initiatives and how they were perceived. Moreover, pinpointing antiquated GAR beliefs in one locality does not negate the fact that tremendous racial and cultural progress resulted from its work, namely a public holiday celebrated irrespective of color or background. When viewed in this context, comrades' firm adoption of shared, integrated remembrance on Memorial Day echoed the GAR's interracial policy while providing a platform for all citizens to showcase their past, present, and future patriotic investments.

While not fully actualized, the GAR's National Headquarters' long-standing repudiation of segregation in its ranks served as major cornerstone of the society's identity on all levels. In her thorough study of white and Black comradeship within the GAR, Gannon highlights that, upon forming and joining the GAR, white Union troops, who survived the four-year-long, horrific war, did not forget soldiers of color and the blood they shed side-by-side.[46] They created and sustained a veterans-only body that granted equal footing to all comrades because it represented their respective "won causes" through memory vindication and parity.[47] It was a conscious choice. African Americans served in the same federal armies as everyone else who swore to preserve the nation's integrity and end slavery.[48] In the eyes of GAR comrades, Black troops deserved to reap the fruits of their struggle. However, this argument asserts that elements of interracial comradeship and justice extended far beyond post walls. By joining the GAR or by remembering the war dead, African Americans attested to their own agency in the new American patriotic paradigm, which Memorial Day affirmed.

In Brooklyn, the Black community's involvement in Memorial Day sprang forth in the late 1870s. The GAR's rehabilitated reputation, as a fraternal society that welcomed Union veterans regardless of race, class, creed, or political affiliation emerged at the start of the Gilded Age and figured heavily in its social and political feats during the era's evolution. With Reconstruction over, Radical Republican control abated, and all secessionist states readmitted, African Americans in the South and around the nation found themselves and their rights under assault via racist ideology, legislation, and terror. Acknowledging this reality at a Memorial Day service in New York, Frederick Douglass reminded all attendees that patriotism not only involved remembering the dead but also ensuring their sacrifice to the newly emancipated

---

46. Gannon, *The Won Cause*, 5.
47. Gannon, 5, 15.
48. It is important to note that while African Americans served in the nation's armed forces during the Civil War and subsequent conflicts, they did so in segregated units. De jure segregation existed in the U.S. military until 1948.

was not in vain.[49] In keeping with Douglass's plea, the appearance of African Americans on Brooklyn's Memorial Day scene predated the establishment of New York State's first all-Black GAR post in 1880.[50] It was not until April of 1881, that the William Lloyd Garrison Post No. 207 became Kings County's first chartered African American GAR unit.[51]

As already noted, the circumstances that delayed the William Lloyd Garrison Post's creation remain murky. The GAR's complex, integrated foundation was not without blemish. Racial bigotry and the blackballing practices were present in GAR posts throughout the North.[52] Moreover, the city at-large and its veterans were not immune from perpetuating racial intolerance. Black and white newspapers were quick to point out injustices committed against African American members and to expose some GAR members for their deep-seated biases.[53] The locality's racial politics also factored into the absence of multiracial posts. Democrats and Republicans, both represented in Brooklyn posts, still fought over matters of reconciliation. Politics shaped the dispersal of the municipality's demographics. Brooklyn's comparatively low Black population, numbering about 5,600 inhabitants as of 1870, was scattered across widely separated neighborhoods, which could have equated to a recruiting issue for the GAR.[54] Additionally, Gannon explains that while they valued their fellowship with whites, African American veterans "consciously created, maintained, and sustained, racially exclusive organizations . . . within the larger, interracial GAR."[55] In light of racial inequity, comrades' work to expunge this from their rituals constituted a progressive, ongoing process.

The initial lack of chartered posts to rally around did not discourage African American veterans, along with their families and the entire community, from paying their respects to the dead and demonstrating their patriotism. The GAR's adoption of Memorial Day as its

49. Frederick Douglass, "Speech delivered in Madison Square, New York, Decoration Day," (New York, N.Y., May 30, 1878), Frederick Douglass Papers, Library of Congress (LOC), Washington, D.C.; GAR, New York City, *Decoration Day, Report of Proceedings, May 30th, 1878* (New York: Geo. F. Nesbitt and Co., 1878), 61–62, Microfilm ZH-1K, p.v. 51, no. 1, NYPL.

50. While there were no Black posts in Brooklyn, members of the Black community, including veterans who were not yet GAR comrades, participated in the day's exercises, whether as bystanders along the parade route or at the cemeteries.

51. The Garrison Post's date of chartering was taken from a database compiled by the Sons of Union Civil War Veterans; see Sons of Union Veterans of the Civil War, "Grand Army of the Republic (GAR) Records Project," April 28, 2023, http://www.garrecords.org.

52. "Blackballing" occurred when white posts voted on prospective new members. Each man would cast his vote anonymously by placing either a white or black marble into the receptacle. Since election had to be unanimous, if the candidate in question received one or more black marbles or balls he would not be admitted into the post. For more context, see McConnell, *Glorious Contentment*, 111–12, 218.

53. "The Color-Line in Theatres," *New York Freeman*, December 18, 1886; "At Fever Heat," *Eagle*, May 7, 1887.

54. Edwin G. Burrows and Mike Wallace, *Gotham: A History of New York City to 1898* (New York: Oxford University Press, 1999), 993; when viewed next to larger cities, like New York, Chicago, and Boston, Brooklyn had a smaller African American population in terms of percentage.

55. Gannon, *The Won Cause*, 37.

own sabbath enshrined in the holiday the same interracial character. Unlike in other urban centers, Brooklyn's integrated remembrance of the dead preceded and nurtured the same among the living. However, there is little doubt that this phenomenon too was steeped in GAR influence, since posts bore responsibility for ensuring proper commemoration. White comrades would have surely included Black veterans and their fallen comrades in the day's rhetoric. According to existing sources, the earliest instances of shared Black and white remembrance occurred in local cemeteries. New York City's "Decoration Day Report of Proceedings" from 1878 details that a crowd of about 10,000, consisting of GAR members and pilgrims from all over the area, decorated Confederate and Union graves at Brooklyn's Cypress Hills Cemetery, including those of U.S. Colored Troops.[56] The program also notes that at nearby Greenwood Cemetery, "The pouring rain did not in the least dampen the patriotic order of the thousands from Brooklyn and New York who crowded every pathway and every avenue . . . from noon until dark."[57]

In addition to the decoration of graves, speeches by GAR veterans centered the meaning of Memorial Day around communal remembrance and patriotism. Speaking to those in attendance at Greenwood on May 30, 1879, James Duncan of New York's J. Lafayette Riker Post, No. 62, reemphasized the GAR's inclusive and freedom-oriented mission:

> My comrades, the mission of the Grand Army of the Republic is, to disseminate the principles of liberty, to teach patriotism, and to put down oppression of every form, and to let all men know that the ties of brotherhood, wedded at the camp-fires still bind together the members of the Grand Army . . . that the nation . . . may still continue to be in reality "The land of the free, and the home of the brave."[58]

Regarding what they had fought for and perceived to be the bedrock of their fraternal society, white members were remarkably consistent in their supportive views of African Americans' service and their place in their ranks—both before and after Garrison Post's creation.[59] As M. Keith Harris observes, "Their devotion to issues and memories of the war years appeared as sharp in the late nineteenth century and early twentieth century as they had in 1865."[60] Under the auspices of Decoration Day, Brooklyn's boys-in-blue marched against Southern mythology, thereby cementing the sacred and victorious Union cause in people's hearts and minds. At the dawn of the Gilded Age, the holiday's place in white but also in Black inhabitants' perceptions of the Civil War and in the nation's annual remembrance of the fallen grew more decisive.

---

56. GAR, New York City, "Decoration Day, Report of Proceedings, May 30th, 1878," 76–77.
57. GAR, New York City, "Decoration Day, Report of Proceedings, May 30th, 1878," 81.
58. "Oration by Comrade Jas. Duncan" in GAR, New York City, *Decoration Day, Report of Proceedings, May 30th, 1879*, (New York: John Polhemus, printer, 1879), 86, Microfilm ZH-IK, p.v. 51, no. 2, NYPL.
59. Harris, *Across the Bloody Chasm*, 7.
60. Harris, 7.

About a month after the GAR's New York Department chartered Brooklyn's first African American unit, the comrades of the William Lloyd Garrison Post marched in step with their white brethren down Clinton Avenue onto Lafayette and Schermerhorn in Brooklyn's hallowed Memorial Day parade.[61] The integrated martial affair was "one of the most imposing ever witnessed in Brooklyn."[62] Under the direction of its first commander, John Little, Garrison members now basked in the warmth of the GAR and their *won cause* with a detail of thirty-six men.[63] Speaking against a backdrop of humble marble headstones, Reverend E. A. Haine eulogized that the city's "fallen comrades sought to restore to the oppressed the God given liberties of their nature."[64] "Freedom in our minds, freedom in our homes, freedom in our country, was a song composed in . . . their every heart."[65] The day-long spectacle centered the fallen and championed the universal freedoms many had died for and Union veterans had fought for. For Black citizens and their white confidants, whether former military or civilian, the parade and nuanced civic recognition of African American devotion confirmed their equal stakes in the Grand Army, Memorial Day, and American patriotism.

Brooklyn's posts placed great importance on sustaining their organization's interracial nature throughout the 1880s. Moreover, comradeship and shared appreciation for the dead and for wartime service extended beyond the temporal confines of Memorial Day. GAR members, their families, and friends held community meetings to listen to guest speakers, revisit memories of the war, and enjoy one another's company. Led by the county's posts, a packed multiracial crowd of over five thousand people met in the Clermont Avenue Temple on September 26, 1881, to celebrate the life of the late President James A. Garfield, who had been assassinated a week earlier.[66] At another crowded church gathering at Brooklyn's Bridge Street African Methodist Episcopal (AME) Church, Black and white attendees listened to a sermon by the church's pastor, Reverend J. B. Stansbury. The GAR, he pronounced, was "the grandest association in existence and thanked our Heavenly Father that he lived to witness this fraternization between the members of the order without respect to race, color, or previous condition of servitude."[67] To celebrate the William Lloyd Garrison Post's third anniversary, dignitaries, such as Mayor Seth Low and Commander James Tanner of the Grand Army of New York State, joined members and their families in the same Bridge Street Church to reflect on the life of the post's namesake.[68] These conspicuous events attest to the reality that the GAR of King's County and the public both appreciated

---

61. "Perpetuated: The Grand Army and Military Parade," *Eagle*, May 30, 1881.
62. "Perpetuated: The Memory of the Soldiers and Sailors of the Union," *Eagle*, May 30, 1881.
63. "Perpetuated: The Grand Army and Military Parade"; Gannon, *The Won Cause*, 7.
64. "Perpetuated: Cypress Hills Cemetery," *Eagle*, May 30, 1881.
65. "Perpetuated: Cypress Hills Cemetery."
66. "Grand Army of the Republic Celebration at the Temple—Address by General Slocum and Rev. Henry Ward Beecher," *Eagle*, September 27, 1881.
67. "William Lloyd Garrison Post G.A.R., No 207," *New York Globe*, February 24, 1883.
68. "William Lloyd Garrison Post," *Eagle*, April 12, 1884.

integration's intrinsic value, but that their true roots lay in the hearts and minds of support-ive local Union veterans and Brooklyn's Decoration Day history.

In the late 1880s, Brooklyn's twenty-three posts, still segregated within post walls, fur-ther devoted themselves to maximizing the observance's interracial value, through ingrain-ing into the public both admiration for the dead and loyalty to the country.[69] With Gen. Ulysses S. Grant's Tomb prominent in the background, Chaplain D. O. Ferris of Brooklyn's U.S. Grant Post No. 327, told his fellow members that, "By this service, without distinction of race or creed, we renew our pledge to exercise a spirit of fraternity among ourselves . . . and of loyalty to the authority and union of the United States of America."[70] Such were the debts the living owed to the dead. Every aspect of the holiday sounded patriotism's bu-gle call to veteran and civilian alike, no matter one's racial identity. GAR commemorative songs, like "The Army of the Grass," "Our Flag at Fort Wagner," and "Morris Island," ex-uded Memorial Day's purpose and interracial overtones.[71] The metropolis-wide campaign to reinforce unionist memory translated into a resounding success in terms of public par-ticipation and displays of reverence for the living and dead. As integration aided in the Grand Army's revitalization after Reconstruction, so too did it help catapult Brooklyn's Decoration Day observances, in terms of both veteran and public involvement, to regional and national fame.

Tabloids proclaimed that every year's Memorial Day tributes and attendance eclipsed their previous iteration. Only a year after congratulating the city's populace on a fantastic commemoration, the *Eagle* claimed in 1886 that the holiday "never had so complete an observance before."[72] "The part of Brooklyn in [Memorial Day] has been conspicuous, im-pressive and pathetic."[73] "Well has Brooklyn done her part," remarked the *Brooklyn Times*.[74] Besides drawing local praise, Brooklyn's sacred and chronicled festivities attracted national

---

69. Kings County GAR, *Annual Tabulated Report of the Proceedings of the Bureau of Employment & Emergency Fund, Also the Report of the Pension Committee of the G.A.R. for Kings County, Under the Articles of the Memorial & Executive Committee, Brooklyn, N.Y., February 25th, 1885* (New York: William De Lacy, 1885), 19, New-York Historical Society

70. *Memorial Day, Monday, May 30th, 1887: Ceremonies at Gen'l Grant's Tomb, at Riverside Park, New York, U.S. Grant Post No. 327, Department of New York, G.A.R.* (New York: Department of New York, G.A.R., 1887), 10, Cranston Family Papers, 1994.013, Box 2, Folder: U.S. Grant Post No. 327, G.A.R.: Clippings and Ephemera, 1884–1887, and undated, Center for Brooklyn History, Brooklyn Public Library.

71. George W. Bungay, *Our Grand Army of the Republic* (New York: Hard and Parsons, 1888), 12, 15, 30 https://hdl.handle.net/2027/loc.ark:/13960/t3708zc5r; African American units gained distinction for their bravery and tenacity in-action at Fort Wagner and Morris Island.

72. *Eagle*, quoted in Grand Army of the Republic, Department of New York, U.S. Grant Post, No. 327, *Memorial Day, May 30th and 31st, 1886: U.S. Grant Post, No. 327, Department of New York, G.A.R.* (New York: G.A.R., 1886), 15, NYPL.

73. *Eagle*, quoted in Grand Army of the Republic, Department of New York, U.S. Grant Post, No. 327, *Memorial Day, May 30th and 31st, 1886*, 15.

74. *Brooklyn Times*, quoted in Grand Army of the Republic, Department of New York, U.S. Grant Post, No. 327, *Memorial Day, May 30th and 31st, 1886*, 15.

attention. Distinguished visitors, such as Civil War generals, high-ranking cabinet members, and multiple presidents, routinely attended to witness a cross section of America gather in the name of loyalty to country and flag. In anticipation of GAR comrade and President Benjamin Harrison's Memorial Day visit in 1889, the *Eagle* declared Brooklyn "a city of homes, a city of hospitality, a city of patriotism and a city of just such wholesome and genuine qualities as American Chief Magistrates should exemplify in their characters and incite in the minds of the people."[75] In retrospect, it owed the GAR for cultivating these qualities and patriotic fervor.

By the late 1880s and 1890s, the GAR, with its unique structure, had dashed segregationist views of Memorial Day and spurred interracial involvement in its "festival of the dead" in Brooklyn.[76] Mary Dearing argues that white Northern GAR members cared little about the inclusion of African American members and eventually adopted a Southern approach to marginalizing them.[77] Members' own actions and words, however, point to their appreciation of Black service and contributions to Brooklyn's patriotic reputation. Ceremonies at the municipality's cemeteries continued not only to display but also to expand their interracial roots. At the New York GAR's annual encampment in 1888, the department's chaplain reported that the rituals at Cypress Hills, where U.S. Colored Troops rested near their white brothers-in-arms, were "impressive and witnessed by over fifty thousand persons" who hailed from various parts of the city and its sister towns.[78] Only ten years earlier, in 1878, Memorial Day attendance at the same Brooklyn cemetery stood at ten thousand persons.[79] In the course of one decade, participation at one event witnessed a 500 percent increase. Not every person at Cypress that day lived in Kings County. Regardless, a large number did, which reflects the overarching value residents placed on remembrance and national loyalty.

In the 1890s, Brooklynites, along with the rest of America, grew indifferent to traditional Memorial Day observations. They were tired of hearing about the war or had severed their personal connections to it. More citizens, instead of visiting cemeteries and reflecting on the rebellion that had occurred some twenty-five years prior, saw the holiday as nothing more than a parade and a day off from work.[80] Embittered by what they witnessed, members of the Kings County and statewide GAR voiced their disappointment and attempted to reverse the degradative tide.[81] Referencing their shared victories of reunion and

75. "President Harrison in Brooklyn," *Eagle*, May 29, 1889.
76. Grand Army of the Republic, Department of New York, U.S. Grant Post, No. 327, *Memorial Day, May 30th and 31st, 1886*, 6.
77. Dearing, *Veterans in Politics*, 411–14.
78. GAR, Department of New York, *Twenty-Second Encampment, 1888* (Albany: Press of Brandow Printing Co., 1888), 88, https://hdl.handle.net/2027/uiug.30112002975073.
79. GAR, New York City, *Decoration Day, Report of Proceedings, May 30th, 1878*, 77.
80. GAR, Department of New York, *Twenty-Fifth Encampment, 1891* (Albany, N.Y.: James B. Lyon, State Printer, 1891), 142, Center for Brooklyn History, Brooklyn Public Library.
81. GAR, Department of New York, 142.

emancipation, Black and white veterans tapped into an age of fear when the Union was at risk of crumbling and slavery's expansion or demise was held in the balance. Others, like one anonymous Brooklyn comrade who suggested the creation of a mixed-race color guard to lead the city's Decoration Day parade, believed aesthetic changes inherent in the GAR's martial and integrated identity would achieve positive effect.[82] These ideas and others achieved limited success in augmenting attendance figures at public ceremonies. However, progress had been made. Over the course of two decades, the GAR's push for integration in Brooklyn's Memorial Day intensified and gained permanence from a growing sense of African American purpose.

African Americans' Patriotic Investment in Memorial Day

I am here to speak . . . and I do so not in the cringing spirit of the slave, but in the manly spirit of an American citizen.
—"Memorials," *Eagle*, May 30, 1881

Hundreds of thousands of African Americans, both those born into freedom and those born into slavery, were among the over one million veterans who fought for the Union and survived. In addition to evading bullets, fighting disease, and confronting the enemy, Black troops dealt with incredible prejudice and discrimination while they served in federal ranks. Segregation was normative. Asked to perform wartime duties similar to and, in some cases, more dangerous than those of white men, "colored units," as they were called at the time, received lower pay and often suffered from receiving inadequate training and supplies. Despite these obstacles, their service demonstrated a yearning for equality and freedom. After the battlefield hostilities ceased, the federal government demanded that secessionist states ratify the Thirteenth and Fourteenth Amendments to the U.S. Constitution to be readmitted to the Union. All signs pointed to a meaningful reconstructive period for African Americans and their white abolitionist allies after the cessation of hostilities. However, even though the war had ended legal slavery, Black veterans discovered that their military service proved incapable of yielding the lasting civic equality they desired.[83]

In Brooklyn, like many cities, villages, and communities throughout the country, African American veterans witnessed the promises of their sacrifices come crashing down; but they did not capitulate. As John Casey states, "They were convinced like their white comrades that the war was highly significant to their identity and to the future of the nation as a whole."[84] Notwithstanding their community's small size in comparison to those in New

---

82. "Suggested by a Veteran: Some New Departures for Decoration Day," *Eagle*, February 22, 1897.
83. John A. Casey Jr., *New Men: Reconstructing the Image of the Veteran in Late-Nineteenth Century American Literature and Culture* (New York: Fordham University Press, 2015), 162.
84. Casey, 162.

York, Chicago, and Boston, Brooklyn's Black former servicemen rallied against waves of change within the national commemorative ethos that dismissed the war's causes as unimportant and espoused total white reconciliation as the way forward. Black and white Union veterans in the County of Kings vowed to remember. Before and after joining the GAR, they labored to ensure that the dead were honored, that they themselves were respected, and that future generations understood why they had gone to war.[85]

While the aforementioned mission burned deep in the hearts of all GAR men, it did so especially in the hearts of Black soldiers, who appealed to a nation that did not fully appreciate their efforts and struggles. Moreover, Black soldiers carried that internal purpose into their postwar civilian careers. When compared to its sister counties, Kings housed a substantial population of educated, middle-class African Americans that increased as more fled neighboring New York.[86] These troops-turned-professionals, in addition to noneducated veterans, dedicated their labors to new pursuits: socioeconomic status, loyalty to country, and community involvement. Beginning in the late 1870s and solidifying over the subsequent decades of the Gilded Age, African American GAR comrades saw Memorial Day as an opportunity to translate their wartime fight into a larger communal movement that promoted Black agency in Brooklyn. At stake stood their place as historical actors on equal footing with whites in the postwar patriotic paradigm.

Before examining how African Americans saw themselves within Decoration Day's commemorative meaning, it is first necessary to acknowledge a crucial aspect of nineteenth-century Black Civil War studies. Across the spectrum, past and present Civil War era research on African Americans during and after the rebellion suffers from a comparative dearth of primary, archival material. Black comradeship in the GAR is no exception. For example, as manifested in this study, the records of Brooklyn's two Black GAR units, the Garrison and Beecher Posts, no longer exist. There is simply not as much available in collections from the perspective of Black veterans and actors as there is from white ones. There is a litany of reasons why, including societal dissuasion, racism in archival construction, actors' illiteracy, and natural deterioration. Given the limits of the sources, it can prove more difficult to write meaningful histories about marginalized groups and minorities.

Effective ways to historicize African Americans in the post–Civil War era abound in the presence of viable alternatives. Newspapers, which play an oversized part in this section and overall argument, serve as a vital source of information. Brooklyn's *Eagle* published full coverage of the city's Memorial Day festivities every year. Columns, chock full of detail, contain scripts of the numerous speeches delivered, and include visual descriptions of the ceremonies themselves. In *Across the Bloody Chasm*, Harris declares that most veterans contributed little to the postwar record, and that, while they participated

---

85. Harris, *Across the Bloody Chasm*, 7.
86. Burrows and Wallace, *Gotham*, 972–73.

in patriotic community events, the majority did not record their sentiments.[87] Yet actions, with or without words attached, still provide a valuable means by which to study history. The lack of personal written reflections should not dissuade historians from drawing evidence-based interpretations that further understanding, even as we must be judicious in drawing conclusions.

As seen in newspaper accounts of the era, President Abraham Lincoln's image as the "emancipator and benefactor" of the Black race held significant weight in African American remembrance and perceptions of their own activism in the American postwar patriotic model.[88] Led in joint fashion by Black and white GAR posts, Memorial Day observances at the Lincoln Statue in Prospect Park attracted substantial interracial participation. It was common ground, a place for self-evaluation and patriotic demonstration. Lincoln's legacy, as the Great Emancipator, commander-in-chief, and revered statesman, represented an object of agreement between Black and white attendees. However, Lincoln's value as a saint in connection with his work struck Brooklyn's Black community in ways more profound than its white counterparts. As Black Brooklynites understood it, Lincoln, in conjunction with their own actions and sacrifices, had helped them to become American citizens and partake in the unfurling of patriotic sentiment no matter the day or year, but especially on Memorial Day.

In commemorating the solemn occasion in 1881, Professor Richard Theodore Greener, Harvard's first African American graduate and a contemporary of Frederick Douglass, asked a multiracial audience at the statue, "'Can the white people of this country ever know what love for Lincoln is?'"[89] On the subject of the martyred president's value to his race, Greener reasoned further that white people "have never known what it is to be ostracized by prejudice of caste, to be trodden down as slaves, and, in my opinion, it is the four million of black men in our land who alone can appreciate he largeness of Lincoln's heart."[90] At the monument, participants paid dual homage to the assassinated president and to the fallen. Greener's purpose was two-fold. He explained that while he "came here to lay the tribute of the colored race upon the monument of their emancipator and benefactor," he was also there "to speak for the 185,000 black men who died that this country might be preserved."[91] In the eyes of Black veterans and those oppressed under antebellum norms that pervaded the United States, Abraham Lincoln's memory deserved invocation and remembrance alongside the Union dead. Both the late president and former soldiers, particularly those who paid the ultimate sacrifice during the rebellion, perpetuated the Union and helped to free enslaved people.

87. Harris, *Across the Bloody Chasm*, 8.
88. "Memorials," *Eagle*, May 30, 1881.
89. "Memorials.".
90. "Memorials."
91. "Memorials."

Emancipated, enfranchised, and empowered African Americans such as Greener saw in Lincoln and in Memorial Day's greater mission of remembrance an opportunity to portray themselves as practitioners of the same patriotism and citizenship as that of their white neighbors. The living veterans gathered and the deceased, whose graves they decorated, presented to those once in bondage and without citizenship a new equality before the law. As he touted the sacrifice of Black soldiers, the Greener revealed to everyone assembled that he spoke "not in the cringing spirit of the slave, but in the manly spirit of an American citizen."[92] By doing so, he challenged not only other Black citizens but also whites to notice and respect that transformation. In closing,. Greener issued a challenge to the crowd: "How can you best keep in eternal remembrance the name of Abraham Lincoln?" His answer, geared toward Black onlookers but particularly toward whites, did not advocate for the raising of monuments.[93] Instead, he believed, the best act of remembrance was "by resolving to take up the sentiment which Lincoln uttered at Gettysburg, by seeing to it that the liberty which he guaranteed to the slave shall be maintained."[94] Theirs was not a passive task, but one that required action and patriotism.

In the same spirit that Greener hoped would wash over the masses in Brooklyn, Memorial Day services at Prospect Park's Lincoln Monument developed into a tradition for the city's GAR posts and residents. Year after year, Brooklyn's Black comrades, joined by their friends, families, and white brethren, celebrated Decoration Day at the statue to remember their president and fallen friends. Black and white posts routinely swapped responsibility for the exercises, which weathered racial divides and maintained a dialogue between the Black and white communities. When in control of the affair, the Garrison and Beecher Posts elected to have Black ministers give benedictions, and they selected orators who gave speeches to project African Americans' place in the day's remembrance.[95] They shared their perceptions of the war's cause and loyalty to the Union dead. For Black veterans, the opportunity to lead and participate in the services reflected several hard-fought victories and affirmed their agency within the city's patriotic discourse.

At is core, the services at the statue provided an occasion for Black comrades to rally their community around a popular historical figure who took action to improve their status and to show that they themselves possessed that power as well. Lincoln's majesty and antislavery goals allowed white veterans to take pride in their small contributions of service, which occurred under his command. "You see those here who were slaves till he struck off their fetters; you see some who were born free and who but for Lincoln would have been born in slavery, and you see men representing the great armies which rose up at his

---

92. "Memorials."
93. "Memorials."
94. "Memorials."
95. For example, see "At the Lincoln Statue," *Eagle,* May 28, 1888.

command," explained James D. Bell of the Brooklyn GAR's committee of public ceremonies.[96] Its public placement allowed Black GAR men to interact with their white brethren, where they held valuable conversations. Most important, there was the opportunity to share wartime sacrifices in the hope of creating a better tomorrow for their children and grandchildren as well as to perpetuate the unionist narrative of the war. Pausing on this very notion, J. R. B. Smith, an African American GAR member and past department chaplain, recalled to his comrades and all present: "By virtue of the fighting done by us—white men and black men—the children of our race are born in freedom and have gone to school."[97] Emancipation's significance would not be forgotten.

Having witnessed the increasing diversity of the crowds at their fraternity's Memorial Day exercises and in the society they fought to protect, white GAR men realized the dual purpose of the North's bloody victory over the Confederacy. Yes, the Union had been saved, but so had enslaved people. Both deserved attention and celebration. They saw in the interracial crowd of faces around them living reminders that attested to slavery's end and a united nation of free men and women.[98] Those who had fought almost exclusively for the Union's integrity now realized a greater conversion to the tangible outcomes of emancipation. On the sloping hills of Cypress and Greenwood cemeteries rested comrades of dark as well as light skin color, who had given all so that others might be free and remain free. The result was emancipation's newfound inclusion in white remembrance rhetoric, especially among those who did not don the uniform.

As time passed and the nation advanced during the Gilded Age, local citizens and visitors to the city alike realized that emancipation, alongside reunion, factored into Memorial Day's public value. Throngs of residents, representing all races and ethnicities, visiting the Black and white Union deceased accounted for this shift in white perception. Irish-born congressman William McAdoo of New Jersey, struck by the sight at Greenwood Cemetery and aware of the war's implications across the Atlantic, proclaimed: "These victor dead wield the destinies of the living, and the humblest grave of the Union soldier has become a pulpit, preaching universal emancipation from feudalism and despotism."[99] At Queens' Calvary Cemetery, Father Sylvester Malone, the pastor of Saints Peter and Paul Church in South Williamsburg, stated that the North belonged to men such as these and those living comrades in attendance.[100] He elaborated further, saying there was "no question of color, for victory to the North was to be the gain of all, as slavery was to be wiped out from this free land forever."[101] One Colonel Jones perhaps said it best: "Above all . . . stands supreme

96. "The Services at the Lincoln Monument," *Eagle*, May 30, 1892.
97. "The Services at the Lincoln Monument."
98. Gannon, *The Won Cause*, 7.
99. "Impressive Ceremonies at the Soldiers' Monument at Greenwood," *Eagle*, May 30, 1890.
100. "The Services at Calvary Cemetery," *Eagle*, May 30, 1892.
101. "The Services at Calvary Cemetery."

the glory of our work—the great fight we made in support of humanity's just rights, the broken shackles of 4,000,000 slaves; a continent redeemed from internecine strife; a principle established for all the world to work up to, that liberty is the inalienable right of all."[102] Not only was victory shared, but the subsequent outcome and commemoration were as well.

Furthermore, it was not mere verbiage that caused this shift in memory. Action was the primary catalyst, as African Americans displayed their equal standing and investment in Memorial Day through openly visible means. Veterans from the Garrison Post often donated flower pots to decorate Union graves.[103] In the city's annual parade, Brooklyn's Black GAR posts gained appreciation from the public, press, and dignitaries, while marching in line with their brother white posts.[104] Separate from veterans, Black members of the public devoted themselves to being present in large numbers at each year's observances in order to support their veterans and vindicate their role as loyal American citizens. For instance, of the five thousand non-GAR participants at the 1892 ceremony at the Lincoln Statue, two-thirds were African American, drawing respect from the attending *Eagle* journalist.[105] The community's active role in Memorial Day and other patriotic activities, showcasing how it saw itself and its role, contributed to a lack of Black protest in Brooklyn during the Gilded Age.[106] In support of their husbands and fathers, African American women joined affiliated interracial groups, like the Women's Relief Corps (WRC) and the Ladies Grand Army of the Republic (LGAR), to express their patriotic devotion.

Written histories and available sources afford historians a limited view of African American women's work in GAR auxiliaries and the relationships they had with white members.[107] Gannon writes that Black women who joined the WRC and the LGAR "used their status as members of these interracial groups to place the African American experience as central to the collective memory of this conflict."[108] John Kennedy argues that white WRC members valued African Americans' place in unionist memory and the work of Black members in honoring the Union cause.[109] Records show that the Corps' New York Department maintained an active presence in patriotic affairs and gained the GAR's trust

102. "At Evergreens Cemetery," *Eagle*, May 30, 1888.
103. "The Floral Contributions," *Eagle*, May 30, 1882.
104. "Memorial Day," *Havana Journal*, June 8, 1889.
105. "The Services at the Lincoln Monument."
106. Frederick Douglass, *Frederick Douglass in Brooklyn*, ed. Theodore Hamm (New York: Akashic Books, 2017), 160.
107. Like class, gender is a not a main category of analysis in this study. It is, however, an invaluable lens with which to study Civil War commemorative culture and deserves further scholarly exploration.
108. Gannon, *The Won Cause*, 57.
109. John C. Kennedy, "Race, Civil War Memory, and Sisterhood in the Woman's Relief Corps," (paper presented at the Third Annual Conference on Veterans in Society, Roanoke, Va., November 12–14, 2015), 209.

and admiration as a result.[110] Brooklyn's representation on the national level mirrored this.[111] On the local level, women of Garrison No. 33, the city's only Black WRC post, carved out their place next to white members in Decoration Day preparations.[112] Their work and the efforts of their GAR relatives informed a distinct Black patriotic consciousness in Brooklyn, which led to greater involvement among African Americans in Memorial Day observances and interracial dialogue.

Concluding Remarks

"History doesn't repeat itself, but it often rhymes" is an adage often attributed to Mark Twain, who lived through all three of the eras encompassed in this study—the Civil War, Reconstruction, and the Gilded Age.[113] These words, although well over a century old, hold a hidden if not neglected importance for the modern United States. Today's America bears an eerie resemblance to the one GAR comrades, their families, and neighbors in Brooklyn, inherited at the start of the Gilded Age. The country is divided along party and ideological lines similar to the sectional lines of the nineteenth-century United States. White supremacism once believed to be quelled is rising from many segments of society. Racism is spreading in communities of all sizes from coast to coast. Revisionist histories are populating newsfeeds. Monuments and other markers to the past are drawing public ire. Domestic and international actors are propagandizing national history in hopes of breaking national unity. The answer, as Twain suggested, is to look to the past.

During the Gilded Age, the citizens of Brooklyn, a mighty northeastern metropolis, faced all these challenges in one form or another. The interracial significance of their Memorial Day observances offers valuable insight to the same city and country well over a century later. Further research needs to be conducted on other major urban centers in the Northern United States. Brooklynites, including veterans, their families, friends, and neighbors, leveraged the integrated structure of a national veterans' powerhouse and a growing Black patriotic consciousness to define Memorial Day's postbellum legacy in their city and to reach a common ground. The result was stunning. Racial divides diminished, and patriotism, not nationalism, abounded to make the city's exercises one of the most popular and

---

110. Ira M. Hedges, "Circular No. 4," Headquarters Department of New York, GAR, New York, N.Y., April 28, 1884, Grand Army of the Republic, Department of N.Y., Collection, Circulars, General Orders, etc. 1884–1927 (SC 361), Syracuse University Libraries; Harrison Clark, "General Orders, No. 11," Headquarters Department of New York, Albany, N.Y., January 14, 1890, GAR, Dept of N.Y., Collection (SC 361), Syracuse University Libraries.
111. *Women's Relief Corps National Convention Proceedings*, 1884–1887, 1889, and 1895, show that the N.Y. Department sent at least one delegate or officer from its Brooklyn posts.
112. Women's Relief Corps, Department of New York, "Abstract of General Orders and Proceedings of the . . . Annual Encampment, Department of New York, Grand Army of the Republic" v. 26 (Albany: James B. Lyon, State Printer, 1892), 352-53, https://hdl.handle.net/2027/hvd.32044090105362.
113. "[Book Review] Q:A," *New York Times*, January 25, 1970.

envied in the Gilded Age United States. Citizens recognized that their task and its accomplishment required social and cultural activism, not political bias.[114] The GAR's mission and indeed that of the whole city that turned out to witness and pay homage to the Union dead had its redemptive qualities in the future. The Memorial Day we celebrate today brings us back to Gilded Age Brooklyn and resembles investments of old that made the solemn day one of remembrance and patriotism. The decorated graves at Cypress Hills, Greenwood, and Evergreen conveyed a call to humility and unification then, as they do now. Realizing this on the holiday's observation in 1888, Gen. Stewart L. Woodford, a proud GAR member and retired commander of the 103rd U.S. Colored Infantry Regiment, foretold for generations to come: "The citizens are fusing and flowing together and approaching the fulfillment of the martyred Lincoln's dream and prophecy of one brotherhood and one citizenship this broad land over."[115]

---

114. For evidence of nonpartisanship, see GAR, Department of New York, *Twenty-Third Encampment, 1889*, 13.
115. "War Memories," *Eagle*, May 28, 1888.

Artifact NY
Industrial Sewing Machine

Ashley Hopkins-Benton

Industrial sewing machine table setups were a common sight in garment workshops across New York City throughout the twentieth century. The machine shown in figure 1 led two distinct lives: first, in a sweatshop in Chinatown, it was used by immigrant women working long hours for a better life; and later, it was used by Tsui Ping Chu, an immigrant from Hong Kong, in her apartment in Brooklyn for hobby sewing, to connect with both her family history and her new city.

The Singer Professional 120u sewing machine was produced from 1972 to 1982 for textile factories. A Tuffy by Consew single phase clutch motor powers the machine. Both sewing machine and motor were made in Japan. The workings are mounted on a table with sturdy, gray steel legs. The top of the table is green laminate with ruler markings across the front. The table is fitted with an adjustable green gooseneck lamp and a mount that holds two cones of thread. A badge on the machine indicates it was sold by Lam Sewing Machine, Inc. (registered in 1975, Centre Street, New York, NY).[1] It is a larger and more cumbersome setup than one would expect to find in a home setting. The colors of the setup—calming greens and blues—bely its original use in a busy garment factory. The paint on the pedal is worn off from many years of use, but otherwise the setup is in excellent condition, and it was clearly well maintained.

The family of Tsui Ping Chu (1948–99), the most recent owner of the sewing machine, contacted the New York State Museum in the spring of 2022. Chu was born in Hong Kong, and after a long relationship by correspondence with Mike (Mon Kwong) Chu (whose family had immigrated to New York in 1966), she immigrated to the United States. The couple married and settled in the Kensington neighborhood of Brooklyn. Unlike many immigrant women at the time, Tsui Ping was able to stay home with their two daughters while

---

1. Gratitude to New York State Museum History Department intern Rebecca Chartier for her in-depth research into the technical aspects of this sewing machine setup as well as into the history of the manufacturers and vendor associated with it.

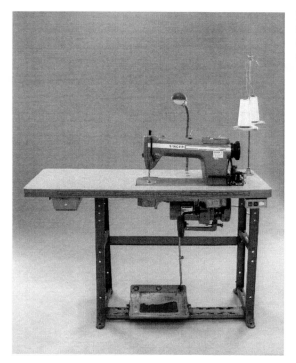

Figure 1. Industrial sewing machine setup, ca. 1972. COURTESY OF THE NEW YORK STATE MUSEUM (H-2022.20.1).

they were young, rather than working outside of the home. Tsui Ping purchased the used sewing machine through contacts in Manhattan's Chinatown garment industry. She sewed as a hobby—primarily making clothing for herself and her two daughters. Theresa Chu Tang, Tsui Ping's daughter, recalls the sewing machine being set up in the eat-in kitchen of their apartment, and she remembers the constant sound of the machine while she and her sister worked on homework in the evenings.

While Tsui Ping never worked in the garment industry, her family in Hong Kong was engaged in textile work, and the practice of sewing in her home provided her a connection to the family she had left. The hobby also allowed her a means to explore her new city. Tsui Ping brought her daughters, Ada and Theresa Chu, on excursions to pick out fabric and patterns, and she engaged them in thinking about fashion. Theresa recalls, "When it came to her consistent hobby, it was always fashion, and getting the fabric, and being creative, and making something usable . . . she definitely had a ton of fun taking us along on the ride—on the bus rides, on the subway rides, exploring the city."[2]

Mike recalls the happiness and pride the sewing machine brought his late wife: "Those year[s], when we [were] in Brooklyn, [were] the best and happy time[s] for her."[3]

---

2. Theresa Chu Tang and Mike (Mon Kwon) Chu, interview by the author, June 13, 2022, New York State Museum Collection.
3. Theresa Chu Tang and Mike (Mon Kwon) Chu, interview by the author.

Figure 2. Tsui Ping Chu with her daughter Ada Chu, who is wearing matching clothing sewn by Tsui Ping, 1977. COURTESY OF THE CHU FAMILY.

When her children were older, Tsui Ping became a social worker with the Special Supplemental Nutrition Program for Women, Infants, and Children (WIC), and she worked with immigrant women. Tsui Ping's family feels that the contrast between her ability to use the sewing machine as a hobby, compared to the relationship of other immigrant women, who toiled at sewing machines for wages, was not lost on her.

Prior to its purchase by Tsui Ping Chu, this same sewing machine setup was used in a sweatshop in Manhattan's Chinatown. Chinatown became a major garment production center in the second half of the twentieth century; garment work jobs there more than doubled from 1969 to 1982.[4] Labor regulations brought about by earlier factory accidents, including the Triangle Shirtwaist Fire, meant that textile factories were safer than they had once been, but garment shop owners in Chinatown pushed back against regulations in an effort to stay profitable as margins shrank. Unionization efforts by the International Ladies Garment Workers Union (ILGWU) began in Chinatown in the 1950s and were largely successful. In addition to benefits for the workers, the union label ensured that jobs continued to flow into Chinatown shops. There was, however, a disconnect between union leadership

---

4. Xiaolan Bao, "The Geographical Movement of Chinese Garment Shops: A Late-Twentieth-Century Tale of the New York Garment Industry," in *A Coat of Many Colors: Immigration, Globalism, and Reform in the New York City Garment Industry*, ed. Daniel Soyer, 67–87 (New York: Fordham University Press, 2005), 70.

Figure 3. Tsui Ping and Mon Kwon Chu with their daughters Theresa and Ada, 1980.
COURTESY OF THE CHU FAMILY.

and both Chinatown garment workers and shop owners. The latter felt that the union was not responsive to the needs of Chinese members.[5]

Garment work provided an important economic opportunity for women in Chinatown, who made up the majority of the workers, but it was not easy. Especially later in the twentieth century, work fluctuated with the fashion seasons, with periods of scant hours and others of around-the-clock work. Wages were directly tied to a person's output, and for new hires, wages could be meager. Despite these conditions, many immigrant women were happy to have the opportunity and freedom to earn money to support their families. To the women who sewed in a sweatshop, this sewing machine may have represented opportunity, but also long, grueling, low-paid work.[6]

The New York State Museum's collection is rich in artifacts from Chinatown, including fixtures and merchandise from three Chinatown stores: Tuck High Company, Sun Goo Shing, and Quong Yee Wo & Co. While they provide a glimpse into the budding economy and social life of Chinatown, theirs is a predominately male story—the stores were founded prior to changes in immigration laws that allowed more Chinese women to immigrate.

---

5. Bao, 72–72.

6. Part II of Bonnie Tsui's *American Chinatown: A People's History of Five Neighborhoods* (New York: Free Press, 2009) provides a helpful glimpse into the experiences of Chinese immigrant women working in the garment factories of Manhattan's Chinatown in the late twentieth century.

Mercantile spaces such as these continued to be considered a male domain, even after there were more women in Chinatown. By contrast, the sewing machine allows us to delve into the stories of the Chinese women who made New York City their new home. The dual lives of this artifact present an opportunity to explore both work life and home life as well as the idea of embracing a new city while also remaining connected to one's past.

Community NY

Battles of Saratoga @ 250: Educate, Engage, Preserve

Lauren Roberts

Many people can still remember when America celebrated the bicentennial of its founding nearly fifty years ago. In 1976, the commemoration of our independence from Britain inspired many citizens to look back through history and learn more about our revolutionary roots. Not only were parades, parties, and events held, but books were published, historical societies created, and general interest in local history hit a high point. Those of us in the history field today still benefit from some of the work done by historians during the bicentennial. Nearly fifty years later, one thing that has not changed is that commemorations offer a unique opportunity to shine a light on our history. Municipal historians should not let this opportunity pass us by.

Saratoga County is proud to be the home of the Battles of Saratoga, known as the Turning Point of the American Revolution. This American victory convinced the French to become our allies and increase the aid they gave to our struggling army, thus ultimately securing our independence from Britain. In order to commemorate the monumental outcome of this campaign, the Saratoga County Board of Supervisors has created the Saratoga County 250th Commission, which has been charged with planning the commemorations related to this anniversary. The Commission, established in 2021, consists of thirteen members and includes stakeholders from the community, including municipal historians, historical societies, living historians, and Veterans groups. As Saratoga County Historian, I am honored to chair this Commission.

The Commission began meeting in 2022 and identified the three main goals that would guide our commemoration. These objectives are as follows:

1. Promote education and civic engagement in the important role our area played as the home of the Battles of Saratoga, America's Turning Point.
2. Increase Heritage Tourism by offering engaging public events showcasing Saratoga County as a historic destination and by organizing a multiyear commemoration to attract visitors to our county at an international level.

Figure 1. Saratoga County 250th Commission reveals their official brand and logo, June 2022. COURTESY OF SARATOGA COUNTY.

   3. Improve the infrastructure dedicated to our historic sites, thus ensuring that our investments throughout these commemorations have a lasting impact on historic preservation in our community for the next generation.

With these principles guiding our mission, we hit the ground running for our first year of programming in 2022. In June, Saratoga County Officials unveiled our official brand, America's Turning Point, and our logo, which was a crucial first step in this effort. Our multiyear commemorative events will take place under this brand, laying the foundation for long-term heritage tourism throughout Saratoga County.

   In July, we had a week-long presence at the Saratoga County Fair. Headquartered in an eighteenth-century-style marquee tent, we offered programming for people of all ages, including crafts and games for children and an area where they could try on replicas of eighteenth-century-style clothing. We featured information about our Revolutionary Era history and engaged the public by having living historians demonstrate both military and civilian life.

   In October, America's Turning Point partnered with the Saratoga National Historical Park to offer the Siege Encampment in Schuylerville during I Love NY's Path through History Weekend. National Park Service rangers offered tours of the Philip Schuyler House, the British 24th Regiment of Foot opened their camp to the public, and the 2nd Continental Artillery gave demonstrations hourly. Other interpreters discussed eighteenth-century

Figure 2. America's Turning Point volunteers participate in the Turning Point Parade in Schuylerville, New York, August 2022. COURTESY OF SARATOGA COUNTY HISTORIAN.

medicine and women's roles in the Saratoga Campaign, while the America's Turning Point Marquee Tent once again housed crafts, games, and an exhibit featuring soldiers who lost their lives during the Battles of Saratoga. Thanks to the support of our many community partners, this event proved to be a resounding success.

Our final event of the year focused on our mission to promote education. We collaborated with the Living History Education Foundation, the Saratoga National Historical Park, and the 2nd Continental Artillery to provide a workshop for social studies teachers and municipal historians throughout Saratoga County to expand their knowledge about the Battles of Saratoga and to introduce them to ways of bringing living history into their classrooms. This workshop was provided to teachers and historians free of cost, and they earned Continuing Teaching and Learning Education credits for their participation. We hope that the connections made between teachers and historians will prove beneficial to both parties for years to come.

In addition to our programming, we also concentrated on researching lesser-known stories of the Revolutionary Era in Saratoga County. When trying to reach a wider audience, expanding the narrative to include people with whom visitors can identify is important. The Saratoga County Historian hosted two interns who worked to explore stories we wanted to highlight. In addition, we were awarded an American Battlefield Protection

Program grant through the National Park Service to create a master interpretation plan. Including stories that focus on Native Americans, African Americans, and women not only adds to our broader understanding of what life was like in our county in the 1770s, but also helps residents and visitors connect with historical figures with whom they can relate.

As we shift our planning efforts to 2023, we continue to look to our guiding principles when deciding which events will be most impactful. Some of these include a symposium focusing on the roles women played in the Revolution, more living history events, and workshops that continue to engage both teachers and students.

For other counties or regions looking to get started on their commemoration planning, I encourage you to set your goals first and let those guide your efforts. Reach out to community partners in your region, and work together to engage your communities; many hands make light work. Finally, start now! Preparations for large-scale events take time and effort, and major anniversary dates will be here before you know it. You may feel like trying to get started on such a huge undertaking is like staring with a blank page the night before your term paper is due; but trust me, just start typing, and you will gain the momentum needed to bring your community's history to the forefront.

BOOK REVIEWS

Amerikanische Aristokraten: Die Van Rensselaer-Familie zwischen Kolonialzeit und Früher Republik, 1630–1857

By Jonas Anderson. Bielefeld: Transcript Verlag, 2020. 318 pages. $51.21 paperback.

With *Amerikanische Aristokraten: Die Van Rensselaer-Familie zwischen Kolonialzeit und Früher Republik, 1630–1857*, which is based on his 2017 dissertation for Ludwig Maximilian University in Munich, Jonas Anderson adds to the literature on Early American Studies an impressive study of the rise and fall of the Van Rensselaer family in upstate New York, between the early New Netherland period and the mid-nineteenth century..

In 1631, Kiliaen Van Rensselaer, an Amsterdam merchant and one of the directors of the Dutch West India Company, laid the basis for the rise of his family in North America by establishing the colonial estate of Rensselaerswyck in New Netherland, without ever setting foot there himself. It covered more than 4,000 km² of present-day New York's Albany and Rensselaer Counties as well as parts of Greene and Columbia Counties. His sons and their descendants managed the land as patroons for roughly the next two centuries. The colony of New Netherland became British a few decades later, and then American following the Revolutionary War. These transitions did not prevent the Van Rensselaers from increasing their wealth and power. The Anti-Rent War following the death in 1839 of the ninth, and by far the most successful and richest, patroon Stephen Van Rensselaer III spelled the end of Rensselaerswyck and the family's influence.

Anderson explains that his study "positions itself against the thesis of an American exceptionalism that has developed since the colonial settling of North America and has found its expression to be a breakthrough and realization of the liberal modern times." He observes that the fact that Americans feel different from Europeans "blocks the way both for a consideration of exchange processes and for an examination of commonalities with Europe and the persistence of European social phenomena in the New World." He determines that "for all the rhetoric of new beginnings, all the emphasis on the great republican experiment, and the renunciation of the Old World, Americans were nevertheless very much entrenched in that very world."

Under the heading *Methodology*, Anderson defends his choice to approach the material he has gathered by dividing it into *Das Land* (The Land) and *Das Leben* (Life). It enables him to apply a chronological and a thematic organization to both parts, and the structure is used to show how landownership and the economic and sociocultural factors associated with it were the foundation of the Hudson Valley aristocracy.

The chronological part in *Das Land*, which covers about one third of the book, traces the history of the Van Rensselaer family through conflicts and changes in its landownership and the resulting social positioning. In addition to the thematic analysis of the role of the land, this part of the book deals with the cultural, economic, sociopolitical, and legal aspects of the Van Rensselaers' landownership.

Das Leben, also roughly covering one third of the book, first shows how patroon and tenant lived their reciprocal relationship of deference and paternalism. A tour of the Van Rensselaer Manor House and its surrounding parkland is used to illustrate how architecture, interior design, and landscaping exemplify the significance of the country house for the colonial elite in North America in terms of social distinction. Subsequent chapters discuss the political role and social engagement of the Van Rensselaer's, culminating in Stephen Van Rensselaer III's establishing the Rensselaer Polytechnic Institute in 1824. Stephen's military role in the War of 1812 concludes this section.

For his sources, Anderson depended heavily on so-called ego documents, particularly the letters found in the Van Rensselaer Manor Papers, as well as on documents from the archives of Historic Cherry Hill in Albany, the Rensselaer Polytech Institute, of the New-York Historical Society, and the New York Public Library.

By giving his study the title *American Aristocrats*, Anderson weighs in on the issue of nobility in America, a controversial topic that is older than the nation that was established following the Revolutionary War. While he informs the reader that "aristocracy must be understood more broadly than in the classical theory of political types," he notes that his study of aristocracies in general, and of the Van Rensselaer's in particular, shows that they become a self-perpetuating circle that manages to concentrate and keep power and wealth and to have a long-term impact, both politically and socioculturally, even during periods of rapid social change. He hopes that his study of New York's large landowners as aristocrats of the North will also contribute to a questioning of the stereotypical dichotomy that considers the planter aristocracies of the South as backward compared to the aristocracies of the North, which are considered progressive, industrialized, and democratic.

An abundance of dissertations, articles, and even conferences shows that recently slavery has claimed a prominent place among the topics to be discussed. In contrast, Anderson devotes just four pages to slavery, concluding that "slavery had already ceased to be of significant economic importance in the northern states when the colonial period ended," and that slave ownership in the North was "more an expression of social distinction and was intended to reflect the socioeconomic status of the owner."

Such an assessment of slavery is problematic, especially in the context of the Van

Rensselaers. Nicole Saffold Maskiel's 2013 dissertation, "Bound by Bondage: Slavery among Elites in Colonial Massachusetts and New York," establishes that in seventeenth-century Rensselaerswyck, "the Van Rensselaer family supplement[ed] the labor supplied by their tenants with the addition of black slaves."

· Anderson has been able to avoid the superficiality that looms large when trying to cover a 200+-year history of an influential family. Stephen Van Rensselaer III, the man who ranks twenty-second on Malcolm Gladwell's list of richest people ever (in *Outliers*) and who was patroon for five decades during turbulent times, definitely was given his due, although one would still like to know more: the increase in the number of rent-paying inhabitants of Rensselaerswyck alone cannot be the answer to how this Stephen became so wealthy.

While Anderson expresses his appreciation for the many seventeenth-century Dutch documents available in English, the ups and downs of the Van Rensselaer family between 1630 and 1857 in this work remain inaccessible for those who cannot read German. An English translation would be welcome, as would an index of subjects and names.

Reviewed by Robert A. Naborn. Naborn holds a PhD in History from the Vrije Universiteit Amsterdam and MA degrees in Applied Linguistics (ESL) and Historical Linguistics from the University of Kansas and the Vrije Universiteit Amsterdam, respectively. His research interests include the Dutch influence on America after the New Netherland period, historical linguistics, and the teaching of composition. Naborn is Director of the Dutch Studies Program at the University of Pennsylvania and an adjunct Assistant Professor of Humanities in Temple University's Intellectual Heritage Program.

Espionage and Enslavement in the Revolution: The True Story of Robert Townsend and Elizabeth

By Claire Bellerjeau and Tiffany Yecke Brooks. London: Lyons Press 2021. 240 pages. $26.95 hardcover, $19.95 paperback, $19.00 e-book.

Espionage and Enslavement in the Revolution: The True Story of Robert Townsend and Elizabeth, a work of historical fiction co-authored by Claire Bellerjeau and Tiffany Yecke, is available on through various outlets and has been presented on multiple virtual platforms. This book opens a window to readers seeking to learn about the Revolutionary War, early espionage tactics and spies, and slavery on Long Island, New York. Based on earlier accounts and new research, this book is a worthy read for newcomers.

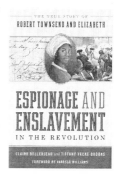

History is an essential examination of humanities that explores and interprets human patterns, life, experience, and conceptional connections. Unfortunately, the record and perspectives of history have gaps and have excluded voices, content, stations, places, and the complexities of many; in other words, history practices othering. The historical record usually tells the story from the victors' point of view, the point of view of the literate, and with bias; even implicit bias overlooks contributions of "others" and diminishes the significance of the whole story. Historiography has proven that the framework and critical analysis of objectivity, materiality, and authorship preference determines subjection. With this is mind, there is an opportunity to reframe and disrupt narratives to include the untold and marginalized stories, which are needed today, a time when books are being banned and curricula are being discarded.

Historical fiction is a great learning tool and a pathway for novice history readers and learners seeking to pique their curiosity and understanding. The primary functions of historical fiction correlate with a factual character's, timeline, and settings. At best, the hope is to view history from a different perspective, to offer contextualized reflections and contemporary connections to the past that informs. Successful examples of widely acclaimed historical drama include Julian Fellowes's *Downton Abbey* and *Turn: Washington's Spies*, a television series that explores the lives everyday citizens who band together to fight for American Independence. This historical period drama period drama situates the timeline within the American Revolutionary War and brings story to life with a modern conceptual relationship and closeness to the characters.

Espionage and Enslavement in the Revolution scrutinizes the terrain of espionage, the construct of slavery, and the underpinning of independence. It recalls contributions of prominent men who played a critical role in American history, such as Benjamin Franklin, Alexander Hamilton, John Jay, Benedict Arnold, John André, and John Adams, and is anchored by Long Island patriots. The book revisits the Boston Massacre and the Battle of Long Island, and it examines documented histories of Franklin's and Arnold's counter-positions. A proponent of the story presents an enslaved character, Liss, and the lesser-known rebirth of abolition of former slaveholder Robert Townsend.

The thrust of the book centers primarily on the Revolutionary War and the activities of Abraham Woodhull, who recruited Long Islanders to spy. The main focus is on Robert Townsend, who became a prominent spy. The story also suggests that a romantic relationship exists between Elizabeth (Liss), the enslaved, and the enslaver. In an American Revolution Institute lecture and other presentations, authors admit to using conjecture and "leaving it up to the reader" when the research goes cold. The situationship between Robert and Liss is presented as either benevolence or humanity; his actions could have been to protect his interests, secrets she was left with, not to be exposed. What autonomy did Liss, or any enslaved person, have in choosing a relationship, or in claiming the rights to their bodies, to bear or to keep their children? Bellerjeau tells Chris Voss, "This book weds the story of patriots, 1776, and slavery into one American story and that you don't have to choose." *Espionage and Enslavement in the Revolution* interjects various concepts and history about American chattel slavery but falls short in that slavery is presented as an additive, subset, an aside rather than as integral to the mosaic of the American story.

In many instances, there is an apologist and then dismissive tone regarding slavery. The discussion that unfolds in the book between generations of Townsend slaveholders as being "people of the time," fighting for human rights while at the same time purchasing enslaved persons, selling human beings, and finally projecting the paternalistic treatment of enslaved persons with care, feels retraumatizing. While the book utilizes primary historical documents, it proports that Liss's story as a true story. But there are too many gaps and projections concerning her that are woven into the narrative, which is misleading, at times. The historical truth about Liss is unknown, and in this book, it is constructed mythically and illustrated literally.

Additionally, language *matters*, and the antiquated language used to describe human beings is harmful and offensive. We should not condone the language used in the historical documents, and we should strive in our own language and references to be as respectful as possible. We do not refer to an individual as "a slave," as that designation does not describe the individual's personhood. We should instead say, a person was "enslaved," "born into slavery," or "was living in slavery," We should use the terms "enslaver" or "slaveholder," not owner or master, and all these terms should not be used interchangeably. We should not subscribe to colonizer's language, such as, "I discovered . . ." How can one discover something, research, documents, or persons who already exist?

Racialized categorization in the book's chapter titles, such as, "Merchants and Masters"; "A Child with Her Then Master"; "Principled against Selling Slaves"; or "Liss a Black Woman," are problematic. From "colored" to "Negro," to Black, to Afro-American, to African American, the identification of groups of people has played a significant role in defining individuals. This is especially true for formerly enslaved persons who were the only involuntary immigrants brought to this country. After the emancipation, people of color had a chance to redefine themselves, their consciousness, and their statuses. As terms evolved, debate ensued over words' origins, derivatives of derogatory racial connotations, and all-inclusive terms. Advocates and proponents sought the realignment of heritage and ancestral homage to denote *ethnicity* and not *race*, as the term Black does. Black is a racial term that negates the contributions of enslaved and captive Africans and American-born Black people who are direct descendants of slavery.

A history of complex terminology exists in primary source documents and, when present, should be used in direct quotes, with proper context and content. Many institutions have cataloged and categorized the documents, artifacts, items, and imagery of Black, Indigenous, people of color (BIPOC) using racial terminology such as "Negro," "mulatto," and "colored" in their depictions. If harmful language is used to describe a record outside of its original title or caption, consideration should be given to replacing the term.

African American is not necessarily interchangeable with Black. Black is a term that is used when referring to the man-made construct of an individual's race. When the term

Black is used, it should be capitalized and used as an adjective, not as a noun. Black can be used regardless of nationality, while African American is specific to Americans of African diaspora, and especially of Black African, descent. Some individuals in the United States self-identify with both terms, while others prefer one term over the other; some may prefer a different but related term (e.g., Afro-Caribbean, Afro-Latino). Descriptions of individuals should use the individual's preferred self-identifier, if known, and a current, nonharmful term. The plural form "Blacks" is considered offensive and should not be used. "Black people" is the preferred plural form for "Blacks."

Espionage and Enslavement in the Revolution introduces a warranted revision of existing research and scholarship on the Townsend family, Long Island spies, and their activities during the time of the American Revolution. An intimate look at Robert Townsend, a spy, and merchant-turned-abolitionist provides us with details often left out of the story. The authors wanted to demystify legends concerning these characters that have been repeated in the written record, and they succeeded. This historical fiction attempts to reimagine and include a fuller history that has been in plain sight but omitted from memory. When we think about the contributions and achievements of the everyday people featured in history, it does not include Liss's story; this book presents a foreshadowing of possibility for future change.

Reviewed by Georgette Grier-Key, Eastville Community Historical Society.

Aristocratic Education and the Making of the American Republic

By Mark Boonshoft. Chapel Hill: University of North Carolina Press, 2020. 296 pages, 1 b&w illus., 8 tables. $99.00 hardcover, $32.50 paperback, $22.99 e-book.

The most revelatory studies in the history of early American education, according to Bernard Bailyn's *Education in the Forming of American Society*, "see education in its elaborate, intricate involvements with the rest of society and . . . its shifting functions, meanings, and purposes" (13). Mark Boonshoft's *Aristocratic Education and the Making of the American Republic* provides a compelling answer to Bailyn's call by arguing that academies became critical infrastructure in the nation-state that formed in the aftermath of the Revolution, and that the initial impulses toward democratic-minded reform were born in opposition to the "aristocratic education" such institutions perpetuated. The work complements a long historiography and

affirms an interconnected history of republicanism, civil society, education, and state formation. While figures like Bailyn, Carl Kaestle, and Lawrence Cremin have argued that republican government promoted the beginnings of public education in America, Boonshoft
inverts this interpretation by suggesting that "the emergence of accessible education, aimed
at producing a self-governing citizenry, . . . was critical to the larger political transformations of the early nineteenth century" (7). Echoing Johann Neem's observation that the
democratic nature of early American schools was contingent on a variety of class, race, and
gender-based qualifications, Boonshoft sees the early national period's fixation on academies as a point of cultural and social transition. The history of both the establishment of
academies and the calls for their reformation paralleled Americans' intellectual, social, and
ideological maturation from an elite-driven society holding onto remnants of a colonial
inheritance to a self-governing, independent nation of people who sought to replace antiquated notions of intellect with a democratic—but not universal—approach to education.

In the colonial period, imperial officials and the clergy who founded academies began
to use them as "engine[s] . . . of elite formation" (15) in the hope that "expanding education
for the elite and empowering educated men would strengthen governance" (22). The union
between these objectives meant that "academies helped to open civil society and the public
sphere" (28), intertwining the mentalities of the Great Awakening with the ambitious aims
of would-be state-makers and governors. During the American Revolution, academies
continued to be "a tool of civil elite formation," as the very elites promoted as future bul-
warks of Britishness became the directors of revolutionary efforts against colonial rule. The
lawyers, surgeons, and militiamen who graduated from Francis Barber's academy in New
Jersey eventually "pushed the paper that allowed the continental army to function" (42)
in the early years of the war. Moreover, figures like the renowned Massachusetts educator
Jacob Green saw academies as prime locations for interdenominational learning that would
help promote republican governance and avoid factional infighting that prevailed in colonial schools (52). Movements toward more secular and civic educational models like those
advocated by Green were intended to unify the young nation's elite individuals around the
republican project instead of dividing it between the interests of Presbyterians or Anglicans
(58). "Shorn of their original denominational purpose," Boonshoft concludes, "academies
proved a durable model for improving associations and institutions that defined American
civil society" (72).

Throughout the 1790s, Federalists used academies to produce a self-perpetuating
corps of future leaders. As figures like Judith Sargent Murray established female seminaries,
and as reformers established charity schools for Black residents in places like New York
City, the education of these groups remained apart from the schooling obtained by white
men who matriculated to the preeminent academies across the nation. Engaged primarily
in the development of literacy, oratory, and philosophy, academies aided Federalist governors in establishing educational precedents that "idealized a certain type of well-to-do
man" (92) and legitimized their vision of an empowered and sovereign United States to

other nations. Moreover, investment in academies undermined the impulses toward egalitarianism that enamored reformers in the late eighteenth and early nineteenth centuries (117). However, academies' centrality to discussions of educational change among advocates and detractors alike solidified schools as public-facing institutions and as key venues for discussions of democratic reform (95).

From 1787 to 1830, Democratic-Republican resistance to the Federalists' intellectual monopoly over class-oriented, elite-driven academies metastasized. For example, George Clinton's 1795 appropriation of £20,000 for elementary education across New York effectively "pitted common schools against academies" by offering an alternative approach to education in the state. Nevertheless, as reform-minded leaders criticized academies for fostering an intellectual aristocracy, their vision of publicly accessible education "was not a racially expansive" proposal, and critics of academies approved of distinct divisions between the education of young men and women in common schools and academies alike (136–38). An educational consensus thus emerged between academy proponents and reformers, based on the continued stratification of each institution's social purpose (147). After 1800, reformers began "imagining universal education in opposition to aristocratic education, [and] they framed reform around the problem of class and privilege in a republic" (176). In the North, both "male and coeducational academies . . . tailored a republican curriculum and trained teachers for common schools" (169). The supply of civically informed instructors, it seems, was fitted to the demand for learning in publicly accessible institutions. In the South, proprietors of academies "fought reform and maintained an essentially aristocratic social and educational system." To promote slavery and prevent "an educated citizenry" from undermining the order of a highly stratified society, leaders in Southern states created educational opportunities particular to the social position of elite landowners, poorer whites, and enslaved African Americans (176). The message of reformers who advocated for common schools resonated, though: in both the North and the South, people associated education with civic institutionalization because it had, since the first academies were founded in the colonial era, been a marker of political, social, cultural, and intellectual status. Ultimately, the political disputes associated with the formation of political parties and the development of a republican society in post-revolutionary America included protracted contests over the extent to which education should reflect "a shared and equalizing civic experience" (183).

In sum, Boonshoft offers a compelling and timely examination of the very nature of America's educational past. The work broadens scholars' understanding of the period by exploring a set of institutions that have likely been misunderstood as logical steppingstones on an overly simplified historical journey toward progressive education in the United States. The book reflects admirable and rigorous research into dozens of academic archives, but Boonshoft does not purport to offer a limited window into academy life. Instead, his work reveals that debates like those over charter schools and educational access today mirror the same arguments over who should have access to different kinds of learning that characterized the colonial, revolutionary, and early national periods of American history. Though Bernard Bailyn concludes that the revolution and the institution of republican government caused "the whole enterprise of education [to] become controversial, conscious, [and] constructed" (43), Boonshoft's work suggests that controversy over conscious efforts to construct a system based on different beliefs about the purpose of education and the people who should receive it was *always*—and continues to be—a foundational component of American civic society.

Reviewed by Zachary Deibel. Deibel is a PhD candidate in American history at Binghamton University and Graduate Student Intern for New York History.

Making the Forever War: Marilyn B. Young on the Culture and Politics of American Militarism

By Mark Philip Bradley and Mary L. Dudziak. Amherst: University of Massachusetts Press, 2021. 232 pages, 1 b&w illus. $90.00 hardcover, $27.95 paperback.

By any measure, Marilyn B. Young was a giant in the field of U.S. foreign relations and war making. Young was one of the foundational historians who wrote from the perspective of the New Left, and her sweeping history, *The Vietnam Wars, 1945–1990*, remains a classic that is widely assigned and read in university undergraduate and graduate history courses even though it was published more than thirty years ago. Young was also a leading academic voice against the twenty-first century U.S. wars in Iraq and Afghanistan. Young passed away in 2017, and historians Mark Philip Bradley and Mary L. Dudziak have assembled a collection of

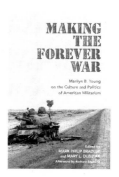

Young's writings to "make them accessible to a new generation, bringing historical insight to some of the most pressing problems" (2) of the current day. The selected essays center on the concept of "forever war," the idea that the United States has not just moved from war to war throughout its history but has continually been militarized and in war mode, always ready and waiting for the next conflict, if not making war. Borrowing from the scholar Richard Slotkin,[1] historian Andrew Bacevich declares in the collection's afterword that

---

1. Slotkin is the author of *Regeneration through Violence: The Myth of the American Frontier, 1600–1860* (Norman: University of Oklahoma Press, 1973); and *Gunfighter Nation: The Myth of the Frontier in Twentieth-Century America* (Norman: University of Oklahoma Press, 1998).

Young's work leads readers to the conclusion that "the political experiment tracing its origins to the founding of the Anglo-American colonies in the first decades of the seventeenth century was from the outset an expansionist enterprise drenched in violence" (212).

Young began her career writing about U.S.-China relations in the nineteenth century, and she also investigated revolutions in Russia and China, the experiences of Russian and Chinese women in socialism, and social change and human rights. The essays in this collection do not demonstrate the breadth of Young's scholarship, as the editors focus narrowly on Young's writings on the Korean and Vietnam wars, in addition to three essays on the wars in Iraq and Afghanistan. If the volume's argument is that militarism has been a fundamental component of U.S. foreign policy since the end of World War II, the choice of essays offers persuasive evidence in support of it. But if the collection is on American militarism broadly, as the title, introduction, and afterword suggest, then the inclusion of at least one of Young's earlier writings on the United States in China or on U.S. expansion more generally is needed to prove it. Taken as they are in this collection, Young's essays draw connections between U.S. interventions in Korea, Vietnam, Iraq, and Afghanistan; but her analysis of those five or six decades as presented in the essays here does not make a convincing case that militarism is inherent to the U.S. character since the nation's founding. That claim might be true, and Slotkin and other scholars have made compelling cases for it; but making the case requires taking a longer view, starting well before the Korean War, of U.S. foreign relations and military interventions.

By emphasizing the Vietnam War as the essential example of U.S. militarism, *Making the Forever War* endorses the New Left critique of U.S. foreign relations. Personal opposition to the Vietnam War informed the worldview of Young and other New Left historians who went on to examine U.S. global engagements through the lens of the conflict (4–5). From this perspective, the U.S. war in Vietnam was proof that the U.S. had always been a violent aggressor. American belligerence was the prime mover of U.S. history and, because of its expansionist drive, of world history since the late eighteenth century. In one of the essays, Young cautions scholars seeking to decenter the United States in global history to follow that agenda, but not too much (34). Perspective and agency are open to interpretation, but U.S. imperialism and the tyranny of the U.S. military abroad are fixed concepts.

If war is central to the American character, then what to make of the ambivalence, if not opposition, to war that U.S. citizens have demonstrated? One of Young's essays included in the collection is titled "Hard Sell: The Korean War" (39–65), and it discusses Americans' opposition to the conflict. Those who disagreed with the war were not all radical pacifists, but "merchants, businessmen, lawyers, farmers, and housewives" (43). Americans across the political spectrum opposed the Vietnam War, too, and Republican Richard Nixon won the presidency in 1968 in part due to his promise to withdraw U.S. forces from Vietnam. Americans also opposed earlier wars, as shown by the formation of the Anti-Imperialism League in 1898, radical labor and socialist opposition to U.S. entry into World War I, and the passage of the Neutrality Acts in the 1930s to keep the United States out of war in Europe and Asia. In light of these examples and others, historians could argue that opposition to war is also part of American identity.

Here we have the start of a conversation that I imagine Young would have relished, which is why *Making the Forever War* is a superb tribute to her professional life and work. The writings included in the collection demand engagement, and they call upon future generations of historians to grapple with the ideas of the forever war and American militarism. Whether scholars confirm Young's viewpoints or suggest different approaches does not matter. What matters is that Young has made us think, as she often did, of war as a necessary point of inquiry into U.S. history. *Making the Forever War* pushes historians to continue to do so.

Reviewed by Heather Marie Stur. Stur is Professor of History at the University of Southern Mississippi and codirector of the Dale Center for the Study of War and Society. Her most recent book is 21 Days to Baghdad: General Buford "Buff" Blount and the 3rd Infantry Division in the Iraq War *(Oxford: Osprey Publishing, 2023).*

Recasting the Vote: How Women of Color Transformed the Suffrage Movement

By Cathleen D. Cahill. Chapel Hill: University of North Carolina Press, 2020. 360 pages. $27.95 paperback.

The narrative of women's suffrage in the United States has been dominated by women such as Alice Paul and Susan B. Anthony. The story typically ends in 1920 with the triumphant passage of the Nineteenth Amendment, maintaining the teleological narratives of white middle-class suffragists. Women of color who also made remarkable contributions are often overlooked in these narratives. Conversely, Cathleen Cahill's *Recasting the Vote* "is not merely an additive project," but seeks to deconstruct the suffrage movement by "[moving] beyond the black/white binary and put different groups in conversation" (6). She traces five women from different 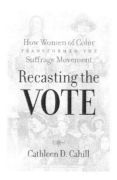 racial and ethnic backgrounds, Gertrude Simmons Bonnin, Mabel Ping-Hua Lee, Nina Otero-Warren, Carrie Williams Clifford, and Marie Louise Bottineau Baldwin and their activism in the women's suffrage movement. Cahill argues that "women from each of these groups therefore had a distinct relationship to citizenship that shaped their suffrage activism" (5). Using an array of primary sources, Cahill presents 1920 as a "pivot when the status of some women changed," rather than marking the Nineteenth Amendment as an end point (5).

In part 1 of her book, Cahill outlines the backgrounds of the five women central to her narrative and examines how they became politically active. She then traces how questions of citizenship shaped these suffragettes' activism. Unlike white middle-class women, women of color were often not considered citizens of the United States. For Native American women like Gertrude Simmons Bonnin and Marie Louise Bottineau Baldwin, sovereignty and land rights where what started their political activism. With legislation preventing, and "othering," Chinese immigrants and Chinese Americans, women such as Mabel Ping-Hua Lee brought attention to female revolutionaries in China who argued for women's rights and who used those arguments to "raise concern about the United States' policies toward China" (25). Nina Otero-Warren, on the other hand, used issues of language rights in order to "[ensure] that Spanish would also be the language of woman suffrage" (56). For African American women like Carrie Williams Clifford, the ongoing concern of Jim Crow catapulted their arguments for suffrage.

In part 2 of her book, Cahill demonstrates that as white supremacy grew during the early twentieth century, suffragettes of color became determined to redefine citizenship. The Wilson administration ushered in a highly discriminatory view against people of color. Cahill successfully highlights how a discriminatory government "had an immediate impact on women of color, especially black women" (7). For African Americans, white politicians used popular culture to instill fear in white Americans over Black enfranchisement and miscegenation. This led Black women to address issues of Black men's suffrage as well. Calling black men to support their cause, Black women connected sex discrimination with racial discrimination. They insisted that anyone who rejected women's suffrage supported racial discrimination. As this section illustrates, suffragists' activism was shaped by the communities from which they came and which, in turn, influenced their broad fight for civil rights.

The onset of World War I provided women of color an opportunity to further push for equality on the basis of race and gender. While for Black and Native American women "the politics of suffrage seemed to have [been] stalled out in the United States" (172), the politics of race were not. Women of color unveiled the government's hypocrisy of fighting a war abroad in the name of democracy while restraining the rights of Americans at home. For women like Bonnin and Clifford, men in their communities who heeded the call to serve proved that they should be granted full citizenship rights. Clifford, along with other African American women on the home front, brought awareness to the racism Black men dealt with while fighting for the United States. By contrast, for Bonnin, the complexities of Native American citizenship were illustrated in the application process. Questions such as "'Are you a citizen?'" and "'Are you a ward of the government?'" left many Native Americans confused as to what they should answer (192). Despite these questions, Native American citizens and noncitizens were still required to register for the draft, and Nina Otero-Warren and Mabel Lee continued to spearhead the suffrage movement.

The passing of the Nineteenth Amendment opens part 4 of the monograph, showing how the new law was a victory for some and a disappointment for others. Women of color, such as Otero-Warren, enjoyed the benefits of the Nineteenth Amendment by using Spain's colonial past "and its legacy of conquest of New Mexico's Indigenous people," to illustrate their similarities with Anglo-Americans. In Native American communities, however, it was not until Congress passed the Indian Citizenship Act in 1924 that Native Americans were granted the right to vote, and not without resistance. At the state level, laws restricted voting rights to taxpaying Native Americans only. As a result, nontaxpayers had to reregister, which proved "exceptionally difficult" (260). Cahill concludes her book with the legacies these women left behind. She argues that the influence Black women had on suffrage is a part of the long civil rights movement (232).

Cahill expertly illustrates the contributions of women of color in the fight for suffrage and racial equality. However, *Recasting the Vote* leaves readers wondering if these women formed alliances or relationships with each other to fight for a common cause. Cahill aimed to bring suffragists of color into conversation with one another, yet the only connection between the characters are politicians and white female suffragists. It is conceivable that these women navigated similar physical and political spaces but, perhaps due to a lack of available sources, each chapter reads as if it is in isolation from the rest. Nonetheless, through this monograph, Cahill reveals important historical actors who helped influence the suffrage movement and who should be part of the story.

Reviewed by Andelina Dreshaj. Dreshaj is a doctoral student in the History Department at SUNY Albany. Her research focuses on capitalism, neocolonialism, human rights, and the creation of asymmetrical geopolitical power.

We Return Fighting: World War I and the Shaping of Modern Black Identity

By Kinshasha Holman Conwill, ed. Washington, D.C.: Smithsonian Books, 2019. 160 pages. $19.95 hardcover.

This companion book to *We Return Fighting*, an exhibition held in 2020 at the National Museum of African American History and Culture (NMAAHC) in Washington, D.C., offers readers rich visual and textual insights into the opportunities and obstacles faced by Black military members and civilians during the Great War. World War I's cataclysmic loss of life, its fracturing and rebuilding of countries and alliances, and the ultimate pathway it laid for World War II have been well documented; less so are the ways in which African American men and women challenged the

deeply segregated parameters of the military and the home front. Indeed, as Secretary of the Smithsonian Lonnie Bunch argues in the book's introduction, "The conflict reshaped black Americans' views of ourselves" (13).

The NMAAHC's temporary exhibition, which closed on September 6, 2020, is still available to view online.[1] Although neither the book nor the website can replicate the more tangible experience of witnessing remarkable objects like the Croix de Guerre medal, awarded by France to each member of the 369th Infantry Regiment (better known as the "Harlem Hellfighters"), the carefully selected photographs, sketches, textiles, and documents that proliferate the book's pages invite close examination and reflection upon the sacrifices and achievements of African Americans in wartime.

The years spanning World War I constitute the primary focus of both the book and the exhibition, with three distinct periods receiving the most attention: Pre-War (1865–1917); During the War (1917–19); and Post-War (1919–63). Edited by NMAAHC deputy director Kinshasha Holman Conwill, the book consists of a collection of essays by various authors, including military historian and exhibit guest curator Krewasky A. Salter; Lisa Budreau, senior curator of military history for the Tennessee State Museum; and Philippe Etienne, ambassador of France to the United States, who wrote the forward. Fittingly, the NMAAHC partnered with France's First World War Centennial Mission and other French cultural institutions in their development of this exhibit.

Woodrow Wilson's call for Americans to enlist and support the war effort divided Black intellectuals and activists. Socialist leaders like A. Philip Randolph, leader of the Brotherhood of Sleeping Car Porters and founder of the magazine *The Messenger*, advocated draft resistance and vociferously critiqued the patriotism of Black leaders like NAACP founder W. E. B. DuBois. For his part, DuBois supported Black participation in the war but called out the hypocrisy of a world in which Jim Crow coexisted with the call to make the world "safe for democracy." Indeed, when Black veterans returned home, they confronted cities that convulsed in racially motivated massacres, as in East St. Louis during the summer of 1917. In his famous refrain, from which the title of the exhibition is drawn, DuBois presented a vision of a "New Negro"—one who had fought with honor and earned deep gratitude abroad, and who now returned home to challenge inequality and discrimination: "We Return. We return from fighting. We return fighting. Make Way for Democracy! We Saved it in France, and by the Great Jehovah, we will save it in the United States of America or know the reason why" (42).

As Krewasky Salter documents, more than 200,000 Black soldiers fought in the war, with most being relegated to "services of supply" (SOS) units. These units, made up of engineers, dockworkers, stevedores, and—in the months after the war's end, gravediggers—kept

1. "We Return Fighting: The African American Experience in World War I," National Museum of African American History and Culture, Smithsonian Institution, accessed April 13, 2023, https://nmaahc.si.edu/explore/exhibitions/we-return-fighting.

the wartime supply effort moving. The Army was the only military unit where Black men were allowed to engage in combat, with around 40,000 African Americans fighting in the infantry. The lauded Harlem Hellfighters fought for an astounding 191 consecutive days in the trenches, and according to historian John Morrow, "ended the war on the banks of the Rhine River" (123). The military valor of the 369th was coupled with its cultural power, as James Reese Europe, leader of the 369th Infantry Regimental Band, brought the sounds of American jazz to eager European audiences. Soon many Black cultural luminaries, like Josephine Baker and Louis Armstrong, flocked to the racially welcoming atmosphere of Paris, igniting what became known as "Paris Noir."

One of the book's most poignant short essays focuses on the "Blue Star" and "Gold Star" families who hung flags in their homes to denote a service member who was enlisted (Blue Star) or who had died during service (Gold Star). Lisa M. Budreau writes that during the 1930s, African American women who had lost relatives during the war were offered the opportunity by the Hoover administration to visit the graves of their loved ones overseas—on the condition that they be escorted separately from grieving white women. Even in death, then, the strictures of Jim Crow held fast. With support from the NAACP, Black women, many of whom were elderly and from the rural South, petitioned against this segregated policy, exercising a method of protest that prefigured Civil Rights Movement activism. In the end, only around 200 African American women made the pilgrimage overseas to visit their dead.

The book misses a few opportunities to insert some deeper critical analysis of Black participation in the U.S. military campaigns outside of the Great War. For example, Salter records how African American Buffalo Soldiers were "crucial to the opening of the American West" in the late nineteenth century (64). Left unexplored is the brutality of this military campaign to subdue and exterminate Indian resistance as well as the ideological link between the white conquest of the American West and the concurrent American imperialist expansion overseas, including within the African Diaspora. Likewise, while the essays celebrate the French admiration of Black cultural figures during the war, there is little reflection on how this admiration simultaneously "Othered" and exoticized Black women like Josephine Baker. The beautifully illustrated book should nonetheless appeal to a broad general audience as well as to specialists in material culture, military history, and African American history who want a deeper understanding of the integral ways in which African Americans both shaped, and were profoundly affected, by this war "to end all wars."

Reviewed by Andrea A. Burns. Burns directs the public history program at Appalachian State University in Boone, North Carolina. She is the author of From Storefront to Monument: Tracing the Public History of the Black Museum Movement *(Amherst: University of Massachusetts Press, 2013).*

Warfare and Logistics along the US-Canadian Border during the War of 1812

By Christopher D. Dishman. Lawrence: University Press of Kansas, 2022. 334 pages. $39.95 hardcover.

The War of 1812 has been interpreted in a surprising variety of ways, largely depending, of course, on an author's perspective. Although classically, or popularly, seen as an American defeat, the last half-century of scholarship has recognized decisive U.S. victories against Native Americans in the Northwest and Southwest. And the United States did win many of its battles in 1814 (and even a few in 1813), suggesting that experience did improve its generals, troop training, and tactical performance. Yet the United States did not achieve the strategic objectives set out by President Madison: to seize Canada (meaning the St. Lawrence Valley and present-day western Ontario, along the shores of Lakes Ontario and Erie) as a bargaining chip to trade for British concessions that would protect American sailors and trade from impressment and seizure. Westerners were delighted by the defeat of Tecumseh and the Red Stick Creeks, but the defense of Baltimore and Lake Champlain might not have been enough to salve the sting of a burned capitol, had it not been for another western victory at New Orleans. The U.S. government recognized the deficiencies of its war effort by rechartering the Bank of the United States and imposing a tariff on foreign manufactured goods in 1816, by retaining and continuing to build several very large warships, by developing plans for a new system of coastal fortifications to build on the success of Fort McHenry, and by instituting a military reform effort that included new standard operating procedures, tactical standardization, and a new emphasis on military education, which would make West Point the commissioning source for almost all new officers during the 1820s.

Among the most important reforms was the retention of a disproportionately large cadre of experienced logisticians—quartermasters, ordnance officers, purchasing officers, and engineers—who would survey new military roads along the frontiers. Christopher Dishman's new book helps explain why. Although most of *Warfare and Logistics along the US-Canadian Border* is a narrative of military battles, campaigns, and strategy, Dishman provides the fullest account of logistics available, and he does so for both sides and for both navies and armies. There are some surprising absences in his sources: he does not cite Richard Barbuto's work—neither *Niagara 1814* (Lawrence: University Press of Kansas, 2000) nor *New York's War of 1812* (Norman: University of Oklahoma Press, 2021)—; nor does he cite the U.S. Army's official history of the Quartermaster Department, by Erna Risch; the biographies of Winfield Scott, by Timothy Johnson and Allan Peskin; or the major works on the U.S. Army before the War of 1812, by Richard Kohn, Theodore Crackel, and James R. Jacobs. Dishman cites J. C. A. Stagg's books, but not his important articles on the officers and soldiers of the U.S. Army. Yet most of these lacunae can be forgiven, for Dishman provides both a very clear, highly detailed, and smoothly written operational narrative and comprehensive context for logistics along the Canadian border.

Warfare and Logistics along the US-Canadian Border is not a technical analysis of logistics, for which many readers will probably be grateful. Many of Dishman's points about logistics will be familiar: due to the limited local population density and agricultural surplus, most supplies had to be sent from outside the region, through limited road networks on both sides of the border, making supplies costly, often scarce, and slow to arrive. Dishman moves quickly from mobilization to war, with a limited analysis of the strategic level of logistics and the financing of the war; here Max M. Edling, *A Hercules in the Cradle: War, Money, and the American State, 1783–1867* (Chicago: University of Chicago Press, 2014) would have been a valuable resource. Dishman's conclusions, that the United States had the advantage in shipbuilding on the Great Lakes due to a greater population density and easier transportation routes south to north (versus those of the British, from east to west), and that naval commanders' caution or aggressiveness was crucial to offensive success, are also known to students of the war. The result was U.S. victory in the northwest, where Oliver Hazard Perry first fought a decisive battle on Lake Erie, and then provided the supply line for William Henry Harrison to the battle on the Thames that broke Tecumseh's Indigenous alliance, but which created a stalemate in the east, where Isaac Chauncey was never willing to risk such a battle, and which resulted in U.S. offensives being repeatedly misdirected toward the strategically irrelevant Niagara peninsula.

My caveats notwithstanding, Christopher Dishman has crafted an excellent study—clear and concise, but well detailed—of operations and battles in the primary theater of the War of 1812, across the entire war, with the most attention to logistics that we have available. It is more accessible that Robert Quimby's *The U.S. Army in the War of 1812* (2 vols.; East Lansing: Michigan State University Press, 1997), and more detailed than the treatment in any of the many surveys of the war. The twenty-six-page index merits special praise. Readers at all levels, from undergraduates to experts, will find *Warfare and Logistics along the US-Canadian Border* well worth reading.

Reviewed by Samuel J. Watson. Samuel Watson is Professor of History at the United States Military Academy, where he teaches Cold War America and nineteenth and twentieth century military history. His books on the army officer corps after the War of 1812, Jackson's Sword and Peacekeepers and Conquerors, won the Society for Military History's Distinguished Book Award.

A Prison in the Woods: Environment and Incarceration in New York's North Country

By Clarence Jefferson Hall Jr. Amherst: University of Massachusetts Press, 2020. 249 pages. $29.95 paperback.

Clarence Jefferson Hall Jr.'s *A Prison in the Woods* examines the role of prison construction in the regional development of the Adirondack North Country from the 1840s to the 2000s. He argues that environmental politics was central in the establishment and operation of the carceral state in the northern Adirondacks (7). Hall deconstructs the bureaucratic quagmire of prison building and racial and class politics by analyzing documents from the Adirondack Park Agency, the Department of Environmental Conservation, local newspapers, and special interest groups. While many have investigated the economic and cultural history of the Adirondacks, Hall centers the carceral state to reveal how environmentalism and the prison-industrial complex developed concurrently. The entanglement of environmental and prison politics shows how rural communities navigated the transformations of the region's political economy caused by environmental reform and deindustrialization.

Hall opens with the establishment of the Dannemora prison in the 1840s to reveal how prison building in the North Country predated the conservation movement of the Progressive Era. The facility exposed the potential and limitations of Progressive Era ideas about the reformatory qualities of nature. Dannemora's isolation, however, also meant the state had to invest in the construction of the infrastructure to support its operation (36). Such work was often completed by incarcerated individuals whose labor contributed to the development of the region's industrial and tourist economy. The presence of prisons, and of incarcerated individuals themselves, would later spark debates over the use, accessibility, and meaning of the environment across the next century.

By the 1970s, prison building was seen as a solution for both overcrowding of pre-established prisons and deindustrialization of the logging and mining industries in the North country. The construction of Ray Brook prison in 1975 revived the Progressive Era idea of locating prisons outside of cities and demonstrated the resilience of nineteenth century attitudes toward crime and punishment. The 1980s Winter Olympics in Lake Placid drew unprecedented global scrutiny over mass incarceration. Organizations such as Stop the Olympic Prison (STOP) drew upon the popularity of the environmental movement to critique New York's role as a bellwether for the war on drugs and prison-industrial complex (50–52). Though STOP failed to prevent the construction of Ray Brook's correctional facility, the organization was one of the first to speak out against the social consequences of prison building (66). The idealization of nature as reformatory elicited conflicts due to changes in the physical and social environment from what officials had previously promised.

Similarly, in 1981, the Department of Correctional Services (DOCS) proposed to build a new penitentiary in the hamlet of Gabriels. The news sparked the formation of op-position groups such as the Citizens Against More Prisons in the Adirondacks (CAMPA). CAMPA consisted of wealthy seasonal homeowners more interested in maintaining the racial and class status quo of the park as a space for white leisure than in challenging mass incarceration. Gabriel's low-income permanent residents resisted the seasonal homeown-ers' "racist brand of environmentalism" because they felt the prison would revitalize the lo-cal economy and infrastructure (94–95). Despite the efforts of CAMPA and the Adirondack Park Agency (APA), the penitentiary opened in 1987. The residents of Lyon Mountain also struggled to sustain their livelihoods in a landscape marred by environmental damage and deindustrialization. By 1983, the building of the penitentiary there served to transition the community from its economic past as a mining town to a future with the prison-industrial complex. For three decades, the community benefited from state investment and incar-cerated labor. However, decreases in incarceration numbers led to the prison's closure in 2010, once again leaving Lyon Mountain residents with an uncertain economic future and ultimately illustrating the tenuousness of postindustrial rural life (162).

The story of Tupper Lake's correctional facility demonstrates how, over the course of the 1980s to the 2000s, the DOCS began supporting the environmental and recreational narratives of anti–prison building advocates. Competing visions of the Adirondack Park as a space of labor or leisure once again emerged along class lines. Rather than navigate the bureaucracy of the APA and public opinion, in 1998, the DOCS for the first time aban-doned a project in the name of environmental protection and chose instead a location out-side the park (168). The DOCS decision reconfirmed seasonal homeowners' vision of the Adirondacks as a place of leisure. Hall concludes by comparing the economic sustainability of Tupper Lake's "Wild Center," a natural history museum built as an economic alternative to the prison, to the economic crisis faced by many rural communities outside the park whose prisons have closed due to lower rates of incarceration.

A Prison in the Woods is an important addition to histories of deindustrialization, en-vironmental justice, and the history of incarceration in New York State. Examining the history of incarceration in the Adirondacks challenges the prevailing narrative of the re-gion's economic transition from extractive industry to a recreation-based economy by em-phasizing the enduring legacy of incarceration. Hall rectifies the erasure of carceral labor in scholarship on the Adirondacks by demonstrating the contributions of unfree laborers to the Adirondack's infrastructure and tourist economy. The racial anxieties in Gabriels exemplify how the low-skill, low-paying work performed by incarcerated men of color re-inforced, rather than disrupted, elites' imagination of the Adirondacks as a space of white leisure. Hall's narrative emphasizes the important of reexamining the Adirondacks through the lens of environmental justice.

Hall outlines the convergence of deindustrialization and mass incarceration to illustrate the exploitative nature of prison building. Struggling Adirondack communities often made ecological concessions, hoping that penitentiary construction would encourage economic development and rectify the hardships of deindustrialization. Yet, locals came to realize the fragility of an economic structure that depended on high incarceration rates for its viability. The stories of organizing by environmentalists and wealthy residents against the prisons demonstrate how the environmental movement and deindustrialization worsened racial and class tensions that already existed in these communities.

For all Hall's appeals to the environment's centrality in the carceral history of the Adirondacks, *A Prison in the Woods* is primarily a policy history of incarceration. Hall's reliance on local newspapers leads him to concentrate on debates between various stakeholders who employed environmentalism as an argumentative tool, rather than including the environment as an active agent in these developments. Further incorporating ecological studies and the perspectives of the inmates would demonstrate how the materiality of the built and nonbuilt environment influenced the decision-making and lived experience of the historical actors examined. Still, Hall convincingly adds to the developing scholarship on the intersection of the environment and incarceration as well as to the field's growing exploration of the limits of environmentalism.

Reviewed by Kaycie Haller. Haller is a doctoral candidate at SUNY Albany. She is currently completing her dissertation titled, "'To Grow Men as Well as Trees': The Making of the Civilian Conservation Corps, American Citizenship, and Environment, 1933–1942," a reimagination of the CCC as both a social and an environmental engineering project across the United States and Puerto Rico.

The Power of Mammon: The Market, Secularization, and New York Baptists, 1790–1922

By Curtis D. Johnson. Knoxville: University of Tennessee Press, 2021. 256 pages. $60.00 hardcover; $60.00 e-book.

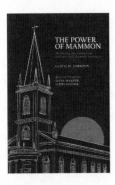

By all appearances, Baptists flourished in nineteenth-century New York. They had migrated to the state as refugees from New England's oppressive religious establishments but grew continuously in both numbers and resources. By the twentieth century, their churches included both the nation's most prosperous capitalist, John D. Rockefeller, and the leading theologian of social reform, Walter Rauschenbusch. But according to a new book by Curtis Johnson, *The Power of Mammon: The Market, Secularization,*

and New York Baptists, 1790–1922, this material success disguised weakened institutions in steady spiritual decline. Johnson carefully analyzes an impressive source base—the minutes, membership rolls, finances, and other records of more than forty congregations and more than fifty associations—to demonstrate that the state's stunning economic growth introduced "values and attractions" such as individualism and acquisitiveness that "collectively eroded Baptist belief and behavior" (xvii). Baptists may have been winners in the free market of religion, but religion lost to commerce in the larger market revolution.

Some readers may balk at labeling a period of extraordinary growth "secularization." Indeed, Johnson's concept of secularization is broad: it is a "process of religious decentering in which an individual or a religious group modifies, rejects, or abandons core principles" (xvi). This definition would seem to encompass almost any religious transformation, whether conversion, revival, reformation, or loss of faith. But Johnson follows Charles Taylor and other theorists in viewing secularization as a process that unfolds over centuries. Even as Baptist adherence grew, he uncovers evidence that distinctiveness faded, institutions weakened, and members lost interest in religion.

By situating the history of Christianity and capitalism within a larger narrative of secularization, Johnson aims to correct an imbalance created by the "business turn in American religious history" (xvii). Many historians have emphasized the way that churches deftly appropriated capitalist logics and commercial methods to rationalize everything from finances to evangelism. But Johnson hastens to add that when "religion began to adopt the values of business to promote its agenda, it also shifted people's attention from the spiritual to the material, from preparation for heaven to prosperity on earth, and from God to mammon" (xxi). His crucial move is to interpret the experience of nineteenth-century congregations in light of the falling membership that began in the 1960s. Compromises that allowed communities to adapt to rapid industrialization and commercialization in the medium term sowed the seeds of their long-term collapse. This is a provocative intervention, though it should be noted that *The Power of Mammon* concludes its narrative in the 1920s, forty years before that declining adherence finally manifested.

Among the strengths of Johnson's secularization argument is that it retrieves many Baptists' own Christian sense that material success breeds spiritual decline. As Francis Wayland—a pastor, university president, and author of the most popular antebellum economics textbook—put it: "The tide of worldliness, the love of gain, and the ambition of expense, which has been for some years, flowing over the Christian world, has overwhelmed us also" (117). Drawing on extraordinary archival research, Johnson demonstrates that this was not mere nostalgia but an accurate assessment of ministry in a world created by the market revolution: the growth rate declined; revivals grew rare; discipline languished; and the laity delegated their authority to committees. Each of these trends is presented with accessible charts and tables as well as with illustrative anecdotes, making the analysis both statistically compelling and richly textured. And all this data points to a more profound development, one more difficult to substantiate but sensed by both Johnson and many of his subjects: that the "multitude of cultural and material distractions tended to blot out notions of the transcendent" (145).

Johnson's fidelity to his substantial source base protects him from the dangers of a simplistic narrative of decline. He is sensitive to ironies, such as the way in which the larger ministerial salaries that allowed ministers to forgo secular occupations actually facilitated secularization, enabling ministers to participate in the economy as consumers and encouraging professionalization (50). He also refuses to flatten complex trajectories, especially regarding the changing roles of women in Baptist churches: whereas women found themselves marginalized in both church and economy as the market shifted production away from the household, they eventually reclaimed essential religious responsibilities as men shifted more of their attention from church affairs to commercial ambitions. Thus, even after readers grasp the shape of Johnson's overarching argument, they will still find remarkable discoveries in each chapter.

Johnson devotes passing attention to New York Baptists' roots in New England's eighteenth-century awakenings; but if explored more deeply, this context would supply even more nuance to his narrative. He portrays the nineteenth-century transformation of Baptist churches as a transition from the robust sociality of "covenanted communities" to more individualistic "voluntary associations"; but Baptists were already championing ecclesiastical voluntarism and individual conscience as early as the 1740s in their struggle against state churches (106). More specifically, Johnson interprets a Baptist revolt in the 1830s against the practice of raising money by church-imposed "tax" on members' assessed worth as evidence that they increasingly viewed personal property as "private." But this practice was already controversial in the eighteenth century because of its resemblance to state-sponsored ecclesiastical taxes. None of this context would upend Johnson's argument, and it seems unfair to expect him to expand a narrative that already covers so much ground in such detail. But it does suggest that Baptists did not merely react to the emergence of a market culture but instead anticipated it in crucial ways.

The depth of research into how the market revolution transformed churches sets *The Power of Mammon*'s contribution apart, appealing to historians of both American secularism and capitalism as well as to anyone whose interests intersect with nineteenth-century Baptists in the Northeast. Johnson's method of studying capitalism via the changing economies of religious communities is worth replicating widely. And here he deftly employs it to demonstrate that in American religious history, market growth was not a rising tide that lifted all boats, and that even some of the boats borne upward eventually found themselves swallowed by the swell.

Reviewed by Erik Nordbye. Nordbye is a ThD candidate in the History of Christianity at Harvard University. He is completing a dissertation entitled "The Cost of Free Religion: Church, State, and Economy in Eighteenth-Century New England." He also holds a MDiv from Harvard and a BA in Religious Studies from the University of Chicago.

Bound by Bondage: Slavery and the Creation of a Northern Gentry

By Nicole Saffold Maskiell. Ithaca, NY: Cornell University Press, 2022.
306 pages, 5 b&w illus., 3 maps, 4 charts. $39.95 hardcover, $25.99 e-book.

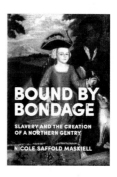

Anyone interested in slavery in early America cannot but rejoice about Nicole Saffold Maskiell's new book, *Bound by Bondage*, for it remarkably pursues the trend that scholars like Graham Russell Hodges, Thelma Wills Foote, Ira Berlin, Leslie Harris, and more recently Andrea Mosterman have set, for the past twenty years, of breaking the North-South division and giving prominence to the study of slavery in Northern colonies. Slavery on American soil is indeed concomitant with the arrival of the first settlers, and its presence is to be found equally in the North and in the South in the colonial times.

If most of the sources that have been used in this book are familiar to specialists of the field, Maskiell distinguishes herself by offering an interpretation "against the grain," reading the personal and administrative correspondence of elite families in a new way to trace their local and regional connections and analyze how they built their prestige and power through the control of enslaved Africans. Even though the book's title mentions the "Northern" gentry, Maskiell specifically focuses on the Dutch colony of New Netherland from which a burgeoning aristocracy had emerged and spread its networks over the Atlantic region, down to the South and the Caribbean. Basically, what she aims at showing is that the early Dutch slave owners and their Anglo-Dutch descendants, like the Stuyvesant-Bayard and Livingston families, were "central to the cultural development of the North," contrary to the widely held representation of New Netherland's slaveholders as "inconsequential players" (6). She not only studies this local community but also investigates how slave-owning literally influenced these families' emigration patterns and the fact that "they appeared all over the Atlantic slaveholding world . . . at key moments of transition" (7). In other words, being slave owners fashioned families' "colonial identities" (55) that were based on what Maskiell very subtly presents as their "racist sensibilities." We can understand here the link between slave-owning and racism, slave-ownership in the seventeenth century having brought about racist behaviors upheld by racialized legal codes in later periods.

The book is divided into seven chapters all bearing titles with key words in Dutch and in English. The introduction presents how these families are connected through two "manhunt" stories of runaway enslaved people owned by two Petrus Stuyvesants, one in 1664 and one in 1777. The first chapter, "Neger," looks at the way the Dutch had very early on differentiated the statuses and sown the seeds of racialization. Then chapters 2 ("Kolonist"), 3 ("Naam"), 4 ("Bond"), and 6 ("Market") all show how these elites built their kinship-based empires and connected "Albany to Maryland and Curaçao to Boston" (40) through slavery. Covering different time periods, from the 1680s to the 1750s, these chapters provide an in-depth analysis of the sprawling personal and commercial connections between Northern enslavers. If the choice of key words in the titles is coherent with the content of the chapters, the switching from Dutch to English words mirroring the decline of the Dutch influence and the emergence of the Anglo-Dutch community one generation after the 1664 conquest, we didn't grasp the clear link, at least not with the title of chapter 3 ("Naam"). Chapters 5 and 7, on "Family" and "Identity," respectively, approach radically different and incredibly fascinating themes: the kinship connections and networks between enslaved people and how these have been constantly endangered and violated but also how they made escaping possible. The charts representing the genealogy of an enslaved family separated by the Livingstons or the reconstruction of Black families on Livingston Manor are really captivating in the way they offer "a multigenerational and migrational portrait of enslaved families and individuals" (12).

What is amazing in this work is how Maskiell manages to write a history of the elites while resurrecting the enslaved. The way she reinterprets the sources (runaway advertisements, slave-to-sale notices, slave-ship documents, court cases, and private correspondence) and reflects on the work of the historian when reconstructing the lives of enslaved people from fragmentary archives is remarkable. Each chapter starts and ends with a biographical vignette that enables the reader to enter the world of the enslaved. In chapter 3, Maskiell chooses to use first names to refer both to enslavers and enslaved people to reinstitute some sense of equality between the two. She also very skillfully shows how the main historical events impacted enslaved people. Leisler's Rebellion, which caused the Livingstons to go back to New York and leave their eldest son and one enslaved man behind in Connecticut, or Isabel being sent to Boston in the aftermath of the 1712 slave rebellion, illustrate how enslavers imposed their power and control by breaking up enslaved families.

If we have clearly understood from the introduction that the focus of the book is intended to be on the elites, the families of higher rank that share "notions of mastery and conceptions of status," land ownership, and a way of life based on slave-ownership, we are wondering why the word "gentry" comes into play at such a late stage in the book with no proper definition. Indeed, many of these heads of families bore the title of "gentleman," which conferred them the aristocratic prestige that brought European titles of nobility to colonial America. Slave-ownership was prestigious because it gave commoners access to a higher rank. So, when Maskiell argues that these elite families shared slave-owning among many other attributes, I would add that many colonists upon arriving in America (Huguenots for instance) used slavery to climb the social ladder and achieve a higher rank. This use of social and racial control existed not only among the wealthiest. Slavery was also practiced among lower social classes, and 41 percent of New York households held enslaved people according to the 1703 census. That slavery fashioned New York colonial society in its most intimate inner workings is no longer difficult to prove, but it in no way detracts from the interest of this brilliant study that manages to write a new history of slavery, one in which not only the gentry but most importantly the enslaved people survive.

Anne-Claire Faucquez. Faucquez is Associate Professor in American civilization and history at University Paris 8. She works on New York's colonial past and on issues of class and race.

Joseph Smith for President: The Prophet, the Assassins, and the Fight for American Religious Freedom

By Spencer W. McBride. New York: Oxford University Press, 2021. 296 pages. $29.95 hardcover.

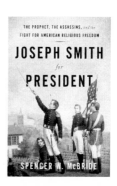

As a trade book, *Joseph Smith for President: The Assassins, and the Fight for American Religious Freedom* will appeal to anyone interested in American history and the struggle to identify religious heterodoxy. By examining the growth of the nascent Church of Jesus Christ of Latter-day Saints and Joseph Smith's improbable bid for the White House in 1844, it tells the story of "mobocracy," institutional religious infringement, and the reaction of an American-born faith to the loss of religious freedom. This book will also be of interest to the readership of this journal because Joseph Smith is an important figure in the antebellum history of the "burned over district."

New York is only the beginning of Smith's journey, since he and his followers quickly moved to the borders of the United States in Missouri; yet, McBride highlights the work of the influential Eastern presses in both Massachusetts and New York to demonstrate the national public case that showed the Latter-day Saints to be religious fanatics. In fact, the press worked toward exposing them as frauds and a threat to democracy. They built a case around the Latter-day Saints as political outsiders and enemies of the state. They evoked a reality in which persecution of the Saints could justify violence as political devotion. Eber D. Howe's book *Mormonism Unvailed* was the single most influential anti-Mormon text in the nineteenth century and includes a compilation of interviews and affidavits of New Yorkers who associated with the Smiths when they lived in New York.

How much these presses caused the ensuing violence is unknown; the outcome was nonetheless the violent suppression and expulsion of the Saints from Missouri, Ohio, and eventually Illinois. McBride tells wrenching stories of how Latter-day Saints endured rape, public torture, military violence, and humiliation. Ultimately, in each case, hundreds of thousands of dollars in property, up to two million dollars worth in Missouri, were destroyed. This left thousands of Latter-day Saints stranded and homeless, seeking refuge from their Protestant neighbors.

In Illinois, the Latter-day Saints found refuge in a swampy bend in the Mississippi River. They sought not to hide or to retreat but to find new footing from which they could participate in local and national politics. They were not the only religious minorities suffering at the hands of their fellow Americans. McBride argues that their environment fostered a "political system seemingly designated to keep them marginalized." They turned to the federal government to fight against mobocracy, as Joseph Smith was interested in a political revolution. He sought religious freedom through local and state government, charters, and political allies. Smith even visited Martin Van Buren at the White House, seeking redress; and his visit was followed up by petitions to Congress, all to no avail. McBride focuses on Smith's run for the presidency as a call for religious freedom, not just for the Latter-day Saints but for Catholics, Shakers, Jews, and other religious minorities. He reveals a compelling side of LDS history that repositions a landscape otherwise fixated on polygamy and the "otherness" of Latter-day Saints to highlight the LDS experience in Nauvoo as one cog in a political contest to protect religious minorities.

McBride argues that even with the guarantees of religious freedom in the First Amendment, Joseph Smith learned by experience that he needed to protect himself and his people rather than depend upon the national rhetoric of religious tolerance. Just as Catholics were a threat to the Whigs because they voted together and congregated together, Mormons were deemed a political threat as a religious minority capable of swaying the vote in Illinois. Smith used Nauvoo and Illinois politics to create a "Kingdom of Nauvoo," where he was legally protected from extradition and arrest warrants. He also repeatedly appealed to the federal government for redress in Missouri through letters to each presidential candidate, several of whom replied to argue that the federal government had no business in state politics. Since he found no representation, Smith produced his own platform and distributed "General Smith's Views of the Powers and Policy of the Government of the United States" in support of his candidacy for President. His national campaign called for the federal government to intervene to protect the constitutional rights of the people. He proposed the expansion of governmental power in the name of protecting religious minorities from violence, and he also proposed the emancipation of slaves, prison reform, and the formation of a national bank. McBride convincingly argues that this was not just a campaign for the Latter-day Saints' redress in Missouri. It was a legitimate campaign, and although doomed to fail, as it may have been, it addressed relevant national issues and moved beyond LDS concerns, marking Smith's bid for President with a national consciousness; it was not just a drive to settle personal grievances. Nonetheless, Smith was murdered before the November election, leaving us wondering what fascinating events may have developed had he continued his campaign.

As the associate managing historian of the Joseph Smith Papers Project, McBride tells Smith's story with archive rich material, yet his prose rises above the minutia his institute has mastered. One can see this in part by his use of the Smith presidential narrative to identify and adjudicate the ongoing problem of religious inequality in American society. Many historians have been interested in this story, but few could have found the balance and relevance McBride offers in *Joseph Smith for President*. Nonetheless, I am left hoping for a second volume, in which the protection of religious minorities fostering atypical non-Protestant religious practices (secret rites, polygamy, hierarchy, new scripture, etc.) inform the divide and factor into American politics. It would be interesting to understand how and which religious differences evoke political unrest, not just that differences led to the suppression of religious minorities. The problem of hierarchy is clear in the presidential candidacy of John F. Kennedy and, more recently, Mit Romney, and it is not far-reaching to wonder how marriage practices work for and against religious minorities today. Smith's story still has more to offer.

Reviewed by Michael Hubbard MacKay. MacKay is Associate Professor of Religion at Brigham Young University and a former historian at the Joseph Smith Papers Project. He is the author of several monographs including Prophetic Authority: Democratic Authority and the Mormon Priesthood, *and he is an editor of several volumes including* Producing Ancient Scripture: Joseph Smith's Translation Projects in the Development of Mormon Christianity.

Philip Payton: The Father of Black Harlem

By Kevin McGruder. New York: Columbia University Press, 2021. 232 pages. $120.00 hardcover; $30.00 paperback; $29.99 e-book.

Philip Payton, the Black real estate entrepreneur who helped Harlem become a famous "race capital" in the early twentieth century, has been comparatively well-known for some time. Classic works on Harlem's growth by scholars such as Gilbert Osofsky recognized Payton's importance and that of his most high-profile business endeavor, the Afro-American Realty Company (AARC). Yet this work by Kevin McGruder, published over 100 years since Payton's death, constitutes the first book-length biography of the Payton story. One reason for the gap is that Payton and his companies did not leave full archives of their activities. As a result, historians have been left to piece together Payton's career from other sources, such as comments from his peers, newspaper accounts, and his occasional brushes with the law. Mc-Gruder tackles the methodological challenge posed by this fragmentary evidential record

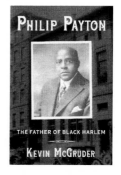

with ingenuity, while the comparatively slim nature of the volume testifies to the unavoidable gaps that remain.

Payton grew up in Westfield, Massachusetts. His parents ran successful businesses catering predominately to the town's small Black community; his father was a barber and his mother a milliner. Payton and his siblings attended the majority-white local high school, and among the novel findings on these formative years is an evocative photo of Philip with his younger brother James as members of the school football team. Yet Philip also briefly attended the all-black Livingstone College in North Carolina, an apparent attempt by his father to stop his son from falling in with the wrong crowd at his local school. Payton, therefore, had lived in the North and the South, and as part of a Black minority and majority, before he subsequently attempted to navigate the evolving color line of New York's real estate market after 1899. As McGruder reminds us, despite Payton's story appearing to conform to that of the classic "self-made man," his success depended on preexisting personal connections, too: his first business partner, for instance, hailed from a nearby Massachusetts town, while his wife, Maggie Lee, also came from Westfield before she became a well-connected member of Harlem society in her own right.

Payton's most famous endeavor, the establishment of the AARC, understandably looms large in this biography. Between 1904 and 1909, the AARC played a key role in helping Black tenants find accommodation in the newer uptown district of Harlem; the AARC used investments from individuals associated with Booker T. Washington and his National Negro Business League (NNBL) to break open houses and apartment blocks previously solely in the hands of white landlords and tenants. Payton was the driving force, and his initial vision was one where white and Black tenants could live side by side. As McGruder reminds us, however, this was a transitory ambition, with racial divisions hardening through the 1900s as white opposition to Black settlement intensified in uptown Manhattan. The story of Payton and the AARC thus reveals the double-edged nature of Black businesses enterprises in this moment: appealing to notion of racial pride formed the basis of a business strategy that offered the prospect of profits while helping build communities, but it also eventually conformed with and perpetuated segregated settlement.

Following an acrimonious court case in 1909 in which he was sued by dissatisfied fellow AARC share-holders, Payton set up a new real estate venture in his own name. McGruder sheds useful light on neglected elements of Payton's career during this period until his death in 1917. His trip to Liberia in 1910 is one interesting episode, an apparent attempt to explore business opportunities in the "little Black Republic." Yet though this voyage is instructive of the transatlantic nature of Black economic and political life in this period, we remain one step removed from Payton's true intentions and feelings. His fellow traveler Bishop Alexander Walters wrote an account of the trip, but Payton did not. McGruder works had to fill in the context, but here, as elsewhere, the archival silences mean that he still cuts an enigmatic and occasionally elusive figure.

Just before his death in 1917, Payton's career appeared to be on another upswing. His name was attached to two large apartment blocks on 141st and 142nd Streets, with an advertisement seeking "refine colored tenants." Once again, though, not all was as it seemed: these large buildings were actually owned by another firm, despite marketing that suggested Payton's firm was in sole control. This in itself revealed the instructive point that by 1917 there remained a perceived business advantage in associating with the Payton "brand." Yet Payton's career was abruptly cut short by his untimely death from liver cancer on August 29 at the age of forty-one. Obituaries and eulogies praised his pioneering efforts, testifying both to the impact of his work and to his success in building and maintaining a public profile of achievement and respectability.

Reflecting on Payton's overall historical significance, McGruder is ultimately sympathetic to the challenges faced by Black business entrepreneurs: of Payton's final deal that traded upon Harlem's hardened racial divides, McGruder acknowledges that "challenging segregated housing and forgoing" higher rents would have been "more honorable," but that financial incentives won through (163). Yet more broadly, for McGruder, Payton's story was part of a wider problem: that Black businesses faced a dearth of alternatives and were frequently starved of access to white capital and markets both in the 1910s and well beyond. Payton, therefore, emerges as an important figure in the history of Harlem who also helps bring into focus the larger ambiguities and dilemmas inherent in twentieth century Black capitalism. One cannot help but lament that the lack of a personal archive stops us from digging into Payton's motivations at various junctures, but this biography does a neat job of setting his experiences into context while serving as a useful primer on Harlem's transformative first decades of the twentieth century.

Reviewed by Oliver Ayers. Olly Ayers is Associate Professor at Northeastern University London with research specialisms in digital mapping and the histories of race and urban space. He is the author of Laboured Protest: Black Civil Rights in New York City and Detroit during the New Deal and Second World War *(Milton, UK: Routledge 2019) and coprincipal investigator on the Mapping Black London digital history project.*

Your Children Are Very Greatly in Danger: School Segregation in Rochester, New York

By Justin Murphy. Ithaca, NY: Cornell University Press, 2022. 312 pages, 10 b&w illus., 2 maps, 5 charts. $32.95 hardcover; $21.99 e-book.

In *Your Children Are Very Greatly in Danger*, Justin Murphy, who is not a historian by profession, offers a fine, well-researched historical and contemporary account of school desegregation activities in Rochester, New York, from the antebellum era to the present. His work fits into the genre of studies that call for true and fair educational equality for all America's children regardless of race, class, gender, or ethnicity. He argues that concerted efforts were employed to institute segregation and that simultaneous and rigorous efforts must be implemented to abate it.

In demonstrating how educational segregation was first institutionalized, Murphy traces the activities of early Rochesterians, such as Austin Stewart and Thomas James, to establish schools for black children who were unwelcome in white schools. When Frederick Douglass establishing residency in Rochester in 1847, desegregation protest activities increased, temporarily causing segregation to end. Similar to other northern locales, Murphy underscores how the Great Migration encouraged Southern blacks to migrate en masse to the Rochester region for jobs. Driven by white racism, white realtors, bankers, and other citizens proactively worked to prevent African Americans from filtering into white neighborhoods, ensuring that Black people were confined instead to exclusively Black enclaves, which fostered the creation of separate Black and white public schools.

With the passage of the 1954 *Brown vs. Board of Education* decision and New York State's education commissioner, James Allen, mandating in 1963 that all New York State public schools be desegregated, the struggle to desegregate schools ensued. This is crux of Murphy's story. He portrays the struggle, which included open enrollment or the allowing of students to attend schools outside their neighborhoods, if space permitted and parents approved; one-way busing of Black children to predominately white schools; a reorganization plan, or a modified version of earlier plans, to quell the disapproval of troubled parents; along with a plethora of other plans that never gained the consensus of most parents, school administrators, teachers, community activists, and local politicians. With the push to ensure that no city schools maintained an enrollment of 50 percent nonwhite students, many middle- and upper-class whites demonstrated their anti-integration stances by fleeing to the suburbs, leaving Rochester city public schools, by 2022, with a population of predominately Black and Brown students, effectively maintaining segregation.

Murphy postulates that Black Rochesterian leaders eventually accepted that whites generally did not want truly integrated schools. Therefore, they focused their energies instead on improving city schools and creating magnet and charter schools that incorporated a results-oriented management style for teachers to ensure that urban students received a quality education. Despite the decades-long battle to achieve school integration, Murphy optimistically advocates that desegregation can still be achieved if a core group of leaders is willing to make it happen. He promotes an integrationist metropolitan approach where public school districts in local suburbs connect to Rochester public schools, creating a single school district in which full integration could and should be institutionalized. To actualize this objective, Murphy concludes by encouraging interested parties to examine the viability of forming a unified countywide school system; to create policies to make the current urban-suburban program more fair (in contrast to the subjective measures suburban administrators have frequently employed to evaluate the applications of urban students); and to provide intensive anti-racism education for children and adults in all Rochester-area school districts. Without these or similar measures, Murphy argues, all Rochester-area students will remain greatly in danger because their educations are skewed.

In the 1960s and after, not all Black Rochesterians favored school integration as a solution for their children receiving a high-quality education. Instead, they supported the efforts to obtain more monetary resources and committed personnel to strengthen inner-city schools. For example, the Nation of Islam had a strong contingent in Rochester in the late 1960s and early 1970s and supported this position. As Murphy shows the strong white opposition to school integration, it would have been good had he also underscored that the Black community was not monolithic. Nonetheless, Murphy's well-written story is supported by a rich primary and secondary source base gathered over years of intensive research, including extensive interviews with key actors in the Rochester integration school process. Moreover, Murphy work hints that a quality urban historical study needs to be written on the Rochester Black community. His work is a must-read for anyone interested in school integration in general and the history of school integration in Rochester, New York, in particular.

Reviewed by Michael B. Boston. Boston is Associate Professor of African and African American Studies at the College at Brockport, State University of New York. He is the author of Blacks in Niagara Falls: Leaders and Community Development, 1850–1985; The Business Strategy of Booker T. Washington: Its Development and Implementation; *and* Dr. Skinner's Remarkable School for Colored Deaf, Dumb, and Blind Children 1857–1860.

The Fulton Fish Market: A History

By Jonathan Rees. New York: Columbia University Press, 2022. 312 Pages.
$30.00 hardcover, $29.99 e-book.

On most mornings, Diego, who runs the fish counter at my local New York City supermarket, goes to the Fulton Fish Market. He proceeds from dealer to dealer, looking for the freshest fish at the best prices. He purchases whole bronzini, trout, and tilapia as well as fillets of Atlantic salmon, cod, and tuna. His routine would be familiar to any of the wholesale buyers who have frequented the market throughout its 200-year history, except that now the market operates in the Bronx instead of in Lower Manhattan, where it stood from 1822 to 2005.

During its long tenure in Manhattan, the Fulton Fish Market gained a reputation as a "never-changing" institution that was symbolic of a vanishing working-class way of life (xix). The mid-twentieth century *New Yorker* writer Joseph Mitchell did more than anyone to promote this nostalgia for the city's fishing industry by chronicling the lives of the ordinary men (fishermen, a boat captain, a restaurant owner, etc.) who worked at "every link" in the market's provisioning chain (xix). What most interests Jonathan Rees in *The Fulton Fish Market*, however, is not historical continuity but the many ways the market has adapted, with varying degrees of success, to urban, technological, and environmental change. For all its seemingly old-fashioned ways, he notes, it managed to outlast every other Manhattan marketplace from the nineteenth century, leaving the island for the Bronx only at the onset of the twenty-first century.

The Fulton Fish Market consisted of three main buildings: the original 1822 structure at the intersection of Fulton and South Streets, and two additional buildings located on South Street by the East River. Its Lower Manhattan neighborhood was a vibrant commercial district bustling with shoppers—many of whom arrived daily via the Brooklyn ferry. The market initially stocked a variety of foodstuffs, including "Meats, Fish, & Game," and was primarily a retail establishment with some wholesale activity (15). Over the course of the nineteenth century, as the market's butchers departed for other areas of the city, the wholesale fish dealers gradually took over. This marked the era of Eugene Blackford, an innovative P. T. Barnum-like figure who sold oysters and Connecticut River shad but who was more famous for his sea-themed spectacles. Near his stand, he maintained an immense aquarium full of "strange living fish" from around the world, while upstairs, on the second floor, he curated exhibits at the Fulton Market Fish Museum (60).

Rees describes the ascendency of the wholesale industry and dealers like Blackford as embodying an "extraordinary change in the way the Fulton Fish Market did business"

(66). Another significant change was the displacement of the ferry by the opening of the Brooklyn Bridge in 1883, which contributed to the gradual decline of the East River's port. As a result, fewer people and boats arrived in the neighborhood, and it became isolated from the rest of the city and its waterways. Fish now had to be shipped to the market by rail and later, in the 1920s, by trucks (both modes of transport were outfitted with modern refrigeration technology to ensure that the fish did not spoil en route).

The market was a predominantly male space, but women could be found there as well. The market's Dorlan & Shaffer oyster house, in fact, owed its popularity to the large number of women who ate there regularly. And an image of shoppers browsing rows of fish (68) prominently features two women. These examples suggest that women may have had a greater presence at the Fulton Fish Market than usually believed, and future studies can explore their influence as consumers.

One of the book's strengths is the attention it pays to the market's animals. Readers learn much about the variety of local fish on display, especially salmon and shad. Over time, overfishing depleted these local species, and they had to be replaced by fish sourced from farther away. In the late nineteenth century, for example, salmon from the Pacific Northwest and shad from the South regularly appeared at the Fulton Fish Market. Oysters had a similar trajectory. During the market's retail heyday, its many small restaurants and stands served an abundance of oysters (reportedly 50,000 a day) from Long Island and Queens's Jamaica Bay. However, pollution decimated local oyster beds, which resulted in the Health Department closing the city's last oyster bed in 1927. Oysters, like fish, now had to be delivered to Lower Manhattan from across the United States.

Rees devotes an entire chapter to the plight of turtles at the Fulton Fish Market. He describes disturbing scenes of giant green turtles "flipped upside on their shells and bound with ropes," many with visible bruises (98). Turtles could also be seen at the entrance to some restaurants, hanging from their rear fins and about to be decapitated. The nascent anti–animal cruelty movement took notice and, in the 1860s and 1870s, had some success convincing New York State to regulate the treatment of turtles aboard ships and at the Fulton Market. Rees astutely points out that fish, which are smaller and less expressive than green turtles, rarely received a similar level of sympathy from civilians, legislators, and animal rights proponents.

He also criticizes the fishmongers' response to local overfishing and pollution. Wholesalers and fisherman consistently resisted attempts at conservation by federal and state agencies, preferring instead to search for more fish elsewhere and to promote experiments in artificial breeding. The latter approach proved only moderately successful at reviving depleted species. If industrial fishing is to have any chance at becoming sustainable, Rees writes, the shortsightedness exhibited at places like the Fulton Fish Market must be jettisoned. It remains to be seen whether the market's move to the Bronx will enable it to respond more responsibly to environmental challenges. The new facility's vast size and remote location might work against this goal, since they provide ideal conditions for selling enormous amounts of fish with minimal public oversight. Thus, the future viability of ocean life and, relatedly, of the Fulton Fish Market is far from assured.

Reviewed by Eric C. Cimino. Cimino is Associate Professor of History at Molloy University in Rockville Center, New York.

The Lost Promise: American Universities in the 1960s

By Ellen Schrecker. Chicago: University of Chicago Press, 2021. 621 pages, 23 b&w illus., 1 table. $35.00 cloth; $24.99 e-pub.

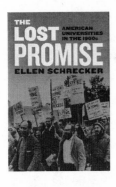

The 1960s was a decade of turbulence for America. Mercifully, the efforts of Sen. Joseph McCarthy and others to find a Communist in every nook and cranny were drawing to a close, but the Civil Rights Movement and the war in Vietnam now dominated public attention. For America's colleges and universities, this decade began in a positive vein and with great hope for the future. There was substantial public and political support for higher education, and it was an era of considerable growth, especially for public institutions. Older schools were becoming larger in size and function, new campuses were being established, and enrollments were rising rapidly. This was especially notable in New York, where Gov. Nelson Rockefeller promoted the extensive expansion of the State University system. These developments led to substantial changes in the student population, both economically and socially. And the professoriate, too, was changing. Traditionally, college faculties had been composed primarily of men from backgrounds of wealth and privilege; now women and men of more diverse backgrounds were aspiring to careers in higher education. However, by the early 1970s support for colleges and universities had diminished, public institutions faced serious cuts to their budgets, and the "golden age" was over. Ellen Schrecker chronicles these developments in her extensively researched and well-written book, *The Lost Promise: American Universities in the 1960s.*

Schrecker attributes the decline in public and political support for universities to student unrest and protest and the participation of some faculty members who joined with them. The protests began with the Free Speech Movement at the University of California at Berkely, but soon other issues dominated. Activist students and faculty were increasingly involved in the Civil Rights Movement and in protests against the war in Vietnam. Antiwar activities included protests against the military draft, the presence of ROTC programs on campuses, and against government grants for defense-related research. For the most part, the earliest activities were nonviolent, but that began to change, and civil disobedience became more common. Disruptions of classes on campus and civil disobedience off campus not only diminished public respect for higher education but also caused serious rifts among faculty. While universities have never really recovered from the damage caused by this period of turbulence, there have been some positive achievements, especially the introduction of new areas of study and the ultimate acceptance of some of the scholarly contributions of radical academics.

Those of us in higher education who lived through these times will find much in this book that is familiar, and it will evoke some unpleasant memories. While many nonradical faculty members agreed with many of the goals of the students and their radical colleagues, they did not condone the methods employed. Workdays could be very stressful. Many New Left faculty and graduate students, so convinced of their righteousness, had little tolerance for more moderate faculty and students, and so treated them with disdain. Schrecker seems to be more concerned with the difficulties encountered by the radical faculty than with those of the more moderate faculty who were trying to perform the tasks expected of their profession. Not only was working at the university trying, but so too was attending a professional association meeting. Schrecker indicates that radical scholars attempted to put their stamp on professional associations, but she downplays the tensions at the annual meetings of those organizations. She specifically mentions the 1969 meeting of the American Historical Association, where, she claims, despite fears of some leaders of the association, there were no disruptions at the business meeting. I am not sure what she would consider a disruption, but I attended that meeting, and I distinctly recall an altercation for possession of a floor microphone.

While the prospects for higher education at the beginning of the 1960s indeed were quite bright, Schrecker sees it as more idyllic than it actually was. Certainly, there were more academic positions available than in later years, but she exaggerates the ease of obtaining one. Since jobs were not posted, it took connections even to know if a position existed. Schrecker claims that it was not difficult to get a good job as long as the candidate remained on good terms with the candidate's dissertation adviser. That may have been true for the people she interviewed, but that was not my recollection, nor was it that of many of my contemporaries. If you were lucky, your mentor might get you a job interview, but then it was up to you, as you competed with several other candidates for that position.

Schrecker has a dim view of the future prospects for higher education in light of the decline of support from the public, the government, and private industry. It is particularly disturbing to see universities dealing with their budget shortfalls by utilizing pitifully paid adjunct faculty to teach many—sometimes the majority—of their classes. But recent events indicate that there are signs of rebellion from this academic underclass. Moreover, faculty unions, at least at public colleges and universities, are not as stagnant as Schrecker claims.

We can hope, at least, that there are some rays of light in the future for higher education in America. To understand how important the 1960s were to America's universities this book is a must-read.

Reviewed by Ivan D. Steen. Steen is Associate Professor of History Emeritus at the University at Albany. He is coauthor, with Nuala McGann Drescher and Willem E. Scheuerman, of United University Professions: Pioneering in Higher Education Unionism *(Albany: SUNY Press, 2019).*

The Market in Birds: Commercial Hunting, Conservation, and the Origins of Wildlife Consumerism 1850–1920

By Andrea L. Smalley with Henry M. Reeves, Baltimore, MD: Johns Hopkins University Press, 2022. 307 pages. $59.95 hardcover and e-book.

The most riveting impression that a reader takes away from *The Market in Birds* is the mental image of millions of bird carcasses—frozen in warehouses, compressed into barrels or piled in boats—all on their way to being eaten or deplumed, or stuffed and mounted.

The book delivers this image in a straightforward, almost dispassionate narrative that nevertheless makes the reader cringe at the sheer extent of the carnage from a particularly grim chapter in this country's environmental history: seventy years of destruction of the country's once-vast populations of wild birds for consumption as delicacies, for decorations on women's hats, and for private collections of eggshells and mounted specimens.

The grim tallies boggle the mind: 35,000 ducks killed in Virginia in 1900 with the help of the newly invented semiautomatic shotgun. Forty thousand passenger pigeons, which were being shipped live for use in target shooting contests, dead from dehydration in a rail car in the 1880s. In Minnesota, 25,810 pounds of dead birds were shipped in just two months alone in 1876. And in one unforgettable passage, the stench of decaying dead birds almost smacks the reader in the face in an account of the frequent failures of early forms of freezer storage. A series of such losses for one dealer culminated with him dumping hundreds of rotting bird carcasses on the prairie from whence many of them had come, with no concept of a teachable moment but plenty of exasperation over his lost profits.

This book is neither a fast read nor a casual, entertaining one. It is also not a book likely to appeal to an amateur birder, with its references to the Progressive Era conservation movement, its detailed accounts of state and federal court battles, and its description of what the authors call "the tangled connections between ecology, economy, culture, and law that the market had thrown into sharp relief." Instead, *The Market in Birds* is more likely to serve as an extremely important reference for academics and conservationists that carefully sets out the authors' theory of the complex relationship between the country's wild resources and the consumers who, had their lives depended on it, could not have identified a living version of the roasted American Woodcock that appeared on their dinner plates in a nineteenth century New York City restaurant.

Completely unregulated in its early years, the market-hunting era decimated bird populations and contributed to the extinction of several species, including the Carolina Parakeet, the Passenger Pigeon, and the Labrador Duck, which was rare even before its carcasses started appearing in urban game markets. The slaughter was slowed by a series of state and federal laws and court decisions, mostly in the twentieth century, and finally came to an end in 1918, with the federal Migratory Bird Treaty Act, which remains in effect today.

The publication of *The Market in Birds* is its own remarkable story. Lead author and historian Andrea L. Smalley, a professor emerita at Northern Illinois University, based the finished manuscript on the work of the late Henry M. Reeves, a renowned biologist with the U.S. Fish and Wildlife Service. Reeves died in 2013 and left an unfinished manuscript and extensive research on the market in birds. Smalley was introduced to Reeves's family, acquired his materials, and used them as the foundation of the final book. Completing another writer's work is exceptionally difficult, and the Reeves family acknowledges that with gratitude in the foreword. As the author of an earlier book on the effect of American colonization on wildlife, Smalley was well-suited to the task.

Every story like this needs a villain or a hero, and Reeves found his villain in Henry Clay Merritt. A nineteenth century market hunter of birds turned dealer in game birds, the hard-bitten Merritt left his native Hudson Valley for Illinois, where he quickly adopted the frontiersman's traits of waste and destruction. Reeves knew about Merritt's autobiography, *The Shadow of a Gun*. It is not clear whether Merritt would have landed such a prominent role in the book Reeves envisioned, but Smalley effectively threads Merritt's life story through the book that she brought to completion. In so doing, she provides a disturbing insight into the mindset of a businessman capable of admiring the birds he was slaughtering. It is not a stretch to say that Merritt probably would have identified as a nature-lover, without any sense of irony.

Merritt also unapologetically felt that his work met an essential need expressed by American consumers, and he distinguished between market hunters and sporting hunters by insisting that market hunters did not engage in profligate killing, because they knew better than to destroy the source of their livelihood. Such a viewpoint displayed a remarkable lack of understanding of a basic fact : if you hunt a breeding population of birds to a tipping point, that population will struggle to survive even if the breeding adults technically continue to reproduce.

By the time Reeves started his research, none of the main players in the market era of bird consumption were alive to be interviewed. In an odd omission, the book does not contain a stand-alone list of references; instead, the references are cited in the chapter notes, and while those notes include editorials and personal accounts written at the height of the legal battles that outlawed market hunting, original interviews were, of course, impossible for a contemporary author. It is also not clear which references Reeves gathered, and which Smalley contributed through her own research, but the source materials—including numerous period photographs—are extensive and often come from obscure accounts in long-ago newspapers, technical journals, and bulletins from agricultural experiment stations.

Pulling together this amount of detail was a prodigious effort for both authors, and Reeves, who did not live to see his idea become a book, gets just credit. In addition to documenting an important period in the country's environmental history, *The Market in Birds* stands as an elegiac ode to Reeves, who gave so much to spend his career protecting birds and who deserves this tribute.

Reviewed by: Darryl McGrath. McGrath is a journalist and the author of Flight Paths: A Field Journal of Hope, Heartbreak, and Miracles with New York's Bird People *(Albany: SUNY Press, 2016).*

Left in the Center: The Liberal Party of New York and the Rise and Fall of American Social Democracy

By Daniel Soyer. Ithaca, NY: Cornell University Press, 2022. 432 pages, 9 b&w illus. $46.95 hardcover, $30.99 e-book.

Contemporary readers, if they remember the Liberal Party at all, are likely to associate it with the newspaper headlines about the arrest of its political boss on corruption charges in the early 2000s. But *Left in the Center*, Daniel Soyer's absorbing, deeply researched account of the party's history, argues that before its sad last years, the Liberal Party played an important role in New York City's political scene—especially in the 1940s and 1950s. Soyer's book goes beyond a narrow account of the party to evoke the distinctive alliances, tensions, institutions, and debates that defined the political world of the city during the heyday of its social democratic institutions—a political culture that has disappeared as thoroughly as the Liberal Party itself.

The Liberal Party had its roots in the city's socialist politics of the early twentieth century and in the ways that these were twisted and transformed by anticommunism in the 1930s and 1940s. Garment worker leaders, most notably David Dubinsky of the International Ladies Garment Workers Union and Alex Rose of the hatters' union, played a key role in founding the party; as late as 1966, the majority of the Manhattan district leaders had once been members of the Socialist Party. Soyer makes the case that many of the Liberal Party's leaders as well as its rank-and-file were driven by what he describes (following Howard Brick) as a "post-capitalist" vision of "social enterprise" and "economic democracy," as the party's founding document put it. This vision also attracted some left-inclined but anticommunist intellectuals such as Adolf Berle (former "brain trust" member and co-author of *The Modern Corporation and Private Property*), civil rights activist Pauli Murray, theologian Reinhold Niebuhr, housing lawyer and advocate Charles Abrams, and Teachers College professor George Childs. Both the intellectuals and the party rank-and-file were alienated by the machine politics of Tammany Hall and sought to follow Eugene Debs and Norman Thomas in promoting an independent political party to endorse what they called "fighting liberalism."

But anticommunism was also central to the creation of the Liberal Party. That the Liberal Party could exist at all is due New York State's provision for "fusion voting," which has itself been infused with antimachine sentiment over the years. Candidates in the state can run on more than one ballot line, with the total votes added together. This permits smaller parties to exert pressure on the Democratic and Republican candidates by either endorsing them or threatening to withhold their support.

In the 1930s, labor activists in the city, led by Alex Rose, were eager to find a way to build support from the left for both Republican Mayor Fiorello H. La Guardia and Franklin Delano Roosevelt. Working with Sidney Hillman of the Amalgamated Clothing Workers, Rose organized the American Labor Party (ALP). Initially, politically left workers in the city were so unaccustomed to voting for mainstream candidates that they had to be persuaded that it was all right to do so on the ALP line. But it did not take long before fierce internal schisms broke out within the ALP, as Communist organizers sought to build their strength within the organization. When a coalition that included Communists was victorious, the right wing of the ALP abandoned the party to start the rival Liberals in 1944.

Accordingly, the Liberal Party was both defined by its efforts to push the Democratic Party on the national level and La Guardia locally to the left, and by its intense anticommunism. Soyer makes the case that its anticommunism reflected a principled revulsion of the Soviet Union's political repression (including the repression of Socialists during the Stalin years) as well as of the real difficulties of working with Communists on local political issues during the Popular Front period. But at the same time, the Liberal Party's anticommunism hampered its own efforts to build an independent left in the city in the 1940s. The Liberals supported the purging of Communist teachers in the city, warning that since the Communist Party was a "conspiratorial group loyal to a foreign state," its members were not "protected by academic freedom" (93). The Party supported the Wilson-Pekula Act at the state level, which barred candidates from running in primaries for parties of which they were not members—an effort to halt the momentum of East Harlem ALP Congressman Vito Marcantonio. When the Democrats tried to unseat Marcantonio, the Liberal Party attacked him as a "Commie stooge" and backed a conservative Democrat whose other allies supported him by saying he was no "New Deal suckling" (121). Two Liberal Party City Council members, Louis Goldberg and Ira Palatin, were elected under the city's short-lived system of proportional representation for council elections in the 1940s. But when this system was attacked from the right—in part because of hostility to two Communist Party council members, Benjamin Davis and Pete Cacchione—the Liberals were not able to mount much of a defense.

Soyer makes the case that the Liberal Party helped to channel the Left's desires into electoral demands, creating a pressure group for rent regulation, cooperative and public housing, cheap mass transit, and public investment in cultural programs, thus playing a critical role in sustaining popular support for the city's extensive public sector. Grassroots political clubs in the city over these years formed a crucial political vehicle for political expression and participation, and Soyer depicts the Liberals as a "year-round party" that tried to advance "ongoing issues and policies" consistently, not just at election time. Neighborhood "clubs" provided political education and social events, linking campaigns for improved bus service or tenant issues to the largest questions of national and international policy. In the late 1940s, for example, members of the West Side Liberal Club might attend talks on rent and price control, racial discrimination in the city and the "Real Facts about Slave Labor in the USSR."

Emphasizing the Liberals' public policy arguments, Soyer shows that they advocated an income tax for the city, years before this became a reality, so that New York's government could provide "full social welfare and educational services consonant with what the daily life of an enlightened, progressive municipality should be." They also pushed for home rule and argued that the fact that a metropolis the size of New York had to go "hat in hand" to Albany to beg for the power to levy its own taxes was a "sorry state of affairs" (107). Mass transit, they insisted, benefited business and real estate interests and should thus be supported by general revenues, not simply paid for by riders. The Liberal Party council members even evolved an early, nuanced critique of Robert Moses, praising his capacity to build public works, parks, and pools as "almost radical" while recognizing that "in matters involving social conflicts, such as upon whom should fall the burden of taxation, or for whose benefit government should be run," he was an "economic royalist" (108).

However, while the Liberals were able to advocate such arguments at least in part because of the political space opened in the city by the Communists and those farther to their left, their enthusiastic participation in the anticommunist crackdown, which grew as the Cold War deepened, helped to shift New York to the right, foreclosing whatever possibilities might have been available for their own politics as well.

The trajectory of the party later in the century underscores this. Despite some efforts to organize in Black and Puerto Rican neighborhoods, the Liberals never regained a constituency after the decline of their old garment union base. (Nor were they able to offer a coherent program to stem the departure of garment factories from the city.) The party leaders continued to haggle over whom to endorse in various races, and often their support was rewarded with patronage and public employment for Liberal Party members, making the party a political machine of its own. The party moved still farther from its roots when it endorsed Rudolph Giuliani for mayor in 1993. Long before the scandals of their final years, the party had become what one observer described as "a law firm with a ballot line" (291).

Soyer suggests that the Liberal Party's sad fate reflects the disappearance of socialist politics in the city, the generational political shifts that led to the rise of Black Power and "community control" politics and the thinning out of the grassroots clubs. Surely all these factors played a role, but the party's collapse might also point to the extent to which the Liberal Party was animated by anticommunist animosity as much as anything else. Once the Communist Party had been marginalized, it is hard to avoid the impression that the Liberals lost their real focus—after those confrontations, they lacked the grassroots energy and political passion to promote the combative social democratic politics they supposedly sought. In providing this detailed narrative of a single third party, Soyer illuminates the myopia and the limits of Cold War liberalism.

Reviewed by Kim Phillips-Fein. Phillips-Fein is the author of Fear City: New York's Fiscal Crisis and the Rise of Austerity Politics *(New York: Metropolitan Books, 2017). She is the Robert Gardiner-Kenneth T. Jackson Professor of History at Columbia University.*

Kitchen Table Politics: Conservative Women and Family Values in New York

By Stacie Taranto. Philadelphia: University of Pennsylvania Press, 2017. 296 pages. $59.95 hardcover and e-book.

Recent social histories, from Lisa McGirr's *Suburban Warriors* to Michelle Nickerson's *Mothers of Conservatism*, have demonstrated the centrality of suburban white women's grassroots activism to the rise of modern conservatism. Stacie Taranto's *Kitchen Table Politics* is an impressive addition to this literature. With a nod to the "kitchen-table activists" depicted by McGirr, Taranto turns our gaze from the South and West to Catholic women in New York who worked from their kitchen tables to organize protest marches and run political campaigns. First-generation suburban Catholic homemakers became the lifeblood of antiabortion

activism in the 1970s, Taranto argues, and contributed to the political realignment of the New York State Republican Party by 1980.

Taranto begins by describing the common trajectory of a generation of Catholic women. Using oral histories and interviews, Taranto illustrates how Catholic women born during the Great Depression grew up as part of New York City's Democratic working class. Many took college classes or worked as secretaries before getting married and turning to a life of homemaking. Once married, they often moved from mixed urban neighborhoods to the all-white, redlined suburbs of New York City. Taranto focuses on four counties—Nassau and Suffolk on Long Island, and Rockland and Westchester to the northwest of the city—which experienced rapid growth in the 1950s and 1960s.

Respecting the Catholic Church's ban on birth control, these Catholic women typically had large families and embraced heteronormative gender roles in their lives as homemakers. If New York City had been a center of liberal and radical feminist activism in the 1960s, Catholic homemakers paid no attention. It was only when feminist activists succeeded in pressuring the New York State legislature to legalize abortion in 1970 that Catholic mothers were galvanized into action, forging a positive politics that sought civil and legal rights for the unborn. Using the Catholic Church's vast network of newspapers and parish groups bolstered by the Vatican II reforms, Catholic mothers mobilized a large base of support throughout the suburbs. They used their authority as "concerned mothers" to bolster their credibility and craft a "maternal populism." They believed abortion was not only state-sanctioned murder but also a selfish means for women to evade their maternal obligations. For Catholic mothers, gender was not a socially constructed identity but rather "divinely inspired and biologically based" (173). Catholic mothers took offense to the feminist idea that homemaking should be a *choice*, as this implied that homemaking was less essential than they believed it to be.

One of the chief achievements of *Kitchen Table Politics* is to demonstrate how Catholic homemakers contributed to the breakdown of the New Deal coalition and produced a political realignment by 1980. Debates over abortion, the state equal rights amendment (ERA), and the Conference on International Women's Year made Catholic homemakers more distrustful of government interventions in the family—leading them to link antifeminist sentiment with calls for smaller government and lower taxes. Catholic mothers further identified electoral politics as a means to support their vision, forming the New York State Right to Life Party and running the candidate Ellen McCormack in the 1976 Democratic presidential primary. Seeing the potential of Catholic homemakers, conservative Republicans partnered with them to marginalize their party's more moderate, pro-feminist wing embodied in Nelson Rockefeller. By the time Rockefeller retired in 1977, the conservative wing had wrested control from the liberals—shifting New York State's Republican Party from a more liberal, feminist politics, to a more conservative, suburban, antifeminist base in 1980. While Taranto sometimes overdraws the contributions of Catholic mothers to this party realignment, the realignment did have outcomes on the national level: while Reagan was barely competitive in New York in 1976, by 1980 the four suburban counties where Catholic homemakers had organized were central to Reagan's victory.

Kitchen Table Politics hinges on the argument that Catholic mothers were only "temporarily political" for a brief period when they mobilized to oppose the ERA and abortion legalization. Once they knew conservative Republicans would protect their interests, Taranto argues, Catholic mothers retreated back to the ostensibly apolitical space of their homes. By taking on this framing, however, Taranto adheres to a divide between private and public that feminist scholars have long questioned. Taranto misses the chance to interrogate the major irony that Catholic homemakers agreed with radical feminists that the personal *was* political and that their work in the home had its own kind of politics. The central problem lies in Taranto's under-theorization of the "political": can subjects be temporarily political? And moreover, can one's growing consciousness of the importance of electoral politics be so easily undone?

Taranto successfully captures how New York's pro-life movement was decidedly more Catholic than the rest of the country, which was dominated by Evangelicals and other conservative Christians. Yet while Taranto points toward Catholic homemakers' "maternal populism," she rarely identifies where their dedication to conservative family values overlapped with antifeminists like Phyllis Schlafly and others. *Kitchen Table Politics* indeed opens up many questions about the post-1970s pro-life mobilization, for instance, how alliances formed between Catholic and Protestant activists, or how grassroots pro-life activism related to efforts to install pro-life judges in the court system.

This book, of course, only prompts these questions because it succeeds in sketching out the local contours of the movement in a way that sparks interest about the national scope of pro-life politics. Ultimately, *Kitchen Table Politics* is a timely and important addition to the scholarship on American conservatism and the history of New York City, reminding us of the significance of local grassroots efforts in shaping modern conservatism.

Reviewed by Whitney McIntosh. McIntosh is a PhD candidate in American History at Columbia University. Her dissertation, "Antipolitics: American Libertarianism, 1960–2003," is a political and intellectual history of the modern American libertarian movement from the counterculture to the Iraq War.

EXHIBIT REVIEWS

A Well Regulated Militia: Citizen, Soldier, and State

Fort Ticonderoga, Ticonderoga, NY

Temporary exhibit, May 2022 through October 2023

Exhibit team: Dr. Matthew Keagle, Curator; T. J. Mullen, Exhibit Design and Fabrication; Miranda Peters, Vice President of Collections and Digital Production; Margaret Staudter, Director of Archaeology; Tabitha Hubbard, Collections Manager; Tyler Ostrander, Registrar

---

A Well Regulated Militia: Citizen, Soldier, and State is a temporary exhibit in the lower level of the Mars Education Center at Fort Ticonderoga. The exhibit, according to the museum's web description, "explores this often misunderstood institution from its formation in the colonial period through its decline in the early 19th century."[1] The exhibit revolves around a small, yet impressive, sampling of Ticonderoga's vast collections of militaria and offers many items of interest for the devoted military history enthusiast. The content is thoroughly researched, and the artifacts are attractively displayed, confirming the Fort's adeptness at engaging visitors with historical material culture.

The exhibit offers visitors an examination of the militia's European antecedents, many of which were in decline at the same time the militia system was being formalized in the North American colonies, and notes how participation in the militia reinforced status within the existing social order and excluded people of color and Native Americans. A brief introductory video offers an overview of the establishment of militia systems in twelve of the colonies that would rebel against British rule in 1775 (only in Quaker Pennsylvania was militia service not codified), but the bulk of the exhibit focuses on the post-Revolutionary militia until the decline of compulsory militia service in the decades after the War of 1812. It is interesting that the exhibit makes scant mention of the challenges and deficiencies within the militia system that were experienced during the conflict with Britain from 1812 to 1815 and that constituted a significant factor in that decline. The exhibition is strongest in its exploration of the passage of the Militia Act of 1792, which codifies the American system of defense and the debates between Federalists and Anti-Federalists over control of the militia as a means of defining state power. The exhibit team also provides a strong overview of

---

1. "A Well Regulated Militia: Citizen, Soldier, and State," Fort Ticonderoga, accessed July 22, 2022, https://www.fortticonderoga.org/a-well-regulated-militia-citizen-soldier-and-state/.

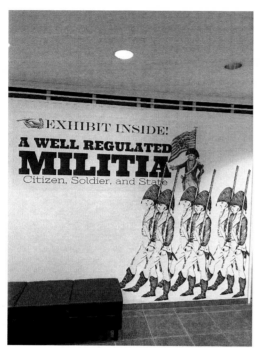

Figure 1. Title wall for "A Well Regulated Militia: Citizen, Soldier, and State" at the Deborah Clarke Mars Education Center, Fort Ticonderoga. PHOTOGRAPH BY AUTHOR.

Figure 2. View of the exhibit hall showcasing Fort Ticonderoga's impressive collection of historical artifacts, including uniforms, small arms, and cannon. Located in the lower level of the Deborah Clarke Mars Education Center, Fort Ticonderoga. PHOTOGRAPH BY AUTHOR.

Figure 3. Text panel for "A Well Regulated Militia." These text-heavy panels, while informative to those steeped in military history, can be daunting for visitors and may provide too much information to be digested. PHOTOGRAPH BY AUTHOR.

the decline of the compulsory militia system in the nineteenth century in favor of volunteer companies. Here, the team could potentially have examined the growing disparity in militia development between urban versus rural communities as part of the broader social context of the period, and they might also have considered the use of the militia as a means of enforcing order and social control in the face of unrest.

A Well Regulated Militia is clearly targeted toward those military history enthusiasts who make the trek to the Champlain Valley to bask in Ticonderoga's material culture. The information is written and presented by and for those with an interest and background in military history rather than for those with a more generalized background. That said, the voluminous text panels may prove daunting to even the most committed visitors. With main text panels at more than 400-words each, the flood of information makes it challenging to fully absorb the exhibit's main themes.

This reviewer was left pondering a couple of decisions made within the gallery. First, it was a curious choice to title the exhibit with language from the politically fraught Second Amendment to the United States Constitution. This amendment is discussed in the body of

Figure 4. Closer view of some of Fort Ticonderoga's world-class collections alongside an intimidating "Arming the Militia" text panel. PHOTOGRAPH BY AUTHOR.

the text panel titled "Arming the Militia" (figure 5), in which the Second Amendment is presented as a "compromise to the Anti-Federalists" to prevent governmental co-optation or neglect of the militia. The prevalence of the text from the Bill of Rights in the exhibit's title was not necessarily reflected within the gallery space, and it was unclear if it was within the exhibit's intended goal to clarify what is oftentimes an overlooked element of the Second Amendment.

Similarly, a juxtaposition of historical images of American militias alongside those of contemporary right-wing militias in the United States and what this reviewer took to be radical jihadist militias in the Middle East or North Africa within the introductory media piece seemed to be pushing for an examination of the ways the term militia has been co-opted or convoluted in the present day, yet this thread is not picked up again anywhere else in the gallery. In neither instance did the omission necessarily detract from the splendid display, but it did seem that the exhibit team brought visitors right up to the line of a broader discussion about the historical context of the militia within our contemporary political discourse before ultimately walking us back. This is not to say that every museum exhibit need be overtly political or have immediate relevance to the present, but the decision to introduce such lines of thought into the gallery without follow-up perhaps raises as many questions as the exhibit answers.

If you are an enthusiast for military history and material culture, *A Well Regulated Militia: Citizen, Soldier, and State* will not disappoint. The exhibit affirms Ticonderoga's claim to one of the finest military collections in the country. For those perhaps less interested in the minutiae of military history presented in the exhibit, the uniforms and accoutrements on display are impressive. Fort Ticonderoga itself remains a fabulous destination for visitors of all ages seeking to learn about military life and warfare along North America's colonial frontier.

Reviewed by Aaron Noble. Noble is Senior Historian for Political, Military, and Governmental History at the New York State Museum. He curated the museum's 2010 exhibition, Citizen Soldier: The New York National Guard in the American Century, *as well as the museum's Civil War and World War I exhibitions.*

Native New York

National Museum of the American Indian, Alexander Hamilton U.S. Custom House, New York, NY

Ongoing (opened 2021)

In 2006, the National Museum of the American Indian (NMAI) in Washington, D.C. opened *Return to a Native Place: Algonquian Peoples of the Chesapeake*, curated by Dr. Gabrielle Tayac (Piscataway). The exhibit, which has an ongoing presence at the NMAI in Washington, D.C., brings attention to the specific Indigenous geographies and histories of the lands now occupied by the museum and many of its local and regional visitors. Long overdue for a similar approach in exhibition, the NMAI in New York City now features *Native New York*, which familiarizes visitors with Indigenous place-based histories of what is now Manhattan, Long Island, the Hudson Valley, and select parts of upstate New York. Of the many thousands of places and sites important to Algonquian and Haudenosaunee histories in what is now New York, the curators selected twelve locales to highlight Lenape, Mohican, Unkechaug, Shinnecock, and Haudenosaunee histories and people. The result is an immersive experience featuring vibrant cartoon illustrations, video clips, a short film, two interactive technology stations, archival and contemporary images, and an impressive (even if it is a little sparse) array of archaeological, historic, and contemporary objects and artwork from the NMAI collections. For 4th- and 7th-graders across New York learning about Indigenous peoples and histories via state curricula, this exhibit offers a tremendous and lively resource.

Stepping inside the gallery space, attractively presented in neutral and jewel tones, *Native New York* takes a novel approach in guiding visitors throughout Algonquian and Haudenosaunee territories without a linear timeline in place. Instead, visitors gain insight into familiar sites around Manhattan and the Bronx before they became bustling cityscapes and how they connect to Indigenous people today. Keskeskick, present-day Van Cortlandt Park, and Kapsee (sharp rock place), now known as Battery Park, were inhabited by Mohican and Lenape peoples, respectively, long before European intrusion, and they continue to be places of significance for Mohican and Lenape histories. A monument to commemorate Chief Nimham and the Mohican and Wappinger people who died in battle alongside American settlers fighting the British can be visited at Van Cortlandt Park. This part of the gallery leads into an area devoted to Kanien'kehaka (Mohawk) ironworkers who helped build the Empire State Building (and thousands of other skyscrapers) after being introduced to ironwork in the late 1800s. So many ironworkers took up work in the construction industry, Boerum Hill became known as Little Kahnawake. In a narrow gallery space in between, visitors will find an obligatory nod to archaeological material, refreshingly bereft

of hypothetical archaeological interpretations; instead, the beautiful stone points, jar fragments, pipe, and pestle on display enhance our understanding of Sapohanikan (canoe
landing place) and Shorakapkok (the sitting down place), as gathering places for Indigenous people to fish, trade, hunt, and visit with each other.

Exhibit text is kept succinct, with generous space devoted to eye-catching cartoon
panels by Weshoyot Alvitre (Tongva) and Lee Francis IV (Laguna Pueblo). One illustration
in the section focused on Indigenous Long Island highlights Unkechaug artist Lydia Chavez
working with drill bits to make wampum beads from Quahog shells for her contemporary
artwork. For people familiar with Shinnecock Nation (host of one of the largest Powwow
gatherings on the East Coast since 1967), a display case features rare and pristine examples
of Shinnecock basketry: an eel basket, a lidded storage basket, and a whisk broom. Jeremy
Dennis, a Shinnecock photographer who created the website On This Site (https://www
.jeremynative.com/onthissite/) features in the exhibit, too, though his more recent work as
founder of Ma's House, a BIPOC artist residency on Shinnecock land, is not mentioned.

Dr. Gabrielle Tayac (Piscataway) began working on *Native New York* in 2012, followed
by David Penney who completed the project for its opening in 2021. Nine years in the making and stymied by the pandemic (originally the exhibit was supposed to open in 2020), the
exhibit's weaknesses can mostly be forgiven. Of the thousands of places and sites significant
for Indigenous people, how and why were twelve selected for the exhibit? Federal- and
state-recognized Indigenous Nations are featured. Montaukett people, who continuously
strive for New York State recognition are not included. The vastness of Haudenosaunee
territory (consisting of most of upstate New York, from east to west) is reduced to two locations on the Onondaga Nation and Niagara Falls. Akwesasne, Kahnawake, Kanasetake,
Tyendinaga, Wahta, Oneida of the Thames, Six Nations, Ganienkeh, and Kanatsiohareke
are omitted, probably due to limited space. Akwesasne and Kahnawake are mentioned only
in connection with Manhattan skyscrapers and ironworkers. Another omission in representation is the lack of Abenaki history, which includes the land around what is now Lake
George and the Adirondacks.

A prominent theme throughout the exhibit is the dismantling of narratives about Indigenous history that have obtained mythic status in American society. A brilliant cartoon
by Alvitre and Francis IV as well as a short film address the lack of documentation for the
historic "sale" of Manhattan to the Dutch. As the film points out, our only information
about any exchange comes from a brief reference in a letter written by Peter Schaghen, an
administrator for the Dutch West India Company. After viewing the short film, it seems
likely the Indigenous people who met with the Dutch, kindly gave them use of lands and
water, and expected an arrangement more akin to leasing than to selling. Similarly, the
exhibit brings to attention the chaos and havoc brought upon Haudenosaunee people by
the American Revolution. In vain, the Haudenosaunee Confederacy attempted to remain
neutral. Eventually, the Oneida and Tuscarora sided with the American colonists, while
the other Haudenosaunee Nations fought alongside the British. In retribution, George

Two images from the Haudenosaunee and Tuscarora beadwork section of the exhibit. Figure 1 is a beaded heart in the Smithsonian collection ("Heart Whimsey"2012 26/9269), made by Grant Jonathan. Figure 2 two features historic pieces of Tuscarora beadwork and a beaded bird in the Smithsonian collection ("Birds of Different Feathers" 2012 26/9259) also made by Grant Jonathan. PHOTOS BY AUTHOR.

Washington sent General Sullivan in 1779 to commit destructive and extremely violent actions against Haudenosaunee people, destroying crops, burning peach trees, and razing villages. For these violent acts, Washington earned the nickname "Town Destroyer," or Hanödaga:yas.

There has been a shift in recent years at the NMAI to producing exhibits that reach non-Native audiences and that push beyond stereotypes to make Indigenous history and peoples more accessible, emphasizing the shared aspects of our lived experiences (e.g. the exhibit *Americans* at NMAI, Washington, D.C.). Given the brutal and ongoing disparities and racisms faced by Indigenous people in the United States, highlighting the humanity and dignity of Indigenous peoples feels necessary. Unfortunately, this approach frequently leaves little exhibition space to bring visitors into conversation with current issues most pressing for Indigenous people, communities, and Nations. What actions are taking place in Native communities to protect lands and waters? To combat climate change? To promote women's rights? To support tribal membership and inclusion? Ironically, several artists whose snapshots can be seen throughout the exhibit and short film (Margaret Jacobs, G. Peter Jemison, Jeremy Dennis, and Natasha Smoke Santiago) are addressing these issues in their artwork, but the visitor does not get to make those connections through seeing their work.

One thing NMAI exhibits do well is share information in multiple formats, and this exhibit is exemplary in that regard. A touch table features a game about negotiating and trade between Indigenous groups; audio files can be accessed on tablets while admiring historic objects from the NMAI collections. An interactive feature shares parts of the epic Haudenosaunee narrative about the beginning of the Confederacy, and a wall hanging made of transparent plastic beads hangs from the ceiling and evokes the splendor of Niagara Falls. In this section of the exhibit, historic and contemporary Tuscarora beadwork glistens under display cases, and an adjacent wall provides visitors with an excellent collection of historic images of Tuscarora women sewing and selling their beaded creations.

The title of this exhibit riffs on the notion of what makes a person "Native" to a place. As the short film inside the exhibit explains, many people can be considered Native New Yorkers; however, to understand and appreciate the first peoples who lived in what we now recognize as New York, we need a more comprehensive map that includes the histories of Indigenous peoples. *Native New York* succeeds in making this point and proving that the histories surrounding Indigenous peoples continue to resonate with Indigenous people today and remain relevant to all New Yorkers.

Reviewed by Gwendolyn Saul. Saul is curator of ethnography at the New York State Museum in Albany.